FINANCIAL & INSURANCE AWARENESS *with* CURRENT AFFAIRS

for Insurance & Bank Exams

- **Corporate Office :** 45, 2nd Floor, Maharishi Dayanand Marg, Corner Market, Malviya Nagar, New Delhi-110017

  Tel. : 011-49842349 / 49842350

Typeset by Disha DTP Team

DISHA PUBLICATION

© Copyright Publisher

For further information about the books from DISHA,

Log on to **www.dishapublication.com** or email to **info@dishapublication.com**

CONTENTS

UNION BUDGET 2019-20

Highlights of Union Budget 2019-20

INTERIM BUDGET 2019

Finance Minister Piyush Goyal presented the Interim Budget for 2019 at the Parliament on February 1. A full-fledged Budget will be presented after the House reassembles after the General Elections.

The Highlights

- Inflation is a hidden and unfair tax; from 10.1% during 2009-14, inflation down to 4.6%, it was down to 2.19% in 2018.

- Fiscal deficit has been brought down to 3.4% in the revised estimates for 2018-19 and fiscal deficit is likely to be 2.5% in 2019-20.

- Farm GST has been continuously reduced, resulting in relief of Rs. 80,000 crore to consumers, and most items of daily use for poor and middle class are now in the 0% to 5% tax bracket.

- One lakh Digital villages planned in the next five years.

- As a tribute to Mahatma Gandhi, the world's largest behavioural change movement Swachh Bharat was initiated by my government.

- Under this more than 98% rural sanitation coverage has been achieved, and more than 5.45 lakh villages declared open defecation free. Mindset change has been achieved, it has become a Jan Andolan.

- Package of Rs. 6000 per annum for farmers with less than 2 hectares of land. Scheme will be called Pradhan Mantri Kisan Samman Nidhi.

- No Income Tax for income up to Rs. 5 lakh.

- Individuals with gross income of up to Rs. 6.5 lakh will not need to pay any tax if they make investments in provident funds and prescribed equities.

- Standard tax deduction for salaried persons raised from Rs. 40,000 to Rs.50,000.

- The ESI cover limit has been increased to Rs. 21,000. Minimum pension was also increased to Rs. 1000.

- Mega pension scheme for workers from the organised sector with income of less than Rs.15,000. They will be able to earn Rs. 3000 after the age of 60 years. The scheme will be called PM Shramyogi Maan Dhan Yojana.

- In the interim budget 2019, Railways has been allocated Rs.1.5 lakh crore for the year 2019-20, This is the highest-ever allocation for the Indian Railways.

TOP HIGHLIGHTS (INCOME TAX)

- No tax for those whose taxable income is less than Rs. 5 lakh

- Standard deduction increased to Rs. 50,000 from Rs. 40,000 for salaried class

- Individuals with gross income up to Rs. 6.5 lakh will not need to pay any tax if they make investments in provident funds and prescribed equities

- TDS threshold for home rent increased

- Interest income up to Rs. 40,000 in post offices and banks made tax free

- Capital gains tax exemptions under Section 54 to be available up to Rs. 2 crore. Capital gains exemption to be available on 2 house properties
- Income tax relief on notional rent from unsold houses extended to 2 years from 1 year
- 10 crore in unorganised sector to get Rs. 3,000 monthly pension
- An assured monthly pension of Rs. 3,000 to workers in the unorganised sector who earn up to Rs. 15,000 per month
- The scheme will be implemented from the current year
- The pension scheme will benefit 10 crore workers
- It might become the world's biggest pension scheme in next 5 years
- The scheme is called Pradhan Mantri Shram-Yogi Maandhan

ASSURED INCOME OF RS. 6000 FOR FARMERS

- The scheme Pradhan Mantri Kisan Samman (PM Kisan) for the assured income support to the farmers
- The scheme would be implemented with retrospective effect from December 2018.
- Rs. 75,000 crore has been earmarked for PM Kisaan scheme.
- Vulnerable farmers having less than two hectare of land will be eligible for the benefit.
- There was speculation that the government would target nearly 40% of BPL population for the direct cash transfer scheme

Swacch Bharat Mission:

- As a tribute to Mahatma Gandhi's 150th birth anniversary in 2019, the NDA Government launched a holistic programme 'Swacch Bharat Mission' in 2014. The programme has been converted into a movement. Under the mission, 98 percent rural sanitation coverage has been achieved. 5.45 lakh villages have been declared Open Defecation Free (ODF). India will be celebrating the 150th birth anniversary of Mahatma Gandhi in October 2019.

Defence Budget:

- Govt increases defence budget to over Rs 3 lakh crore. Govt will provide additional funds for Defence, if needed.
- Disbursed 35,000 crore rupees under #OROP scheme in the last few years.

Railways Budget:

- Rs 64,587 crore allocated to Railways for FY20.
- Railway's operating ratio seen 96.2% in FY19 Vs 95% FY20.
- Railway capex for FY20 set at record Rs 1.6 lakh crore.

For workers:

- Rs 3,000 per year pension for unorganised sector workers
- New Pradhan Mantri Shram Yogi Maandhan Yojana for unorganised sector workers with income up to Rs 15,000 per month. Beneficiaries will get Rs 3,000 per month pension with a contribution of Rs 100 per month after retirement. Govt allocates Rs 500 crore for the scheme
- Gratuity limit increased for workers to Rs 30 lakh.

Education Sector:

- National Education Mission allocation increased by about 20% to Rs. 38,572 cror in BE 2019-20
- 25% additional seats in educational institutions to meet the 10% reservation for the poor
- 10% reservation for the poor in educational institutions and government jobs
- EWS Reservation To ensure 10% res-

ervation in educational institutions and Government jobs for economically weaker sections, the Government will provide for 25% extra seats i.e. around 2 lacs, while maintaining the existing reservation for SC/ST/Other Backward Classes.

Fiscal Deficit:

- For FY19, government has revised the fiscal deficit target to 3.4 percent in FY 19. Fiscal deficit for 2019/20 estimated at 3.4 percent of GDP.
- Government's stated commitment earlier was to bring down the fiscal deficit to 3.1 percent of GDP by the end of March 2020, and to 3 percent by March 2021
- Current account deficit at 2.5% of the GDP.

Miscellaneous Highlights:

- Growth in the last 5 years has been higher than that by any other govt. Spent Rs 2.6 lakh crore in recap of PSU Banks.
- Domestic air traffic doubled in the last 5 years
- Over 90 percent of the country covered under sanitation coverage.
- In the past, false promises were made but we have taken targeted expenditure on all dimensions
- Ayushman Bharat, the world's largest healthcare programme, was launched to provide medical care to almost 50 crore
- people, resulting in Rs 3,000 crore savings by poor families
- Lower costs of Stents & Knee implants have benefitted people. Government has announced 14 new AIIMS since 2014
- Loans worth Rs 7.23 lakh crore have been given under Mudra Yojana
- Monthly mobile data consumption has increased 50x in last 5 years; cost of data & voice calls in India is possible the lowest in the world.
- Allocation for the north eastern region has been proposed to be increased to Rs 58,166 crore

Modi Govt's 10-point 'Vision 2030'

1. Physical and social infrastructure
2. Digital India
3. Clean and green India
4. Rural industrialisation
5. Clean rivers
6. Oceans and coastline
7. Space
8. Self-sufficiency in food production
9. Health
10. Minimum government, maximum governance

POLICIES & SCHEMES 2018-19

POLICIES & SCHEMES (2018-19)

Cabinet approves Agriculture Export Policy, 2018:

The Union Cabinet chaired by Prime Minister has approved the Agriculture Export Policy, 2018.

Aim of the policy:

To double agricultural exports from present US$ 30+ Billion to US$ 60+ Billion by 2022 and reach US$ 100 Billion in the next few years thereafter, with a stable trade policy regime. To diversify our export basket, destinations and boost high value and value added agricultural exports including focus on perishables.

Atal Solar Krushi Pump Yojana:

Under the scheme, the government of Maharashtra has decided to give two LED bulbs, a DC fan and a mobile charging socket as freebies to farmers. The scheme provides a subsidy of up to 95% on solar pump sets. The State plans to install one lakh solar pumps.

Personal Laws (Amendment) Bill, 2018:

The Lok Sabha has passed the Personal Laws (Amendment Bill), 2018, which seeks to remove leprosy as a ground for divorce. Leprosy is being removed as a ground for divorce as it is now a curable disease as against the earlier notion of it being incurable.

National Policy on Domestic Workers:

In a bid to give recognition to domestic workers besides making them eligible for minimum wages, social security and safe working conditions, labour ministry is drafting the national policy.

Pravasi Teerth Darshan Yojana:

Govt. has launched the Pravasi Teerth Darshan Yojana, under which a group of Indian diaspora will be taken on a government-sponsored tour of religious places in India twice a year. The group will be taken to the religious places of all major religions in India. The tour would be completely government sponsored.

Yuva Swabhiman Yojana:

Madhya Pradesh government has launched 'Yuva Swabhiman Yojana' for the youths of the weaker section in urban areas of the state. It aims to provide employment to the youth belonging to the weaker section of the society mainly in urban areas of the state.

Sujalam Sufalam Jal Sanchay Abhiyan:

The government of Gujarat launched the second edition of the water conservation scheme Sujalam Sufalam Jal Sanchay Abhiyan.The scheme aims to deepen water bodies in the state before monsoon to increase storage of rainwater to be used during times of scarcity.

Shreyas Program:

The Ministry of Human Resources Development has launched the Scheme for Higher Education Youth in Apprenticeship and Skills (SHREYAS) for providing industry apprenticeship opportunities to the general graduates exiting in April 2019 through the National Apprenticeship Promotional Scheme (NAPS).The program aims to enhance the employability of Indian youth by providing 'on the job work exposure' and earning of stipend.

'Jal Amrutha' Scheme Launched By Karnataka Government:

A water conservation scheme 'Jal Amrutha' was launched by Karnataka chief minister H D Kumaraswamy, in Bengaluru. A function was organized by the Rural Development and Panchayat Raj department at Dr. B R Ambedkar Bhavan in Bengaluru. The scheme plans to make people aware of the importance of conserving water and to prompt them to come up with ways to avoid wastage of water. The state government has declared 2019 as the Year of Water.

Haryana Government Announces Mukhyamantri Parivar Samman Nidhi Scheme:

Mukhyamantri Parivar Samman Nidhi' scheme was launched by Haryana Chief Minister Manohar Lal Khattar in Chandigarh. It is primarily meant for farmers of the state who cultivate on land with areas up to 5 acres and the families with an income of less than Rs. 15,000 per month.

Cabinet Approves 'Pradhan Mantri JI-VAN Yojana':

The Cabinet Committee on Economic Affairs, chaired by Prime Minister Narendra Modi approved the 'Pradhan Mantri Jaiv Indhan- Vatavaran Anukool fasal awashesh Nivaran (JI-VAN) Yojana' for providingfinancial support to the Integrated Bioethanol Projects.The scheme aims to incentivise the Second Generation (2G) Ethanol sector and support the industry by creating a suitable ecosystem for setting up commercial projects and increasing R&D in this area. The PM JI-VAN Yojana will be supported with the total financial outlay of Rs 1969.50 crore for the period 2018-19 to 2023-24.

Kisan Urja Suraksha evam Utthaan Mahaabhiyan or KUSUM scheme:

The government has cautioned against fake websites claiming to be registration portal for Kisan Urja Suraksha evam Utthaan Mahabhiyan (KUSUM) scheme and said such websites may be misusing the collected data. It is a Rs. 1.4 lakh-crore scheme for promoting decentralised solar power production of up to 28,250 MW to help farmers.

National Mineral Policy, 2019:

The Union Cabinet has approved National Mineral Policy 2019. The policy is aimed at bringing about more effective regulation to the mining sector as well as a more sustainable approach while addressing the issues of those affected by mining. It focuses on Make in India initiative and Gender sensitivity in terms of the vision.

Yuva Swabhiman Yojana

Date: 28th January 2019

Madhya Pradesh government has launched 'Yuva Swabhiman Yojana' for the youths of the weaker section in urban areas of the state.

Key Points:

- The scheme was launched in Chhindwara district of the state. It aims to provide employment to the youth belonging to the weaker section of the society mainly in urban areas of the state.
- Under this scheme, 100 days of employment will be provided.
- Apart from this 100 days employment, they will also be given skill training by the government.

HEALTHCARE

Daman Initiative: Model for Malaria Control

Date: 28th January 2019

According to the World Health Organisation's World Malaria Report of 2018 – India is the only country among the 11 highest-burden countries that saw substantial progress in reducing disease burden. India saw a 24% decrease in 2017 compared to 2016.

Key Points:

- Odisha has emerged as an inspiration in the fight against malaria.
- It has dramatically scaled-up efforts to prevent, diagnose and treat malaria through its Durgama Anchalare Malaria Nirakaran (DAMaN) initiative
- It involved accredited social health activists (ASHAs), who helped distribute approximately 11 million bed nets in 2017, which was enough to protect all the residents in areas that were at the highest risk.
- Odisha recorded an 80% decline in malaria cases and deaths in 2017.

Pradhan Mantri Shram-Yogi Maandhan Yojana

- **Date:** 2nd February 2019

Pradhan Mantri Shram-Yogi Maandhan Yojana social security scheme announced in the interim budget 2019

Key Points:

- The scheme for the unorganised sector workers with monthly income up to Rs 15,000. A sum of Rs 500 crore has been allocated for the Scheme.
- This scheme shall provide an assured monthly pension of Rs 3,000 from the age of 60 years on a monthly contribution of a small affordable amount during their working age.
- An unorganised sector worker joining pension yojana at the age of 29 years will have to contribute only Rs 100 per month till the age of 60 years. A worker joining the pension yojana at 18 years, will have to contribute as little as Rs 55 per month only.
- The Government will deposit equal matching share in the pension account of the worker every month.
- It is expected that at least 10 crore labourers and workers in the unorganised sector will avail the benefit of the scheme within next five years making it one of the largest pension schemes of the world.

Pradhan Mantri Kisan Samman Nidhi

Date: 2nd February 2019

Highlights:

- Under this programme, vulnerable landholding farmer families, having cultivable land up to 2 hectares, will be provided direct income support at the rate of Rs. 6,000 per year.
- This income support will be transferred directly into the bank accounts of beneficiary farmers, in three equal instalments of Rs. 2,000 each.
- Around 12 crore small and marginal farmer families are expected to benefit from this.
- It would not only provide assured supplemental income to the most vulnerable farmer families, but would also meet their emergent needs especially before the harvest season.
- It would pave the way for the farmers to earn and live a respectable living.

New e-commerce policy comes into effect

Date: 2nd February 2019

India's new e-commerce policy came into effect on February 1, 2019. A new set of policy rules have been formed for the e-commerce companies. DIPP gave them a 60-day window period for aligning themselves to the government's modified foreign direct investment (FDI) rules.

Highlights:

- The police bars online retailers from selling products through vendors in which they have an equity interest.
- It also bars them from entering into exclusive deals with brands for selling products only on their platforms.
- All online retailers will be required to maintain a level playing field for all the vendors selling their products on the platform, and it shall not affect the sale prices of goods in any manner.
- Disallows e-commerce players to control the inventory of the vendors. Any such ownership over the inventory will convert it into inventory based model from marketplace based model, which is not entitled to FDI.
- Under the new rules, the e-commerce retailer shall be deemed to own the inventory of a vendor if over 25 per cent of the purchases of such a vendor are through it.
- Restricts marketplaces from influencing prices in a bid to curb deep discounting. With this, special offers like cashback, extended warranties, faster deliveries to some brands will be prohibited, with the view to provide a level playing field.

RASHTRIYA GOKUL MISSION

Date: 2nd February 2019

The Finance Minister Piyush Goyal announced the allotment of Rs. 750 crore to the Rashtriya Gokul Mission (RGM).

Highlights:
- Government has launched 'Rashtriya Gokul Mission' under the National Programme for Bovine Breeding and Dairy Development (NPBBD).
- Rashtriya Gokul Mission will be implemented through the "State Implementing Agency (SIA viz Livestock Development Boards). State Gauseva Ayogs will be given the mandate to sponsor proposals to the SIA's (LDB's) and monitor implementation of the sponsored proposal. All Agencies having a role in indigenous cattle development will be the "Participating Agencies" like CFSPTI, CCBFs, ICAR, Universities, Colleges, NGO's, Cooperative Societies and Gaushalas with best germplasm.
- Funds under the scheme will be allocated for the establishment of Integrated Indigenous Cattle Centres viz "Gokul Gram".
- Gokul Gram will act as Centres for development of Indigenous Breeds and a dependable source for supply of high genetic breeding stock to the farmers in the breeding tract.

Ujjwala Utsav

Date: 8th February 2019

Ujjwala Utsav observed to celebrate the stellar role played by various stakeholders in making Pradhan Mantri Ujjwala Yojana (PMUY) a success.

Key Points:
- The event was organised under the aegis of Ministry of Petroleum & Natural Gas to encourage, motivate as well as felicitate all frontline field force for their outstanding contribution to PMUY.
- The occasion also saw the launch of the PMUY anthem – Ujjwala Bharat Ujjwala – composed and developed by Kailash Kher.
- PMUY is the central government's flagship program to provide LPG (liquefied petroleum gas) connections to poor households.

Pradhan Mantri Kisan Samman Nidhi

Date: 25th February 2019

The Government has unveiled the Pradhan Mantri Kisan Samman Nidhi (PM-KISAN).

Key Points:
- Under this programme, vulnerable landholding farmer families, having cultivable land up to 2 hectares, will be provided direct income support at the rate of Rs. 6,000 per year.
- This income support will be transferred directly into the bank accounts of beneficiary farmers, in three equal instalments of Rs. 2,000 each.
- The complete expenditure of Rs 75000 crore for the scheme will borne by the Union Government in 2019-20.
- Around 12 crore small and marginal farmer families are expected to benefit from this.
- It would not only provide assured supplemental income to the most vulnerable farmer families but would also meet their emergent needs especially before the harvest season. It would pave the way for the farmers to earn and live a respectable living.

Draft e-commerce policy

Date: 25th February 2019

The Department of Industry and Internal Trade has released the draft National e-commerce Policy that sends a clear message that India and its citizens have a sovereign right to their data.

Key features:
- It bars the sharing of sensitive data of Indian users with third party entities, even with consent.
- All e-commerce websites, apps available for download in India to have a registered business entity here. Non-compliant e-commerce app/website to be denied access here.
- Location of the computing facilities like data centres, server farms within India. Firms to get 3 years to comply with local data storage requirements.
- FDI only in marketplace model. No FDI in inventory model.
- Curbs on Chinese e-commerce exports. Gifting route, often used by Chinese apps, websites, banned for all parcels except life-saving drugs. Integrating

Customs, RBI and India Post to improve tracking of imports through e-commerce.

- E-commerce startups may get 'infant industry' status raising the limit for courier shipments from Rs 25,000 to boost e-commerce export.

National Mineral Policy, 2019

- **Date:** 1st March 2019
- The Union Cabinet has approved National Mineral Policy 2019. The policy is aimed at bringing about more effective regulation to the mining sector as well as a more sustainable approach while addressing the issues of those affected by mining.

Highlights:

- It focuses on Make in India initiative and Gender sensitivity in terms of the vision.
- National Mineral Policy 2019 replaces the National Mineral Policy 2008. In 2017, the Supreme Court had directed to review NMP 2008.
- Important features of the new policy include:
- Introduction of Right of First Refusal for RP (Reconnaissance Permits)/PL (Prospecting Licenses) holders.
- Encouraging the private sector to take up exploration and attract private investment through incentives.
- Auctioning of virgin areas on a revenue sharing basis.
- Development of online public portal with provision for generating triggers at higher level in the event of delay of clearances.
- Encourages dedicated mineral corridors to facilitate the transportation of minerals
- Introduces the concept of Inter-Generational Equity that deals with the well-being of present as well as future generations.
- Proposes to constitute an inter-ministerial body to institutionalize the mechanism for ensuring sustainable development in mining.

FAME-II Scheme

Date: 22nd April, 2019

The Inter-Ministerial Steering Committee of the National Mission for Transformative Mobility led by Niti Aayog chief executive officer Amitabh Kant has decided to incorporate localisation conditions to avail benefits under the FAME-II Scheme.

Key Points:

- The Inter-Ministerial Committee of the National Mission for Transformative Mobility was formed following a cabinet decision to promote clean and sustainable mobility initiatives in the country. It consists of secretary of nine stakeholder ministries and director general of the Bureau of Indian Standards as its members.
- The steering committee has mandated that only companies that meet the 50% localisation threshold will be eligible for the incentives that will be available under the Faster Adoption and Manufacturing of Hybrid and Electric Vehicles (FAME-II) scheme to boost electric mobility as well as the 'Make in India' initiative.

Unnat Bharat Abhiyan

Date: 4th May 2019

Common Service Centers (CSC) e-Governance Services India Limited, under the Ministry of Electronics & IT, has tied up with IIT-Kanpur to upscale 'Unnat Bharat Abhiyan'.

Key Points:

- IIT-Kanpur has brought together 15 leading higher education institutions from Uttar Pradesh to work with CSC for the development of villages under the Unnat Bharat Abhiyan scheme.
- These institutions will adopt gram panchayats and equip them with all citizen-centric services through CSCs.
- 'Unnat Bharat Abhiyan' is an initiative of the Ministry of Human Resource Development (MHRD).
- It aims to create a vibrant relationship between the society and the higher educational institutions, with the latter providing the knowledge and technology support to improve livelihoods in rural areas and to upgrade the capabilities of both public and private organizations in the society.

BASICS OF ECONOMICS

INTRODUCTION

Economics, often referred to as the "**dismal science**", is a study of certain aspects of society. Adam Smith, the "father of modern economics" and author of the famous book "An Inquiry into the Nature and causes of the wealth of Nations", spawned the discipline of economics by trying to understand why some nations prospered while others lagged behind in poverty. Alfred Marshall, author of "The Principles of Economics", reflects the complexity underlying economics: "Thus it is on one side the study of wealth; and on the other, and more important side, a part of the study of man."

Meaning of economics

- The term 'economics' comes from the *Greek term oikonomia*, which is composed of *oikos* (house) and nomos (law), meaning rules of the household.
- Economics is concerned with the factors that determine the production, distribution, and consumption of goods and services.

BRANCHES OF ECONOMICS

Micro Economics

- It examines the behaviour of basic elements in the economy, including individual agents and markets, their interactions, and the outcomes of interactions.
- It shows us how individuals and firms respond to changes in price and why they demand what they do at particular price levels.

Macro Economics

- It looks at the total output of a nation and the way the nation allocates its limited resources of land, labor and capital in an attempt to maximize production levels and promote trade and growth for future generations.
- It analyses the entire economy and issues affecting it, including unemployment of resources (labour, capital and land), inflation, economic growth, and the public policies that address these issues (monetary, fiscal, and other policies).

ECONOMICS BASICS: DEMAND AND SUPPLY

- **Demand** refers to how much (quantity) of a product or service is needed by buyers at various prices. The relationship between price and quantity demanded is known as the demand relationship.
- **Supply** represents how much the market can offer. It is the producer's willingness and ability to supply a given good at various price points. The correlation between price and how much of a good or service is supplied to the market is known as the supply relationship.

> **Price, is a reflection of supply and demand**

A. The Law of Demand

- The law of demand states that, if all others factors remain equal, the higher the price of a good, the less people will demand that good. Demand curve illustrates

- Negative relationship between price and quantity demanded.

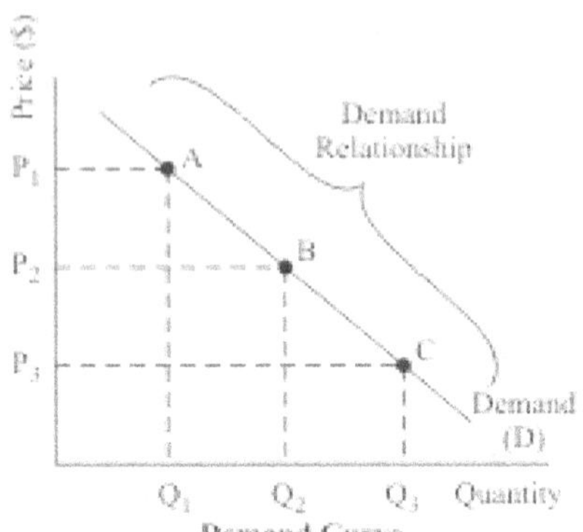

B. The Law of Supply

- The law of supply demonstrates the quantities that will be sold at a certain price.

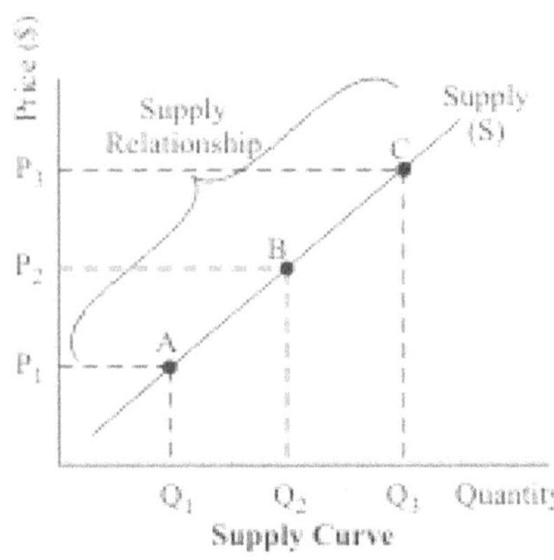

- Supply curve shows an upward slope. This means that the higher the price, the higher the quantity supplied.

C. Equilibrium

- When demand and supply are equal the economy is said to be at equilibrium.
- At this point, the amount of goods being supplied is exactly the same as the amount of goods being demanded.

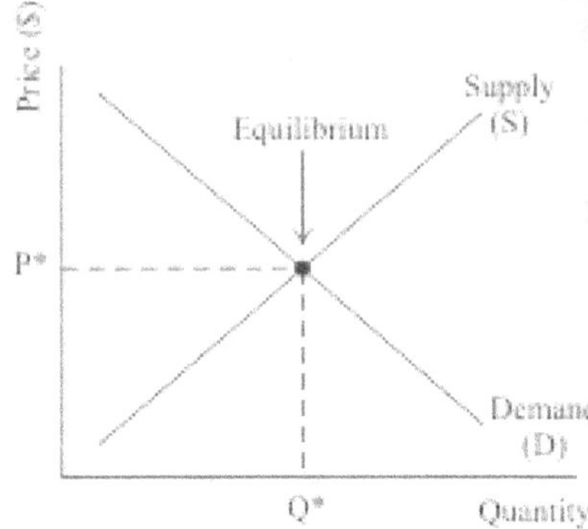

D. Disequilibrium

- Disequilibrium occurs whenever the price or quantity is not equal to P* or Q*.
- If price is set to high, **excess supply** will be created within the economy.
- Excess demand is created when price is set below the equilibrium price.
- A movement along the supply curve will occur when the price of the good changes and the quantity supplied changes in accordance to the original supply relationship.
- A shift in a demand or supply curve occurs when a good's quantity demanded or supplied changes even though price remains the same.

E. Elasticity

- The degree to which a demand or supply curve reacts to a change in price is the curve's elasticity.

Elasticity of the supply or demand curves equation:

$$\left(E = \frac{\% \text{ change in quantity}}{\% \text{change in price}} \right)$$

F. Utility

- Utility explains how individuals and economies aim to gain optimal satisfaction in dealing with scarcity.
- **Total Utility** is the aggregate sum of satisfaction that an individual gains from consuming a given amount of goods or services.

- **Marginal Utility** is the additional satisfaction, or amount of utility gained from each extra unit of consumption.

G. Monopolies, Oligopolies and Perfect Competition

- A **monopoly** is a market structure in which there is only one producer/seller for a product. For example, in **Saudi Arabia** the government has sole control over the oil industry.
- In an **oligopoly,** there are only a few firms that make up an industry. This group of firms has control over the price.
- **Perfect competition** is characterized by many buyers and sellers, many products that are similar in nature and, as a result many substitutes. In a perfectly competitive market prices are determined by supply and demand.

Meaning of an Economy

- An economy is a man-made organization for the satisfaction of human wants.
- It is a framework where all economic activities are carried out.

TYPES OF ECONOMIES

- Typically, economies are divided into different types based on the extent of government involvement in econmic decision-making. Based on above criteria, the following are the major types of economies.

Traditional Economy

- There is very little government involvement in this type of economy. Allocation of resources here relies on customs, rituals and time-honored belief.
- There is very little individual choice in this system and people work together for the common good.
- This type exists in tribes in Amazon, Aborigines in Australia, etc.

Command Economy

- A command economy is a system where the government determines what goods should be produced, how much should be produced and the price at which the goods are offered for sale.
- Cuba, North Korea and the former Soviet Union are examples of countries that have command economies.

Free Market Economy

- It refers to an economy where the government imposes few or no restrictions and regulations on buyers and sellers.
- More, participants determine what products are produced, how, when and where they are made, to whom they are offered, and at what price - all based on supply and demand.

Capitalistic Economy

- In this system capital goods are owned by private individuals or business partners.
- Individuals are free to determine where to invest, what to produce or sell, and at which prices to exchange goods and services.

Socialist Economy

- In the socialist or centrally planned economies all the productive resources are owned and controlled by the government.
- Countries such as Russia, China and many eastern European countries are said to be socialist countries.

Mixed Economy

- A mixed economy combines the best features of capitalism and socialism.
- This system protects private property and allows a level of economic freedom in the use of capital, but also allows for governments to interfere in economic activities in order to achieve social aims.

Open Economy

- It is an economy in which there are economic activities between the domestic community and outside.

- It is characterized by the absence of tariffs, taxes, licensing requirements, subsidies, unionization and any other regulations.

Closed Economy

- In this economy no activity is conducted with outside economies. A closed economy is self-sufficient, meaning no imports are brought in and no exports are sent out.

CLASSIFICATION OF COUNTRIES

Developed Country

- A **developed country**, i.e. industrialized **country** is a sovereign state that has a highly **developed** economy and advanced technological infrastructure relative to other less industrialized **nations**.
- Common criteria for evaluating a country's degree of development are per capita income or gross domestic product (GDP), level of industrialization, general standard of living, and the amount of widespread infrastructure.
- The most well-known current examples of developed countries include the United States, Canada and most of western Europe, including the United Kingdom and France.

Developing Country

- **Developing countries"** are commonly used to refer to countries that do not enjoy the same level of economic security, industrialization and growth as developed countries.

- These are nations with a less developed industrial base, and a low Human Development Index (HDI).

Least Developed Country

- The **least developed countries** (LDCs) are a group of **countries** that have been classified by the UN as **"least developed"** in terms of their low gross national income (GNI), their weak human assets and their high degree of economic vulnerability.

SECTORS OF THE ECONOMY

There are three main sectors of the economy are:

Primary Sector

Primary sector refers to that sector of the economy which uses natural resource to produce goods, like mining, fishery, forestry, dairy and poultry etc.

Secondary Sector

Secondary sector is also called as manufacturing sector or industrial sector. The sector which transforms one physical good into another is called secondary sector. The manufacturing, electricity, gas, water supply etc. are included in this sector.

Tertiary Sector

In the tertiary sector, activities that assist the development of the primary and secondary sectors are carried out. Services of various kinds like education, health, banking, insurance, trade and transport are included in this sector.

EXERCISE

1. Who is called as the 'founding father of modern economics'?
   - (a) Adam Smith
   - (b) John Maynard Keynes
   - (c) F. Hayek
   - (d) Samuelson

2. Macroeconomics is a study of economics that deals with which 4 major factors:
   - (a) households, firms, government, and demand-supply
   - (b) households, firms, government and external sector
   - (c) firms, government, free-market, and regulations
   - (d) none of the above

3. The law of demand states that
   - (a) as the quantity demanded rises, the price rises
   - (b) as the price rises, the quantity demanded rises
   - (c) as the price rises, the quantity demanded falls
   - (d) as supply rises, the demand rises

4. Which of the following is a characteristic of pure monopoly?
   - (a) one seller of the product
   - (b) low barriers to entry
   - (c) close substitute products
   - (d) perfect information

5. Consider the following statements
   1. In a Capitalist economy there is private ownership of means of production
   2. In a communist nation, the means of production are owned by the State
   3. In a free-market economy there is minimum role of the Government

4. Which of the above 3 statement is/are true?
   - (a) Only 1 and 3
   - (b) Only 2 and 3
   - (c) Only 3
   - (d) All are true

6. Demand is a function of
   - (a) Price
   - (b) Quantity
   - (c) Supply
   - (d) None of these

7. A mixed economy is characterised by the co-existence of
   - (a) Modern and traditional industries
   - (b) Public and private sectors
   - (c) Foreign and domestic investments
   - (d) Commercial and subsistence farming

8. Microeconomics deals with the
   - (a) Allocation of resources of the economy as between production of different goods and services
   - (b) Determination of prices of goods and services
   - (c) Behaviour of industrial decision makers
   - (d) All of the above

9. Equilibrium in the market for good A obtains
   - (a) when there is no surplus or shortage prevailing in the market
   - (b) where the demand and supply curves for A intersect
   - (c) when all of what is produced of A is consumed
   - (d) all of the above

10. Which one of the following activities can be included in the primary sector?
    (a) Giving lans to the farmer
    (b) Making Sugar from sugar cane
    (c) Cultivating Sugar cane
    (d) Providing storage facility for the grains

11. Point where market demands will be same to market supply
    (a) equilibrium in perfect competition
    (b) equilibrium in imperfect competition
    (c) equilibrium competition
    (d) all of answers are correct

12. The tribe relied on hunting and farming for food. The boy knew he would be a farmer just like his dad had been. What kind of economic system does this describe?
    (a) command economy
    (b) traditional economy
    (c) free market economy
    (d) mixed economy

13. There is little or no government control in a ______________ economy.
    (a) mixed
    (b) free market
    (c) command
    (d) traditional

14. In the former Soviet Union consumers had to wait in long lines to buy everyday items like bread. They did not have many choices and the government controlled factories. What type of economy did they live in?
    (a) traditional economy
    (b) free market economy
    (c) command economy
    (d) mixed economy

15. Which of the following is NOT a type of economic system?
    (a) command economy
    (b) free market economy
    (c) public market economy
    (d) traditional economy

16. An underdeveloped economy is characterized by
    (a) High per capita real income
    (b) Large proportion of labor force in the tertiary sector
    (c) State of deprivation of large proportion of population
    (d) All the above

17. Utility means—
    (a) Power to satisfy a want
    (b) Usefulness
    (c) Willingness of a person
    (d) Harmfulness

18. **Adam Smith in his book,** *The Wealth of Nations*, **developed a theory about:**
    (a) communism
    (b) capitalism
    (c) regulating foreign investment
    (d) ensuring internal order

19. In a capitalist economy, the question of how society chooses to employ the resources to produce goods and services is determined **by**
    (a) business
    (b) government
    (c) government & business
    (d) all of the above

20. At the current price there is a shortage of a product. We would expect price to:
    (a) increase, quantity demanded to increase, and quantity supplied to decrease
    (b) increase, quantity demanded to decrease, and quantity supplied to increase
    (c) increase, quantity demanded to increase, and quantity supplied to increase
    (d) decrease, quantity demanded to increase, and quantity supplied to decrease

HINTS & EXPLANATIONS

1. (a) Adam Smith's 1776 book "An Inquiry into the Nature and Causes of the Wealth of Nations" many of the major ideas that we use in economics today

2. (b) Macroeconomics is a branch of *economics* dealing with the performance, structure, behavior, and decision-making of an *economy* as a whole rather than individual markets.

3. (c) There is negative relationship between price and quantity demanded

4. (a) A monopoly is a market structure in which there is only one producer/seller for a product.

5. (d)

6. (a)

7. (b) **A mixed economy** is defined as an *economic system* consisting of a mixture of either *markets* and *economic planning, public ownership* and *private ownership*.

8. (d) *Microeconomics* is a branch *of economics* that studies the behavior of individuals and *firms* in making decisions regarding the allocation of *limited resources*.

9. (a) **Equilibrium** is a state where **economic** forces such as supply and demand are balanced and in the absence of external influences the (**equilibrium**) values of **economic** variables will not change.

10. (b) The **primary sector** of the economy is the sector of an economy making direct use of natural resources. This includes agriculture, forestry, fishing and mining.

11. (a) Equilibrium is a state where economic forces such as supply and demand are balanced and in the absence of external influences the (equilibrium) values of economic variables will not change.

12. (b) A traditional economy is one that is built around the way a society lives. The goods and services are determined based on the livelihood of the people.

13. (b) A free market is a *system* in which the prices for goods and services are determined by the open market and *consumers*, in which the laws and forces of *supply and demand* are free from any intervention by a *government*.

14. (c) **A command economy** is a system where the government, rather than the free market, determines what goods should be produced, how much should be produced and the price at which the goods are offered for sale.

15. (c) A **Public Market** is a year-round, carefully crafted, intentional and diverse medley of owner-operated shops, stalls and/or "daytables".

16. (c) Underdeveloped countries face the problem of deprivation of large section of the population, low per capita real income etc.

17. (a) **Utility** is a term used by **economists** to describe the measurement of "usefulness" that a consumer obtains from any good.

18. (b) *An Inquiry into the Nature and Causes of the Wealth of Nations* is the full name of the famous book by Scottish economist and moral philosopher Adam Smith. Known more commonly by its shortened name, *The Wealth of Nations* was published in 1776.

19. (a) **Capitalism** is an **economic** system based on private ownership of the means of production and their operation for profit.

20. (a) A shortage is a situation in which demand for a good or service exceeds the available supply.

CHAPTER 4

BASIC ECONOMIC/ FINANCIAL DATA

INDIAN ECONOMY - SNAPSHOT

- The Indian economy grew at 7.7 per cent in fourth quarter (Q4) FY 2017-18, as per the Second Advance Estimates of National Income by Central Statistics Office (CSO).
- Foreign direct investment (FDI) inflows stood at US$ 35.94 billion during April-December 2017.
- India's foreign exchange reserves were US$ 423.58 billion in the week up to April 20, 2018, as compared to US$ 426.08 billion over the past week.
- Mutual Funds asset base stood at Rs 23.21 lakh crore (US$ 33.09 billion) at the end of April 2018, as against Rs 23.26 trillion (US$ 360.90 billion) at the end of April 2017.
- India's Index of Industrial Production (IIP) advanced by 4.4 per cent in March 2018, as against a rise of 7.0 per cent in February 2018. The cumulative IIP growth for 2017-18 was 4.3 per cent over the same period in 2016-17.
- The eight key infrastructure sectors rose 4.7 per cent year-on-year in April 2018 as against 4.4 per cent in March 2018, with cement exhibiting the maximum growth of 16.6 per cent. The cumulative growth during 2017-18 was 4.3 per cent.
- Domestic passenger vehicle sales increased 7.50 per cent in April 2018 over April 2017.
- India's current account deficit (CAD) was 1.9 per cent during April-December 2017. The current account deficit (CAD) for the financial year 2016-17 narrowed to 0.7 per cent of GDP, as against a deficit of 1.1 per cent in 2015-16.
- India's Wholesale Price Index (WPI) inflation index increased by 0.2 per cent to 116 in March 2018 compared to 115.8 in February 2018.
- India's Consumer Price Index (CPI) inflation rate decreased to 3.97 per cent in April 2018 as compared to 4.36 per cent in March 2018.
- Total Merger and Acquisition (M&A) activity grew 53.3 per cent year-on-year to reach US$ 77.6 billion in 2017. M&A activity stood at US$ 19.1 billion in April 2018.
- Total value of Private Equity (PE)/ venture capital (VC) investments reached a record high of US$ 26.8 billion in value terms in 2017. PE/VC investments in Jan-Mar 2018 stood at US$ 7.9 billion.

Base Year
The year agains which the performance of an index is measured. It is also called reference year. Currently this is 2011-12. Basically after every 10 years. It is changed.

Percentage share of major Imports Es. 2016-17

Commodities/Group		Share %
1.	Fuel	26.7%
2.	Capital Goods	13.6%
3.	electronic Goods	11.2%
4.	Gold & Silver	7.6%
5.	Chemicals	6.3%

Percentage share of major Exports. Es. 2016-17

	Commodities/Group	Share %
1.	Gems & Jewellerly	15.7%
2.	Agriculture & allied	12.3%
3.	Ores & Minerals	1.8%
4.	Crude & Petroleum Products	11.8%
5.	Transport Equipments	7.7%

Direction of exports by Region E.S. 2017-18

	Region	Share (%)
1.	Europe	19.3%
2.	Africa	8.4%
3.	America	19.9%
4.	Asia	49.9%
5.	CIS & Baltics	1.0%

Direction of Exports by Countries E.S 2017-18

	Countries	Share %
1.	USA	15.3%
2.	China	3.7%
3.	Hong-Kong	5.1%
4.	UAE	11.3%
5.	U.K	3.1%
6.	Singapore	3.5%

India's Share in World Exports by Commodities. E.S (2016)

	Commodities	Share (%)
1.	Rice	24.5%
2.	Spices	17.1%
3.	Pearls and Precious stones	17%
4.	Unmanufactured Tobacco	5.9%

Direction of Imports by Regions E.S (2017-18)

	Regions	Share (%)
1.	Europe	16%
2.	Africa	7.5%
3.	America	12.1%
4.	Asia	60.0%
5.	CIS & Baltics	2.4%

Direction of Imports by Countries E.S (2017-18)

	Countries	Share (%)
1.	China	15.9%
2.	U.S.A	5.8%
3.	U.A.E	5.6%
4.	Saudi Arab	5.2%
5.	Switzerland	4.5%

EXERCISE

1. The Ministry of Finance is an important ministry within the Government of India. It concerns itself with
   (a) taxation
   (b) financial legislation
   (c) financial institutions
   (d) All of the above

2. Gross National Product equals:
   (a) Net National Product adjusted for inflation
   (b) Gross Domestic Product adjusted for inflation
   (c) Gross Domestic Product plus net property income from abroad
   (d) Net National Product plus net property income from abroad

3. Net National Product equals:
   (a) Gross National Product adjusted for inflation
   (b) Gross Domestic Product adjusted for inflation
   (c) Gross Domestic Product plus net property income from abroad
   (d) Gross National Product minus depreciation

4. Real national income measures:
   (a) Nominal national income adjusted for population change
   (b) Nominal national income adjusted for unemployment
   (c) Nominal national income adjusted for inflation
   (d) Nominal national income adjusted for exchange rates

5. GDP measures:
   (a) A country's income
   (b) A country's wealth
   (c) Consumer spending
   (d) Net trade income

6. FDI is an acronym that stands for:
   (a) federation of direct investors
   (b) federal diversification initiative
   (c) foreign direct investment
   (d) formal direct internationalization

7. Which one of the following groups of items is included in India's foreign-exchange reserves?
   (a) Foreign-currency assets, Special Drawing Rights (SDRs) and loans from foreign countries
   (b) Foreign-currency assets, gold holdings of the RBI and SDRs
   (c) Foreign-currency assets, loans from the World Bank and SDRs
   (d) Foreign-currency assets, gold holdings of the RBI and loans from the World Bank

8. Which of the following would include Foreign Direct Investment in India?
   1. Subsidiaries of companies in India
   2. Majority foreign equity holding in Indian companies
   3. Companies exclusively financed by foreign companies
   4. Portfolio investment
   Select the correct answer using the codes given below:
   (a) 1, 2, 3 and 4
   (b) 2 and 4 only
   (c) 1 and 3 only
   (d) 1, 2 and 3 only

9. India has retained its ranking as the 11th highest recipient of FDI in 2016, according to which UNCTAD report?
   (a) World Investment Report 2017
   (b) World Investment Report 2015
   (c) World Investing Report 2016
   (d) World Investing Report 2015

10. What is the India's rank in terms of Foreign Direct Investment (FDI) inflows, as per the latest 2017 World Investment Report?
    (a) 15th   (b) 11th
    (c) 10th   (d) 19th

11. Which of the following countries feature in top 5 in both Destinations of Exports from India as well as imports from those countries to India (financial year 14-15)

1. Saudi Arabia
2. Hong Kong
3. UAE
4. Switzerland

(a) 1,2,3   (b) 1,3,4
(c) 2,3   (d) 1,3

12. Which of the following commodities are both Principal Commodities of Export as well as Import for India(15-16)
    1. Gems and Jewellery
    2. Machinary
    3. Chemicals and related Products
    4. Textiles and allied products

    (a) 1,2,3   (b) 1,3,4
    (c) 1,3   (d) 1,2
    (e) 2,3

13. Find the correct statements.
    1. India's largest trade dealing is with European region.
    2. Share of gems and jewellery is highest in India's imports.

    (a) 1only   (b) 2only
    (c) Both   (d) None

14. Economic Survey 2016-17 projects that the real GDP growth for the current financial year and for 2017-18 will be in the range of _________.
    (a) 7 – 8 %   (b) 7.5 – 8 %
    (c) No Change   (d) 6.75 – 7.5 %

15. CPI inflation seen around ______ in 2017-18
    (a) 3.3%   (b) 6%
    (c) 7%   (d) 6.5%

16. What is the rank of India among the world's Top-Ten largest manufacturing countries in the latest United Nations Industrial Development Organization (UNIDO) report?
    (a) Fourth   (b) Fifth
    (c) Sixth   (d) Seventh

17. Which of the following accounts for the maximum share in India's foreign exchange reserves?
    (a) Gold reserves
    (b) NRI deposits
    (c) Special depository receipts
    (d) Foreign currency assets

18. A debt which is irrecoverable and is therefore written off as loss in the accounts of an institution or bank is known as __________
    (a) external debt
    (b) good debt
    (c) bad debt
    (d) internal debt

19. Which one of the following institution publish the report of 'World Investment Report'?
    (a) World Bank   (b) IMF
    (c) UNCTAD   (d) WTO

20. Which one of the following countries has the highest share in the World Export among the Asian countries?
    (a) South Korea   (b) Singapore
    (c) India   (d) China

HINTS & EXPLANATIONS

1. (d) The Ministry of Finance is an important ministry within the Government of India concerned with the economy of India.

2. (c) Gross national product (GNP) is an estimate of total value of all the final products and services produced in a given period by the means of production owned by a country's residents.

3. (d) NNP is the amount of goods that can be consumed within a nation each year without reducing the amount that can be consumed in following years.

4. (c) Real national income is nominal or money national income (output) adjusted for inflation, also called 'at constant prices.

5. (a) Gross domestic product (GDP) is a monetary measure of the market value of all final goods and services produced in a period (quarterly or yearly).

6. (c) Foreign direct investment (FDI) is an investment in a business by an investor from another country for which the foreign investor has control over the company purchased.

7. (b Foreign-exchange reserves (also called forex reserves or FXreserves) is money or other assets held by a central bank or other monetary authority so that it can pay if need be its liabilities,

8. (d) Foreign direct investments can be made in a variety of ways, including the opening of a subsidiary or associate company in a foreign country, acquiring a controlling interest in an existing foreign company, or by means of a merger or joint venture with a foreign company.

9. (a) India has retained the ranking as the tenth highest recipient of FDI in 2015 receiving USD 44 billion in investment that year compared to US $35 billion in 2014, as per the UN
World Investment Report 2016 released by UNCTAD found India also jumped a place in terms of attractiveness as a business destination in 2015 to sixth place with 14% of respondents naming it as destination of their choice

10. (b) India has been ranked 10th in the Foreign Direct Investment (FDI) inflows in the world, as per the latest 2016 World Investment Report by the United Nations Conference for Trade and Development (UNCTAD). The list is topped by United States followed by Hong Kong, China, Ireland, Netherlands, Switzerland, Singapore, Brazil and Canada.

11. (d) Top 5 Export destinations serially – USA, UAE, Hong Kong, China, Saudi Arabia

12. (c) Principal Exports – Petroleum (Crude and Products), Gems and Jewellery, Textiles and Allied Products, Chemicals and related products, Ari and allied products

    Principal Imports – Petroleum (Crude and Products), Gems and Jewellery, Chemicals and related products,,Electronic items and Machinary.

13. (d) India's largest export and import is with Asian region. Share of petroleum products is highest in both imports and exports.

14. (d)

15. (a)

16. (c) Top 5 countries: China, United States, Japan, Germany and South Korea.

17. (d)

18. (c) The term bad debts usually refers to accounts receivable (or trade accounts receivable) that will not be collected.

19. (c)

20. (d) The term export means shipping in the goods and services out of the jurisdiction of a country. The seller of such goods and services is referred to as an "exporter" and is based in the country of export whereas the overseas based buyer is referred to as an "importer".

INDIAN ECONOMY

INDIAN ECONOMY

- The **economy of India** is the *seventh-largest* economy in the world measured by *nominal GDP* and the *third-largest* by *purchasing power parity* (PPP).

- The country is classified as *newly industrialised country*, one of the *G-20 major* economies, a member *BRICS* and *adeveloping economy* with an average growth rate of approximately 7% over the last two decades.

- Maharashtra is the wealthiest Indian state and has an annual GDP of US$220 billion, nearly equal to that of *Portugal*, and accounts for 12% of the Indian GDP followed by the states of *Tamil Nadu* (US$140 billion) and *Uttar Pradesh* (US$130 billion).

- India's economy became the world's fastest growing *major economy* in the last quarter of 2014, replacing the *People's Republic of China*.

Features of Indian Economy

> Per capita income level is much low in India as compared with other developed countries.

(1) Low Per Capita Income

- According to **World Development Report**, India's per capita income was $1974.76 in 2018. The per capita income in United States is $59,484 and hence India's per capita income is about 1/30 of US level of per capita.

(2) Disparities in Income Distribution

- According to the data shown by NSSO, 39% of rural population possesses only 5% of all the rural assets while, on the other hand, 8% top households possess 46% of total rural assets.

(3) Heavy Population Pressure on Agriculture

- Income disparities are some what more intensive in urban areas as compared with those of rural areas.

- Land-labour ratio is not favourable in India. Per capita land availability is very low and, on the contrary, labour use per hectare is very high in India.

- Agriculture and allied sector even today provides livelihood to about 65 to 70% of the total population but according to the new series of national income released by CSO at 2011-12 prices, the share of agriculture in total GDP is 17.9% in 2014.

(4) Over-Population

- In every decade Indian population gets increased by about 20%. With this high growth rate of population about 1.8 crore new persons are added to Indian population every year.

- According to 2011 census, the total Indian population stands at a high level of 121.02 crore which is 17.7% of the world's total population.

(5) Unbalanced Economic Development

- According to latest data available for the year 2011-12 about 49% of total labour force is dependent on agriculture, 24% on industries and the rest about 27% on trade, transport and other services.

(6) Lack of Capital

- Savings are low in India, i.e. low national income and high consumption expenditure. Gross domestic savings declined to 34.3% in 2008-9, it again improved to 36.6% in 2009-10, but again declined to 32.3% in 2013-14.

(7) Industrialisation Backwardness

- India lacks in large industralisation based on modern and advanced technology, which fails to accelerate the pace of development in the economy.

- The latest gross domestic product (GDP) estimates show that industry grew by just 1.1% in 2012-13 and slowed further in 2013-14, posing a negative growth rate of 0.1%. During 2014-15, (April-Dec.) IIP growth has been estimated to be 2.1%.

(8) Service Sector

- The services sector has emerged as the second fastest growing in the world, with a CAGR of 9% during the period from 2001 to 2012.

(9) Operation of Economic vicious circles

- Economic vicious circles are still in operation in Indian economy and as a result poverty has become both cause and effect in the country. **"India is poor because economy is poor"**–indicates a true economic scene of the country. The intensity of poverty has made these vicious circles unbreakable in the country.

(10) Market Imperfections

- Indian economy faces a number of market imperfections like lack of mobility among production factors from one place to the other and lack of specialisations which hinder the optimum utilisation of available resources.

(11) Limited Availability of Transport and Communication Facilities –

- Transport facilities are not available in remoter areas of the country due to which industrial development is not equally distributed among various part of the economy. It also hinders the process of exploiting available resources in the country.

Existence of Traditional Society

- The Indian traditional society is still facing a number of social problems like traditions and customs, malpractices, superstitious, etc. which adversely effect the process of economic development, because these social obligations do increase the unproductive expenditure of the masses and hardly spare any saving for capital formation process.

Structure of the Indian Economy

Indian Economy consists of 3 important aspects:

- Agricultural
- Industry
- Service

Occupational Structure

- The distribution of working population among " different occupations" or "productive activities".

Types of Occupations

Primary	Secondary	Tertiary
Agriculture	Industries	Banking
Plantations	Construction Activities	Hotels
Mining		Computers
		Communications

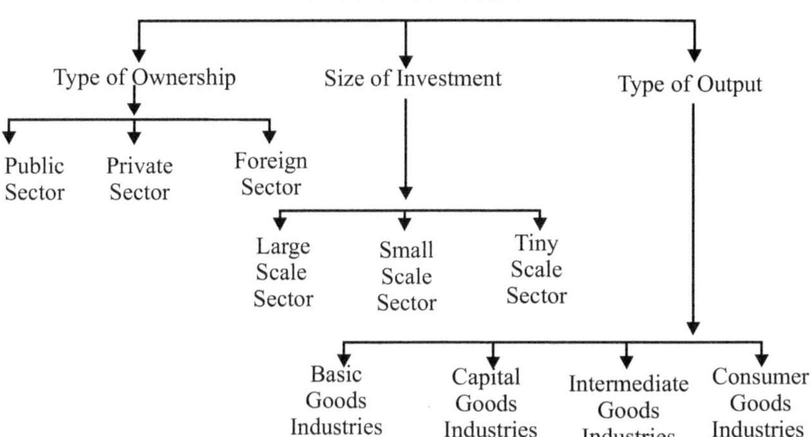

National Income

National Income of a country is the total value of all final goods and services produced in the country in a particular period of time usually, one year. The growth of National Income helps to know the progress of the country. National Income is a flow, not a stock. In India, National Income estimates are related with the financial year, i.e. April 1 to March 31.

Measures/Concepts of National Income

1. **Gross Domestic Product (GDP):** GDP is the total money value of all final goods & services produced within the geographical boundaries of the country (produced by resident citizens + foreign nationals) during a given period of time, generally one year.

$$GDP = Q \times P,$$

Q = Total quantity of final goods & services.
P = Price of final goods & services.

2. **Gross National Product (GNP):** GNP is the money value of total output or production of final goods & services produced by the nationals of a country during a given period of time, generally a year. In this case, the income of all the resident & non-resident citizens of a country is included whereas the income of foreign nationals who reside within the geographical boundary of the country is excluded.

$$GNP = GDP + (X - M)$$

X = Export of goods & services
M = Import of goods & services
$X - M$ = Net Factor Income from Abroad (NFIA)
So, $$GNP = GDP + NFIA$$

3. **Net National Product (NNP): can be calculated in 2 ways:-**
(i) NNP at market price:

$$NNP = GNP - Depreciation$$

Depreciation means wear & tear of goods produced.
NNP at market price includes Indirect taxes and excludes subsidies.
(ii) NNP at factor cost: NNP at factor cost calculates National Income only on the basis of cost incurred to produce the goods & services. This cost is the payment made to the factors of production.

$$NNP_{fc} = NNP_{mp} - \text{Indirect Taxes} + \text{Subsidy}$$

When NNP is obtained at factor cost, it is known as National Income.

Likewise, GDP at factor cost also can be calculated.

$$GDP_{fc} = GDP_{mp} - \text{Indirect Taxes} + \text{Subsidy}$$

4. **Personal Income :** It is that income which is actually obtained by nationals in one year.

P.I. = National Income – Undistributed Profits of Corporation – Payments for Social Security Provisions – Corporate Taxes + Government Transfer payments + Business Transfer payments + Net Interest paid by government.

SOCIAL SECURITY PROVISIONS = Payments made by employees towards pension & provident fund

TRANSFER PAYMENTS = payments made not against any productive activity. eg. – old age pension, unemployment compensation, disaster relief payment, etc.

5. **Disposal Personal Income (DPI):** Income that is available to individuals that can be disposed at their will.

$$DPI = \text{Personal Income} - \text{Direct Taxes.}$$

6. **National Income at constant price & current price**

$$\text{NI @ Constant Price} = \text{Total quantity of all final goods & services produced in a particular year} \times \text{Price of base year.}$$

Base year of National Income accounts is the year chosen to enable inter – year comparisons. The new series changes the base to 2011–12 from 2004–05

$$\text{NI @ Current Price} = \text{Total quantity of all final goods & services produced in a particular year} \times \text{Price of goods & services in that particular year.}$$

Measurement of National Income

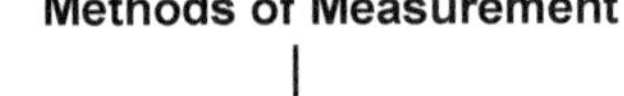

Product/Output/Production method

1. Gross value added = Output of final goods & services – Intermediate Consumption

2. GDP = Gross value added + Indirect Taxes – Subsidy

Income method

N.I. = Total Rent + Total wages + Total Interest + Total profit

Consumption/Expenditure method

GDP = Consumption Expenditure of Consumers + Consumption Expenditure of investors or entrepreneur called investment + consumption of government

EXERCISE

1. What is the mainstay of Indian economy ?
   (a) Manufacturing (b) Business
   (c) Public sector   (d) Agriculture
2. The data of estimation of India's National income is issued by ?
   (a) Planning Commission
   (b) National Data Center
   (c) Central Statistical Organsation
   (d) None of above
3. The most important source of capital formation in India has been?
   (a) Household savings
   (b) Public sector savings
   (c) Government revenue surpluses
   (d) Corporate savings
4. Which of the following is not a method of estimating national income?
   (a) Income method
   (b) Value - added method
   (c) Expenditure method
   (d) Export - import method
5. Following are the features of underdevelopment in India.
   (a) Majority of the people depend on agriculture
   (b) Low per capita income
   (c) Incidence of unemployment
   (d) All the above
6. Following are the features of mixed economy in India.
   (a) Existence of private and public sectors
   (b) Dominant role of public sector
   (c) Decentralized planning
   (d) All the above
7. Following are the roles of agriculture in India
   (a) Providing employment
   (b) Contributing to national income
   (c) Supporting industry
   (d) All the above
8. Industrial sector depends on agriculture sector because
   (a) Agriculture provides food grains to industrial works
   (b) Agriculture supplies raw materials to industries
   (c) Agricultural sector provides market for industrial products
   (d) All the above

9. As per the CSO classification, which of the following does not fall under finance and real estate category?
   (a) Banking   (b) Construction
   (c) Insurance   (d) Real estate
10. Consider the following statements and identify the right ones.
    I. The data for NI and PCI are collected at current prices.
    II. They are deflated using the deflator index to get value at constant prices.
    (a) I only   (b) II only
    (c) both   (d) none
11. The most appropriate measure of a country's economic growth is
    (a) GDP   (b) NDP
    (c) Per capita real income
    (d) GNP
12. The largest proportion of national income comes from
    (a) Public Sector
    (b) Private Sector
    (c) Local Sector
    (d) None of the above
13. National Income is
    (a) Net National Product – Indirect Taxes + Subsidies
    (b) Gross National Product – Direct Taxes
    (c) Gross Domestic Product – Imports
    (d) Net Domestic Product + Products
14. At the present rate of growth of population, by which year is India expected to overtake China?
    (a) 2022   (b) 2015
    (c) 2020   (d) 060
15. It is deducted from GNP to get NNP:
    (a) Indirect taxes
    (b) Depreciation
    (c) Direct taxes
    (d) Transfer payment
16. Which is the largest figure:
    (a) NNP   (b) GNP
    (c) DPI   (d) PI
17. It is avoided to make correct estimate of national income:
    (a) Free services
    (b) Double counting
    (c) Export earnings
    (d) All of the above

18. It is not included in estimation of national income:
    (a) Illegal income
    (b) Services of house wife
    (c) Imports
    (d) All are not included
19. A country is poor if it has:
    (a) Less production of goods per capita
    (b) Less amount of gold
    (c) Less amount of foreign currency
    (d) Less exports
20. Which of the following would increse level of national income?
    (a) An increase in taxation.
    (b) A reduction in government spending
    (c) A reduction in consumer spending
    (d) An increase in exports

HINTS & EXPLANATIONS

1. **(d)** Agriculture is demographically the broadest economic sector and plays a significant role in the overall socio-economic fabric of India.

2. **(c)** The Central Statistical Organisation (CSO) of India is responsible for coordination of statistical activities in India, and evolving and maintaining statistical standards.

3. **(a)** Household saving is defined as the difference between a household's disposable income (wages, income of the self-employed and net property income) and its consumption (expenditures on goods and services.)

4. **(d)** 5. **(d)**

6. **(d)** The features of a mixed economy which exist in India are: Private ownership of means of production: This is observed in most of the agricultural, industrial and service sectors. ... The public sector plays a crucial role in strategic sectors such as arms and ammunitions.

7. **(d)** India is mainly an agricultural country. Agriculture is the most important occupation for most of the Indian families. In India, agriculture contributes about sixteen percent (16%) of total GDP and ten percent (10%) of total exports.

8. **(d)** The agriculture sector is the backbone of an economy which provides the basic ingredients to mankind and now raw material for industrialisation.

9. **(b)** As per the CSO classification, construction falls under the category of industrial sector.

10. **(c)** This is done so because the national income can increase either due to increase in production of goods and services or in prices.

11. **(c)** Per capita income is the average income of the country. Per capita real income takes inflation into consideration.

12. **(b)**

13. **(a)** National income is the total value a country's final output of all new goods and services produced in one year.

14. **(a)** Already containing 18% of the world's population, India is projected to be the world's most populous country by 2022, surpassing China, its population reaching 1.6 billion by 2050.

15. **(b)** Depreciation is only deducted from GDP when calculating net national income, not when calculating gross national income.

16 **(b)** Gross national product (GNP) is a broad measure of a nation's total economic activity. GNP is the value of all finished goods and services produced in a country in one year by its nationals.

17. **(b)** To avoid the problem of double counting, only the value of the final stage, the retail price, is included, and not the value added in all the intermediate stages - the costs of production, plus profits.

18. **(d)** 19. **(a)**   20. **(d)**

6
CHAPTER

Jawahar Rozgar Yojana

- Jawahar Rozgar Yojana was launched on April 1, 1989 by merging National Rural Employment Program (NREP) and Rural Landless Employment Guarantee Programme (RLEGP).
- Since April 1, 1999 this Yojana was replaced by Jawahar Gram Samridhi Yojana. Later from September 25, 2001 Jawahar Gram Samridhi Yojana was merged with Sampoorna Grameen Rozgar Yojana.

Indira Gandhi National Old Age Pension Scheme

- The **Indira Gandhi National Old Age Pension Scheme (IGNOAPS)** is a non-contributory old age pension scheme that covers Indians who are 60 years and above and live below the poverty line. The pension scheme is part of the National Social Assistance Programme (NSAP) that was launched by the Ministry of Rural Development in August, 1995.
- All IGNOAPS beneficiaries aged 60-79 receive a monthly pension of ₹200. Those 80 years and above receive a monthly pension amount of ₹500.

Annapurna

- This scheme was started by the government in 1999-2000 to provide food to senior citizens who cannot take care of themselves and are not under the National Old Age Pension Scheme (NOAPS), and who have no one to take care of them in their village.

- This scheme would provide 10 kg of free food grains a month for the eligible senior citizens. The allocation for this scheme as off 2000-2001 was ₹ 100 crore.

Integrated Rural Development Program (IRDP)

- IRDP in India is among the world's most ambitious programs to alleviate rural poverty by providing income-generated assets to the poorest of the poor. This program was first introduced in 1978-79 in some selected areas, but covered all the areas by November 1980.
- The main objective of IRDP is to raise families of identified target group below poverty line by creation of sustainable opportunities for self-employment in the rural sector. The program is implemented in all blocks of the country as centrally sponsored scheme funded on 50:50 basis by the Center and the states.
- The target group under IRDP consists of small and marginal farmers, agricultural laborers and rural artisans having annual income below ₹ 11,000 defined as poverty line in the Eighth Plan.

National Rural Employment Guarantee Act (NREGA)

- The *NREGA* bill notified in 2005 and came into force in 2006 and further modified it as the Mahatma Gandhi National Rural Employment Guarantee Act (MGNREGA) in 2008. This scheme guarantees 150 days of paid work to people in the rural areas.

- The scheme has proved to be a major boost in Indian rural population's income. The Ministry of Rural Development (MRD) is the nodal Ministry for the implementation of NREGA. It will also ensure that the implementation of NREGA at all levels is sought to be made transparent and accountable to the public. Now 100 to 150 days work for all is provided.

Pradhan Mantri Suraksha Bima Yojana

- **Pradhan Mantri Suraksha Bima Yojana** is a government-backed accident insurance scheme in India. It was originally mentioned in the 2015 Budget speech by Finance Minister Arun Jaitley in February 2015.
- It was formally launched by Prime Minister Narendra Modi on 9 May in Kolkata. As of May 2015, only 20% of India's population has any kind of insurance, this scheme aims to increase the number.
- Pradhan Mantri Suraksha Bima Yojana is available to people between 18 and 70 years of age with bank accounts. It has an annual premium of ₹12 excluding service tax, which is about 14% of the premium. The amount will be automatically debited from the account.
- In case of accidental death or full disability, the payment to the nominee will be ₹2 lakh and in case of partial Permanent disability ₹1 lakh.

Pradhan Mantri Jeevan Jyoti Bima Yojana

- It was formally launched by Prime Minister Narendra Modi on 9 May 2015 in Kolkata. As of May 2015, only 20% of India's population has any kind of insurance, this scheme aims to increase the number.
- Pradhan Mantri Jeevan Jyoti Bima Yojana is available to people between 18 and 50 years of age with bank accounts. It has an annual premium of ₹330 excluding service tax, Which is above 14% of the premium.

Atal Pension Yojana

- It was formally launched by Prime Minister Narendra Modi on 9 May 2015 in Kolkata.
- In Atal Pension Yojana, for every contribution made to the pension fund, the Central Government would also Co-contribute 50% of the total contribution or ₹ 1,000 per annum, whichever is lower, to each eligible subscriber account, for a period of 5 years.
- The minimum age of joining APY is 18 years and maximum age is 40 years. The age of exit and start of pension would be 60 years. Therefore, minimum period of contribution by the subscriber under APY would be 20 years or more.

Pradhan Mantri Mudra Yojana

- **Pradhan Mantri Mudra Yojana** under the Micro Units Development and Refinance Agency (MUDRA) Bank launched in 8 April 2015, is a new institution being set up by Government of India for development and refinancing activities relating to micro units.
- The purpose of MUDRA is to provide funding to the non corporate small business sector. Loans worth about ₹1 lakh crore have been sanctioned to small entrepreneurs under the Pradhan Mantri MUDRA Yojana, Prime Minister Narendra Modi said today, emphasising that the government wants youth to be job creators and not job seekers

- Under the scheme three categories of interventions has been named which includes
1. **Shishu:** Loan up to ₹150,000
2. **Kishore:** Loan ranging from ₹50,000 to ₹5 lakh
3. **Tarun:** Loan above ₹5 lakh and below ₹10 lakh

Pradhan Mantri Garib Kalyan yojana (PMGKY)

The Garib Kalyan Yojana was officially launched by Prime Minister Narendra Modi in April 2015, when he announced that for development of any country, the welfare of weaker and poor people of the country is utmost important.

- The primary objectives of PMGKY are to attract investments in irrigation system at field level, develop and expand cultivable land in the country, enhance ranch water use in order to minimize wastage of water, enhance crop per drop by implementing water-saving technologies and precision irrigation.
- The goal is to open the doors for optimal water budgeting in all sectors. Tagline for PMGKY is "more crop per drop".

National Nutrition Mission (POSHAN Abhiyan)

- National Nutrition Mission was launched as an expansion of Beti Bachao Beti Padhao programme by Prime Minister Narendra Modi at Jhunjhunu in Rajasthan on the occasion of the International Women's Day on March 8, 2018.
- The main objectives of this scheme are to attain proper nutritional status among children from 0-6 years, adolescent girls, pregnant women and lactating mothers in a timely manner; reduce stunting, under-nutrition, and anaemia among young children, women, and adolescent girls; and lowering low birth weight by at least 2% per annum.

Samagra Shiksha Scheme

- The Samagra Shiksha Scheme was launched by the Union Ministry of Human Resource Development (HRD) on May 24, 2018, in view of improving the quality of education at school level in India.
- It is an overarching program which will incorporate digital technology and introduce skill development in the school education system.
- An annual grant of five thousand to twenty thousand rupees will be provided for strengthening libraries in schools under the program.
- The scheme unifies the elements of Sarva Shiksha Abhiyan (SSA), Rashtriya Madhyamik Shiksha Abhiyan (RMSA), and Teacher Education (TE) to treat school education holistically, from pre-school to Class 12 levels.

Atal Bhujal Yojana

- Atal Bhujal Yojana is Central Government's ₹ 6,000-crore ambitious water conservation scheme launched to deal with the ever-deepening crisis of depleting groundwater level.
- The main objectives of this scheme are to revitalize groundwater level and create sufficient water storage for agricultural purposes; rejuvenation of surface water bodies so that groundwater level can be increased, especially in the rural areas; recharging sources of groundwater and ensure effective use of water by involving people at local level.
- The scheme was launched in water-stressed states such as Gujarat, Haryana, Karnataka, Maharashtra, Uttar Pradesh, Rajasthan and Madhya Pradesh.

First "Khelo India School Games"

- The Central Government of India inaugurated the first edition of the Khelo India School Games (KISG) at the Indira Gandhi Indoor Stadium in New Delhi from January 31 to February 8, 2018.
- This program highlighted India's young sporting talent and their potential in sports. The main objectives behind KISG were to revive the sports culture in India at the grass-root level, to build a strong foundation of all the sports played in the country, and make India a great sporting nation.
- This mega event was held across 16 disciplines in the under-17 age category. Around 5,000 school children from all the 29 states and 7 union territories participated in the event.

National Bamboo Mission (Restructured under Budget 2018)

- National Bamboo Mission has been restructured by the government in the Union Budget 2018 in order to promote commercial bamboo cultivation in the northeastern states to boost the income of the bamboo farmers.
- The Union Government has allocated Rs. 1,290 crore towards the mission to promote holistic development of bamboo production as an industry in the country. It will offer a continuous source of income to the bamboo farmers and communities owning bamboo groves.
- There is a proposition of utilizing this mission under the Pradhan Mantri Awas Yojana, the government's flagship programme for housing to set up bamboo houses.

Ayushman Bharat Yojana or National Health Protection Mission

- Ayushman Bharat Yojana or National Health Protection Scheme was launched on April 14, 2018, by the Central government to focus on the wellness of the poor families and providing medical benefits to them.
- Under this scheme, around 10 crore poor families will be provided an insurance cover of Rs. 5 lakh every year and will undergo cashless treatment at all the government and private empanelled hospitals across the country for the secondary and most tertiary care procedures.
- The scheme will include the on-going centrally sponsored schemes-Rashtriya Swasthya Bima Yojana (RSBY) and the Senior Citizen Health Insurance Scheme (SCHIS).

GOBAR-Dhan Yojana

- GOBAR-Dhan is abbreviation of The Galvanising Organic Bio-Agro Resources Dhan (GOBAR-DHAN). It was launched by Haryana's Chief Minister Manohar Lal Khattar and Uma Bharti (Union Minister for Sanitation and Drinking Water) on April 30 this year.
- The GOBAR-Dhan scheme is an effort by the government to improve the living conditions in the Indian villages and make them open-defecation free.
- A segment of the Swachh Bharat initiative, this scheme will focus on useful conversion of solid waste and cattle dung into manure and biogas.

Swatchh Bharat Abhiyan

Prime Minister Narendra Modi launched the ' Swatchh Bharat Mission' or 'Clean India Campaign' from the Valmiki Basti in New Delhi on 02 October, 2014.

This campaign aims to accomplish the vision of 'clean India' by 150th birthday of Mahatma Gandhi, i.e. by 02 October 2019. The urban component of the Mission is proposed to be implemented over 5 years starting from 02 October 2014 in all 4041 statutory towns.

The urban component includes elimination of open defecation, conversion of insanitary toilets to pour flush toilets, eradication of manual scavenging, municipal solid waste management and bringing about a behavioural change in people regarding healthy sanitation practices.

The total expected cost of the programme is ₹ 62,009 crore, out of which the proposed central assistance will be of ₹ 14,623 crore. The "Nirmal Bharat Abhiyan" (NBA) is restructured into "Swachh Bharat" Mission (rural).

Saansad Adarsh Gram Yojana (SAGY)

The scheme was launched on 11th October, 2014 on the occasion of birth anniversary of Lok Nayak Jai Prakash Narayan. The goal of the programme is to develop three Adarsh Grams by March 2019 of which one would be achieved by 2016.

Thereafter, five such would Adarsh Grams (one per year) will be selected and developed by 2024.

Under the scheme, each MP will take the responsibility of developing physical and institutional infrastructure in three villages by 2019.

The MP would be free to identify a suitable Gram Panchayat for developing it into an Adarsh Gram, other than his/her own village or that of his/her spouse.

A Gram Panchayat would be the basic unit. It will have a population of 3,000-5,000 in plain areas and 1,000-3,000 in hilly, tribal and difficult areas.

Labour Reforms Introduced by The Government:

- **The Deen Dayal Upadhyaya Shramev Jayate program** was launched to emphasize the dignity of labour, especially that performed by blue-collared workers referring to them as "shram yogi".

- **The Universal Account Number scheme (UAN) or 'Shram Suvidha'** for all Provident Fund (PF) contributors will allow portability of PF benefits and online tracking of PF benefits. The UAN is provided for all 4.17 crore PF users.

- To support the graduates from Industrial Training Institutes (ITIs) across the country, who undergo vocational training after completing class X, the government will reimburse 50% of the stipend paid to apprentices during first two years of their training. There are 2.82 lakh apprentices undergoing training against 4.9 lakh seats. The program will aim to increase this to 24 lakhs apprentices.

- **The Rashtriya Swasthya Bima Yojana (RSBY),** which insures families of unorganised sector workers for up to Rs. 30,000 of medical care, is to be transferred from the Ministry of Labour and Employment to the Union Health Ministry.

Housing for All by 2022

With an aim to provide housing for all by 2022, the government will soon launch an urban housing mission named after Sardar Patel by merging and improving existing housing schemes.

The focus of the mission is Low Cost Affordable Housing to be anchored in the National Housing Bank with a view to increase the flow of cheaper credit for affordable housing to the urban poor.

Currently, there are several schemes including Jawaharlal Nehru National Urban Renewal Mission, Rajiv Awas Yojana, Indira Awas Yojana, Rajiv Rinn Yojana meant for providing housing facilities to economically weaker sections.

Pradhan Mantri Jan Dhan Yojana

Launch Date – 28 July 2014

Objective – To provide access of banking facilities and financial services to the poor people. This is a national mission for the financial inclusion of all households.

Achievements –

- 60% bank accounts opened in rural areas (As on 25 April 2018)
- 31.52 crore Jan Dhan accounts opened (As on 25 April 2018)
- Total balance in Jan Dhan accounts is Rs. 80871.67 crores (As on 25 April 2018)
- Over 23.71 Crore Rupay Cards issued (As on 25 April 2018)
- Share of zero-balance Jan Dhan accounts dropped to 24% in December 2016 from 73% in December 2014
- Over 1.26 lakh bank-mitras appointed by banks
- 2.5 lakh Gram-Dak-Sewaks will function as banking correspondents

Atal Pension Yojana

The important features and highlights of this scheme are as follows:-
- **Launch Date** – 9 May 2015
- **Objective** – Govt. will provide financial security in old age through guaranteed minimum monthly pension for all people who are working in informal sector or daily wagers in the age group of 18 to 40 years. Govt. contribution is 50% of beneficiaries premium (up to Rs. 1000) for 5 years in new accounts opened before 31 December 2015.

- **Achievements** – As on 5 January 2018, about 80 lakh subscribers have been enrolled under APY.

Pradhan Mantri Ujjwala Yojana

- The important features and highlights of this scheme are as follows:-
- **Launch Date** – 1 May 2016
- **Objective** – To provide deposit free 5 crore cooking gas (LPG) connections to women from below-poverty-line (BPL) households over 3 years from 2016-17 to 2018-2019.

Achievements –

- 2.07 crore LPG connection provided to BPL Households (As on 5 April 2018)
- Scheme spread all over the country, now in 694 districts
- This scheme targets to provide 5 core LPG connections in 3 years during 2016-19
- Rs. 8000 crores have been earmarked for this scheme
- 24X7 Helpline for LPG Consumers – Dial 1906

Swachh Bharat Mission

- The important features and highlights of this scheme are as follows:-

Swachh Bharat Mission Gramin (SBM-G)

- **Launch Date** – 2 October 2014
- **Objective** – To fulfill Mahatma Gandhi's dream of a clean and hygienic India.
- **Achievements** –
- Over 6.26 crore household toilets constructed since the launch of the Mission (as on 21 March 2018)
- 3,23,560 villages, 314 districts and 11 States(9States+2UTs) declared ODF (as on 21st March, 2018)
- 4,464 open defecation free villages under Namami Ganga

- Sanitation Coverage increased from 38.70% in 2014 to 78.98 % as on 21.03.2018
- Incentive for individual toilet increased to Rs. 12,000

Swachh Bharat Mission (Urban)

- **Launch Date** – 2 October 2014
- **Objective** – To make 4,041 cities and towns Open Defecation Free and clean by October, 2019
- **Achievements** –
- 46,36,158 individual household toilets constructed so far
- 3,06,064 Community and Public Toilet seats constructed so far
- 2477 cities have been so far declared Open Defecation Free
- 61,846 urban wards covered under 100% Door to Door collection of solid waste
- Waste to Compost total achievement 13.11 lakh TPA from 145 Plants
- Around 88 Mega Watts of energy is being produced from waste

Pradhan Mantri Awas Yojana (Urban)

- The important features and highlights of this scheme are as follows:-
- **Launch Date** – 25 June 2015
- **Objective** – To address the gap in housing demand and supply in urban areas in respect of Economically Weaker Sections, Low and Middle Income Groups and meet the target of "Housing for All" by 2022, with an aim to provide a decent pucca home
- **Achievements** –
- Cabinet approved creation of National Urban Housing Fund (NUHF) for ₹ 60,000 crores
- As on 31st March 2018, Ministry has sanctioned 43.87 lakh houses under Pradhan Mantri Awas Yojana (Urban)

- More than 21.28 lakh houses have been grounded and about 5.2 lakh houses have been completed. (Including RAY component)
- Beti Bachao Beti Padhao Yojana
- The important features and highlights of this scheme are as follows:-
- **Launch Date** – 22 January 2015
- **Objective** – The goal of the BBBP scheme is to celebrate the girl child and enable her education. The specific objectives of the scheme include preventing gender biased sex selective elimination, ensuring survival and protection of the girl child and ensuring education and participation of the girl child.
- **Achievements** –
- Hon'ble Prime Minister had launched All India coverage 640 districts (as per Census 2011) of BBBP Scheme on 8th March, 2018 at Jhunjhunu, Rajasthan
- Two major components of the Scheme are (i) Multi-sectoral intervention and media advocacy in 405 districts (including 161 districts) is being implemented under the leadership of DCs / DMs and (ii) 360 degree approach in alert media advocacy and outreach activities in remaining 235 districts.
- The BBBP is 100% central sector scheme with total outlay of Rs. 1132.5 Cr from 2017-18 to 2019-2020
- Improving trend in SRB is visible in 104 BBBP
- 119 Districts have reported progress in first trimester registration against the reported Anti Natal Care registrations
- 146 districts have reported improvement in Institutional deliveries
- Unified District Information System for Education (U-DISE) 2015-16, girls enrolment in secondary education was 80.97% against 76% in 2013-14. Now the revised target of GER has been proposed to 82% by 2018-19.

Pradhan Mantri Sukanya Samriddhi Yojana

The important features and highlights of this scheme are as follows:-

- **Launch Date** – 22 January 2015
- **Objective** – A small deposit savings scheme to promote the welfare of girl child and ensure them a secure future.
- **Achievements** –
- More than 1.26 crore accounts have been opened
- Amount of over Rs. 19,183 crores deposited till November 2017

Mission Indradhanush

The important features and highlights of this scheme are as follows:-

- **Launch Date** – 25 December 2014
- **Objective** – To achieve full immunization of at least 90% children by 2020 (now by 2018). Full immunization coverage to missed out and left out children and pregnant women during routine immunization rounds, against 7 life threatening diseases.
- **Achievements** –
- 2.55 crore children vaccinated
- 66.57 lakh children fully immunized
- 68.78 lakh pregnant female immunized
- 73.49 lakh vitamin A doses administered
- 68.57 lakh ORS packets distributed
- 2.345 crore zinc tablets distributed
- **Intensified Mission Indradhanush** – Launched by PM on 8th October 2017 at Vadnagar, Gujarat to cover 121 districts, 17 urban areas and 52 districts of NE states (total 190 districts/urban areas across 24 states) for intensified immunization campaign.

Deen Dayal Upadhyaya Gram Jyoti Yojana

The important features and highlights of this scheme are as follows:-

- **Launch Date** – 25 July 2015
- **Objective** – 100% Rural Electrification with reliable, adequate & quality electricity supply and also to provide access to electricity to villages/ habitations & households. It includes Strengthening and augmentation of sub transmission and distribution infrastructure, Separation of agriculture and non-agriculture feeders and Metering for feeders, distribution transformers & consumers along with Micro-grid and off-grid distribution network.
- **Achievements** – Out of 597,464 census villages, 597,464 villages (100%) have been electrified

Stand Up India Yojana

The important features and highlights of this scheme are as follows:-

- **Launch Date** – 5 April 2016
- **Objective** – To support entrepreneurship among women and SC & ST communities by facilitating bank loans between 10 lakh and 1 Crore to them. This scheme will benefit at least 2.5 lakh entrepreneurs.
- **Achievements** –
- The number of loans given by Public Sector, Private and Regional Banks under the Stand-up India Scheme are 51,888, 2,445, and 1,009 respectively up to 07.03.2018 since inception of the Scheme
- Regional Rural Banks sanctioned 180 loans to borrowers of Scheduled Castes (SC) category as on 07.03.2018 since inception of the Scheme

- 56260 Self Unemployment Insurance, SUI applications sanctioned for 12194 crores
- 44460 SUI applications disbursed for 6641 crores
- 7424 online SUI loan applications submitted of which 2641 SUI online loans have been sanctioned

Pradhan Mantri Kaushal Vikas Yojana (PMKVY)

The important features and highlights of this scheme are as follows:-

- **Launch Date** – 15 July 2015
- **Objective** – To provide formal short term training to impart skills to and recognition of skills through certification, to enhance employability of the youth.

- **Achievements** –
- 8479 training centers opened in 596 districts and training is given in 375 trades.
- 19.85 Lakh youth trained and 2.49 Lakh placed as part of PMKVY (2015-2016)
- For PMKVY (2016-2020), 16.37 Lakh targets have been allocated to training providers under Short Term Training, Recognition of Prior Learning, and Special Projects with 2.72 Lakh enrollments as on date.
- Women constitute approx. 50% of all enrolled candidates under PMKVY
- PMKVY 1 trained 40% higher number of candidates than STAR

EXERCISE

1. Which of the following is not one of the International Development Targets of the Millennium Development Goals?
   (a) Reducing the number of persons living in extreme poverty by one half of 2015
   (b) Universal primary education by 2015
   (c) Reduction of infant and child mortality by 2/3rd by 2015
   (d) Reducing the total population by 1/3rd

2. Chronic unemployment is measured using:
   (a) US data
   (b) CWS data
   (c) None of the two
   (d) Both (a) and (b)

3. Structural Planning refers to:
   (a) laying down broad goals and strategies
   (b) centralised planning
   (c) fixing flexible targets
   (d) changing existing institutions or creating new ones

4. Structural unemployment arises due to:
   (a) deflationary conditions
   (b) heavy industry bias
   (c) shortage of raw materials
   (d) inadequate productive capacity

5. Aam Admi Bima Yojana provides social security to-
   (a) All labours in rural areas
   (b) All landless labours living below poverty line in rural areas
   (c) All labours in urban areas
   (d) All labours in both rural as well as urban areas

6. Sector wise, maximum employment in the public sector in
   (a) electricity, gas, and water
   (b) community, social, and personal services
   (c) finance, insurance, and real estate
   (d) transport, storage, and communication

7. Which Indian plan ensured high growth rate as compared with targeted growth rate ?
   (a) Fifth Plan   (b) Fourth Plan
   (c) Second Plan   (d) Eighth Plan

8. What was the aim of Antyodaya Programme?
   (a) Elimination of Urban Poverty
   (b) Improving the standards of scheduled castes
   (c) Uplifting minorities
   (d) Helping the poorest among poor

9. The Employment Assurance Scheme envisages financial assistance to rural areas for guaranteeing employment to at least
   (a) 50 per cent of the men and women seeking jobs in rural areas
   (b) 50 per cent of the men seeking jobs in the rural areas
   (c) one man and one women in a rural family living below the poverty line
   (d) one person in a rural landless house hold living below the poverty line

10. Among the following who are eligible to benefit from the "Mahatma Gandhi National Rural Employment Guarantee Act"?
    (a) Adult members of only the scheduled caste and scheduled tribe households
    (b) Adult members of below poverty line (BPL) households
    (c) Adult members of households of all backward communities
    (d) Adult members of any household

11. _____ sector was the largest contributor to GDP during the Ninth Plan?
    (a) Manufacturing
    (b) Trade
    (c) Information technology
    (d) Financial services

12. Which of the following is not a millennium development goal?
    (a) The eradication of extreme poverty and hunger.
    (b) Universal primary and secondary education.
    (c) Gender equality and empowerment of women.
    (d) Reducing the child mortality rate.

13. Which one of the following statements is not correct?
    (a) Under the Targeted Public Distribution System, the families below Poverty Line are provided 50 kg of food grains per month per family at subsidized price.
    (b) Under Annapurna Scheme, indigent senior citizens of 65 years of age or above eligible for National Old Age Pension but not getting pension can get 10 kg of food grains per person per month free of cost.
    (c) Ministry of social justice and empowerment has a scheme in which indigent people living in welfare institutions like orphanages are given 15 kg of foodgrains per person per month of BPL rates.
    (d) Ministry of Human Resource Development gives financial support to mid-day meal scheme for the benefit of Class I to V students in government or government aided school.

14. Who among the following is NOT a part of National Development Council?
    (a) Finance Commission of India Chairman
    (b) Vice Chairman of Planning Commission
    (c) Secretary of Planning Commission
    (d) Secretary of Planning & Implementation Ministry

15. 'Pradhan Mantri Jan-Dhan Yojana' has been launched for
    (a) providing housing loan to poor people at cheaper interest rates
    (b) promoting women's Self-Help Groups in backward areas
    (c) promoting financial inclusion in the country
    (d) providing financial help to the marginalized communities

16. The Government of India has established NITI Aayog to replace the
    (a) Human Rights Commission
    (b) Finance Commission
    (c) Law Commission
    (d) Planning Commission

17. Which of the two employment programmes are being merged in newly introduced Prime Minister's Employment Generation Programme?
    1. PMRY   2. NREP
    3. REGP   4. RLEGP
    Choose the right option
    (a) 1 only   (b) 1 and 2
    (c) 1 and 3   (d) 2 and 4

18. With reference to the government's welfare schemes, consider the following statements.
    1. Under the Antyodaya Anna Yojana, the foodgrains are available to the poorest of the poor families at ` 2 kg for wheat and ` 3 kg of rice.
    2. Under the National Old Age Pension Scheme, the old and destitute are provided ` 75 month as Central Pension, in addition to the amount provided by most State Governments.
    3. Government of India has allocated 25 kg foodgrains per below poverty line family per month, at less than half the economic cost.
    Which of these statements are correct?
    (a) 1 and 2   (b) 1 and 3
    (c) 2 and 3   (d) 1, 2 and 3

19. With reference to "Aam Admi Bima Yojana", consider the following statements
    1. The member insured under the scheme must be the head of the family or an earning member of the family in a rural landless household.

2. The member insured must be in the age group of 30 to 65 years.
3. There is a provision for free scholarship for upto two children of the insured who are studying between classes 9 and 12.

Which of the statements given above is/are correct?

(a) 1 only　　(b) 2 and 3
(c) 1 and 3　　(d) 1, 2 and 3

20. _____ is/are not matched correctly?

1. First Plan　　1950-55
2. Third Plan　　1961-66
3. Fourth Plan　　1966-71
4. Seventh Plan　　1985-90

(a) 1 and 2　　(b) 3 only
(c) 1 only　　(d) 1 and 3

21. Which plans and features are wrongly matched?

1. First Plan - Community development projects
2. Second - Heavy industries
3. Third - Green Revolution
4. Fourth Plan

(a) 1 and 4　　(b) 3 and 4
(c) 3 only　　(d) 1 and 3

22. National Rural Employment Guarantee Act ensures that the

1. Centre bears 75% of the cost of wages of unskilled manual workers.
2. State government provides 100 days of work to every member of a household in a financial year.

(a) 1 only　　(b) 2 only
(c) Both 1 and 2　　(d) Neither 1 nor 2

23. Inclusive growth would necessitate :

(a) Development of infrastructural facilities
(b) Revival of agriculture
(c) Increase availability of social services such as education and health.
(d) All the above.

24. Consider the following statements :

(1) MNREGA was launched in the 11th five year plan.
(2) Indira Awas Yojana was launched in the 9th Five Year Plan.

Which of the statements given above is/are correct?

(a) only 1　　(b) only 2
(c) Both 1 and 2　　(d) Neither 1 nor 2

25. Consider the following statements :

(1) Indo-China war had hampered the proper progress and implementation of Fourth Five Year Plan in India.
(2) In the Indian Economy, the plan Holiday took place during 1966 to 1969.

Which of the statements given above is/are correct?

(a) 1 only
(b) 2 only
(c) Both 1 and 2
(d) Neither 1 nor 2

26. Consider the following statements :

(1) The state sets broad parameters and goals for the economy.
(2) The targets to be achieved are broadly set by the state.
(3) The plan is made for the specific time period of about 15 years.

Which of the statements given above is/are correct about the Indicative planning?

(a) 1, 2 and 3　　(b) 1 and 2
(c) 1 and 3　　(d) only 1

27. Consider the following statements:

1. Indira Gandhi Matritva Sahyog Yojana (IGMSY) has been launched to improve the health and nutrition status of pregnant, lactating women and infants.
2. The scheme envisages Cash Incentives for the above beneficiaries
3. All Government Women Employees are beneficiaries of the IGMSY

Which among the above statements is are correct?

(a) Only 1 & 2 are correct
(b) Only 2 & 3 are correct
(c) Only 1 is correct
(d) All are correct

28. **List-I**

(A) Development
(B) National Council of
(C) Indira Gandhi Institute
(D) World Bank

List-II

(1) UN India Human Programme Development Report
(2) India Development Applied Economic Report Research
(3) World Development of Development Report Research
(4) Human Report Development

(a) A – 4 ; B – 1 ; C – 2 ; D – 3
(b) A – 4 ; B – 2 ; C – 1 ; D – 3
(c) A – 2 ; B – 3 ; C – 4 ; D – 1
(d) A – 2 ; B – 1 ; C – 4 ; D – 3

29. Consider the following statements
1. Since 1993-94, the benefit of Indira Awas Yojana is being provided even to those rural poor of non-schedule caste/schedule tribe who are living below the poverty line.
2. A minimum of 60% of funds is to be utilized for construction of houses for the SC/ST people.
3. From 1995-96, IAY benefits have been extended to widows or next to kin of defence personnel killed in action.
4. Benefits have also been extended to ex-servicemen and retired members of Para military forces as long as they fulfil the normal eligibility conditions of IAY.
Which of the following is / are correct
(a) 1 and 2   (b) 3 and 4
(c) 1 and 4   (d) 1, 2, 3, 4

30. Scheme _______ is a Government of India program aimed at providing 24×7 uninterrupted power supply to all homes in Rural India
1. Deendayal Disabled Rehabilitation Scheme
2. Deen Dayal Upadhyaya Gram Jyoti Yojana
3. Digital India Programme
Select the name of the scheme
(a) 1 only   (b) 2 only
(c) 3 only   (d) 2 and 3

31. The Economic Planning Committee was established in the chairmanship of
(a) J.L. Nehru
(b) Dr. Rajendra Prasad
(c) Ramkrishna Mudaliyar
(d) K.C. Niyogi

32. Which five year plan was focused on poverty and unemployment for the first time?
(a) Third Five Year Plan
(b) Fourth Five Year Plan
(c) Fifth Five Year Plan
(d) Sixth Five Year Plan

33. Socio-economic planning is a part of _____?
(a) Union List   (b) State List
(c) Concurrent List   (d) Reserved List

34. The 'Bombay Plan' drafted by GD Birla and JRD Tata emphasized:
(a) that the economy should be left to the dynamic investments by the private sector in heavy industries, etc.
(b) the public sector investment in infrastructure and heavy industries
(c) annual planning
(d) that the private sector should foot the Bill for intensive and low return investments in the industrial sector.

35. _____ is an achievement of Indian planning.
1. development of infrastructure
2. diversification of industry and exports
3. high growth in national in-come
4. control over prices
(a) 1 and 2   (b) 1, 2 and 3
(c) 1, 2 and 4   (d) 2 and 3

36. Which among the following is not correct with regard to Sampoorna Garmeena Rozgar Yojana?
1. The cash component of the programme is borne exclusively by the Central Government.
2. Foodgrains are provided free of costs to the States/Union Territories.
Select the answer using the code given below:
(a) 1 only   (b) 2 only
(c) Both 1 and 2   (d) Neither 1 Nor

37. Match the following

Year of starting		**Name of programme**
I.	1971-72	a. Pilot Intensive Rural Employment
II.	1972-73	b. Crash Scheme for Rural Employment
III.	1973-74	c. Food for work Programme
IV.	1977-78	d. Drought Prove Areas Programme

    (a) I-a, II-b, III-c, III-d
    (b) I-b, II-a, III-d, IV-c
    (c) I-d, II-c, III-b, IV-a
    (d) I-a, II-d, III-a, IV-b

38. Consider the following statements
    1. Food for Work Programme was launched in India during the 10th Five Year Plan.
    2. The Planning Commission in India is a constitutional body.
    Which of the statements given above is/are correct?
    (a) Only 1   (b) Only 2
    (c) Both 1 and 2   (d) Neither 1 nor 2

39. Consider the following statements:
    1. Indira Gandhi Matritva Sahyog Yojana (IGMSY) has been launched to improve the health and nutrition status of pregnant, lactating women and infants.
    2. The scheme envisages Cash Incentives for the above beneficiaries
    3. All Government Women Employees are beneficiaries of the IGMSY
    Which among the above statements is / are not correct?
    (a) 1 and 2   (b) 2 and 3
    (c) 3 only   (d) 1, 2, 3

40. Match the following

List-I	**List-II**
(Five Year Plan)	**(Emphasis)**
A. First empowerment	1. Food security and women
B. Second	2. Heavy industries
C. Fifth	3. Agriculture and community development
D. Ninth	4. Removal of poverty

    Codes :

	A	B	C	D
(a)	1	2	4	3
(b)	1	4	2	3
(c)	3	2	4	1
(d)	3	4	2	1

HINTS & EXPLANATIONS

1. (d) 2. (d) 3. (d) 4. (d) 5. (b)
6. (b) 7. (d) 8. (d) 9. (c)
10. (d) All adult members of the household who registered can apply for work. To register, they have to be local residents.
11. (a) 12. (b) 13. (a) 14. (a)
15. (c) Pradhan Mantri Jan-Dhan Yojana (PMJDY) is National Mission for Financial Inclusion to ensure access to financial services, namely, Banking/ Savings & Deposit Accounts, Remittance, Credit, Insurance, Pension in an affordable manner.
16. (d) The Government of India has established NITI Aayog to replace the Planning Commission. The Union Government of India announced formation of NITI Aayog on 1 January 2015 and the first meeting of NITI Aayog was held on 8 February 2015.
17. (c) 18. (d)
19. (c) The statements 1st and 3rd are correct, but 2nd statement is wrong because, the member should be aged between 18 and 59 years not 30 and 65 years.
20. (d) 21. (b) 22. (b)
23. (d) Inclusive growth is a concept which involves equitable allocation of resources during the process of economic growth with benefits incurred by every section of society. Inclusive growth necessitates development of infrastructural facilities, revival of agriculture and also increases availability of social services such as education and health.
24. (b) The Mahatma Gandhi National Rural Employment Guarantee Act (MNREGA) is an Indian law that aims to guarantee the 'right to work' and ensures livelihood security in rural areas by providing at least 100 days of guaranteed wage employment in a financial year to every household whose adult members volunteer to do unskilled manual work. MNREGA was launched in 200 select districts in 2006. However Indira Awas Yojana was lauched in the 9th Five Year Plan to provide housing for the rural poor in India.
25. (b) Despite big investments during the first three Plans the living standards of the poor could not be raised and poverty and inequity in distribution of state resources remained stark. Consequently, the period between 1966 and 1969 marked the shift from a 'growth approach' to a 'distribution from growth approach'. Looking at the failures and pitfalls the planners suspended the impending Fourth Plan, which was due in 1966, until 1969 for a revision of objectives and targets. This was called as the 'Plan Holiday' extending from 1 April 1966 to 31 March 1969.
26. (b) Indicative planning is a form of economic planning implemented by a state in an effort to solve the problem of imperfect information in market and mixed economies in order to increase economic performance. Regarding the indicative planning, state sets broad parameters and goals for the economy and the targets to be achieved are broadly set by the state.
27. (a) 28. (a)
29. (d) 1. Since 1993-94, the benefit of Indira Awas Yojana is being provided even to those rural

poor of non-schedule caste/ schedule tribe who are living below the poverty line.

2. A minimum of 60% of funds is to be utilized for construction of houses for the SC/ST people.

3. From 1995-96, IAY benefits have been extended to widows or next to kin of defence personnel killed in action.

4. Benefits have also been extended to ex-servicemen and retired members of Para military forces as long as they fulfil the normal eligibility conditions of IAY.

30. (b) Deen Dayal Upadhyaya Gram Jyoti Yojana is a Government of India program aimed at providing 24 × 7 uninterrupted power supply to all homes in Rural India. It was launched in 2015.

31. (a) After India gained independence, a formal model of planning was adopted, and the Planning Commission, was established on 15 March 1950, with Prime Minister Jawaharlal Nehru as the chairman.

32. (c) Fifth five year plan was focused on poverty and unemployment for the first time. The slogan of 'poverty abolition' was given by Indira Gandhi in 1971 and it was implemented during the fifth five year plan(1974–79). Gandhi promised to reduce poverty by targeting the consumption levels of the poor and enact wide ranging social and economic reforms.

33. (c) 34. (b) 35. (a) 36. (b)

37. (b)

S. No.	Name of the Programme	Year of Starting	Main Objectives
1.	Crash Scheme for Rural Employment	1971-72	Generation of new employment rural development.
2.	Pilot Intensive Rural Employment	72-73	Construction work in Villages.
3.	Drought Prove Areas Programme	73-74	To develop natural resources in drought prove rural areas.
4.	Food for work Programme	77-78	To provide food for work in development process

38. (a) According to The National Food for Work Programme, food subsidy should be better targeted through targeted public distribution system and specific programmes for the poor like Food for Work Programme. The National Food for Work Programme was launched on 14 November 2004 in 150 of the most backward districts of India with the objective of generating supplementary wage employment. The Planning commission is not a constitutional body.

39. (c) Indira Gandhi Matritva Sahyog Yojana (IGMSY) has been launched to improve the health and nutrition status of pregnant, lactating women and infants. The scheme envisages Cash Incentives for the above beneficiaries.

40. (c) 1. First Five Year Plan (1951-56)- Agriculture and community development

2. Second Five Year Plan (1956-61)- Heavy Industry

3. Fifth Five Year Plan (1974-79)- Removal of Poverty

4. Ninth Five Year Plan (1997-2002)- Food Security and woman empowerment

COMMISSIONS & ORGANISATIONS

1. Finance Commission

The constitution of the Finance Commission is laid down in Art. 280, which has to be read with the Finance Commission (Miscellaneous Provisions) Act of 1951. The Commission has to be constituted by the President, every five years.

The Chairman must be a person having 'experience in public affairs'; and the other four members must be appointed from amongst the following —

a) A High Court Judge or one qualified to be appointed as such;

b) person having special knowledge of the finances and accounts of the Government;

c) a person having wide experience in financial matters and administration;

d) a person having special knowledge of economics.

Functions

It shall be the duty of the Commission to make recommendations to the President as to–

(a) The distribution between the Union and the States of the net proceeds of taxes which are to be, or may be, divided between them under this Chapter and the allocation between the States of the respective shares of such proceeds;

(b) The principles which should govern the grants-in-aid of the revenues of the States out of the Consolidated Fund of India;

(c) The measures needed to augment the Consolidated Fund of a State to supplement the resources of the Panchayats in the State;

(d) The measures needed to augment the Consolidated Fund of a State to supplement the resources of the Municipalities in the State;

(e) Any other matter referred to the Commission by the President in the interests of sound finance.

Finance Commission	Year of Establishment	Chairman	Operational Duration	Year of Submitting Report
I	1951	K.C. Niyogi	1952-57	1952
II	1956	K. Santhanam	1957-62	1956* and 1957
III	1960	A.K. Chanda	1962-66	1961
IV	1964	P.V. Rajamannar	1966-69	1965
V	1968	Mahaveer Tyagi	1969-74	1968* and 1969
VI	1972	Brahma Nand Reddy	1974-79	1973
VII	1977	J.M. Shellet	1979-84	1978
VIII	1983	Y.B. Chawan	1984-89	1983* and 1984
IX	1987	N.K.P.Salve	1989-95	1989
X	1992	K.C. Pant	1995-2000	Nov. 26, 1994

XI	1998	A.M. Khusro	2000-2005	Jan. 15, 2000* & 7 july, 2000 & 31 Aug. 2000
XII	2003	C.Rangrajan	2005-10	Report submitted on Nov. 30, 2004.
XIII	2007	Vijai L. Kelkar	2010-15	Submitted Report on December 30, 2009
XIV	2014	Y V Reddy	2015-20	Submitted its report to the President of India on 15 December 2014.
XV	2017	N.K.Singh	2020-25	....

* Interim Report

14th Finance Commission

- The 14th Finance Commission was constituted in January 2014. Commissions chairman was former RBI governor Y V Reddy and its members were Sushma Nath, M. Govinda Rao, Abhijit Sen, Sudipto Mundle. In December 2014, Commission had submitted its report to the President Pranab Mukherjee.
- The 14th Finance Commission has submitted its report to the President Pranab Mukherjee.
- Finance Commission in its report has given their views on the devolution of tax receipts from the Centre to the states from 1st April 2015 to 31st March 2020. Earlier, the Finance Commission was appointed in January 2013 to give its report by October 31 this year.

Recommendations of 14th Finance Commission

- Union government has accepted recommendations of the 14th Finance Commission (FC) as per its agenda of cooperative federalism. The accepted recommendations are for the five-year period 2015-16 to 2019-20.

Key facts

- Government has accepted FC's recommendation to increase the devolution of tax receipts from the Centre to the states to 42 %. Previously, 13th FC had pegged the states' share at 32 per cent.
- The share of States in the Centre's net tax receipts will go up by Rs 1,78,000 crore in 2015-2016. It is the largest ever change in percentage of devolution.
- As per the increased devolution suggested by 14th FC, States will get Rs 3.48 lakh crore in 2014-15 and Rs 5.26 lakh crore in 2015-16.
- Higher tax devolution will allow states greater autonomy in financing and designing of schemes as per their needs and requirements.
- FC also recommended the distribution of grants of Rs 2 .88 lakh crore to states for strengthening duly elected gram panchayats and municipal bodies for five years.
- FC also has identified 11 revenue deficit states and granted them Rs 48,906 crore as additional resources for the year 2015-16.

Highlights of 14th Finance Commission Report

Grant-in-aid for Revenue Deficit States (2015-2020)

States	2015-20(₹crores)
Andhra Pradesh	22, 113
Assam	33, 79
Himachal Pradesh	40, 625
Jammu and Kashmir	59, 666
Kerala	9,519
Manipur	10,227
Meghalaya	1,770
Mizoram	12,183
Nagaland	18,475
Tripura	5,103
West Bengal	11,760
Total States	1, 94,821

Criteria and Weights for Calculating Tax Devolution

Criteria	Weight (%)
Population	17.5
Demographic Change	10
Income Distance	50
Area	15
Forest Cover	7.5

15th Finance Commission:

- The 15th Finance Commission constituted in November 2017 will recommend central transfers to states. It has also been mandated to: (i) review the impact of the 14th Finance Commission recommendations on the fiscal position of the centre; (ii) review the debt level of the centre and states, and recommend a roadmap; (iii) study the impact of GST on the economy; and (iv) recommend performance-based incentives for states based on their efforts to control population, promote ease of doing business, and control expenditure on populist measures, among others.

- This Commission will be headed by Shri. N.K.Singh, former Member of Parliament and former Secretary to the Government of India. Shri Shaktikanta Das, former Secretary to the Government of India and Dr. Anoop Singh, Adjunct Professor, Georgetown University shall be the members of the Commission. Dr. Ashok Lahiri, Chairman (Non-executive, part time), Bandhan Bank and Dr. Ramesh Chand, Member, NITI Aayog shall be the Part time members of the Commission. Shri Arvind Mehta shall be the Secretary to the Commission.

- The new Finance Commission will cover five-year period commencing April 1, 2020.

National Statistical Commission

- The Government of India through a resolution dated 1st June, 2005 set up the National Statistical Commission (NSC). The setting up of the NSC followed the decision of the Cabinet to accept the recommendations of the Rangarajan Commission, which reviewed the Indian Statistical System in 2001.

- The NSC was constituted with effect from 12th July 2006 with a mandate to evolve policies, priorities and standards in statistical matters.

- Basically NSC is the apex advisory body on statistical matters and the government has proposed the National Statistical Commission Bill to strengthen its existing institutional and legal framework which have been found to be inadequate for producing India's official statistics.

- Core statistics such as national income and growth data, industrial production and inflation numbers besides budgetary data related to capital and revenue currency and deposit-related indicators and capital market instruments could come under the commission's auditory scanner if the policy makes its way through.

- The Chief Executive Officer (CEO) of the NITI (National Institution for Transforming India) Aayog is the ex-officio Member in the Commission.

- The NSC has four Members besides a Chairperson, each having specialization and experience in specified statistical fields.

- Dr. Radha Binod Barman is its current chairperson, will remain on his post till 31 July 2018.

Khadi and Village Industries Commission

- The Khadi and Village Industries Commission (KVIC) is a statutory body formed by the Government of India, under the Act of Parliament, 'Khadi and Village Industries Commission Act of 1956'.

- It is an apex organization under the Ministry of Micro, Small and Medium Enterprises, with regard to khadi and village industries within India, which seeks to - "plan, promote, facilitate, organise and assist in the establishment and development of khadi and village industries in the rural areas in coordination with other agencies engaged in rural development wherever necessary."

- In April 1957, it took over the work of former All India Khadi and Village Industries Board.

- The First Director of KVIC was Late Sardar KA Venkataramaiya, a veteran freedom fighter from Karnataka. Its head office is based in Mumbai, with its six zonal offices in Delhi, Bhopal, Bnagalore, Kolkata, Mumbai and Guwahati. Other than its zonal offices, it has offices in 29 states for the implementation of its various programmes

The objectives of KVIC is-

1. The social objective of providing employment.

2. The economic objective of producing saleable articles.

3. The wider objective of creating self-reliance amongst the poor and building up of a strong rural community spirit

National Commission for Enterprises in the Unorganized Sector, India

- The National Commission for Enterprises in the Unorganized Sector (NCEUS) was established by the Government of India as an advisory body on the informal sector to bring about improvement in the productivity of informal enterprises for generation of large scale employment opportunities on a sustainable basis, particularly in the rural areas.
- The Commission was mandated to recommend appropriate measures to enhance the competitiveness of the informal sector in the global economy and to link the sector with the institutional framework in areas such as credit, raw material, infrastructure, technology up-gradation skill development, and marketing.
- In its 2007 report, the Commission recommended a broad policy agenda, including:

National Commission for Enterprises in the Unorganized Sector, India

- The National Commission for Enterprises in the Unorganized Sector (NCEUS) was established by the Government of India as an advisory body on the informal sector to bring about improvement in the productivity of informal enterprises for generation of large scale employment opportunities on a sustainable basis, particularly in the rural areas.
- The Commission was mandated to recommend appropriate measures to enhance the competitiveness of

the informal sector in the global economy and to link the sector with the institutional framework in areas such as credit, raw material, infrastructure, technology up-gradation skill development, and marketing.

Commission for Agricultural Costs and Prices (CACP)

- CACP is an expert body which recommends minimum support prices (MSPs) to Government (CCEA) by taking into account cost of production, trends in domestic and international prices. It is an attached office of the Ministry of Agriculture and Farmers Welfare. It came into existence in January 1965.
- Currently, CCEA comprises Chairman, Member Secretary, one Member (Official) and two Members (Non-Official). The non-official members are representatives from farming community and usually have active association with farming community.
- As of now, CACP recommends MSPs of 23 commodities, which comprise 7 cereals (paddy, wheat, maize, sorghum, pearl millet, barley and ragi), 5 pulses (gram, tur, moong, urad, lentil), 7 oilseeds (groundnut, rapeseed-mustard, soyabean, seasmum, sunflower, safflower, nigerseed), and 4 commercial crops (copra, sugarcane, cotton and raw jute).
- CACP submits its recommendations to the government in the form of Price Policy Reports every year, separately for five groups of commodities namely Kharif crops, Rabi crops, Sugarcane, Raw Jute and Copra.

Central Statistical Organisation (CSO)

- The Central Statistical Organisation (CSO) was set up in the cabinet secretariat on 2 May 1951. CSO is responsible for coordination of statistical activities in the country, and evolving and maintaining statistical standards.

- CSO activities include national income accounting, conduct an annual survey of industries, economic census and its follow up surveys, compilation of index of industrial production, as well as Consumer Price Indices for urban non-manual employees, human development Statistics, gender statistics, imparting training in official statistics, five year plan work relating to development of statistics in the States and Union territories, dissemination of statistical information, work relating to trade, energy, construction and environment statistics, revision of national industrial classification, etc.

- The CSO is headed by the Director-General who is assisted by 2 Additional Directors-General and 4 Deputy Directors-General, Directors & Joint Directors and other supporting staff.

- The Central Statistical Organisation (CSO) is located in Delhi. Some portion of industrial statistics work pertaining to an annual survey of industries is carried out in Kolkata.

The National Sample Survey Organization (NSSO)

The National Sample Survey Office(NSSO) in India is a unique setup to carry out surveys on socio-economic, demographic, agricultural and industrial subjects for collecting data from house holds and from enterprises located in villages and in the towns. It is a focal agency of the Govt. of India for collection of statistical data in the areas which are vital for developmental planning.

The National Sample Survey Directorate was first setup in the country in the ministry of finance in 1950. The directorate was subsequently transferred to the cabinet secretariat in 1957 and subsequently in 1970 it became a part of NSSO in the department of statistics under the ministry of planning. Since 1999 it is under the newly created Ministry of Statistics and Programme Implementation.

NAFED

- National Agricultural Cooperative Marketing Federation of India Ltd. (NAFED) was established 2nd October 1958. It is registered under the Multi State Co-operative Societies Act.

- Nafed was setup with the object to promote Co-operative marketing of Agricultural Produce to benefit the farmers. Agricultural farmers are the main members of Nafed, who have the authority to say in the form of members of the General Body in the working of Nafed.

- The Department of Agriculture and Cooperation is implementing a Price Support Scheme (PSS) for the procurement of oilseeds and pulses at the Minimum Support Price (MSP) declared by the Government, through NAFED, which is the central nodal agency for this purpose.

- NAFED is the national level marketing agency for agricultural products in the Cooperative Sector.

- The core objective of NAFED is to organise, promote and develop marketing, processing and storage of agricultural, horticultural and forest produce, distribution of agricultural machinery, implements and other inputs, undertake inter-State, import and export trade, wholesale or retail as the case may be and to act and assist for technical advice in agricultural production for the promotion and the working of its members and cooperative marketing, processing and supply societies in India. (NAFED website)

TRIFED

- TRIFED is Tribal Cooperative Marketing Development Federation of India Limited (TRIFED). It was established in August 1987 by the then Ministry of Welfare, Government of India, under the Multi State Cooperative Societies Act 1984 (which has now been replaced by the Multi-State Cooperative Societies Act, 2002).

- The core objective was institutionalizing the trade of Minor Forest Produce (MFP) and Surplus Agriculture Produce (SAP) collected/cultivated by tribals as tribals are heavily dependent on these natural products for their livelihood. However, they did not use to get remunerative prices due to middle-men and unscrupulous traders exploiting the naiveté of Tribals. TRIFED also works as an agency to the FCI for procurement of Wheat and Rice.

EXERCISE

1. Whose duty is it to recommend to the President of India on the issue of the distribution and allocation of the net proceeds of taxes in the context of Centre-State fiscal relations?
   (a) Planning Commission
   (b) National Development Council
   (c) Union Ministry of Finance
   (d) Finance Commission

2. Match the **List-I** with **List-II** and select the correct answer using the codes given below the Lists.
   List-I
   A. Public Interest Litigation
   B. Distribution of powers
   C. Article 268-281
   D. Article 280
   List-II
   1. No Plaintiffs no Defendants
   2. Distribution of revenue
   3. Finance Commission
   4. Federal feature
   Code

	A	B	C	D
(a)	2	4	3	1
(b)	2	4	2	3
(c)	3	4	2	1
(d)	1	2	3	4

3. Who among the following recommend the Union Government that grant of financial assistance to the Sates ?
   1. The President of India.
   2. The Comptroller and Auditor-General of India
   3. The Finance Commission
   4. The Planning Commission
   (a) 1 and 2   (b) 2 and 3
   (c) 3 and 4   (d) 1 and 4

4. The role of the Finance Commission in Centre-State fiscal relations has been undermined by
   (a) The State Government
   (b) The Zonal Councils
   (c) The Planning Commission
   (d) The Elections Commission

5. Match the **List-I** (institutions) with **List-II** (Article) of Constitution and select the correct answer by using the codes given below the lists
   List-I
   A. Comptroller and Auditor General of India
   B. Finance Commission
   C. Administrative Tribunals
   D. Union Public Service Commission
   List-II
   1. Article 315   2. Article 280
   3. Article 148   4. Article 323(A)
   Code

	A	B	C	D
(a)	3	4	2	1
(b)	1	2	4	3
(c)	3	2	4	1
(d)	1	4	2	3

6. Who among the following is responsible for the final compilation of the accounts of the Union Government
   (a) Finance Minister
   (b) Secretary (Finance)
   (c) Controller General of Accounts
   (d) Comptroller and Auditor General

7. Which one of the following statements about the Finance Commission in India is not correct?
   (a) The Commission comprises a Chairman and four other members
   (b) The Parliament is authorized to determine by law the qualifications of the members of the Commission
   (c) All the appointments are made by the President of India
   (d) All the members have to be form Indian Economic Service or Indian Statistical Service

8. Consider the following statements
   The Finance Commission in India is created
   1. By the President of India on the advice of the Union Cabinet.
   2. Under Article 280 of the Constitution of India.
   3. To suggest ways and means to augment the financial resources of the Union and States.
   4. To make recommendations to the President defining the principles which should govern the grants-in-aid of the revenues of the states out of the Consolidated Fund in India.
   Which of the statements given above are correct?
   (a) 2, 3 and 4   (b) 1, 2 and 3
   (c) 1, 3 and 4   (d) 1, 2 and 4

9. Consider the following statements
   The Finance Commission of India is differs from the Planning Commissions because
   1. The former is a constitutional body and latter a Cabinet creation.
   2. The former determines the principles of allocation of grants-in-aid to the states and the latter allocated funds for the Central and the State Government.
   3. The former emphasizes the distinction between plan and non-plan expenditure and the latter maintains it.
   4. The former's report is submitted to the Union Finance Minister and the latter's to the Cabinet.
   Which of the statements given above is/are correct?
   (a) 1 and 2   (b) 3 and 4
   (c) 2, 3 and 4   (d) 1, 2, 3 and 4

10. The Central Administrative Tribunal deals with
    (a) Recruitment matters
    (b) Promotion matters
    (c) Disciplinary matters
    (d) Recruitment and all service matters

11. A new All India Service can be created by
    (a) A resolution of the Rajya Sabha
    (b) An act of Parliament when Rajya Sabha authorises by a resolution
    (c) An order of the President
    (d) A resolution of the UPSC

12. Which of the following are constituted by the President?
    1. The Finance Commission
    2. The Planning Commission
    3. The Commission of Official Languages
    4. The Union Public Service Commission
    Which of the statements given above is/are correct?
    (a) 1 and 2   (b) 3 and 4
    (c) 1, 3 and 4   (d) 2, 3 and 4

13. Which of the following is a source of income of the Gram Panchayats?
    (a) Income tax
    (b) Sales tax
    (c) Professional tax
    (d) Levy duties

14. The Institution of Ombudsman was first introduced in:
    (a) New Zealand   (b) Norway
    (c) Finland   (d) Sweden

15. According to the Constitution of India, it is the duty of the President of India to cause to be laid before the Parliament which of the following?
    1. The Recommendations of the Union Finance Commission
    2. The Report of the Public Accounts Committee
    3. The Report of the Comptroller and Auditor General
    4. The Report of the National Commission for Scheduled Castes
    Select the correct answer using the codes given below :
    (a) 1 only   (b) 2 and 4 only
    (c) 1, 3 and 4 only (d) 1, 2, 3 and 4

16. Consider the following statements:
    1. An amendment to the Constitution of India can be initiated by an introduction of a bill in the Lok Sabha only.
    2. If such an amendment seeks to make changes in the federal character of the Constitution, the amendment also requires to be ratified by the legislature of all the States of India.

    Which of the statements given above is/are correct?
    (a) 1 only   (b) 2 only
    (c) Both 1 and 2   (d) Neither 1 nor 2

17. Match List-I with List-II and select the correct answer using the codes given below the lists:

    List-I (Publisher)
    A. Ministry of Industry
    B. Central Statistical Organisation
    C. Reserve Bank of India
    D. Ministry of Finance

    List-II (Publication)
    1. Report on Currency and Finance
    2. Economic Survey
    3. Wholesale Price Index
    4. National Accounts Statistics

    Codes:
    (a) A-4, B-3, C-2, D-1
    (b) A-3, B-4, C-1, D-2
    (c) A-4, B-3, C-1, D-2
    (d) A-3, B-4, C-2, D-1

18. In India, the interest rate on savings accounts in all the nationalized commercial banks is fixed by
    (a) Union Ministry of Finance
    (b) Union Finance Commission
    (c) Indian Banks' Association
    (d) None of the above.

19. When the annual Union Budget is not passed by the Lok Sabha ?
    (a) The Budget is modified and presented again
    (b) The Budget is referred to the Rajya Sabha for suggestions
    (c) The Union Finance Minister is asked to resign
    (d) The Prime Minister submits the resignation of Council of Ministers.

20. With reference to the Finance Commission of India, which of the following statements is correct?
    (a) It encourages the inflow of foreign capital for infrastructure development
    (b) It facilitates the proper distribution of finances among the Public Sector Undertakings
    (c) It ensures transparency in financial administration
    (d) None of the above

21. The Government of India has established NITI Aayog to replace the
    (a) Human Rights Commission
    (b) Finance Commission
    (c) Law Commission
    (d) Planning Commission

22. Which Article in the Indian Constitution provides for the Finance Commission?
    (a) Article 323
    (b) Article 280
    (c) Article 256
    (d) Article 378

23. What is the constitution of the Finance Commission?
    (a) Chairman and nine elected (by Lok Sabha) members
    (b) Chairman, Vice-chairman and eight nominated members
    (c) Chairman, and four other members appointed by the President
    (d) Ten elected members of the Lok Sabha

24. Consider the following statements
    1. NAFED is one of the largest procurement as well as marketing agencies for agricultural products in India.

2. National Spot Exchange is a Commodities exchange in India, and is a joint venture of Financial Technologies India Ltd. (FTIL) and National Agricultural Cooperative Marketing Federation of India (NAFED).

Which of the above statements is/are correct?

(a) Only 1 (b) Only 2
(c) Both (d) None

25. Which among the following sentence is not correct about NAFED?

(a) NAFED is apex organization of marketing cooperatives for agricultural produce in India.

(b) Its headquarters is located in Kolkata.

(c) It was founded in October **1958** to promote trade of agricultural produce and forest resources across the nation.

(d) It functions under **Ministry of Agriculture.**

26. TRIFED is Tribal Cooperative Marketing Development Federation of India Limited (TRIFED) and was established in August 1987 by which of the ministry of India?

(a) Ministry of Welfare, Government of India

(b) Ministry of Agriculture, Government of India

(c) Ministry of finance, Government of India

(d) None of the Above

27. TRIFED organizes National Tribal Craft Expo called-

(a) AADISHILP (b) AadiChitra
(c) OCTAVE (d) Melas

28. How many zonal offices are of Khadi and Village Industries Commission in India?

(a) 4 (b) 5
(c) 6 (d) 7

29. Commission for Agricultural Costs and Prices (CACP) is a decentralized agency of the Government of India. It was established in ..... as the Agricultural Prices Commission

(a) 1965 (b) 1968
(c) 1969 (d) 1985

30. As of now, CACP recommends MSPs of 23 commodities, which comprise 7 cereals. Which of the cereals among following is not included in this list?

(a) Paddy (b) Wheat
(c) Maize (d) lentil

31. CACP submits its recommendations to the government in the form of Price Policy Reports every year, separately for how many groups of commodities?

(a) five groups (b) six groups
(c) seven groups (d) eight groups

HINTS & EXPLANATIONS

1. (d) 2. (b) 3. (c) 4. (c) 5. (c)
6. (c) 7. (d) 8. (d) 9. (a) 10. (d)
11. (b) 12. (c) 13. (d) 14. (d)

15. (c) It is not the duty of the President of India to cause to be laid report of public Accounts Committee before the Parliament.

16. (d) An amendment to the constitution of India is introduced as a bill in the Parliament. It then must be approved by both the houses of Parliament. The amendments must then be ratified by the legislatures of at least one half of the states (not all the states). Once all these stages are complete the amendment is bound to receive the assent of the President of India.

17. (b)

18. (d) It is fixed by Reserve Bank of India. In 2011, RBI permitted the commercial banks to fix interest rate on saving account independently. Rate of interest up to ` 1 lakh has to be same for every bank.

19. (d) If annual Union Budget is not passed by the LOK SABHA, it is tantamount to no confidence motion. So the Govt submits the resignation of his Council of Ministers.

20. (d) The Commission shall make recommendations as to the following matters, namely :

(i) The distribution between the Union and the States of the net proceeds of taxes which are to be, or may be, divided between them under Chapter I Part XII of the Constitution and the allocation between the States of the respective shares of such proceeds;

(ii) The principles which should govern the grants-in-aid of the revenues of the States out of the Consolidated Fund of India and the sums to be paid to the States which are in need of assistance by way of grants-in-aid of their revenues under article 275 of the Constitution for purposes other than those specified in the provisions to clause (1) of that article; and

(iii) The measures needed to augment the Consolidated Fund of a State to supplement the resources of the Panchayats and Municipalities in the State on the basis of the recommendations made by the Finance Commission of the State.

21. (d) The Government of India has established NITI Aayog to replace the Planning Commission. The Union Government of India announced formation of NITI Aayog on 1 January 2015 and the first meeting of NITI Aayog was held on 8 February 2015.

22. (b) 23. (c) 24. (c) 25. (b) 26. (a)
27. (a) 28. (c) 29. (a) 30. (d) 31. (a)

AGRICULTURE

INTRODUCTION

- Agriculture contributes about 16% of total GDP and 10% of total exports in India.
- Over 60 % of India's land area is arable making it the second largest country in terms of total arable land.
- Agricultural products of significant economic value include rice, wheat, potato, tomato, onion, mangoes, sugarcane, beans, cotton, etc.
- India exported $39 billion worth of agricultural products in 2013, making it the **seventh** largest agricultural exporter worldwide and the **sixth** largest net exporter.
- Indian agricultural/horticultural and processed foods are exported to more than 100 countries, primarily in the Middle East, Southeast Asia, SAARC countries, the EU and the United States.

Features of Agriculture in India

- Agriculture is India's largest Private sector industry.
- Agriculture sector includes Agriculture, Forestry & Logging and Fishing.
- Despite of industrialization and liberalizations it provides employment to around **60%** of the country's population.
- Agriculture is also "most free" private sector industry and it is the only profession that carries no burden of Income Tax.
- Agriculture is Biggest Unorganized sector of Indian economy and accounts for around 90% of the unorganized work force of the country.

Agriculture in Five year Plans

Five year Plan	Major Features
1st (1951-56)	• Launch of the *Community development Programme, abolition of Zamindari system*, campaigns for growth in food and other related areas like fisheries, forestry, animal husbandry, soil conservation, etc. were the major features. • Growth in agriculture was 2.71%.
2nd (1956-61)	• Industrial sector was given more importance in this plan. • Agricultural Expenditure was only 20% of the actual plan expenditure. • The agricultural growth, however, was high at 3.15%.
3rd (1961-66)	• Achieving self- sufficiency in foodgrains and increase in agricultural production was one of the main aims of this plan. • Higher priority was given to agricultural and allied areas as compared to industrial development. • However, the plan did not achieve its goals and agricultural growth fell to 0.73%. • *Land reforms, land ceiling* and *Green Revolution* were some of the major initiatives in this plan.

Annual Plans (1966-69)	• Priority was given to minor irrigation projects and *High Yielding Variety* of seeds was preferred so as to increase agricultural productivity. • Agricultural growth was high at 4.16%.
4th (1969-74)	• The results of the introduction of Green revolution and HYV seeds were good. • Expenditure on agriculture was 22% of annual expenditure. • Agricultural growth was 2.57%.
5th (1974-79)	• Emphasis was laid on spread of HYV seeds, use of fertilizers, pesticides and insecticides to increase production. • Expenditure on agriculture was around 21% of annual expenditure. • Agricultural growth was 3.28%.
6th (1980-85)	• It was realised by this plan that growth of Indian economy depends on rural and agricultural development. • The growth rate in agricultural production was a *high 4.3%* against a target of 3.8%. • Overall growth in agricultural sector was 2.52%.
7th (1985-90)	• Expenditure on agriculture was 22% of annual expenditure. • Growth in agriculture was 3.47%
8th (1992-97)	• The growth *target was 4.1%* but the agricultural sector showcased an impressive *growth of 4.68%*.
9th (1997-2002)	• This plan was a failure in the agricultural sector and it registered an agricultural *growth rate of 2.44%*.
10th (2002-07)	• Against a target of 4%, the average agricultural growth rate was only 2.3%.
11th (2007-12)	• The major emphasis was on increasing agricultural productivity and profitability by making available *affordable institutional credit, farm mechanisation, biotechnology, cold storages, and marketing.* • Growth in agriculture was 3.5%.
12th (2012-17)	• This plan, like its predecessors, has a target of 4% agricultural growth rate, with growth in food-grains at 2% and non- food grains at 5.6%. • The plan puts an emphasis on *improvement in technology, use of public- private partnership, greater road connectivity, development of horticulture, dairying,* and *other related agricultural fields.*

INDIA'S NATIONAL AGRICULTURAL POLICY (2000)

• This is the first ever national agriculture policy (2000) of India

• The policy seeks to promote technically sound, economically viable, environmentally non-degrading, and socially acceptable use of country's natural resources for sustainable development of agriculture.

- It seeks to actualise the vast untapped growth potential of Indian agriculture, strengthen rural infrastructure to support faster agricultural development.
- It promote value addition, accelerate the growth of agro business, create employment in rural areas.

Over the next two decades, it aims to attain:

- A growth rate in excess of 4% per annum in the agriculture sector;
- Growth that is based on efficient use of resources and conserves our soil, water and bio-diversity;
- Growth with equity, i.e. growth which is widespread across regions and farmers;
- Growth that is demand driven and caters to domestic markets and maximises benefits from exports of agricultural products in the face of the challenges arising from economic liberalization and globalisation;
- Growth that is sustainable technologically, environmentally and economically.

MAJOR AGRICULTURE PROGRAMS

NMSA

Under the National Action Plan on Climate Change, India has launched a dedicated National Mission on Sustainable Agriculture (NMSA) to define its strategies for climate mitigation and adaptation within the agriculture sector.

NFSM

- National Food Security Mission (NFSM) is a Central Scheme launched in 2007 for 5 years.
- It aims to increase production and productivity of wheat, rice and pulses on a sustainable basis so as to ensure food security of the country.
- The aim is to bridge the yield gap in respect of these crops through dissemination of improved technologies and farm management practices.

Rashtriya Krishi Vikas Yojna

- Rashtriya Krishi Vikas Yojana is a special Additional Central Assistance Scheme launched in 2007 to orient agricultural development strategies.
- It reaffirms its commitment to achieve 4% annual growth in the agricultural sector during the 11th plan.
- The scheme was launched to incentivize the States to provide additional resources in their State Plans over and above their baseline expenditure to bridge critical gaps. RKVY closed in 2012.

NHM

- National Horticulture Mission (NHM) is a horticulture Scheme launched under the 10th Five-Year Plan in the year 2005-06.
- While Government of India contributes 85%, 15% share is contributed by State Governments.
- The NHM's key objective is to develop horticulture to the maximum potential available in the state and to augment production of all horticultural products (fruits, vegetables, flowers, coco, cashew nut, plantation crops, spices, medicinal aromatic plants) in the state.

ISOPOM

Integrated Scheme of Oil Seeds, Pulses, Oilpalm and Maize (ISOPOM)

- The first programme on Oilseeds was launched in 1986 as Technology Mission on Oilseeds (TMO).
- The core idea was to increase the production and productivity of oilseeds to make the country self-reliant in this vital sector.
- Later Pulses, Oil Palm & Maize were brought in its ambit in the 1990s.

RADP

Rainfed Area Development Programme (RADP)

- To ensure agriculture growth in the rainfed areas, RADP was launched in the year 2011-12.
- It aims at improving quality of farmers' life especially, small and marginal farmers by offering a complete package of activities to maximize farm returns.
- RADP focuses on Integrated Farming System (IFS) for enhancing productivity and minimizing risks associated with climatic variabilities.
- During 2011-12, RADP was piloted in 10 states with an outlay of ₹ 250 crore.

NeGP

- The National e-Governance Plan (NeGP) is an initiative of the Government to make all government services available to the citizens of India via electronic media.
- NeGP was formulated by the Department of Electronics and Information Technology (DEITY) and Department of Administrative Reforms and Public Grievances (DARPG).
- The Government approved the National e-Governance Plan, consisting of 27 "Mission Mode Projects" (MMPs) and Ten components, on 18 May 2006.

NMFP

- National Mission on Food Processing (NMFP) was approved by the Cabinet Committee on Economic Affairs in August 2012.
- The scheme was announced in Union Budget 2012-13.
- The objective of the scheme is to have a better outreach and to provide more flexibility to suit local needs.
- The food processing sector has been growing at an average rate of over 8% over the past 5 years.

MAJOR AGRICULTURAL REVOLUTIONS IN INDIA

Green Revolution

- The Green Revolution at first started in India in the late 1960s.
- With this, India attained food self-sufficiency within a decade by the end of the 1970s (the first 'wave' of the Green Revolution).
- The key pillars of this revolution were high yielding variety (HYV) seeds, chemical fertilizers, pesticides and promoted irrigation facilities.
- Green revolution was introduced as a package programme with seed-water-fertilizer-pesticide-technology components and was originally called High Yielding Variety Programme (HYVP). Introduction of new high yielding varieties of improved seeds and enhanced application of the fertilizers and extended use of pesticides were its main features.
- The farmers were also extended finance through a relaxed mechanism.

Second Green Revolution

- The first green revolution ran out of steam mainly because it was focussed only on grain production; it did not help the dry land farming and it was not scale neutral.
- The call for second green revolution focuses on these issues by adopting a different strategy to follow.
- In India, the second green revolution has been called for in Eastern States via the BGREI programme in recent years.
- However, Second Green Revolution currently remains as a concept only. It has not translated into a reality so far.

The White Revolution in India

- The White Revolution, also known as **Operation Flood**, was a plan of three phases by the **National Dairy**

Development Board to revitalize India's dairy production until India became self-sufficient in milk.

- The program was so successful that by 1998, India was the world's largest milk producer.

- It transformed India from a milk-deficient nation into the world's largest milk producer, surpassing the USA in 1998, with about 17% of global output in 2010–11.

- It was launched to help farmers direct their own development, placing control of the resources they create in their own hands.

- **Verghese Kurien**, the chairman and founder of Amul, was named the chairman of NDDB by the then Prime Minister of India Lal Bahadur Shastri.

Blue Revolution

- Blue Revolution is the water equivalent of the green revolution and primarily refers to the management of water resources that can steer humanity to achieve drinking water and crop irrigation security.

- Blue Revolution is a continuation of the same kind of environmental and political reforms that catalyzed its Green Revolution in the 1960s.

Evergreen Revolution

- The term 'Green Revolution' was coined in **1968** to indicate revolutionary improvements in crop yield in several Asian countries.

- Many of these improvements came at the cost of adverse environmental effects in areas subjected to intensive farming.

- However, where population pressure is high, there is no option except to produce more food.

- Productivity must increase, but in ways which are environmentally safe, economically viable and socially sustainable. This has been christened an 'Evergreen Revolution'.

Yellow Revolution

- The term "Yellow Revolution" has been used to describe the dramatic increase in **oilseed** production in India which began in 1986.

- The growth, development and adoption of new varieties of oilseeds and complementary technologies nearly doubled oilseeds production from 12.6 mt in 1987-88 to 24.4 mt in 1996-97, catalyzed by the Technology Mission on Oilseeds, brought about the Yellow Revolution.

LAND REFORMS

- Land title formalization has been part of India's state policy from the very beginning.

- Independent India's most revolutionary land policy was perhaps the abolition of the Zamindari system (feudal land holding practices).

- Land-reform policy in India had two specific objectives:

- The first is to remove such impediments to increase in agricultural production as arise from the agrarian structure inherited from the past.

- The second is closely related to the first, which is to eliminate all elements of exploitation and social injustice within the agrarian system, to provide security for the tiller of soil and assure equality of status and opportunity to all sections of the rural population."

Land Bill 2015

The Right to Fair Compensation and Transparency in Land Acquisition, Rehabilitation and Resettlement (Amendment) Bill 2015, also known as Land Bill 2015 has been passed by the Lok Sabha on March 10, 2015.

Highlights of the Land Bill 2015

The nine amendments that were adopted in the land bill 2015 are:

1. Government to acquire land for government bodies, corporations,
2. Farmers may get right to appeal/complain over land acquisition hearing and redressal of grievances at the district level,
3. Panchayat's nod may be compulsory for acquiring tribal land,
4. Social Infrastructure under PPP, not anymore in exempted category,
5. Replacing the term 'private entity' with 'private enterprise',
6. Compulsory employment to one member of the affected family of farm labourers,
7. Limiting the industrial corridor to one kilometer on both the sides of the highways and railways,
8. Ceiling on land for acquisition in industrial corridors,
9. Hassle free mechanism for grievances redressal of land losers.

RURAL CREDIT & EXTENSION SERVICES

Rural Banking

- Rural banking has become an integral part of the Indian financial markets with a majority of Indian population still living in rural or semi-urban areas.
- The government and the RBI have been continuously working to achieve complete financial inclusion, i.e. timely and sufficient access to financial services and credit at an affordable cost, in the vast expanse of the country.
- **Pradhan Mantri Jan Dhan Yojana** is one of the recent initiatives by the new government which has definitely contributed to bring banking to every household.
- This scheme with time will significantly reduce the gap between rural and urban areas in terms of financial inclusion

- However, the fact that about 70% of population of India is still rural and the penetration of banking facilities is as low as only 24%.
- The credit to weaker sections is to be made hassle-free and given at cheap or concessional rates.

Microcredit in India

- Microcredit is the extension of very small loans (microloans) to impoverished borrowers who typically lack collateral, steady employment and a verifiable credit history.
- Microcredit is designed to support entrepreneurship and alleviate poverty.
- It also aims to empower women and uplift entire communities by extension.
- As of 2009 an estimated 74 million men and women held microloans that totalled US$38 billion.
- Grameen Bank reports that repayment success rates are between 95 and 98 %.

Agriculture Loans

- Agricultural loans are available for a multitude of farming purposes.
- Farmers may apply for loans to buy inputs for the cultivation of food grain crops as well as for horticulture, aquaculture, animal husbandry, floriculture and sericulture businesses.
- There are also special loans to finance the purchase of agricultural machinery such as tractors, harvesters and trucks.
- Construction of biogas plants and irrigation systems as well as the purchase of agricultural land may also be financed through special types of agricultural finance.

Major Sources of Rural Credit

Co-Operative Credit Societies

- The cooperative societies are supposed to be the cheapest and most important source of rural credit.

- All credit Societies engage in Deposit schemes like Member, Saving Account, Compulsory Saving, Fix deposit (FD), Recurring Deposit (RD), Monthly Recurring (MR), Daily Deposit (DD), Pension schemes, etc.
- After collecting money from depositors they start giving loans as Housing Loan, Vehicle Loan, Gold Loan, Festival Loan, General Loan, Consumer Loan, Agriculture Loan etc. and decide the Loan EMI.
- These Societies give high return on deposits schemes and give loan at reasonable rate of interest as they have low running cost and every year declare Dividend for its members.

Land Development Banks

- Land development bank (formerly known as **land mortgage banks**) mainly provide long-term loans to farmers against the mortgage of their lands at low rates of interest over a period of 15 to 20 years.
- Farmers find borrowing from such banks attractive if costly land improvement programmes (such as digging or deepening of wells) are to be undertaken.

Commercial Banks

- Commercial banks now provide both direct and indirect finance to agriculture.
- Direct finance is provided for short and medium terms to enable farmers carry out agricultural operations smoothly.
- Indirect finance is provided in the form of advances for the purchase of inputs like seeds and fertilisers. Such loan is also provided through PACs.
- Commercial banks also provide finance to the FCI, and the State Government agencies for food procurement operations. Banks also provide credit for storing and distribution of agricultural inputs.

Regional Rural Banks (RRB)

- In 1975, the Government set up a network of regional rural banks to look into the special needs of small and marginal farmers, landless workers, rural artisans and the rural poor in general.
- The unique feature of the **196 RRBs** operating since September 1990 is that they cater exclusively to the weaker sections of the rural community through nearly 14,800 branches spread over India.

NAFED

Stablished - 2 October, 1958

The National Agricultural Co-operative Marketing Federation of India (NAFED)

- NAFED is an apex organisation of marketing cooperatives in the country.
- It deals in procurement, processing, distribution, export and import of selected agricultural commodities.
- The NAFED is also the central nodal agency for undertaking price support operations for pulses and oilseeds and market intervention operations for other agricultural commodities.

TRIFED

Stablished - August, 1987

The tribal cooperative marketing development federation of India limited (TRIFED)

TRIFED functions as a Service provider, Facilitator, Coordinator and a Market Developer for tribal products instead of its earlier activity of procurement and sale of Minor Forest Produce & Surplus Agricultural Produce.

NCDC

Stablished - 1963

The National Cooperative Development Corporation (NCDC)

Its main functions include planning, promoting and financing programmes for production, processing, marketing, storage, export and import of agricultural produce, food stuffs, certain other notified commodities, supply of consumer goods and collection, processing, marketing, storage and export of minor forest produce through cooperatives.

Loan Facilities for Short Term Agricultural Operations

- Crop loans are also called short term loans for "Seasonal Agricultural Operations."
- The Seasonal Agricultural Operations connote such activities as are undertaken in the process of raising various crops and are seasonally recurring in nature.
- The activities include, among others, ploughing and preparing land for sowing, weeding, transplantation where necessary, acquiring and applying inputs such as seeds, fertilizers, insecticides, etc. and paying for labour.
- Thus, the credit required to meet the current expenditure for raising the crops on land till the crops are harvested is construed as production or short term credit for seasonal agricultural operations.

Kisan Credit Card Scheme (KCC)

Launched - 1998

- Crop loans are generally disbursed by the banks through the mode of Kisan Credit Card (KCC).
- The Kisan Credit Card Scheme is in operation throughout the country and is implemented by Commercial Banks, Cooperative Banks and RRBs.
- All farmers including small farmers, marginal farmers, share croppers, oral lessees and tenant farmers are eligible for issuance of KCC.
- Bank assesses farmer's eligibility on the basis of land available for cultivation and the scale of finance fixed by the District Level Technical Committee in that district and the credit history of the farmer.

NABARD

Stablished - 12 July, 1982

National Bank for Agriculture and Rural Development (NABARD)

- NABARD is responsible for refinance disbursement to commercial banks, State cooperative banks, State cooperatives, rural development banks, Regional Rural Banks (RRBs) and other eligible financial institutions.
- It also sanctions money through its Rural Infrastructure Development Fund for projects covering irrigation, rural roads and bridges, health and education, soil conservation and drinking water schemes.
- NABARD also offers a Kisan Credit Card Scheme and crop loans under the Rashtriya Krishi Bima Yojana.

Agricultural Insurance in India

Agriculture in India is highly susceptible to risks like droughts and floods. It is necessary to protect the farmers from natural calamities and ensure their credit eligibility for the next season. For this purpose, the government introduced many agricultural schemes throughout the country.

Pradhan Mantri Fasal Bima Yojana

- The Pradhan Mantri Fasal Bima Yojana (Prime Minister's Crop Insurance Scheme) was launched by Prime Minister of India, Narendra Modi on 18 February 2016.
- It envisages a uniform premium of only 2% to be paid by farmers for Kharif crops, and 1.5 % for Rabi crops.
- The premium for annual commercial and horticultural crops will be 5 %.

NAIS

National Agriculture Insurance Scheme (NAIS)

- It was introduced in 1999-2000.

- NAIS envisages coverage of all food crops (cereals and pulses), oilseeds, horticultural and commercial crops. It covers all farmers, both loanees and non-loanees, under the scheme.
- The premium rates vary from 1.5 % to 3.5% of sum assured for food crops.

CCIS

- The Comprehensive Crop Insurance Scheme (CCIS) covered 15 states and 2 union territories.
- Participation in the scheme was voluntary.
- If the actual yield in any area covered by the scheme fell short of the guaranteed yield, the farmers were entitled to an indemnity on compensation to the extent of the shortfall in yield.

Agricultural price policy (APP) in India

- Agricultural pricing framework has gradually evolved in India ever since 1960s.
- The objective of the Government's price policy for agricultural produce is to set remunerative prices with a view to encourage higher investment and production.
- Theoretically, APP accounts for various economic factors, such as the rate and quality of economic growth, in identifying and promoting the optimal crop mix.
- APP includes the following instruments:
    – MSP (minimum support price)
    – Procurement prices
    – Public distribution system
    – Zonal restrictions

WTO & Agricultural Subsidies

- The Agreement on Agriculture (AoA) is an international treaty of the World Trade Organization.
- India has been member of GATT since 1948; hence it was party to Uruguay Round and a founding member of WTO.

- In India about 80% of farming is subsistence and hence, India & other developing countries can use this opportunity.

The Three Boxes of WTO

The three boxes of World Trade Organisation come under its Agreement on Agriculture. These boxes denote different kinds of domestic subsidies provided in a country. The three boxes are-

Green Box Subsidies

- Green box subsidies are those subsidies which cause either no, or at most minimal, trade distorting effects or effects on production.
- These include the amounts spent on Government services such as research, disease control, and infrastructure and food security.
- This also includes the subsidies given to the farmers that directly don't affect international trade badly.
- The Green Box contains fixed payments to producers for environmental programs, so long as the payments are "decoupled" from current production levels.

Blue Box Subsidies

- Blue Box contains direct payment subsidies which can be increased without limit, so long as payments are linked to production-limiting programs.

Amber Box Subsidies

- All domestic support measures considered to distort production and trade (with some exceptions) fall into the amber box.
- The provisions accepts 5% of agricultural production for developed countries, 10% for developing countries.

PDS

- Public distribution system (PDS) means distribution of essential commodities to larger section of the society, mostly vulnerable people, through a network of fair Price Shops on a recurring basis.

- The essential commodities under PDS at present are wheat, rice, sugar and Kerosene.
- The first government intervention in the PDS in India started in 1940 during the interwar period.
- FCI was established in 1964 to handle the shortage of food grains clubbed with black marketing of the food grains by hoarders.
- Today, with the network of around 5 Lakh fair price shops PDS is virtually world's largest system of its kind.

Food Corporation of India (FCI)

- FCI was set up on 14 January 1965.
- The following objectives of the National Food Policy are:
  - (a) Effective price support operations for safeguarding the interests of the farmers,
  - (b) Distribution of foodgrains throughout the country for Public Distribution System,
  - (c) Maintaining satisfactory level of operational and buffer stocks of foodgrains to ensure National Food Security,
  - (d) Regulate market price to provide foodgrains to consumers at a reliable price.

Targeted Public Distribution System (TPDS)

- The "Targeted" means that the focus is really poor and vulnerable sections of society.
- Targeted Public Distribution System (TPDS) was introduced in June 1997.
- The focus of the Targeted Public Distribution System (TPDS) is on "poor in all areas" and TPDS involves issue of 10 Kg of food grains per family per month for the population Below Poverty Line (BPL) at specially subsidized prices.

- Its distribution in a transparent and accountable manner at the FPS level. So we can say that "Since 1997 the PDS in India has become pro-poor.
- The identification of the poor under the TPDS is the responsibility of the state governments.
- Poverty estimates of states in India by Planning Commission are estimated by the formula developed by late Prof. Lakdawala Committee.

Agriculture in Budget 2018-19

It is to be noted that at this point of economic history, Doubling farm income is imperative rather than being an option. The government has much stressed on "Doubling Farm Income" and it has been one of the major selling points of the present day government. The budgetary allocation of the agriculture and farmers welfare ministry for 2018-19 has been kept at Rs. 58,080 crore as against Rs. 51,576 crore for 2017-18, for the emancipation of the sector this year, but there are many wings of this sole bird called : Agriculture. The various sectors of the economy directly or indirectly are dependent on each other. Let us explore the various fronts :

Infrastructure : A plan has been drafted to build roads to connect rural India's farms and schools which will augment the better access to the markets. With the increased allocation for the sector, the government will promote establishment of specialized agro-processing financial institutions and to set up state-of-the-art testing facilities in all the 42 mega food parks.

Increased allocation for building warehouses and Institutional credit to raise for agriculture sector to 11 lakh crore for 2018- 19 from 10 lakh crore in 2017-18.

Pricing MSP : One of the most welcomed and appreciated points in this year's budget is the announcement of 1.5 times the expenses borne by farmers. The support price of the kharif crops has been increased aiming to increase the incomes from farm.

Market : "The government would strengthen e-NAM — the e-trading platform for the National Agriculture Market and would expand coverage of e-NAM to 585 APMCs. Out of that, 470 APMCs have already been connected to the e-NAM network and the rest will be connected by March 2018. Also, an agri-infrastructure fund with a corpus of Rs.2,000 crore will be set up for developing and upgrading agricultural marketing infrastructure in the 22,000 grameen agricultural markets and 585 APMCs," said Mr. Jaitley. Upgradation of 22,000 rural haats into grain agricultural markets is another appreciable attempt.

Machinery & Automobiles: Increased spending in rural areas and agri sector is supposed to make a vibrant growth in the two wheeler and tractor companies. Better farm outputs and better prices would eventually hike up the purchasing power of the farmers and more investments would be caught in the machinery and advancements for the field.

MSME : Reduction of corporate tax rates and increased credit support to boost employment and profitability in the sector, could be proved to vanish disguise employment from the farms. Encouraging FPOs through 100% tax deduction, promoting cluster based organic farming by SHG and roll out of "operation greens" is a necessary shot in the arm for increasing agricultural productivity.

Towards Rural India & Women Emancipation: Free cooking gas to be distributed to rural women through "Ujjawala Yojana" considering the health of the women is another prudent highlight of the budget, when the contribution of women in the sector has been increasing at a high pace. The government has agreed to contribute 12% of the wages of the new employees to the EPF for all the sectors. This takes care of the organised sector. Though no thought has been given to the large pool of workers in the unorganised sector. Women SHG would be encouraged to take up organic agriculture in clusters under national rural livelihood programme.

Horticulture : Encourage clustering in horticulture production and marketing increase the allocation for organic farming provide cheaper credit to small farmers and create infrastructure funds for fisheries and animal husbandry. Higher spends on e-nam in more mandis, special focus in food processing agricultural exports (from current $30 billion to its potential of $100 billion) fisheries and aqua culture and animal husbandry.

Dairy & Fisheries : To meet the working capital needs of small and marginal farmers in fisheries and animal husbandry sector, the government has extended the facility of Kisan Credit Cards (KCC) to the sector. "This would give benefit of crop loan and interest subvention, so far available to agriculture sector only under KCC, for rearing of cattle, buffalo, goat, sheep, poultry and fisheries," said Mr. Jaitley.

Finance Minister also announced setting up of a Fisheries and Aquaculture Infrastructure Development Fund fisheries sector and an Animal Husbandry

Infrastructure Development Fund for financing infrastructure requirement of animal husbandry sector. Total Corpus of these two new Funds would be Rs.10,000 crore.

The deacon to integrate fisheries and animal husbandry with Kisan credit cards and restructure of National Bamboo Mission to enhance the cultivation and consumption of bamboo :)

Organic Farming : Sum of 200 crore has been allocated to support organized cultivation of highly specialized medicinal and aromatic plants and aid small and cottage industries that manufacture perfumes, essential oils and other associated products .

Allied Sectors : Allocation of 1,290 crore for restricted national bamboo mission raise hopes for bamboo based industries, NE grows 67% of India's bamboo, but the resource has been mostly wasting since the population could not make use of the bamboo due to the Forest Act.

Operation Green : This addresses price volatility of perishable commodities such as potatoes, tomatoes and onions at an outlay of 500 crore. This shall promote FPO, agri logistics and processing facilities and professional management in the sector. Announcing a 100% deduction in respect of profits to farmer producer companies having turn over upto 100 crore for a period of 5 years from the financial year 2018-19 in order to encourage professionalism in

EXERCISE

1. Which one of the following agencies is not included in the operation of the Kisan Credit Cards?
   (a) Co-operative Banks
   (b) Regional Rural Banks
   (c) Scheduled Commercial Banks
   (d) NABARD

2. The price at which the Government purchase foodgrains for maintaining the public distribution system and for building up buffer stocks are known as
   (a) Minimum support prices
   (b) Procurement prices
   (c) Issue prices
   (d) Coiling prices

3. Which one of the following agencies assigns the Agricultural Income Tax to states in India?
   (a) Inter – State council
   (b) National Development Council
   (c) Agriculture Finance Corporation
   (d) Finance commission

4. Which one of the following agencies of Indian Government implements the price support scheme (PSS)?
   (a) FCI
   (b) NAFED
   (c) Agriculture pricing agency of India
   (d) None of the above

5. In which five year plan in Indian Economy, the targets for the crop function were not fixed for the first time-
   (a) Seventh five year plan
   (b) Eighth five year plan
   (c) Ninth five year plan
   (d) Tenth five year plan

6. The importance of agriculture in Indian Economy is indicated by its contribution to which of the following?
   (a) National income and employment
   (b) Industrial development and international trade
   (c) Supply of foodgrains
   (d) All of the above

7. When the Kisan Credit Card schemes for the farmers started in India?
   (a) 1995–1996   (b) 1998–1999
   (c) 2005–2006   (d) 2007–2008

8. Which one of the following states is the first state to impose Agriculture Income Tax in India?
   (a) Madhya Pradesh
   (b) Uttar Pradesh
   (c) West Bengal
   (d) Bihar

9. Which one of the following five year plans has the highest growth rate in Agriculture sector in India ?
   (a) Sixth Five Year Plan
   (b) Seventh Five Year Plan
   (c) Eighth Five Year Plan
   (d) Ninth Five Year Plan

10. In which of the following years was the Food Corporation of India (FCI) set up ?
    (a) 1955   (b) 1960
    (c) 1965   (d) 1970

11. Rashtriya Krishi Vikas Yojna was launched in the year?
    (a) 2003   (b) 2004
    (c) 2006   (d) 2007

12. The head office of the National Bank for Agriculture and Rural Development (NABARD) located in
    (a) Lucknow   (b) Hyderabad
    (c) New Delhi   (d) Mumbai

13. Which is not a source of Agriculture finance in India?
    (a) Co-operative societies
    (b) Commercial Banks
    (c) Regional Rural Banks
    (d) None of these

14. NABARD was established in the
    (a) Fourth Five Year Plan
    (b) Fifth Five Year Plan
    (c) Sixth Five Year Plan
    (d) Eighth Five Year Plan
15. In India, which of the following has the highest share in the disbursement of credit to agriculture and allied activities?
    (a) Commercial Banks
    (b) Co-operative Banks
    (c) Regional Rural Banks
    (d) Microfinance Institutions
16. What will be the ultimate impact on the poor and landless farmers if all of a sudden, government decides to raise the Minimum Support Prices of rice & foodgrains inexorably or excessively?
    (a) The poor farmers will become rich
    (b) The markets will crash
    (c) The poor farmers will get poorer
    (d) This will encourage the exports of rice and food grains
17. What is the main motive of the government behind having a dual price system & setting up of fair price shops?
    (a) To demote speculation and hoarding
    (b) To incentivise the trading of essential commodities
    (c) To eliminate the monopoly of the traders and speculators
    (d) To make the essential commodities available to the weaker sections of the society
18. Which among the following is an example of Green Field Investment?
    (a) Investment made by a real estate company in agriculture land to develop it later when the land prices increase
    (b) Investment made by a company in a new factory complex in a remote land of the country where there was no facilities
    (c) Investment made by a company to clean up a cement factory located in populated area because of its pollution and using it for a commercial office purpose
    (d) Investment made by a company to clean up a cement factory located in populated area because of its pollution and using it for a residential purpose
19. The central nodal agency for implementing the price support operations for commercial crops is:
    (a) NAFED   (b) NABARD
    (c) TRIFED   (d) FCI
20. Which among the following has been discontinued after the Cabinet decision in small saving schemes?
    (a) National Saving Certificates (NSC)
    (b) Kisan Vikas Patras (KVP)
    (c) Monthly Income Scheme (MIS)
    (d) Recurrent Deposit Schemes
21. Which of the following is an apex financing agency for the institutions providing investment and production credit for promoting the various developmental activities in rural areas?
    (a) RBI   (b) NABARD
    (c) SIDBI   (d) RRB
22. In 1982, the Rural Planning and Credit Cell (RPCC) of Reserve Bank of India was merged to which of the following banks?
    (a) SIDBI   (b) NABARD
    (c) IDBI   (d) RRB
23. The Rural Infrastructure Development Fund (RIDF), which is used by the state governments to develop infrastructure in rural areas, is managed by which among the following?
    (a) IDBI
    (b) RBI
    (c) NABARD
    (d) Rural Ministry of India

24. Which among the following facility has been started in India for refinance assistance for small irrigation, IRDP, Dairy Development and Mechanism of farms?
    (a) National Credit Fund
    (b) National Rural Credit Fund
    (c) National Credit Stabilization Fund
    (d) Rural Infrastructure Development Fund

25. Which programme targets integrated farming, on- farm water management, storage marketing and value addition of farm produce in order to enhance farmers' income in rainfed areas?
    (a) Integrated Scheme for Oilseeds, Pulses, Oil Palm and Maize
    (b) National Mission for Sustainable Agriculture
    (c) Mission for Integrated Development in Horticulture
    (d) Rainfed Area Development Programme

26. Green Revolution has led to:
    1. Spurt in production of all food grains.
    2. Greater regional inequalities
    3. Reduction in inter-personal inequalities.
    4. Increase in production of wheat.
    (a) 1 and 3
    (b) 1, 2 and 3
    (c) 2, 3 and 4
    (d) 2 and 4

27. With reference to Indian agriculture, consider the following statements:
    1. Agriculture provides direct livelihood to 59% of the labour force in India.
    2. It contributes more than 20% to the GDP
    3. It accounts for about 10% of the total value of India's commodity exports
    4. Almost 80% of the area under agriculture is irrigated.
    Which of the above statement/s is/are correct?
    (a) 1, 2, 3 and 4
    (b) 1, 2 and 3
    (c) 3 only
    (d) 4 only

28. Consider the following statements regarding the objectives of the Second Green Revolution announced in 2005:
    1. It seeks to minimise post-harvest wastage
    2. It will focus on improved storage
    3. It will help the Indian farmers meet phyto-sanitary conditions
    4. It will equip the Indian farmers to participate more fully in global agricultural trade
    Which of these statement/s is/are correct?
    (a) 1, 2, 3 and 4
    (b) 1, 3 and 4
    (c) 4 only
    (d) 2, 3 and 4

29. Consider the following statements.
    1. The loans disbursed to farmers under Kisan Credit Card Scheme are covered under Rashtiya Krishi Bema Yojna of Life Insurance Corporation of India
    2. The Kisan Credit Card holders are provided personal accident insurance of ₹ 50,000 for accidental death and ₹ 25,000 for permanent disability.
    Which of the statements given above is/are correct?
    (a) 1 only
    (b) 2 only
    (c) Both 1 and 2
    (d) Neither 1 nor 2

30. Which of the following are the objectives of the Commission for Agricultural Costs and Prices (CACP)?
    1. To stabilize agricultural prices
    2. To ensure meaningful real income levels to the farmers
    3. To protect the interest of the consumers by providing essential agricultural commodities at reasonable rates through public distribution system.
    4. To ensure maximum price for the farmer
    (a) 1, 2 and 3
    (b) 1, 2 and 4
    (c) 1, 3 and 4
    (d) 2, 3 and 4

31. Which of the fallowing are responsible for the decrease of per capita holding of cultivated land in India?
    1. Low per capita income.
    2. Rapid rate of increase of population.
    3. Practice of dividing land equally among the heirs.
    4. Use of traditional techniques of ploughing.

    Select the correct answer using the codes given below
    (a) 1 and 2   (b) 2 and 3
    (c) 1 and 4   (d) 2,3 and 4

32. As a policy to boost the agricultural sector, the GOI has taken special measures over time. Which of the following are not a measure with a direct impact on the agricultural sector?
    1. Setting up of a National Food Processing Bank
    2. Opening irrigation, sanitation and water projects for Private Participation.
    3. Efforts to reduce fiscal deficit to 5.5 per cent level of GDP
    (a) 1 only   (b) 2 only
    (c) 3 only   (d) 1 and 2

33. With reference to the agriculture sector of India, consider the following statements
    1. Rural infrastructure Development Fund disperses loans to the states to complete the minor irrigation projects.
    2. Rural infrastructure Development Fund is managed by the public sector Commercial Banks.

    Which of the statements given above is/are correct?
    (a) 1 only   (b) 2 only
    (c) Both 1 and 2   (d) Neither 1 nor 2

34. Consider the following statements :
    1. Regional Rural Banks grant direct loans and advances to marginal farmers and rural artisans.
    2. NABARD is responsible for laying down policies and to oversee the operations of the RRBs.

    Which of the statements given above is/are correct?
    (a) 1 only   (b) 2 only
    (c) Both 1 and 2   (d) Neither 1 nor 2

35. Consider the following statements :
    1. India is the 4th largest producer of Natural Rubber in the world.
    2. India in the world, shares more than 8.0% in the Natural Rubber Production.

    Which of the statements given above is/are correct?
    (a) 1 only   (b) 2 only
    (c) Both 1 and 2   (d) Neither 1 nor 2

36. Consider the following statements :
    1. India is the 6th largest producer of coffee.
    2. India's share in Global Area under coffee is about 2%.
    3. India contributes about 4% to world coffee production as well as in the International trade.

    Which of the statements given above is/are correct?
    (a) 1 only   (b) 2 only
    (c) 1 and 2   (d) 1, 2 and 3

37. Consider the following statements:
    1. All kinds of Development Banks in India appeared Post-Independence
    2. NABARD is the only agricultural Development Bank in India

    Which among the above statements is / are correct?
    (a) Only 1 is correct
    (b) Only 2 is correct
    (c) Both 1 and 2 are correct
    (d) Neither 1 nor 2 is correct

38. Consider the following statements:
    1. Price Stabilization Fund Scheme was launched for Coffee, Tea, Rubber and Tobacco growers in the country

2. In this scheme Government procures the commodities when the prices fell below a certain level to support the growers

Which among the above statements is/are correct ?

(a) Only 1 is correct
(b) Only 2 is correct
(c) Both 1 and 2 are correct
(d) Neither 1 nor 2 is correct

39. What are long term loans?

I. These are provided for a period of less than 15 months to meet out expenses of routine farming and domestic consumptions

II. These are provided for a period of 15 months to 5 years to purchase agricultural equipments, animals and for land improvements.

III. These are provided for a period of more than 5 years.

(a) Only II
(b) Only I
(c) Only III
(d) None of the above

40. Which statement is correct according to the growth and productivity of agriculture?

I. The total irrigated area increased from less than one million hectares per annum before the green revolution to about 2.5 million hectares per annum during the 1970's

II. The total gross irrigated area now is 40 million hectares.

III. The yield per hectare of food grains has shown remarkable increase in the pre Green Revolution period.

(a) Only I
(b) I & II
(c) I & III
(d) None of the above

41. Which of the following is correct statement?

I. Agriculture is the primary occupation in India as it provides direct livelihood to 59% of its labour force

II. In India, 75% of below the poverty line (BPL) population lives in rural areas, and is directly or indirectly dependent on agriculture.

III. Agriculture contributes to more than 13.7% (2013) of GDP, although this share has progressively declined from 57% in 1950-51.

IV. In developed countries, like the UK and USA, the share of agriculture in GDP is only around 2%.

(a) I & II
(b) I & III
(c) I, II & III
(d) All the above

42. Which of the statement is correct regarding Land Development Banks?

I. It provides long-term rural credit for land improvement, soil conservation and other investments of a capital nature.

II. LDBs have now been renamed as State Co-operative Agricultural and Rural Development Banks (SCARDBs)

III. They raise their funds through long-term debentures offering state government guarantee, and refinancing from NABARD.

(a) I & II
(b) II & III
(c) Only II
(d) All the above

43. Which of the following statements are correct in accordance to Kisan Credit Cards?

I. NABARD formulated a model scheme for issue of Kisan Credit Cards (KCCs) to farmers so that they may use them to readily purchase agricultural inputs such as seeds, fertilizers, pesticides, etc.

II. These are operated by only commercial banks.

III. The scheme has helped in augmenting the flow of short-term crop loans for seasonal agricultural operations of farmers.

IV. From January 31, 2006, the scheme has been extended to all types of loan requirements of borrowers of State Cooperative Agriculture Rural Development Banks (SCARDBs).

(a) I & II   (b) Only IV

(c) I, III & IV   (d) All the above

44. What are short term loans?

I. These are provided for a period of less than 15 months to meet out expenses of routine farming and domestic consumptions.

II. These are provided for a period of 15 months to 5 years to purchase agricultural equipments, animals and for land improvements.

III. These are provided for a period of more than 5 years.

(a) Only II

(b) Only I

(c) Only III

(d) None of the above

45. What is procurement price?

I. It is that price at which government purchases the crop after harvesting, while MSP is the minimum price at which government declares it will buy the crop.

II. It is that price at which people purchases the crop after harvesting, while MSP is the maximum price at which government declares it will buy the crop.

III. It is the price at which people purchase the product from the government

(a) Only I

(b) II & III

(c) Only III

(d) None of the above

46. What are Co-operative Credit Societies?

I. They are apex institution for providing credit facility to agricultural and rural areas.

II. These are the most important source of rural credit.

III. They are finance rural credit directly through Regional Rural Banks (RRBs).

(a) I & II

(b) Only III

(c) Only II

(d) None of the above

47. What is NABARD?

I. They are apex institution for providing credit facility to agricultural and rural areas.

II. These are the most important source of rural credit.

III. They provide finance rural credit directly through Regional Rural Banks (RRBs).

(a) I & II

(b) Only I

(c) Only II

(d) None of the above

48. NABARD took over the function of which all institutes?

I. Agricultural Credit Development (ACD)

II. Rural Planning and Credit Cell (RPCC) of RBI

III. Agricultural Refinance Development Corporation (ARDC)

IV. State Co-operative Agricultural and Rural Development Banks (SCARDBs).

(a) I, II & III   (b) I & II

(c) Only IV   (d) All the above

49. What are the functions of NABARD?
    I. It is associated with policy, planning, operation and even monitoring levels for providing agricultural credit.
    II. Its primary task is to function as refinancing institution for all types of lending for agricultural and rural development.
    III. In addition to this, it provides term credit to state co-operative banks, regional rural banks, land development banks and state governments (only for share capital contribution to co-operative credit societies).

    (a) Only I
    (b) I & II
    (c) II & III
    (d) All the above

50. What are medium term loans?
    I. These are provided for a period of less than 15 months to meet out expenses of routine farming and domestic consumptions
    II. These are provided for a period of 15 months to 5 years to purchase agricultural equipments, animals and for land improvements.
    III. These are provided for a period of more than 5 years.

    (a) Only II
    (b) Only I
    (c) Only III
    (d) None of the above

HINTS & EXPLANATIONS

1. **(d)** A Kisan Credit Card is a credit card to provide affordable credit for farmers. It was started by the Government of India, Reserve Bank of India (RBI), and National Bank for Agricultural and Rural Development (NABARD) in 1998–99 to help farmers access timely and adequate credit. The credit is available to farmers in most of the banks like commercial banks cooperative banks and regional rural banks. However in day to day operations NABARD is not included.

2. **(b)** The price at which the Government purchases foodgrains for maintaining the public distribution system and for building up buffer stocks are known as procurement prices.

3. **(d)** Finance commission

4. **(b)** In Order to help the farmers in getting remunerative prices for their produce with a view to encourage higher investment and as also to increase production and productivity of a commodity, the government declares Minimum Support Price (MSPs) for 25 notified agricultural commodities for each Kharif & Rabi crop season. National Agricultural cooperative Marketing Federation of India Ltd (NAFED) is one of the Central Nodal Agencies which implements PSS.

5. **(d)** Tenth five year plan

6. **(d)** The importance of agriculture in Indian Economy is indicated by its contribution to national income, industrial development and supply of foodgrains. It contributes around 13.7% to GDP, supplies raw material for development of industries along with supplying food grains for livelihood.

7. **(b)** A Kisan Credit Card is a credit card to provide affordable credit for farmers. It was started by the Reserve Bank of India (RBI), and National Bank for Agricultural and Rural Development (NABARD) in 1998–99 to help farmers access timely and adequate credit.

8. **(d)** Bihar is the first state to impose agricultural income tax in India. Agricultural income tax is levied on the income from Agriculture. At present agriculture is subjected to two direct taxes and they are Agricultural Income tax and Land Tax. They are levied by the state governments. Bihar was the first state in India to levy a tax on agricultural income in 1938.

9. **(c)** The growth performance of the agriculture sector has been fluctuating across the plan periods. It witnessed a growth rate of 4.8 per cent during the Eighth plan period (1992–97).

10. **(c)** The Food corporation of India (FCI) was set up in 1965. Its objectives are Effective price support operations for safeguarding the interests of the farmers. Distribution of food grains throughout the country for public distribution system and maintaining satisfactory level of operational and buffer stocks of foodgrains to ensure National Food Security.

11. (d) Rashtriya Krishi Vikas Yojana was launched in August 2007 as a part of the 11th Five Year Plan by the Government of India. Launched under the aegis of the National Development Council, it seeks to achieve 4% annual growth in agriculture through development of Agriculture and its allied sectors during the period under the 11th Five Year Plan (2007–11).

12. (d) The head office of the National Bank for agriculture and Rural Development (NABARD) is located in Mumbai. It helps farmers access timely and adequate credit.

13. (d) Co-operative societies, Commercial Banks and Regional Rural Banks are source of agriculture finance in India. They provide finance under various schemes run by central government and state governments to purchase seeds, implements, fertilizer, pesticides etc.

14. (c) National Bank for Agriculture and Rural Development (NABARD) is an apex development bank in India having headquarters based in Mumbai. It was established on 12 July, 1982 in sixth five year plan by a special act by the parliament and its main focus was to uplift rural India by increasing the credit flow for elevation of agriculture & rural non farm sector.

15. (a) In India, commercial banks have the highest share in the disbursement of credit to agriculture and allied activities. The commercial banks disburse around 60% credit followed by cooperative banks around 30% and RRB and others.

16. (c) 17. (d) 18. (b) 19. (a) 20. (b)
21. (b) 22. (b) 23. (c) 24. (c)

25. (d) RADP was launched by the government as a pilot scheme under RKVY, focusing on small and marginal farmers and farming systems. It targets integrated farming, on- farm water management, storage marketing and value addition of farm produce in order to enhance farmers' income in rainfed areas.

26. (d) 27. (b) 28. (a) 29. (b) 30. (a)

31. (b) Rapid rate of increase of population and practice of dividing land equally among the heirs are responsible for the decrease of per capita holding of cultivated land in India.

32. (c)

33. (a) Rural Infrastructure Development Fund (RIDF) was instituted in NABARD with an announcement in the Union Budget 1995-96 with the sole objective of giving low cost fund support to State governments and state owned corporations for quick completion of ongoing projects relating to medium and minor irrigation, soil conservation, watershed management and other forms of rural infrastructure.

34. (c) National Bank for Agriculture and Rural Development (NABARD) is an apex development bank in India . It was established on 12 July 1982 in sixth five year plan and its main focus was to uplift rural India by increasing the credit flow for elevation of agriculture and rural non-farm sector and laying down policies and to oversee the operations of the RRBs. Moreover Regional Rural Banks grant direct loans and advances to marginal farmers and rural artisans. So both statements are correct.

35. (c) India is the fourth largest producer, of natural rubber and fifth largest consumer of natural rubber and synthetic rubber together in the world. India in the world, shares more than 8.0% in the Natural Rubber Production.

36. (d) India is the 6th largest producer of coffee in the world having a share of around 2% in terms of global area. India contributes about 4% to world coffee production as well as in the International trade.

37. (d) 38. (a)

39. (c) These are provided for a period of more than 5 years. This type of loan is taken by farmers to purchase land and expensive agricultural equipments and for repayment of old loans.

40. (a) The total irrigated area increased from less than one million hectares per annum before the green revolution to about 2.5 million hectares per annum during the 1970's. The total gross irrigated area now is 80 million hectares.

41. (d)

42. (d) Land Development Banks (LDBs) provide long-term rural credit for land improvement, soil conservation and other investments of a capital nature. LDBs have now been renamed as State Co-operative Agricultural and Rural Development Banks (SCARDBs). They raise their funds through long-term debentures offering state government guarantee, and refinancing from NABARD.

43. (c) NABARD formulated a model scheme for issue of Kisan Credit Cards (KCCs) to farmers so that they may use them to readily purchase agricultural inputs such as seeds, fertilizers, pesticides, etc. These are operated by commercial banks, RRBs and co-operative banks.

44. (b) These are provided for a period of less than 15 months to meet out expenses of routine farming and domestic consumptions.

45. (a) Procurement price is that price at which government purchases the crop after harvesting, while MSP is the minimum price at which government declares it will buy the crop. Since 1968-69, the MSP is usually the procurement price.

46. (c) These are the most important source of rural credit.

47. (b) NABARD is the apex institution for providing credit facility to agricultural and rural areas. It came into existence on July 12, 1982 and took over the functions of the erstwhile Agricultural Credit Development (ACD), Rural Planning and Credit Cell (RPCC) of RBI and the Agricultural Refinance Development Corporation (ARDC).

48. (a)

49. (d) Its primary task is to function as refinancing institution for all types of lending for agricultural and rural development. In addition to this, it provides term credit to state co-operative banks, regional rural banks, land development banks and state governments (only for share capital contribution to co-operative credit societies).

50. (a) These are provided for a period of 15 months to 5 years to purchase agricultural equipments, animals and for land improvements.

FISCAL AND MONETARY POLICY

INTRODUCTION

Fiscal Policy deals with the taxation and expenditure decisions of the government covered in the annual budget. Monetary Policy deals with the supply of money in the economy and the rate of interest. In India, the government deals with fiscal policy, while the Central bank (RBI) is responsible for monetary policy.

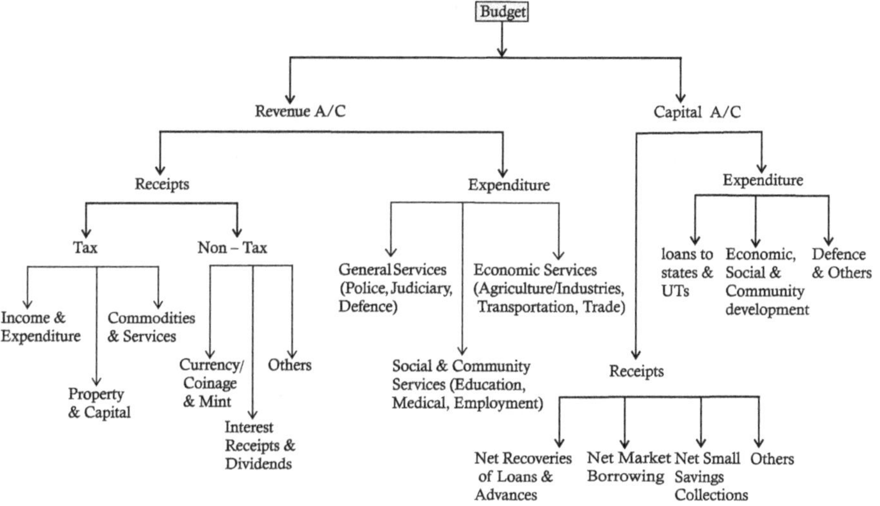

FISCAL POLICY

Fiscal policy or budgetary policy refers to the use by the government of the various instruments such as taxation, expenditure and borrowing in order to achieve the objectives of balanced economic development, full employment or to establish a welfare state. In the context of economic liberalization, the major themes of the fiscal policy comprises:

(i)   a systematic effort to simplify tax structure and tax laws

(ii) a deliberate move to a regime of reasonable direct tax rates and better administration and enforcement.

- The budget or the annual financial statement of the government gives expression to its fiscal policy.

- Union budget or **Annual financial statement** is a statement of estimated receipts and expenditures of the Government of India. The annual financial statement gives the following details:

   (a)   An outline of the results of the last financial year compared with the previous budget estimates.

   (b)   Government forecasts of receipts and payments for the next year.

   (c)   Proposed changes in taxes and expenditure allocations.

Types of Fiscal Policy

Expansionary Fiscal Policy

The policy in which the government minimizes taxes and increase public spending.

Contractionary Fiscal Policy

The policy in which the government increases taxes and reduce public expenditure.

Fiscal Policy (Budget) Tools

Government Spending

- Government spending includes all government consumption, investment, and transfer payments.

Taxes

- Taxes are a fiscal policy tool because changes in taxes affect the average consumer's income, and changes in consumption lead to changes in real GDP.

  The budget shows the receipts and payments of the Government under three heads:

(i) **Consolidated fund**

  It consists of all revenues and loans received by the government.

(ii) **Contingency fund**

  It comprises of the sum placed at the disposal of the President to meet unforeseen expenditure.

(iii) **Public Account**

  It consists of receipts and payments, which are in the form of deposit account with the Government, such as provident funds, small savings, etc.

Parts of Budget

There are two parts of budget, i.e. Revenue Account and Capital Account.

Revenue Account

Revenue Account contains all current receipts, such as taxation, (central excise, custom duty, corporation tax) dividends of public sector units (PSU's) and expenditure of the Government.

Capital Account

Capital Account consists of all capital receipts and expenditure such as domestic and foreign loans, loan repayment, foreign, etc.

Public Expenditure

Total expenditure of the government can be classified into two categories- Developmental or Non-developmental. Developmental expenditure includes government spending with the aim of creating economic and social infrastructure like transport, roads, communication, hospitals, school, etc.

Non-developmental does not directly contribute to development of economy, for example expenditure for loan repayment, interest payable on internal and external loans, defence expenditure, subsidies, etc. In the Indian budget management, this classification is not used.

In India, the public expenditure is of two types – Plan and Non-plan.

Plan Expenditures

Expenditure on central plans such as agriculture, rural development, irrigation, transport, communications, environment and welfare schemes are considered plan expenditure.

Non-plan Expenditures

Non-plan expenditure is further divided into **Revenue expenditure**, which includes interest payments, subsidies, defence expenditure and **Capital expenditure**, which includes loans to PSUs, states, foreign governments.

In short, all asset creating and productive expenditure is part of plan expenditure, and all non- productive, consumptive and non-asset building expenditure is part of non-plan expenditure.

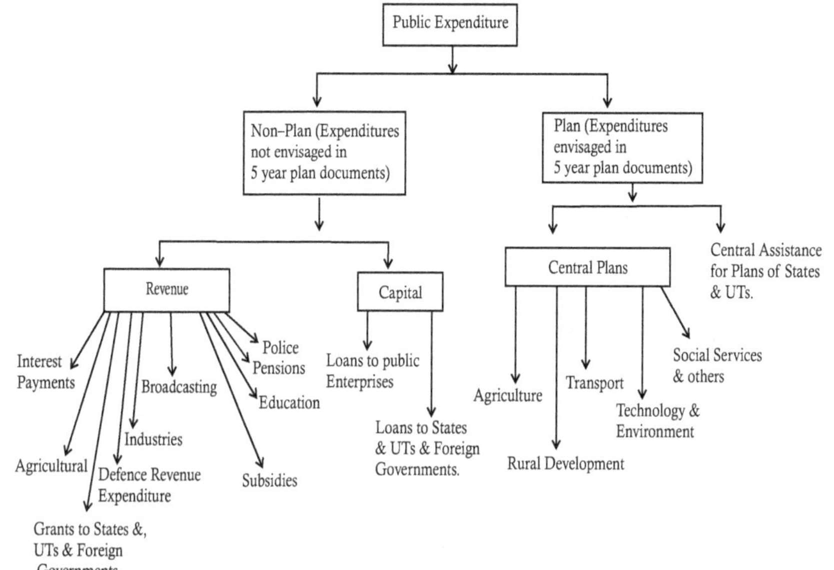

On the recommendations of the **Sukhomoy Chakravarti Committee**, from the financial year 1987-88, Indian budget started being classified as plan and non-plan expenditure, instead of developmental and non-developmental. But now **NDA Government is dropping the classification of expenditure as plan and Non-Plan**.

BUDGET DEFICIT

Deficit means shortage. The gap between Revenue and Expenditure is called Deficit.

> Budget Deficit = Total Expenditure – Total Receipt

Types of Deficit

Revenue deficit

Revenue deficit means the excess of current revenue expenditure over current revenue receipts. Revenue deficit indicates that the government cannot meet its current expenditure from its current revenue.

> Revenue Deficit = Revenue expenditure – Revenue receipts

Fiscal Deficit

It is budget deficit plus borrowings and other liabilities. Fiscal deficit indicates the total borrowing requirements of the government from all sources, whereas budgetary deficit only indicated government's borrowing from RBI.

> Fiscal deficit = Total Expenditure – Revenue Receipts + Recoveries of loans + other receipts

or

> Fiscal deficit = Budget deficit + Government's market borrowing and liabilities.

The FRBM Act, 2004 laid down that the government's revenue deficit should be brought down to zero and its fiscal deficit should not be allowed to exceed 3% of the GDP by 2008-09, but this has still not been achieved.

A high fiscal deficit is also inflationary because it is mainly due to the government's high non plan expenditure which is unproductive. Besides, a high fiscal deficit imposes huge burden by way of repayment of interest and principal. As such, the **Kelkar panel** in 2012 on fiscal consolidation recommended a series of measures like disinvestment, raising diesel prices, auction of spectrum, pruning some plan schemes and rationalising of subsidies.

Primary Deficit

India started using this term since 1997-98. Primary deficit is considered a very useful tool in helping bring more transparency in the government's pattern of expenditure. It shows the current state of government finances. If interest payments are deducted from fiscal deficit, then it will obviously show a lesser deficit for that year as the interest payments are on account of loans taken in the past and not in the present year.

> Primary Deficit = Fiscal Deficit–Interest Payments.

Monetised Deficit

- It refers to that part of deficit for which the government borrows from the RBI.
- To meet the government's such requirements, the RBI prints fresh currency, as a result of which the economy gets monetised.
- This term was adopted by India in 1997-98.

Deficit Financing

The process of bridging the gap between the revenue and expenditure is called deficit financing. In other words, Deficit financing refers to the ways in which the budgetary gap is financed.

Deficit financing was first done in the USA in 1930s as a tool to get out of the effects of the Great Depression. India tried this in 1969 and it gradually became a routine phenomenon in Indian fiscal management.

Objectives of Deficit financing

1. It is used as a tool for meeting financial needs of government, especially in times of war.

2. In under-developed countries, deficit-financing has been considered essential for financing the plans of economic development.

3. It is used for the mobilisation of surplus, non-utilised and idle resources in the economy.

4. It is used as an instrument of economic policy for removing the conditions of depression and to raise the level of output and employment.

Public debt

Governments in developing countries borrow internally under various attractive schemes of capital accumulation. Public debt has three components:

(i) **Internal debt:** It includes market loans from banks and financial institutions, short-term borrowings on treasury bills and other bonds and certificates issued by the government.

(ii) **Other internal liabilities:** It includes small saving schemes, provident fund, reserve fund of the railways, post and telegraph on which the Central Government has to pay interest.

(iii) **External debt:** It includes loan from foreign countries and international financial institutions like the World Bank, IMF, ADB, etc.

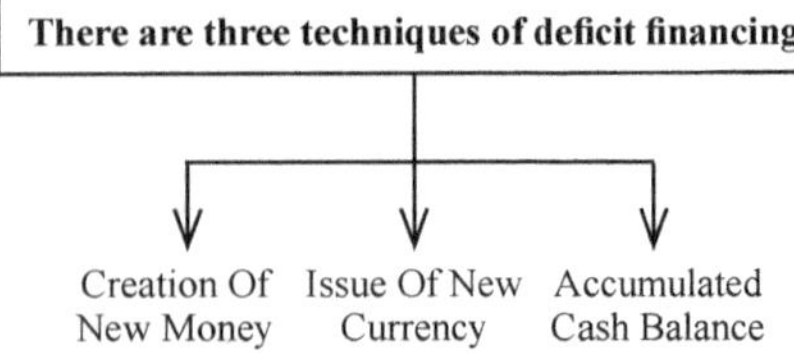

External aid and borrowings

A developing country often resorts to foreign aid if it finds that domestic sources are not large enough. But a country going for foreign aid has to take two precautions:

(i) Keeping the borrowing level low so that country does not fall in a debt trap, and

(ii) Keeping foreign aid strings-free.

- External grants and borrowings are different things. External aids and grants may come free or with very low or even zero interest rates. However, these may come with many terms and conditions attached which are usually not good for a country's economy and autonomy.

- External borrowings means taking loans from other countries.

- External borrowing is often preferred as it brings foreign currency which may help the government in various ways.

- It is also preferred over internal borrowings because if the government itself starts borrowing from the banks of the country, there might not be enough left for other borrowers.

Internal Borrowings

These are not usually preferred because they might hamper the investment scenario of the public and corporate sector of India. But, it may be resorted to as and when required.

Printing currency

- It is usually the last resort for the government in managing its deficit. It might help the government in times of need but it should be undertaken only in case of extreme necessity as it has many damaging effects on the economy.

- It increases inflation proportionally. It may also lead to a pressure on the government for an upward revision in salaries of government employees, which in turn will lead to an increase of government's expenditure, further necessitating printing of currency and more inflation.

TAXES

- Taxes are the main source of government revenues.

- The primary purpose of taxation is the mobilisation of resources and channelising the same for productive investment.

- Taxation can also be used as a measure to promote equity and reduce disparities or to encourage or discourage consumption of particular items.

- Taxation is in the nature of a compulsory levy and there is no **quid pro quo** between the amount paid and the services provided by the government.

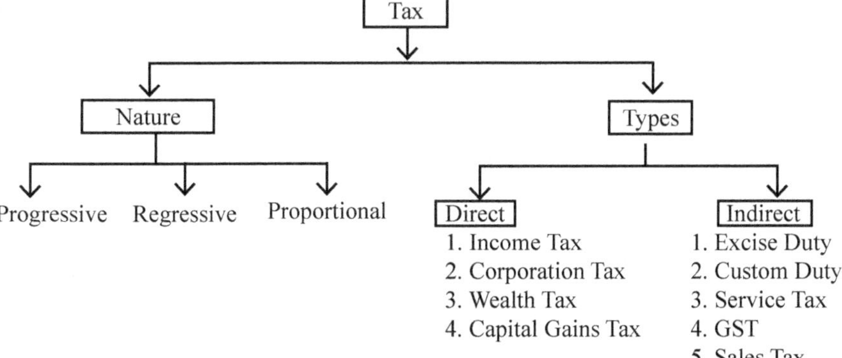

Nature of Taxes

(1) Progressive Tax

- Progressive tax means rates of tax increase for increasing values or volumes on which the tax is levied.

- Income tax is a progressive tax as it has exemptions for very small incomes, low rates for the first slab of taxable income, and higher rates for the largest incomes.

- Indirect taxes can be progressive if there are exemptions or low tax rates for goods heavily consumed by the poor, and higher rates on luxury items, mostly consumed by the rich.

- India has adopted this system for income tax. This is pro-poor way of taxation and is popular in the whole world.

(2) Regressive tax

- Regressive tax is one where the proportion of tax paid falls as income rises.

- The most regressive tax is a poll tax, levied at a fixed rate per person regardless of income.

- A tax system can be made regressive by having indirect taxes levied at relatively high rates on goods heavily consumed by the poor.

(3) Proportional Tax

Proportional tax is one by which the revenue collected rises proportionally with income. A tax system could be made approximately proportional by having a uniform rate of income tax with very few exemptions, and indirect taxes levied at similar rates on as many goods and services as possible.

At some level, progressive and regressive taxes have to be made proportional, otherwise there will be no limit to increase or decrease as the case may be.

TYPES OF TAXES

(A) Direct taxes

- These are taxes that are directly paid to the government by the taxpayer.

- It is a tax applied on individuals and organizations directly by the government.

- Examples of these taxes are income tax, corporation tax, wealth tax, etc.

Income Tax

- Income Tax is paid by an individual based on his/her taxable income in a given financial year.

- Under the Income Tax Act, the term 'individual' also includes Hindu Undivided Families (HUFs), Co-operative Societies, Trusts and any artificial judicial person.

- Taxable income refers to total income minus applicable deductions and exemptions.

- Tax is payable if the taxable is above the minimum taxable limit and is paid as per the differing rates announced for each tax slab for the financial year.

Corporation Tax

- Corporation Tax is paid by Companies and Businesses operating in India on the income earned worldwide in a given financial year.

- The rates of taxation vary based on whether the company is incorporated in India or abroad.

Wealth Tax

- Wealth tax is applicable on individuals, HUFs or companies on the value of their assets in a given financial year on the date of valuation.

- It is taxed at the rate of 1% of the net wealth of any assessee exceeding ₹ 30,00,000.

- 'Net wealth' includes, unproductive assets like cash in hand above ₹ 50,000, second residential property not rented out, cars, gold jewellery or bullion, boats, yachts, aircrafts or urban land.

- It does not include productive assets like commercial property, stocks, bonds, fixed deposits, mutual funds etc.

Capital Gains Tax

- The profits made on sale of property are taxable under Capital Gains Tax.

- Property here includes stocks, bonds, residential property, precious metals etc.

- It is taxed at two different rates based on how long the property was owned by the taxpayer – Short Term Capital Gains Tax and Long Term Capital Gains Tax.

- This deciding period of ownership varies greatly for different classes of property.

(B) Indirect Taxes

Central excise duty

- Excise duty is applicable on the manufacture of goods sold in India.

- Once goods are manufactured, it is originally paid by the manufacturer directly to the Central Government.

- When the goods change hands from the manufacturer to the buyer, this tax is bundled by the manufacturer along with the cost of goods and passed on to the buyer.

Customs duty

- It is the tax imposed on commodities imported into India (import duty) or those exported from India (export duty).

- Since imposing duties on exports reduced the competitive position of the country, the government withdrew export duties.

Service tax

- Service tax is applicable on all services provided in India except a specified negative list of services that are exempt.

- It is paid by the service provider to the government who in turn collects it from the end user by the service provider at the time of provision of such service.

Sales Tax

- Sales Tax is charged on the sale of movable goods.

- It is collected by the Central Government in case of inter-state sales (Central Sales Tax or CST) and by the State Government for intra-state sales (Value Added Tax or VAT).

- The rates of taxation vary depending on the product type.

GOODS AND SERVICES TAX- 2017

Features

- Uniform regime of taxes across India
- Common market of goods & services across India
- GST has two components, viz. central GST (CGST) and the state GST (SGST).
- States will collect service taxes (SGST)
- Centre will collect Integrated Goods & Service Tax (IGST) on inter-state suppliers
- IGST rate will be equal to CGST plus SGST
- It will subsume 16 central & states's taxes
- Goods and services are divided into five tax slabs for collection of tax- 0%, 5%, 12%, 18%, 26%.,

GST Replaces

States Taxes:

(i) VAT/Sales Tax

(ii) Entry Tax/octroi

(iii) Local Tax

(iv) Entertainment Tax

(v) Purchase Tax

(vi) Mandi Tax/Local levies

(vii) Luxury Tax

(viii) Tax on lottery & Betting

(ix) Inter-State Sales Tax

Central Taxes:

(i) Central Excise Duty

(ii) Excise duty on Medicine & Toiletries

(iii) Additional Custom Duty

(iv) Sp. Add. Custom Duty

(v) Countervailing Duty

(vi) Service Tax

(vii) Cesses & Surcharges

GST Excludes

(i)　Alcohol (i.e. remains with states)

(ii)　Petroleum (for 2 years with states)

(iii)　Real Estate:

- Stamp duty with states

- Service tax with GST

BLACK MONEY

It is unaccounted money which is concealed from tax authorities. All illegal economic activities are dealt with this Black Money. Hawala market has deep roots with this black money. Black money creates parallel economy. It puts an adverse pressure on equitable distribution of wealth and income in the economy.

Why Black Money?

Some of the reasons for the spread of black money in India are:

- The shortage and consequent black marketing during the war years and the troubled days of partition;

- The launching of the five-year plans with large expenditure on projects and the consequent enlargement of bureaucracy;

- The regime of controls over economic activity providing scope for corrupt practices;

- Heavy taxation and cumbersome procedures which prompt the evasion;

- Rent control and other regressive laws which led to concealment of actual values in real estate transaction;

- Dishonest foreign trading involving under-invoicing of exports and over-invoicing of imports;

> The Black Money and Imposition Act, 2015, which came into effect from 1 july 2015, lends 90-days compliace window. This gives the person having undisclosed foreign assets and income, a chance to come clean by declaring all such assets and paying a total of 30% tax and penalty.

General Anti Avoidance Rules (GAAR)

GAAR has been introduced as a very important component of Direct Tax code with the objective of preventing such deals and transactions that are carried out to evade and avoid paying taxes. In other words, GAAR seeks to prevent such transactions that are carried out by way of aggressive tax planning so as to avoid paying taxes. GAAR has been prompted by practices of 'round-tripping' whereby a company operating in India may deliberately incorporate its office in a tax haven country, moves its assets there and invests back in India, thereby avoiding paying tax in India.

The announcement to implement GAAR from 2012-13 caused panic among foreign investors and led to massive outflow of foreign funds, which led the **government to set up Shome Committee to review GAAR.** The Committee recommended, among other things, postponement of GAAR and also recommended that it should not be imposed on investments from Mauritius and Singapore. It also recommended that GAAR should not be imposed if the tax liabilities are less than 3 crores. It also suggested doing away with the arbitrary powers given to tax authorities in India.

Methods to Reduce Tax Liability

The methods adopted to reduce tax liability can be broadly put into four categories :

(i) **Tax Evasion:** Tax evasion is illegal means to reduce tax liabilities, i.e. falsification of books, suppression of income, overstatement of deductions, etc.

(ii) **Tax Avoidance:** Tax Avoidance means an attempt to reduce tax liability through legal means, i.e. to regulate one's financial affairs in such a way that one pays the minimum tax imposed by the law.

(iii) **Tax Mitigation:** Tax Mitigation is a situation where the taxpayer takes advantage of a fiscal incentive afforded to him by the tax legislation by actually submitting to the conditions and economic consequences that the particular tax legislation entails.

(iv) **Tax Planning:** Tax Planning is defined as "arrangement of a person's business and / or private affairs in order to minimize tax liability".

MONETARY POLICY

Monetary policy refers to the set of measures adopted by the Central bank (RBI) for monetary management.

Monetary Policy Objectives

- **Stability of external value**
  Fluctuation in exchange rate of a currency affects foreign trade and investment. It is, therefore, important that the rate of exchange is maintained without violent fluctuations.

- **Maintenance of domestic price level**
  Fluctuation in prices affects investment decisions. It also leads to increasing income disparities. However, monetary policy alone cannot ensure the maintenance of domestic prices, as several other factors such as erratic monsoons, changes in tastes, fluctuation in world prices, etc. affect domestic prices.

- **Reducing the impact of business cycles (slumps and booms)** by manipulation of credit and interest policy. However, economists are not of the same opinion on whether business cycles are primarily caused by monetary factors.

Indian Monetary Policy

Planned economic development adopted by India required an active monetary policy. The two stated aims of this policy were:

- boost economic development.
- control inflationary pressure.

Role of RBI in functioning of Monetary Policy

- RBI works as the monetary authority of India and operates the monetary policy.
- RBI announces Monetary Policy every year in the Month of April.
- This is followed by three quarterly

Reviews in July, October and January. However, it at its discretion can announce the measures at any point of time.

- The Annual Monetary Policy is made up of two parts viz. Part A: macroeconomic and monetary developments; Part B: Actions taken and fresh policy measures.

The functions of RBI in the context of monetary policy are as follows:

- Using the monetary policy tools, RBI increases and reduced the money supply in the system in order to maintain price stability and check too much inflation.

- RBI makes efforts for the controlled expansion of bank credit and helps commercial banks in credit creation. It also makes decisions regarding credit allocation to priority and marginal sector.

- RBI tries to increase the productive investments in the country by retraining non-essential investments and creating an enabling environment for productive investments.

CREDIT CONTROL

- Credit control is an important tool used by Reserve Bank of India to control the demand and supply of money **(liquidity)** in the economy.

- Central Bank administers control over the credit that the commercial banks grant.

- Such a method is used by RBI to bring "Economic Development with Stability". It means that banks will not only control inflationary trends in the economy but also boost economic growth which would ultimately lead to increase in real national income with stability. In view of its functions such as issuing notes and custodian of cash reserves, credit not being controlled by RBI would lead to Social and Economic instability in the country.

Credit Control Measures

Qualitative control

- **Margin Requirement-** refers to difference between the securities offered and amount borrowed by the banks.
- **Rationing of Credit** - RBI controls the credit granted/ allocated by commercial banks.
- **Moral suasion** - Psychological means and informal means of selective credit control.
- **Direct Action** - Refers to the step taken by the RBI against banks don't fulfil conditions and requirements.

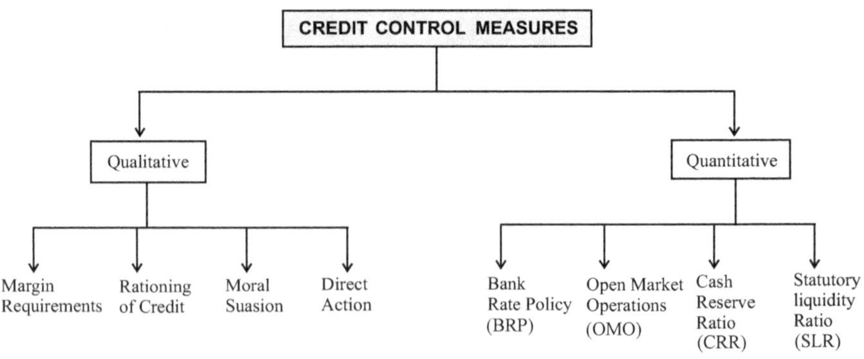

Qualitative control

Bank Rate

- Bank rate is the rate charged by the central bank for lending funds to commercial banks.
- Bank rates influence lending rates of commercial banks.
- Higher bank rate will translate to higher lending rates by the banks.
- To curb liquidity, the central bank can resort to raising the bank rate and vice versa.

Base Rate

- Base rate is the minimum rate set by the Reserve Bank of India below which banks are not allowed to lend to its customers.
- Base rate is decided in order to enhance transparency in the credit market and ensure that banks pass on the lower cost of fund to their customers.
- Loan pricing will be done by adding base rate and a suitable spread depending on the credit risk premium.

Call Money Rate

- Call money rate is the rate at which short term funds are borrowed and lent in the money market.
- The duration of the call money loan is 1 day.
- Banks resort to these type of loans to fill the asset liability mismatch, comply with the statutory CRR and SLR requirements and to meet the sudden demand of funds.
- RBI, banks, primary dealers etc are the participants of the call money market.
- Demand and supply of liquidity affect the call money rate.
- A tight liquidity condition leads to a rise in call money rate and vice versa.

Repo Rate

- Repo (Repurchase) rate also known as the benchmark interest rate is the rate at which the RBI lends money to the banks for a short term.
- When the Repo rate increases, borrowing from RBI becomes more expensive.
- If RBI wants to make it more expensive for the banks to borrow money, it increases the Repo rate.
- However, if it wants to make it cheaper for banks to borrow money it reduces the Repo rate.

Reverse Repo Rate

- Reverse Repo rate is the short term borrowing rate at which RBI borrows money from banks.
- The Reserve bank uses this tool when it feels there is too much money floating in the banking system.
- An increase in the reverse repo rate means that the banks will get a higher rate of interest from RBI.
- As a result, banks prefer to lend their money to RBI which is always safe instead of lending it others (people, companies etc) which is always risky.

Cash Reserve Ratio (CRR)

- It is a tool used by RBI to control liquidity in the banking system.
- Banks in India don't hold much cash with themselves; they deposit such cash **(aka currency chests)** with Reserve Bank of India, which is considered as equivalent to holding cash with themselves.
- This minimum ratio (that is the part of the total deposits to be held as cash) is stipulated by the RBI and is known as the CRR or Cash Reserve Ratio.
- Therefore, higher the ratio, the lower is the amount that banks will be able to use for lending and investment.

Statutory Liquidity Ratio (SLR)

- All banks are required to maintain at the close of business every day, a minimum proportion of their Net Demand and Time Liabilities as liquid assets in the form of cash, gold and un-encumbered approved securities.

- The ratio of liquid assets to demand and time liabilities is known as Statutory Liquidity Ratio (SLR).

- RBI is empowered to increase this ratio up to 40%. An increase in SLR also restricts the bank's leverage position to pump more money into the economy.

Marginal Standing facility (MSF)

- It is a special window for banks to borrow from RBI against approved government securities in an emergency situation like an acute cash shortage.

- MSF rate is higher than Repo rate.

- Current MSF Rate is 7%.

Open Market Operations (OMO)

- Open Market Operations include the purchase and sale of the Government securities (G-Secs) by RBI from / to market.

- The objective of Open Market Operations is to adjust the rupee liquidity conditions in the economy on a durable basis.

- When RBI sells government security in the markets, the banks purchase them.

- When banks purchase Government securities, they have a reduced ability to lend to the industrial houses or other commercial sectors.

- This reduces surplus cash, contracts the rupee liquidity and consequently credit creation / credit supply.

Capital Account Convertibility (CAC)

- CAC means the freedom to convert local financial assets into foreign financial assets and vice versa at market determined rates of exchange.

- This implies that Capital Account Convertibility allows anyone to freely move from local currency into foreign currency and back.

- Basics Capital account is made up of both the short-term and long-term capital transactions.

- The Capital Transaction may be Capital outflow or capital inflow.

- Convertibility on the capital account is usually introduced after a certain period of introducing the Current account convertibility.

- The most important effect of introducing the capital account convertibility is that it encourages the inflow of the foreign capital, because under certain conditions, the foreign investors are enabled to repatriate their investments, wherever they want.

Policy Rates of RBI – July 2018

Bank Rate	6.5%
Repo Rate	6.25%
Reverse Repo Rate	6.00%
CRR	4%
SLR	19.5%
MSFR	6.5%

EXERCISE

1. Which of the following will elevate 'demand pull inflation' in the economy?
   1. Increase in subsidy on LPG
   2. Rise in fuel prices
   3. Fall in income tax rates
   Choose the correct option from the codes:
   (a) 1 and 2 only (b) 1 and 3 only
   (c) 2 and 3 only (d) 1, 2 and 3

2. What could be the possible effect of expansionary fiscal policy:
   1. Fiscal deficit rise
   2. Labor wage rise
   3. income tax rate rise
   choose the correct option from the codes:
   (a) 1 only   (b) 1 and 2 only
   (c) 1 and 3 only (d) 1,2 and 3

3. The Economic Survey is compiled by which of the following:
   (a) National Sample Survey Organization
   (b) Department of economic affairs
   (c) Central Statistical office
   (d) none of these

4. Which among the given instrument(s) assist in financing a company?
   1. Bonds
   2. Shares
   3. Debentures
   select the correct answer using the codes given below.
   (a) 1 and 2 only
   (b) 2 only
   (c) 2 and 3 only
   (d) 1, 2 and 3

5. What would be the consequence of increasing the indirect taxes in any economy?
   1. Increases in GDP at factor cost
   2. Fall in GDP at factor cost
   3. Rise in GDP at market price
   4. Fall in GDP at market price
   choose the correct option from the codes:
   (a) 1 only   (b) 2 and 3 only
   (c) 3 only   (d) 4 only

6. 'Narrow banking' comes into effect when:
   (a) banks lend only to risk free sectors
   (b) there are limited areas of operation by banks
   (c) banking takes place by non-banking financial companies
   (d) banks acts only as payment banks

7. Which among the given option(s) are the functions performed by Reserve Bank of India?
   1. RBI manages inflation
   2. RBI acts as the banker's bank
   3. RBI manages India's Foreign Exchanges
   4. RBI handles the borrowing program of government
   Select the correct answer using the codes given below.
   (a) 2, 3 and 4 only
   (b) 1, 2 and 3 only
   (c) 2 and 3 only
   (d) 1, 2, 3 and 4

8. With reference to the Indian tax structure:
   1. Corporation tax has the largest contribution.
   2. Contribution from direct taxes is more than that of indirect taxes.
   Which of the statements given above is/are correct?
   (a) 1 only
   (b) 2 only
   (c) Both 1 and 2
   (d) Neither 1 nor 2

9. Which of the following would help to increase the Gross capital formation of a country:
   1. Rise in gross domestic savings
   2. Rise in gross domestic consumption
   3. Rise in GDP

choose the correct option from the codes:
- (a) 1 only
- (b) 1 and 2 only
- (c) 1 and 3 only
- (d) None

10. Which among the given statement(s) is/are true?
   1. Gross domestic product of India is more than its Gross National Product.
   2. India's Net Factor Income from Abroad is positive.
   - (a) 1 only
   - (b) 2 only
   - (c) Both 1 and 2
   - (d) Neither 1 nor 2

11. What is the meaning of Gross budgetary support:
   - (a) expenditure in budget on social schemes
   - (b) Centre's contribution to budget
   - (c) assistance provided by the Centre to five year plan.
   - (d) None of the given choices

12. Which of the following statement defines the 'Bank rate'?
   - (a) The rate at which commercial banks lend money to customers
   - (b) The rate at which commercial banks lend money to RBI
   - (c) The rate at which commercial banks borrow money from RBI
   - (d) None of the given choices

13. In monetary terminology, what is 'monetary base' or 'high powered money'?
   - (a) the total assets of RBI
   - (b) the total liability of RBI
   - (c) the total debt of the government
   - (d) the total foreign exchange of RBI

14. How could RBI increase the money supply in the market?
   - (a) Buying government securities
   - (b) selling government securities
   - (c) Borrowing money from commercial banks
   - (d) none of the given choices

15. How could RBI reduce the money supply in the market?
   - (a) borrowing money from commercial banks
   - (b) buying government securities
   - (c) selling government securities
   - (d) None of the given choices

16. Which of the following is the effective process by which RBI or any Central bank protects the economy against adverse economic shocks:
   - (a) stabilization
   - (b) liberalization
   - (c) sterilization
   - (d) protection

17. Which of the following is not an example of 'public goods'?
   - (a) National Forests
   - (b) Roads
   - (c) National defense
   - (d) Cars

18. Which one of the given choices is the most important part of "The Government Budget"?
   - (a) Capital Budget only
   - (b) Revenue Budget and Capital Budget
   - (c) Revenue Budget only
   - (d) None of the given choices

19. Which of the following comes under India's foreign-exchange reserves ?
   - (a) Foreign-currency assets, Special Drawing Rights and loans from foreign countries.
   - (b) Foreign-currency assets, gold holdings of the Reserve Bank of India and loans from the World Bank.
   - (c) Foreign-currency assets, gold holdings of the Reserve Bank of India and SDRs.
   - (d) Foreign-currency assets, loans from the World Bank and SDRs

20. Which among the following constitute Capital Account? (2013)
   1. Private Remittances
   2. Portfolio Investments
   3. Loans from foreign countries
   4. FDI
   Select the correct answer using the codes given below.
   - (a) 2, 3 and 4
   - (b) 1, 2 and 4
   - (c) 1, 2 and 3
   - (d) 1, 3 and 4

21. Which of the following set the value of currencies in global market:
    1. Economic potential of the country in question
    2. Stability of the government of the concerned country
    3. Demand for goods/services provided by the country concerned
    4. World Bank
    Which of the statements given above are correct?
    (a) 1 only
    (b) 2 and 4
    (c) 2 and 3
    (d) 1 and 4

22. There has been a persistent deficit budget year after year. What action could be taken by the government to reduce the deficit?
    1. Expanding industries
    2. Introducing new welfare schemes
    3. Rationalizing subsidies
    4. Reducing revenue expenditure
    choose the correct option from the code.
    (a) 3 only
    (b) 3 and 4
    (c) 1 only
    (d) 1, 2, 3 and 4

23. Which of the following best describes the "Primary deficit"?
    (a It is the difference between capital receipts and Interest Payment
    (b) It is the difference between the Fiscal Deficit and Interest Payment
    (c) It is the addition of Fiscal Deficit and Interest Payment
    (d) It is the difference between Revenue receipts and Revenue Expenditure

24. What is the process through which the Reserve Bank of India estimates the demand for banknotes?
    (a) RBI evaluates the rate of growth of Indian Economy
    (b) Demand and Reserve requirements are replaced by RBI
    (c) Application of various Statistical and Economic principles
    (d) All of these

25. Which of the following is also known as "Banker of all the Banks"?
    (a) World Bank
    (b) Reserve Bank of India

    (c) Asian Development Bank
    (d) State Bank of India

26. One rupee note in India is signed by:
    (a) Governor of Reserve Bank of India
    (b) President of India
    (c) Finance Secretary
    (d) Prime Minister of India

27. Which among the following constitutes the direct instruments of Monetary Policy?
    (a) Cash Reserve Ratio
    (b) Statutory Liquidity Rate
    (c) Repo Rate
    (d) Both A and B

28. Which of the following statement is correct?
    1. Commercial banks are advised in the monetary matters by the RBI.
    2. Commercial banks retain their deposits with the Reserve Bank of India
    3. In times of need the Reserve Bank lends funds to the commercial banks.
    Select the correct answer below:
    (a) 2 and 3 only
    (b) 1 and 2 only
    (c) 1 and 3 only
    (d) 1, 2 and 3

29. Which of the following is/are the possible reasons for continuous rise in food inflation in India?
    1. There are structural constraints in the food supply chain
    2. Due to the effect of increase in incomes, the patterns of consumptions of the people have changed significantly.
    3. Gradual switchover towards the cultivating the commercial crops, and continuous decrease in the area under the cultivation of food grains.
    Which of the statements given above are correct?
    (a) 1 and 2 only.
    (b) 2 and 3 only.
    (c) 1 and 3 only.
    (d) 1, 2 and 3.

30. Who could participate in the Open Market transactions?
    (a) Reserve Bank of India and the Government
    (b) Market and Reserve Bank of India
    (c) Government and the Market
    (d) Global Markets and Reserve Bank of India

31. Who could be the clients borrowing under "long-term lending under Bank Rate"?
    I. Government of India
    II. State Governments
    III. Non Banking Financial Corporations
    IV. Commercial banks in India
    Choose the correct answer from the codes below.
    (a) 1 and 4 only
    (b) 2 and 3 only
    (c) 1, 2 and 4 only
    (d) All of the above

32. Which among the following rate(s) is/are is not controlled by the Reserve Bank of India directly?
    (a) CRR
    (b) Reverse repo rate
    (c) Repo rate
    (d) WPI

33. Under which of the give circumstance(s) RBI might sell the Government Securities in open market?
    (a) In a condition when inflow of Foreign Funds is very low.
    (b) In a condition when inflow of Foreign Funds is very high.
    (c) In a condition when banks have require liquidity.
    (d) None of the given choices

34. Which of the following policies of the financial sectors is basically designed to transferring local financial assets into foreign assets freely and at market determined exchange rates?
    (a) Capital account convertibility
    (b) Financial deficit management
    (c) Minimum support price
    (d) None of these

35. What would be the effect on fiscal policy if the RBI tries to promote economic stability?
    (a) Decrease in taxes
    (b) Increase in taxes
    (c) Decrease in spending
    (d) Decrease in borrowing

36. What does the term "paper gold" mean?
    (a) it is a reserve assets in the International Monetary Fund designed to supplement reserves of gold and convertible currencies used to maintain stability in the foreign exchange market
    (b) it is special type of paper made out of gold
    (c) it is a currency prevailing only in Europian Union
    (d) None of the above options.

37. What does Special Drawing Rights (SDR) mean?
    (a) A measure of a country's reserve assets in the international monetary system.
    (b) A specified minimum fraction of the total deposits of customers, which commercial banks have to hold as reserves either in cash or as deposits with the central bank.
    (c) A comprehensive measure used for estimation of price changes in a basket of goods and services representative of consumption expenditure in an economy
    (d) none of the above

38. A great deal of Foreign Direct Investment(FDI) to India comes from Mauritius than from any other major economies like UK and France.Why?
    (a) India has preference for certain countries as regards receiving FDI
    (b) India has double taxation avoidance agreement with Mauritius
    (c) Most citizens of Mauritius have ethnic identity with India and so they feel secure to invest in India

    (d) Impending dangers of global climate change prompt Mauritius to make huge investment in India.

39. Which of the following is not an argument for protectionism?
(a) To protect infant industries
(b) To increase the level of imports
(c) To protect strategic industries
(d) To improve the balance of payments

40. Foreign Direct Investment involves:
(a) A speculator trying to make a profit by buying company shares on a foreign stock exchange.
(b) A UK energy company buying territory abroad where it expects to find oil reserves.
(c) A tourist purchasing foreign currency to spend on a holiday abroad.
(d) A company signing an agreement with a wholesaler to distribute its products in foreign markets.

41. AoA in context with World Trade Organization is ___?
(a) Article of Association
(b) Agreement on Agriculture
(c) Agreement on Association
(d) Administration of Agriculture

42. FDI in Multi-Brand Retail Trade (MBRT) in all products is now permitted in India subject to
1. a ceiling of 51%
2. minimum amount to be brought in as FDI by the foreign investor is US $ 100 million.
3. atleast 50% of the procurement of manufactured/processed products should be sourced from 'small industries'.
4. retail sales locations set-up only in cities with a population of more than 10 lakh.
Select the correct answer using the codes given below
(a) 1, 2, 3 and 4 (b) 1 and 4
(c) Only 2 (d) 1, 2 and 4

43. Which of the following pairs is not correctly matched?
(a) Increase in—Monetary expansion
(b) Low import growth rate in India-Recession in Indian industry
(c) Portfolio investment—Foreign institutional investors.
(d) Euro-issues—Shares held by Indian companies in European countries

44. Which of the following would include Foreign Direct Investment in India?
(a) Subsidiaries of foreign companies in India
(b) Majority foreign equity holding in Indian companies
(c) Companies exclusively financed by foreign companies
(d) All of the above

45. Which of the following statement is not correct about World Trade Organization (WTO):
(a) The WTO deals with the global rules of trade between nations.
(b) The goal of the WTO is to help producers of goods and services, exporters, and importers conduct their business.
(c) The WTO, which is a successor body of the General Agreement on Tariffs and Trade, came into being following the Uruguay Round of Negotiations.
(d) The WTO distances itself in framing of rules on trad in intellectual property rights.

46. Consider the following statements:
1. The Foreign Exchange Management Act FEMA became an act on the 1st day of June, 2002.
2. It replaced FERA.
3. It made all offenses regarding foreign exchange civil offenses, as opposed to criminal offenses as dictated by FERA.
Which of the statements given above is/are correct?
(a) 1 and 2   (b) 2 and 3
(c) 1 and 3   (d) None

47. Consider the following statements:
    1. Kelkar Committee is associated to oil and gas.
    2. Kelkar Committee has to prepare a roadmap for enhancing import of oil and gas.
    Which of the statements given above is/are correct?
    (a) 1 only (b) 2 only
    (c) 1 and 2 (d) None

48. Consider the following statements:
    1. The Petrapole-Benapole border checkpoint controls the foreign trade between India and Bangladesh.
    2. Petrapole is on Bangladesh side and Benapole is on Indian side.
    Which of the statements given above is/are correct?
    (a) 1 only (b) 2 only
    (c) 1 and 2 (d) None

49. Which of the following statement would not include Foreign Direct Investment in India?
    (a) By incorporating a wholly owned subsidiary or company anywhere
    (b) By acquiring shares in an associated enterprise
    (c) Through a merger or an acquisition of an unrelated enterprise
    (d) Participating in an equity joint venture with same investor or enterprise

50. Consider the following statements:
    1. International Monetary Fund (IMF) was initiated in 1944 at the Bretton Woods Conference and formally created in 1945.
    2. IMF grants loan to member country and other developing countries.
    Which of the statements given above is/are correct?
    (a) 1 only (b) 2 only
    (c) 1 and 2 (d) None

51. Consider the following statements regarding the Federation of Indian Export Organisation (FIEO).
    Which of the statements given is/are correct?
    (a) FIEO was set up in 1965 under the aegis of Ministry of Commerce.
    (b) It is an apex body of Export Promotion Organisations
    (c) FIEO renders an integrated package of services to various organizations connected with export promotion.
    (d) All of the above

52. Which sentences are correct regarding special drawing rights?
    I. It was created in 1980
    II. It is also known as "paper gold".
    III. Its value is based on a basket of five key international key currencies and SDRs can be exchanged for freely usable currencies
    (a) Only II (b) I & III
    (c) II & III (d) All the above

53. Match the following current accounts with their examples:
    CA
    I. Visible Trade a. Gifts
    II. Invisible Trade b. Tea
    III. Unilateral Transfer c. Insurance
    (a) I – b, II – c, III – a
    (b) I – a, II – c, III – b
    (c) I – c, II – a, III – b

54. Which statement is correct regarding capital account?
    (a) On the credit side of this account receipt of foreign exchange due to Foreign Direct Investment (FDI), Foreign Capital Investment (FCI) and Foreign Borrowing (FB) is recorded.
    (b) On the debit side of capital account payment of foreign exchange due to Direct Investment Abroad (DIA), Portfolio Investment Abroad (PIA) and Foreign Lending (FL) is recorded.
    (c) Both (a) and (b)
    (d) Neither (a) not (b)

55. Which of the below statements are correct?
    (a) Reverse account balance makes an adjustment between current account balance and capital account balance.

(b) If surplus in the Capital Account is more than deficit in the Current Account, there is net increase in the Forex Reserves of the country at the end of the year.

(c) If deficit in the current account is more than surplus in the Capital Account then there is net decrease in Foreign Reserves of the country at the end of the year.

(d) All of the above

56. What are the factors on which import substitution strategy was based on?
(a) Non-price
(b) Physical- interventionist policies like licensing, quotas and other physical restrictions on imports
(c) All of the above
(d) None of the above

57. Choose the correct sentence regarding the trade policy.
(a) Mahalanobis strategy adopted during the First plan
(b) Export increased at an average rate of 29% per annum in dollar terms between 1986 and 1990
(c) A combination of factors such as bad policy, weak government and external factors led to the decline of this performance to nine per cent in 1990-91 and 4 per cent in the subsequent years.
(d) None of these

58. Which points are correct regarding SEZ act?
I. Exemption to SEZ developer and units from Minimum Alternate Tax.
II. Constitution of an authority for each SEZ with a view to providing greater administrative, financial and functional autonomy to these zones.
III. Establishment of designated courts and a single enforcement agency to ensure speedy trial and investigation of offences committed in SEZs.
(a) I & II   (b) Only II
(c) Only III   (d) All the above

59. Match the area with the state where there are EPIPs in India:
Column I   Column II
I.   Rajasthan   a.   Amingaon
II. Maharashtra b.   Sitapura
III. Kerala   c.   Ambarnath
IV. Assam   d.   Kakkinad
(a) I-b, II-c, III-d, IV-a
(b) I-a, II-c, III-d, IV-b
(c) I-d, II-c, III-b, IV-a
(d) I-c, II-b, III-a, IV-d

60. Which statement is correct regarding FDI?
I.   FDI is a non-debt capital flow, is a leading source of external financing, especially for the developing economies.
II. It not only brings in capital and technical know-how but also increases the competitiveness of the economy.
III. Overall it supplements domestic investment, much required for sustaining the high growth rate of the country.
IV. Since 2000, significant changes have been made in the FDI policy regime by the government to ensure that India becomes an increasingly attractive and investor-friendly destination.
(a) I & II   (b) II & III
(c) Only IV   (d) All the above

61. With reference to the foreign portfolio investments (FPI):
1. FPI's have more volatility as compared to the loans from international financial institutions,
2. FDI's are an integral constituent of the FPIs.
Which among the above statement/s is/are correct?
(a) 1 only   (b) 2 only
(c) Both 1 and 2 (d) Neither 1 nor 2

HINTS & EXPLANATIONS

1. **(b)** Increase in subsidy of LPG would reduce the pocket expenditure of people on LPG, making more money available with them, thereby increasing demand pull inflation. Similarly decrease in income tax rates will lead to more money availability. Increase in fuel prices would lead to cost-push inflation.

2. **(a)** Expansionary fiscal policy is a macroeconomic policy that looks to expand the money supply to encourage economic development or combat inflation (price increases). One form of expansionary policy is fiscal policy, which comes in the form of tax cuts, rebates and increased government spending. Expansionary policies could also come from central banks, which focus on increasing the money supply in the economy. Such a fiscal policy would increase the expenditure, thereby increasing fiscal deficit. Increase in wages of labor is unrelated. There could be a decrease (not increase) in income tax rates, so statement 3 is false.

3. **(b)** The Economic Survey is complied by Department of economic affairs, Ministry of Finance. Office of economic advisor publishes WPI, while Central Statistical office publishes the matters about IIP and CPI.

4. **(b)** Shares are equity instruments, while bonds and debentures are debt instruments. Debt instruments are assets that require a fixed payment to the holder, usually with interest. Examples of debt instruments include bonds (government or corporate), debentures and mortgages. Equity financing allows a company to acquire funds (often for investment) without incurring debt, e.g. shares.

5. **(c)** An indirect tax is a tax that is paid to the government by one entity in the supply chain, but it is passed on to the consumer as part of the price of a good or service. GDP (market price) = GDP (factor cost) + indirect taxes – subsidies. Which clearly shows that any increase in indirect taxes would increase the GDP at market prices.

6. **(a)** A 'Narrow Bank' could be defined as the system of banking under which a bank places its funds in risk-free assets with maturity period matching its liability maturity profile, so that there is no problem relating to asset liability mismatch and the quality of assets remains intact without leading to emergence of sub-standard assets.

7. **(d)** The Reserve Bank of India has the sole right to issue currency notes except one rupee notes which are issued by the Ministry of Finance. As banker to the government the Reserve Bank manages the banking needs of the government. It has to-maintain and operate the government's deposit accounts. It collects receipts of funds and makes payments on behalf of the government. It represents the Government of India as the member of the IMF and the World Bank. The commercial banks hold deposits in the Reserve Bank and the latter has the custody of the cash reserves of the commercial

banks. The Reserve Bank has the custody of the country's reserves of international currency, and this enables the Reserve Bank to deal with crisis connected with adverse balance of payments position.

8. (c) Since 2007-08, the contribution of direct tax has been more than indirect tax. Before this, the trend was opposite. Corporation tax is the largest contributor among other taxes.

9. (d) Gross capital formation, in simple terms is equivalent to total investment made. It was earlier called gross domestic investment. The part of GDP that is used is called gross domestic consumption, while the part that is saved is gross domestic savings (GDS). Some part of this GDS would be re-invested back, and that is called gross capital formation. Now, an increase in GDP or GDS would not necessarily lead to an increase in capital formation. Because how much is invested back would depends on many other factors.

10. (a) GNP = GDP + NFIA. India's NFIA is negative. Thus India's GDP is more than its GNP. NFIA = Factor income earned from abroad by residents – Factor income of non-residents in domestic territory.

11. (c) The Government's support to the Central plan is called the Gross Budgetary Support. In the recent years the GBS has been slightly more than 50% of the total Central Plan. The share of the GBS in Central Plan has been rising since 2008-09.

12. (c) Bank rate is the rate at which commercial banks could borrow money from the RBI. If the rate is higher, then taking money from

RBI becomes difficult, so the banks would have lesser money to lend to public. The vice-versa in this case is also true.

13. (b) This includes the currency (notes and coins in circulation and vault cash of commercial banks) along with the deposits held by the Government of India and commercial banks with RBI.

14. (a) RBI controls the money supply in the market by tools known as CRR and SLR. By reducing CRR and SLR, banks have more money to lend, and therefore money supply is increased. RBI can also change the Repo rate and the bank rate. Both of these are the rates at which banks borrow from the RBI. Decreasing these rates decrease the cost of borrowing, thereby inducing the banks to maintain a healthy cash balance.

15. (c) RBI controls the money supply in the market by tools known as CRR and SLR. By increasing CRR and SLR, banks have less money to lend, and therefore money supply is reduced. RBI can also change the Repo rate and the bank rate. Both of these are the rates at which banks borrow from the RBI. Increasing these rates increases the cost of borrowing, thereby inducing the banks to maintain a healthy cash balance.

16. (c) RBI does this by performing a host of operations, for example controlling the Bank Rate, buying or selling government securities, etc.

17. (d) Public goods are those goods that cannot be provided by market mechanisms.

18. (b) Revenue Budget consists of the revenue receipts of the government

(tax revenues and other revenues) and the expenditure met from these revenues. Tax revenues comprise proceeds of taxes and other duties levied by the Union

Capital budgeting is the process in which a business determines and evaluates potential expenses or investments that are large in nature. These expenditures and investments include projects such as building a new plant or investing in a long-term venture.

19. (c) Foreign Exchange reserves are foreign currency assets held by the central banks of countries. These assets include foreign marketable securities, monetary gold, special drawing rights (SDRs) and reserve position in the IMF. The main purpose of holding foreign exchange reserves is to make international payments and hedge against exchange rate risks.

20. (a) A portfolio investment is a hands-off or passive investment of securities in a portfolio, and it is made with the expectation of earning on return. Portfolio investment is distinct from direct investment, which involves taking a sizable stake in a target company and possibly being involved with its day-to-day management.

Foreign debt is an outstanding loan that one country owes to another country or institutions within that country. Foreign debt also includes due payments to international organizations such as the International Monetary Fund (IMF). The debt may be comprised of fees for goods and services or outstanding credit due to a negative balance of trade.

Foreign direct investment (FDI) is an investment made by a company or individual in one country in business interests in another country, in the form of either establishing business operations or acquiring business assets in the other country, such as ownership or controlling interest in a foreign company.

21. (c) Stability of the government of the concerned country and the demand for goods/services provided by the country concerned set the value of currencies in global market.

22. (b) Introducing new welfare schemes would increase expenditure and thus would increase the budget deficit. Reducing revenue expenditure and rationalizing subsidies would cut down on the budget deficit. Expanding industries would also need investments which would increase expenditure.

23. (b) Primary deficit refers to difference between fiscal deficit of the current year and interest payments on the previous borrowings. Primary Deficit = Fiscal Deficit − Interest Payments

24. (d) The reserve bank estimates the demand for Banknotes on the bases of the growth rate of economy along with the replacement demand as well as reserve requirements by using various statistical and economic principles.

25. (b) RBI is known as Banker's Bank as it holds a part of the cash reserves of banks, lends them funds for short periods, and provides them with centralized clearing and cheap and quick remittance facilities. In the early stages of the

development of central banking, banks used to keep some of their cash reserves voluntarily with a leading bank which gradually took over the role of a central bank.

26. (c) Under section 22 of the Reserve Bank of India Act, RBI has role to issue currency notes of various denomination except one rupee notes. It bears the signature of finance secretary.

27. (d) Cash Reserve Ratio, Statuary Liquidity Ratio and Refinance facilities are the instruments of monetary policy. Under CRR a certain percentage of the total bank deposits have to be kept in the current account with RBI which means banks do not have access to that much amount for any economic activity or commercial activity. Banks can't lend the money to firms or individual borrowers, banks can't use that money for investment purposes. So, that CRR remains in current account and banks don't earn anything on that.

28. (d) commercial bank is a financial institution that provides various financial services, such as accepting deposits and issuing loans. Commercial bank customers can take advantage of a range of investment products that commercial banks offer like savings accounts and certificates of deposit. The loans a commercial bank issues can vary from business loans and auto loans to mortgages.

29. (a) Food price inflation has remained persistently elevated for over a year now, reflecting in part the structural demand-supply mismatches in several commodities. The trend of food inflation points at not only structural demand-supply mismatches in commodities and essential consumption basket but also at changing consumption patterns.

30. (c) OMOs are conducted by the RBI via the sale/purchase of government securities (G-Sec) to/from the market with the primary aim of modulating rupee liquidity conditions in the market. OMOs are an effective quantitative policy tool in the armory of the RBI, but are constrained by the stock of government securities available with it at a point in time.

31. (d) The interest rate which the RBI charges on its long-term lending is known as the Bank Rate. The clients who borrow through this route are the Union Government, State Governments, Financial Institutions, Banks, NBFC's and co-operative banks.

32. (d) Wholesale Price Index (WPI) represents the price of goods at a wholesale stage i.e. goods that are sold in bulk and traded between organizations instead of consumers. WPI is used as an important measure of inflation in India. Fiscal and monetary policy changes are greatly influenced by changes in WPI. Inflation rate is the difference between WPI calculated at the beginning and the end of a year.

33. (b)

34. (a) Current account convertibility allows free inflows and outflows for all purposes other than for capital purposes such as making investment and loans. It allows residents to make and receive

trade-related payments receive dollars (or any other foreign currency) for export of goods and services and pay dollars for import of goods and services, make sundry remittances, access foreign currency for travel, studies abroad, medical treatment, etc.

35. (a) Fiscal policy deals with taxation and government spending and is often administered by an executive under laws of a legislature, whereas monetary policy deals with the money supply, lending rates and interest rates and is often administered by a central bank.

36. (a) Paper Gold is a reserve assets in the International Monetary Fund designed to supplement reserves of gold and convertible currencies used to maintain stability in the foreign exchange market. The term paper gold means you have a piece of paper acting as a substitute for the physical gold. With paper gold, you don't own the gold; you own a promise to receive physical gold.

37. (a) The SDR is an international reserve asset, created by the IMF in 1969 to supplement its member countries' official reserve.It is a measure of a country's reserve assets in the international monetary system.

38. (b) India has comprehensive Double Taxation Avoidance Agreement (DTAA) with 23 countries. This means that there are agreed rates of tax and jurisdiction on specified types of income arising in a country to a tax resident of another country. India gives relief to taxpayers of Mauritius which helps them to invest hugely in India.

39. (b) Protectionism would reduce the level of imports into an economy.

40. (b) The energy company will own and control the territory and the oil reserves it contains.

41. (b) Different agreements of WTO are:
   1. Multi-Fiber agreement (MFA).
   2. Agreement on agriculture (AOA).
   3. Trade related investment measures (TRIMS).
   4. Trade related intellectual property right (TRIPS).
   5. General agreement on trade and services (GATS)

42. (d) In respect to multi-brand retail trading, changes made in 2012 permitted up to 51 % FDI with prior government approval. The foreign investor has to bring in a minimum investment of USD 100 million in an entity engaged in multi brand retail trading. Similar to the requirement of mandatory local sourcing as applicable in single brand product trading (prior to Cabinet meeting) at least 30% of the procurement of manufactured/ processed products shall be sourced from `small industries`. The reach of retail sales outlets of foreign multi brand retail trader will be limited to only those cities with a population of 1 million (including an area of 10 kilometres around the municipal/ urban agglomeration limits of such cities).

43. (d) Euro issue includes issue of ADR (American Depositary Receipts) and GDR (Global Depositary Receipts). A scheme has been initiated during 1992 under which Indian companies are permitted to raise foreign currency resources through issue of Foreign Currency Convertible Bonds (FCCBs)

and/or issue of ordinary equity shares through Global Depositary Receipts (GDRs)/American Depositary Receipts (ADRs) to foreign investors i.e. institutional investors or individuals (including NRIs) residing abroad.

44. (d)

45. (d) The World Trade Organization (WTO) is the only global international organization dealing with the rules of trade between nations. At its heart are the WTO agreements, negotiated and signed by the bulk of the world's trading nations and ratified in their parliaments. The goal is to help producers of goods and services, exporters and importers conduct their business. The Uruguay Round led to the creation of the World Trade Organization, with GATT remaining as an integral part of the WTO agreements. The agreements fall into a simple structure with six main parts, intellectual property (Agreement on Trade-Related Aspects of Intellectual Property Rights (TRIPS)) was one of them.

46. (b) The Foreign Exchange Management Act (FEMA) has been introduced as a replacement for earlier Foreign Exchange Regulation Act (FERA). FEMA became an act on the 1st day of June, 2000. FEMA made all offenses regarding foreign exchange civil offenses, as opposed to criminal offenses as dictated by FERA.

47. (a) Vijay Kelkar Committee is prepared to prepare a road map for enhancing domestic production of oil and gas so as to reduce the nation's import dependency by 2030.

48. (a) The Petrapole-Benapole border checkpoint controls the foreign trade between India and Bangladesh. It is in North 24 Parganas district of West Bengal. Out of them, Petrapole is on Indian side and Benapole is on Bangladesh side.

49. (d) Foreign direct investment (FDI) is a direct investment into production or business in a country by an individual or company of another country, either by buying a company in the target country or by expanding operations of an existing business in that country. Foreign direct investment is in contrast to portfolio investment.

50. (a) International Monetary Fund (IMF) was initiated in 1944 at the Bretton Woods Conference and formally created in 1945 to foster global growth and economic stability. IMF grants loan to member country only.

51. (d) FIEO an apex body of Export Promotion Organisations was set up in 1965 to renders an integrated package of services to various organizations connected with export promoting undertaken to stimulate and diversify the country's export trade.

52. (c) SDR is an international monetary reserve currency, created by International Monetary Fund (IMF) in 1969. It operates as a supplement to the existing reserves of member countries. It is also known as "paper gold".

53. (a)

54. (c) On the credit side of this account receipt of foreign exchange due to Foreign Direct Investment (FDI), Foreign Capital Investment (FCI)

and Foreign Borrowing (FB) is recorded. On the debit side of capital account payment of foreign exchange due to Direct Investment Abroad (DIA), Portfolio Investment Abroad (PIA) and Foreign Lending (FL) is recorded.

55. (d) If surplus in the Capital Account is more than deficit in the Current Account, there is net increase in the Forex Reserves of the country at the end of the year. On the other hand if deficit in the current account is more than surplus in the Capital Account then there is net decrease in Foreign Reserves of the country at the end of the year.

56. (c) The import substitution strategy was based on non-price, physical-interventionist policies like licensing, quotas and other physical restrictions on imports.

57. (c) Mahalanobis strategy adopted during the Second Plan and continued with modifications till the early 1980s. It was only from 1985-86 that a genuine attempt was made towards trade liberalisation. The result was spectacular as export increased at an average rate of 17 per cent per annum in dollar terms between 1986 and 1990. A combination of factors such as bad policy, weak government and external factors led to the decline of this performance to nine per cent in 1990-91 and 4 per cent in the subsequent years.

58. (d)

59. (a)

60. (d) A non-debt capital flow, is a leading source of external financing, especially for the developing economies. It not only brings in capital and technical know-how but also increases the competitiveness of the economy. Overall it supplements domestic investment, much required for sustaining the high growth rate of the country. Since 2000, significant changes have been made in the FDI policy regime by the government to ensure that India becomes an increasingly attractive and investor-friendly destination.

61. (a)

INDIAN FINANCIAL SYSTEM

INTRODUCTION

A well established financial system plays very important role in economic development of any country. A financial system consists of financial institutions, financial markets, financial instruments and financial services. This system provides a framework by which savings and surplus funds are mobilized in a productive manner. A financial system servers as a link between savers and investors

It promotes the capital formation by bringing together supply of savings and demand for funds.

This system provides detailed information about the players in the market such as individuals, corporate houses, government agencies etc.

It also provides a mechanism for controlling risks involved in managing savings and allocating funds.

It covers the whole gamut of demand for and supply of funds for productive purposes. The financial system promotes economic development through mobilising savings and channelising these to investment avenues.

The Indian financial system consists of both short term and long term finances.

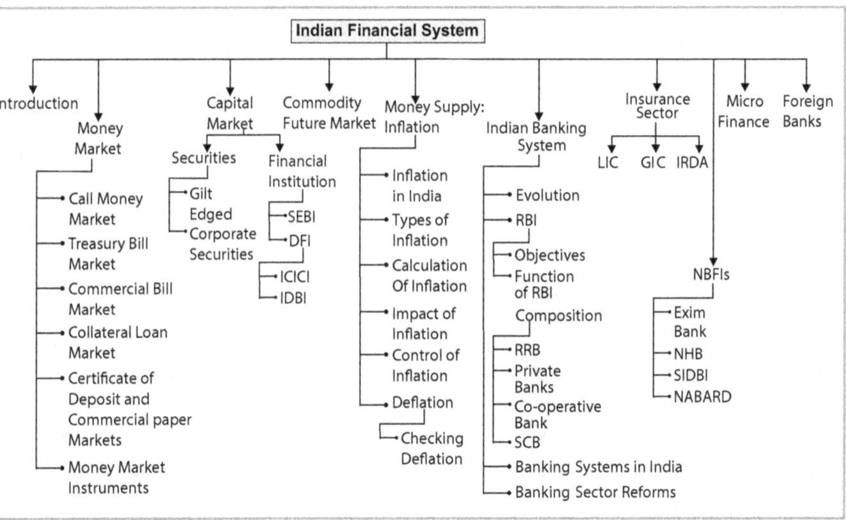

MONEY MARKET

Call Money Market

- A money market, which involves financial transaction (lending and borrowing) for only a small period of time, is termed as Call Money Market, or short – term money market. Call money transactions are limited between a day and a fortnight and are most applied in the case of inter – bank exchanges.

- Call Money, Notice Money and Term Money markets are vital components of the Indian Money Market.

- Call money involves monetary transaction for a day; notice money refers to the borrowing and lending of funds for 2 – 14 days and term money refers to financial transactions with a time frame exceeding a fortnight.

- For such markets, the interest rates are subjected to the market conditions and bizscapes. For instance, in India, the public sector banks account for 80% of the demand whereas the foreign and the private players result for the remaining 20%. To cater to these demands, institutions like IDBI and LIC supply majority of the short term funds to the state banks vis – a - vis other banks.

- Since banks feature as lenders and borrowers in this process, it is called Inter – Bank Market.

- Call money is mostly liquid money and policies are framed with regards to the RBI intervention. These short–term policies are located in established cities like Chennai, Kolkata, Mumbai and Delhi.

Treasury Bill Market

- Short–term securities that mature within an year from their issue date are called Treasury Bills or T – Bills. These policies are effectively deployed by the US Government to raise money from the public.

- Initially, T – Bills are purchased at prices lower than their par (Face) value and after maturity, the government pays the bearer, the full par value. Mathematically, the interest is actually the difference between the purchase price of the security and the amount received post maturity.

- A competitive bidding or auction process is employed to issue T – Bills; either non – competitive wherein the return is specified post the bidding process and competitive wherein the bidder needs to specify the expected return.

- Individuals, Firms, Trusts, Institutions and banks can purchase T-Bills.

- The advantages of such bills are as follows:

    (a) Zero Risk: T–Bills are issued by the Government and thus, the investor has no botheration

    (b) High Liquidity: Short–term investments (3 months, 6 months, 9 months)

    (c) Transparency: Regulated by the Government.

    (d) High Tradability: The secondary market of T–Bills is highly organized

- The Central Government of India issues such bills, for a minimum amount of ₹25, 000 and in multiples of the same.

Commercial Bill Market

- The commercial bill market relates to the seller and buyer equation over the purchased goods.

- Commercial bills are issued by the seller (drawer) on the buyer (drawee) for the value of the goods or products delivered by him.

- Commercial bills are considered as marketable investments. The process involves a seller (in need of funds) sending a bill to the buyer, who in turns accepts the same and promises on – time payment. The bank can also be approached to accept the bill. The bank levies a commission for the acceptance of the bill and vows to pay if the buyer defaults. Following this protocol, the seller can sell his goods in the market.

- Such bills are instrumental in providing short-term financial impetus to businesses. However, these bills failed to be effective as cash credit scheme is the prime form of bank lending and big corporate firms do not abide by the principle of timely payments.

- The difference between the commercial and the T-bill is that the latter is issued by the Government whereas the former is imposed by the seller.

Collateral Loan Market

- Providing and availing loans is a primary factor of the financial market. In those cases where the principal amount of the loan is in massive proportion, the lender (banks mostly) imposes a collateral on the borrower.

- Collateral represents the asset which can be pledged, as a security to the creditor by the borrower. The collateral amount depends according to the value of the loan.

- The collateral policies are implemented in case of real estate purchase or car purchase. Here, the property itself or the vehicle will act as collateral, until the loan is paid in full.

- Complete information related to such loans is furnished in a contract, which is signed by the lender and the borrower.

- For loans on vehicles, the vehicle itself is kept as security. In the condition of a default in the borrower's repayment, the vehicle would be legally seized by the financial institution, which it is hypothecated to.

- Jewelry and other securities can also be used as collateral in giving loans. In such cases, the ownership of these securities remains with the borrower but in case of a failure to repay, the ownership rights are transferred to the bank.

- The collateral process provides a level of confidence and assurance at the time of giving the loan.

Commercial Paper Market

- Commercial paper is an unstructured or rather unsecured bond, issued by a corporation, based on receivables and inventories. Maturities on such bonds are no longer than nine months.

- These alternatives are actually targeted by organizations, aiming at borrowing short–term money from banks. The conventional process, being very tedious and process–oriented, has led to the fame of commercial paper.

- This method is otherwise very safe, as it easily indicates the financial condition of a company within a few months. There has not been many cases of defaulters in the last four decades, because commercial papers are issued to companies with high credit ratings and good reputation only.

- The commercial paper market provides a means for corporations to borrow money to cover short-term debt obligations, such as payroll.

Money Market Instruments

- Chakravarthy committee and Narasimhan committee recommended certain money market instruments to reform Indian money market. Some of these are:

- 182 days treasury bills which are sold through fortnightly auctions. They carry attractive rates of interest and practically no risk and are therefore popular with commercial banks.

- 364 days treasury bills were also introduced in 1992.

- Dated government securities with maturities up to 10 years have also been introduced primarily to develop a secondary market.

- Money market mutual funds have been permitted to be floated by commercial banks.

- Repurchase options (repos) and reverse repos have been introduced in order to even out sharp fluctuations in the money market. Repos provide an opportunity for RBI to repurchase government securities from commercial banks. Reverse repos are government securities sold through auction at fixed cut-off rate of interest.

- Liquidity Adjustment Facility (LAF) refers to RBI's policy of using Repos and Reverse Repos to adjust liquidity on a day-to-day basis.

CAPITAL MARKET

Capital market deals with long-term finance (more than 365 days) funds. It includes all facilities and institutional arrangements available for borrowing and lending of term funds (including medium-term).

The difference between money market and capital market is not so much in the institutions involved as in their term of borrowing or lending. Long-term funds are raised either by borrowing from certain institutions or by issuing securities.

The main players in Indian capital markets are:

- Banks, indigenous and commercial.

- Insurance companies

- Development Finance Institutions (DFI),

- Non-Banking Finance Companies, (NBFCs)

- Non-Banking Financial Institutions.

The capital market may be divided into

(i) the securities market; and (ii) the financial institutions.

Securities

(a) Gilt–edged

- There are securities issued by the government to borrow money from the market. These government issued securities are called *gilt* or *gilt edged securities*.

- Should there arise a situation where in the Government creates a security for raising a public loan, an intimation regarding the same is notified in the Official Gazette under the Government Securities Act, 2016.

- Gilt–edged securities are a high – grade investment with very low risk.

- High–grade bonds can also be issued by private firms too, which flaunts a long record of consistent earnings and possess ability to pay its obligations on time and not accrue any bad debts in business transactions.

- The term, 'gilt–edge' initially originated from Britain; then referred to the debt securities issued by the Bank of England, on behalf of His/ Her Majesty's Treasure.

- Depending upon expiry date, government securities are classified into the following:

Short – term gilt: Maturity: >1 year	Long – term gilt: Maturity: 5 /10 /15 yrs.

- Additionally, these gilt–edged securities provide safety due to the zero income default, 100% liquidity and bulk investment opportunity owing to the high rate of return.

(b) Corporate

- Corporate security identifies and effectively mitigates, at an early stage, any developments that may threaten the resilience and survival of a corporation. It is a corporate function that oversees and manages the close coordination of all functions within the company that are concerned with security, continuity and safety.

- Corporate securities or company securities are known to be the documentary media for mobilising funds by the joint stock companies.

- The need for corporate securities arises in the following:
  - (a) Successful establishment of business functions
  - (b) Sponsoring of fund–intensive expansion plans
- There are two types of corporate securities:

Ownership Securities	Creditorship Securities

- Ownership securities consist of preference shares and equity shares. Preference shares are those shares which carry priority rights related to dividend payment at a fixed rate and repayment of capital, in the event of a company being wound up. The advantages of preference shares include mobilizing funds from investors who prefer stable earnings with assurance, flexibility in capital structure as desired, complete control of business transactions within an organization and increase in the profits of the shareholders. Disadvantages include not allowing investors to carry voting rights, shares being expensive, income tax problems and redemption issues at the time of depression.

- Equity shares are ordinary shares, devoid of special attributes with respect to dividend or return of capital, as in preference shares. Equity shareholders are the residual claimants against the assets and income of the corporation."The financial risk is more with equity share capital, also called 'risk capital.' Some of the advantages of these shares are long shelf – life of funds, shareholders' right to participation in the affairs of the company, increase in shareholders' assets and ownership rights of the shareholders.

- Creditorship securities are also called debentures and accounts for the debt of a company. Debenture holders are regarded as the creditors of the company and debentures account for the borrowed capital. A debenture may be defined as an instrument executed by company under its common seal, acknowledging indebtedness to an individual or a group, to secure the sum advanced. Debentures are usually bonds issued by the company in series of a fixed denomination e.g., ₹100, ₹200, ₹500, ₹1,000 of face value and are offered to the public, by means of a prospectus.

FINANCIAL INSTITUTIONS

(a) SEBI

- Established in 1988 and provided statutory powers in 1992, the Securities and Exchange Board of India (SEBI) is the regulator for the Indian security market.

- The Indian Parliament passed the SEBI Act on 12 April, 1992.

- SEBI is headquartered in Mumbai, Maharashtra.

- Before the Government of India enforced the existence of SEBI, Controller of Capital Issues was the regulatory authority.

- The main motto behind constructing SEBI was to regulate and control the function of capital markets in India under the intervention of the Indian Government.

- The SEBI is managed by: (a) The Chairman – nominated by the Union Government of India; (b) two officers from the Union Finance Ministry; (c) one member from the RBI and five members nominated by the Union Government, among which three should be whole – time members.

- The present Chairman of SEBI is Mr. Upendra Kumar Sinha, who replaced C. Bhave in 2011.

- The Preamble defines SEBI's immediate responsibility to protect the interests of the investors, promote goodwill, usher development and regulate proceedings pertaining to the securities market.

- SEBI caters to the needs of the security issuers, the investors and the market intermediaries.

- SEBI also has additional responsibilities to draft SOPs and regulations (legislative), conducts investigation and verification for proper enforcement (executive) and passes rulings and orders (judicial)

- In order to streamline, regulate and monitor its duties, the SEBI has been bestowed with the following powers:

  (a) To approve by–laws of stock exchanges;

  (b) To instruct stock–exchanges to modify their by–laws;

  (c) To inspect the accounts and ledgers and call for periodical returns from major stock exchanges;

  (d) To inspect the accounts and ledgers of financial intermediaries;

  (e) To register brokers after validating their background verification.

- Some of the important SEBI Committees are the Primary Market Advisory Committee (PMAC), Secondary Market Advisory Committee (SMAC), Mutual Fund Advisory Committee and Advisory Committee for the SEBI Investor Protection and Education Fund.

(b) DFI

- A Development Finance Institution (DFI) is a subsidiary financial establishment which includes microfinance institutions – agencies which sponsor budding entrepreneurs and small businesses, especially in the semi – urban areas which lack access to banks and related services; community development financial institution which provides credit and financial services to the deprived markets and populations and revolving loan funds, which assists micro, small, medium and rural projects by providing loans to individuals who does not otherwise qualify for conventional financial benefits.

- Some of the important characteristics of these institutions are providing credit in the form of higher risk loans and equity positions.

- DFIs are commonly seen in the developed countries, supported by the states.

- For markets with severe restriction and lack of financial access, DFIs are very useful for providing finance for inclusive growth and development.

(c) IFCI

- In 1947, shortly after the Independence, it was observed the India's capital market was relatively underdeveloped due to lack of policies, benchmarks and service providers. However, the demand was relatively high. To add to the woes, there were no merchant bankers or underwriting firms and neither were proper commercial banks to provide long – term investment options or portfolios.

- Against such a backdrop, the Industrial Finance Corporation of India (IFCI) was constituted on July 1, 1948. IFCI, at its inception was meant to provide access to cost – effective funds through the Central Bank's Statutory Liquidity Ratio (SLR).

- IFCI, thus became an India Government owned development bank to provide long – term financial leverage to the industrial sector.

- IFCI's contribution to the modernization of Indian Industry, export promotion, import substitution, entrepreneurship development, pollution control, energy conservation and generation of both direct and indirect employment is noteworthy.

- IFCI was reinstated as an organization in 1993 (under the Companies Act, 1956), to impart higher degree of operational benefits, and access the capital markets directly.

- With effect from 1999, IFCI changed to IFCI Limited.

- The modus operandi of IFCI Limited was to facilitate provision for medium and long term financial support to large scale industries, especially when banks do not have the authority for an undertaking or issuing shares.

- Some of the vital responsibilities include providing loans and advances to major industrial projects, facilitating loan sanction in domestic and international currencies, underwriting the issue of stocks, bonds and shares.

(d) ICICI

- ICICI, an acronym for **Industrial Credit and Investment Corporation of India**, is a multinational banking and financial services company , based out of Mumbai and registered office in Vadodara.

- Over the years since inception, ICICI Bank has accumulated several accolades. In 2014, it was declared as the second largest bank in terms of assets and third in terms of market capitalization.

- Out of the vast portfolio of products and services, few worth mentioning are investment banking, life insurance, venture capital and asset management.

- The ICICI empire has a network of 4450 branches and 13995 ATMs in India and is globally present in 19 countries.

- Along with giants like SBI, PNB and BoB, ICICI is noted among the big four banks of India.

- ICICI Bank was established by the Industrial Credit and Investment Corporation of India (ICICI), an Indian financial institution, as a wholly owned subsidiary in 1994. The parent company was formed in 1955 as a joint-venture of the World Bank, India's public-sector banks and public-sector insurance companies to provide project financing to Indian industry

- ICICI was the first Indian bank to be enlisted under the NYSE in 1999, being a non – Japanese institution.

- Over the last two decades, ICICI has witnessed several important mergers with other banks and private partners to consolidate its business foundation.

- As a stalwart, it influences regulators such as the National Stock Exchange, the Credit Rating Information System of India Limited, National Commodities and Derivatives Exchange Ltd. and NABARD.

- Some of the vital portfolios include **'Money2India'** – an online money transfer and tracking facility provided to non resident Indians by the bank, 'Extra Home Loans' – mortgage – guaranteed supported loans for retail customers aiming at purchasing their homes in the economical housing segment, 'Smart Value' – the automated system of 24X7 lockers, including weekends and wee hours; 'Saral Loans' – to provide loans at nominal rate of interests to the rural folks, including women; 'Video Banking for NRIs'; 'Contactless Debit and Credit Cards' and 'iWish' – the flexible recurring deposit scheme to allow customers deposit feasible amounts of their choice each month.

- ICICI is a brand known for its CSR initiatives like the 'Go Green Initiative', 'Jiyo Khulke' contest and 'Read to Lead.'
- A noble lady, a visionary, ICICI's CEO, Chanda Kochhar is one of India's most powerful corporate tycoon, of recent times and has been influential in creating the success story. Some of her milestones are appropriate case studies for inspiring the youth.
- Under Kochhar's leadership, ICICI has won the title of the 'Best Retail Bank in India' thrice consecutively.
- However, amidst such appreciation, ICICI has been criticized for several money laundering scams and inhuman debt recovery methods using goons.
- Chanda Kochhar allegedly favoured Videocon Group in lending practices. ICICI Bank has decided to institute an independent enquiry into the allegations. SEBI favours adjudication proceeding against ICICI Bank and Chanda Kochhar.

(e) IDBI

- The Industrial Development Bank of India (IDBT), as it was formerly known, is a government–owned financial service company, headquartered in Mumbai.
- The main motto behind its establishment was to supply credit and financial stability to the Indian industrial sector.
- With 1853 branches and 3350 ATMs and is a significant player under the aegis of commercial banks owned by the Indian Government.
- The Bank has an aggregate balance statement of INR 3.74 trillion, at the closure of the last Financial Year.
- IDBI is classified as a development bank. Turning the pages of history, development banking emerged after the Second World War. India had a fair development banking system and was mainly targeted towards financing short–term capital requirements of the industrial projects. On the contrary, DFI – listed institutions like the NABARD,

SIDBI and NHB, were catering to the long – term financing requirements, under the RBI guidelines.

- In 1976, the statutory ownership of IDBI was transferred to the Government of India, which was initially a wholly–owned subsidiary of the RBI, since the inception in 1964, under an Act of the Parliament.
- IDBI can be accounted for the various reforms during the 1964–1991 period, and has assisted in setting institutions like the Securities and Exchange Board of India (SEBI), National Stock Exchange of India (NSE), the EXIM Bank and the Small Industries Development Bank of India (SIDBI).
- With the Industrial Development Bank (Transfer of Undertaking and Repeal) Act, 2003, IDBI was bestowed with the status of a limited company viz., IDBI Ltd. Shortly thereafter, IDBI was incorporated as a 'scheduled bank' under the RBI Act, 1934.
- IDBI, just like ICICI has been crowned with many jewels; one worth mentioning is Dun & Bradstreet rating of the 'Best Public Sector Bank' in 2011, a period where customers were dissatisfied with the offerings of the government banks.
- Mr. Kishor Kharat is captaining the ship, being the CEO and MD.
- Some of the important portfolios include consumer banking, corporate banking, investment banking, mortgage loans, wealth management and private equity.
- The Insurance Regulatory Development Authority of India (IRDAI) has allowed LIC (Life Insurance Corporation of India) to invest up to 51% in IDBI Bank.

COMMODITY FUTURE MARKET

In the aftermath of the 2008 global financial crisis, some regulatory reforms have been initiated in the US, European Union (EU) and some other countries to enhance market transparency and coordination among regulatory authorities in the public interest, commodity future market is one of them.

Commodities are the primary products that can be bought, sold or traded in different kinds of markets. These are the raw materials that are used to make secondary products which are consumed in everyday life around the world, from food products to building material commodities. These are grouped into:

i. **Soft commodities:** These are agricultural produ..cts such as corn, wheat, coffee, cocoa, sugar and soybean; and livestock.

ii. **Hard commodities:** These are natural resources that need to be mined or processed such as crude oil, gold, silver and rubber.

Commodity markets are of two types: **i. Spot (physical)** and **ii. Derivatives** (such as futures, options and swaps).

In a **spot market**, a physical commodity is sold or bought at a price negotiated between the buyer and the seller. The spot market involves buying and selling of commodities in cash with immediate delivery.

Contracts in Derivative Markets

a. **Forward Contract:** It is a non-standardized or customized contract between two parties to undertake an exchange of the underlying asset at a specific future date at a pre-determined price. It is a bilateral agreement whose terms are negotiated and agreed upon between two parties. It is transacted over-the counter and is not traded on an exchange. The contract is executed by both parties on the due date by delivery of asset by the seller and payment by the buyer.

b. **Future Contracts:** These are agreements made on a futures exchange to buy or sell a commodity at a pre-determined price in the future.

   For example, if one wants to buy *5* tonne of rice today, one can buy it in the spot market. But if one wants to buy or sell 15 tonne of rice at a future date, i.e. after three months, one can buy or sell the same through futures contracts at a commodity futures exchange.

   Let's understand, a farmer enters into a futures contract to sell 20 tonne of rice at \$ 50 per tonne to a miller on a future date. On that date, the miller will pay the full purchase price (\$ 1,000) to the farmer and in exchange will receive the 20 tonne of rice.

   However, under the **cash-settled futures contract**, the farmer and the miller would simply exchange the difference between the spot price of rice on the settlement date and the agreed upon price as mentioned in the futures contract and there would be no actual delivery of rice. Following the above example, if on the settlement date the price of rice was \$ 40 per tonne, while the agreed upon price of futures contract was \$ 50 a tonne, the miller will pay \$200 to the farmer in cash and there will be no delivery of rice to the miller. If, on the settlement date, the price of rice was \$ 60 a tonne, the farmer will pay \$ 200 to the miller in cash and no delivery of rice will take place.

c. **Options Contracts:** These are the contracts that give the owner the right, but not the obligation, to buy or sell an agreed amount of a commodity on or before a specified future date.

d. **Swaps Contract:** This contract is an agreement between two parties to exchange cash (flows) on or before a specified future date based on the underlying value of commodity, currency, stock or other assets. Unlike futures, swaps are not exchange-traded instruments. Swaps are usually designed by banks and financial institutions that also arrange the trading of these bilateral contracts.

e. **Over-The-Counter (OTC) derivatives:** These contracts are privately negotiated and traded between two parties, without going through an exchange. The market players trade with one another through telephone, email, and proprietary electronic trading systems.

Regulations of Commodity Futures Markets in India

The Commodity Futures Markets in India are regulated through a three-tiered regulatory structure, i.e. Central Government, Forward Markets Commission (FMC), and Commodity Exchanges.

i. **The Central Government:** In addition to determining regulatory policies, the Central Government has the legislative powers to pass, amend and repeal laws related to futures trading in India subject to the approval of the Parliament.

ii. **The Forward Markets Commission (FMC):** The FMC is a statutory body set up under Forward Contracts (Regulation) Act, 1952. Its headquarter is at Mumbai. It is the regulatory and supervisory authority for commodity futures market in India. Over the years, most of the regulatory powers of the central government have been delegated to FMC. It now functions under the administrative control of the Ministry of Finance. All terms and conditions of a futures contract have to be approved by the FMC before it can be launched on commodity futures exchanges.

iii. **Commodity Derivatives Exchange (CDE):** A commodity exchange (i.e. bourse) is an organized physical or virtual marketplace where different tradable securities, commodities and derivatives are sold and bought. Commodity derivatives exchanges are places where trading of commodity futures and options contracts are conducted.

The main functions of CDE are:

a. Providing and enforcing rules and regulations for uniform and fair trading practice.

b. Facilitating trading in a transparent manner.

c. Recording trading transactions, including circulating price movements and market news, to the participating members.

d. Ensuring execution of contracts.

e. Providing a system of protection against default of payment (clearing).

f. Providing a dispute settlement mechanism.

g. Designing the standardized contract for trading which cannot be modified by either parties

Commodity Exchanges in India

The most important out of currently 19 commodity derivatives exchanges in India are:

i. Multi Commodity Exchange of India **(MCX)** – Mumbai

ii. National Commodity and Derivatives Exchange of India **(NCDEX)** – Mumbai

iii. National Multi Commodity Exchange **(NMCE)** – Ahmedabad

iv. Indian Commodity Exchange **(ICEX)** - New Delhi

v. ACE Derivatives & Commodity Exchange Limited – Mumbai

vi. Universal Commodity Exchange Limited - Navi Mumbai

Foreign Portfolio Investment (FPI)

It is an investment by non-residents Indians in Indian securities, i.e. shares, government bonds, corporate bonds, convertible securities, infrastructure securities, etc. The class of investors who make investment in these securities are known as Foreign Portfolio Investors.

- SEBI has made the criteria for Foreign Portfolio Investment. As any equity investment by non-residents which is less than 10% of capital in a company is portfolio investment and above 10%, the investment will be counted as Foreign Direct Investment (FDI).

- All FPI taken together cannot acquire more than 24% of the paid up capital of an Indian Company.
- Foreign Portfolio Investors are Asset Management Companies, Pension Funds, Mutual Funds, and Investment Trusts as Nominee Companies, Incorporated / Institutional Portfolio Managers or their Power of Attorney holders, University Funds, Endowment Foundations, Charitable Trusts and Charitable Societies.
- Qualified Foreign Investor is an individual, group or association which is a resident in a foreign country.

Acronym:

BIS	=	Bank for International Settlements
CDS	=	Credit Default Swap
CFTC	=	Commodity Futures Trading Commission
FII	=	Foreign Institutional Investor
FMC	=	Forward Markets Commission
ICEX	=	Indian Commodity Exchange
MCA	=	Ministry of Corporate Affairs
MCX	=	Multi Commodity Exchange of India
NAFED	=	National Agricultural Co-operative Marketing Federation of India Limited
NBOT	=	National Board of Trade
NCDEX	=	National Commodity and Derivatives Exchange of India
NMCE	=	National Multi Commodity Exchange
OCEIL	=	Online Commodity Exchange India Limited
UCC	=	Unique Client Code
UNCTAD	=	United Nations Conference on Trade and Development

MONEY SUPPLY

M_1 measure represents the most liquid form of money among four money stock measures adopted by RBI. As we move from M_1 to M_4, the liquidity gets reduced.

In other words, M_4 possesses the lowest liquidity among all these measures. The reduction in liquidity indicates the shifting from 'medium of exchange' to *'store of value'*. All these four money stock measures are not of equal importance. Their relative importance varies from the point of view of monetary policy

Generally, in developed countries, the bank deposits are the most important component in money supply, while due to less banking habits in under-developed countries people want to keep their money in the most liquid form i.e., currency.

M3 is the most important component among all money stock measures and is generally termed as '**Broad money**'.

In economics, the **money supply** or **money stock** is the total amount of monetary assets available in an economy at a specific time. There are several ways to define 'money' but standard measures usually include currency in circulation and *demand deposits*.

Money supply data are usually recorded and published by the **government** or the **central bank** of the country. Public and private sector analyst have long monitored changes in money supply because of its possible effect on the price level inflation, exchange rate and the business cycle.

Inflation

- As per economics concept, there might arise a condition where there is a steep increase in the general price of goods and services, over a time span. During such a crisis, a conventional currency unit buys lesser goods and services. Thus, there is a reduction in the purchasing power and affordability. Also, the currency value might dip and this could hit export and import and wreck and economy.

- The positive effects could be reduction of debt of the public and the private sector, keeping nominal interest rates above zero, so that the central banks can adjust interest rates to stabilize the economy and reducing unemployment.

- However, the negatives weigh more. Inflation creates a major set – back for investment and savings, production and promotion, thereby resulting in shortage of goods and resources. In a way, the opportunity cost of holding money, increases.

- The Consumer Price Index (CPI), the Personal Consumption Expenditures Price Index (PCEPI) and GDP deflator are some of the examples of broad price indices.

- Inflation does not only increase prices of commodities such as food and fuels, but also hike prices of financial assets (stocks, bonds), tangible assets (such as real estate), services (healthcare and education) and manpower resources (labour).

- For calculating the inflation rate, the percentage rate of change of price index over a period of time, needs to be gauged.

- To study the effects of inflation, Robert Gordon's triangle model can be utilized. As per the study, there are three types of inflation, namely:

    (a) **Demand–pull inflation:** There is an increment in the aggregate demand, due to an increase in the public and private spending. A typical example is the kind of disposable income which youth today are exposed to. However, demand inflation encourages economic growth since excess demand privileges investment and expansion.

    (b) **Cost–push inflation:** Also called 'supply shock inflation.' It is featured by a drastic fall in the overall output. A typical example would be that of insurance losses during recession, due to fraudulence or disasters.

    (c) **Built–in inflation:** Such inflation is ushered by adaptive expectations, related to the price/wage spiral. Price/wage spiral is a humongous cyclic process, where wage increase, increases the price. It could happen either because business owners try to push profit margins from rising expenses or the wage earners try to push their nominal after – tax wages upward to maintain equilibrium with the rising prices.

- Inflation can be checked if the economic growth is at par with the increase in the money supply. Some of the allied factors are investment in market production, infrastructure, education, healthcare, wherein investment should be hiked; even defence.

Deflation

- Deflation is a commonly witnessed economical picture when improvements in production efficiency, lower the overall price of the goods. In such a condition, the hard currency per head count drops, in effect making money scarce.

- Generally, deflation is a detriment in the price level of goods and services.

A 0% (negative inflation rate) is also called deflation.

- Economists believe that deflation increases the debt value, leading to recession and hence do not endorse it.

- In the IS–LM Model, a fall in the aggregate level of demand can cause deflation, due to a shift in the demand – supply curve for the goods and the services. As the prices of goods fall, consumers tend to delay purchase decisions which in turns hampers the overall economic activity. This condition also negatively affects investments and product innovation. Such a condition is called the **deflationary spiral**.

- There was inflation during World War I, but deflation returned immediately after the war had ended, almost close to the 1930s Depression.

- Ideally, deflation might also result from an inequilibrium; i.e. the supply of goods going up and the supply of money coming down.

- Demand-based deflation are categorized as follows:

  (a) **Growth Deflation–** A deflation resulting out of decrease in the production and distribution cost of the goods and services, accompanied by competitive price cuts, resulting in demand rise.

  (b) **Cash Deflation–** A decrease in the overall consumption to save money, leads to decrease in the velocity of money, otherwise termed as cash deflation.

- The most dangerous impact of deflation is non–investment or reduced investment.

- Deflation can be controlled by special liquidity policies to be strategized by the central banks, alongside regulating the value of the capital assets.

Indian Banking System

Introduction & Evolution

- The origin of the Indian banking system dates back to the last decades of the 18th century.

- The State Bank of India, which was initially known as the Bank of Calcutta, started in 1806 and was then renamed as the Imperial Bank of India, which was partially nationalized on 1st July, 1955, and further converted into being what is called as SBI today.

- However, much earlier to this, the first officially established records as per records, was the Bank of Hindostan which operated from 1770 – 1832, followed by the General Bank of India, which was functional from 1786 – 1791.

- The Indian Banking System is broadly classified into Scheduled and Non – Scheduled Banks. The banks which are included under the 2nd Schedule of the Reserve Bank of India Act, 1934, are the Scheduled Banks; further classified into nationalized banks, foreign banks and Indian private sector banks.

- In India, as nationalized banks have vast coverage, they are the majority lenders in the Indian economy. Eg: SBI

- The Indian Banking Act was passed in March 1949 and on the 1st January, of the same year; the Reserve Bank of India was nationalized.

- In 1955, 8 other banks were converted into SBI's associate banks, and the State Bank Group was formed.

- The list of the 8 banks include: The State Bank of Bikaner and Jaipur, The State Bank of Hyderabad, The State Bank of Indore , The State Bank of Mysore, The State Bank of Saurashtra, The State Bank of Patiala and The State Bank of Travancore.

- In 1969, 14 large commercial banks, with reserves more than 50 crores each, were nationalized, in order to establish an authority and proper regulation. The nationalized banks include: The Central Bank of India, Bank of India, Punjab National Bank, Canara Bank, United Commercial Bank, Syndicate Bank, Bank of Baroda, United Bank of India, Union Bank of India, Dena Bank, Allahabad Bank, Indian Bank, Indian Overseas Bank and the Bank of Maharashtra

- In 1980, 6 private banks, with reserves more than 200 crores each were nationalized. Those banks were: Andhra Bank, Punjab and Sindh Bank, New Bank of India, Vijaya Bank, Corporation Bank and Oriental Bank of Commerce.

- However, as in 1993, the New Bank of India merged with the Punjab National Bank, the total number of nationalized banks in the country, is as of now 19.

Reserve Bank of India

- With a capital of 5 crores, the Reserve Bank of India; abbreviated as RBI, was established in 1935.

- The entity originated as 5 lakh equity shares of 100 each, with the share capital being with the non – government share holders.

- In order to streamline the assets and prevent monopoly, the Reserve Bank of India was nationalized on January 1, 1949.

- RBI, also known as India's Central Bank has the following as its Preamble, "To regulate the issue of the Bank notes and the keeping of reserves with a view of securing monetary stability in India and generally to operate the currency and the credit system of the country to its advantage.

- The general administration and the direction of the RBI is governed by a central board of directors, which is nominated by the Government of India, with regards to the Reserve Bank of India Act.

- The Central Board is appointed for a span of 4 years and includes Official Directors (1 Governor and 4 Deputy Governors) and Non – Official Directors (10 Directors and 2 Government Officials; nominated by the Government and 4 Directors elected from the Local Boards).

- The RBI is headquartered in Mumbai and Dr. Urijit Patel is the Governor.

- Some of the objectives include: monitoring the issue of bank notes and stock – keeping reserves, for securing monetary stability and regulating the credit system; supervising the monetary policy in India (which involves formulating the SOPs, framework and institutional composition) and supporting cash flow for industrial development; publishing legal notices in the cases of bank fraudulence and consolidating accounts (money, debt and foreign exchange).

- The RBI performs a number of other developmental functions, such as arranging credit for agriculture (now taken over by NABARD), collecting and publishing periodic economic data, providing loans to the Government by buying and selling Government's securities and trade bills.

- The RBI also represents the membership of India in the International Monetary Fund.

Composition of the Indian Banking System

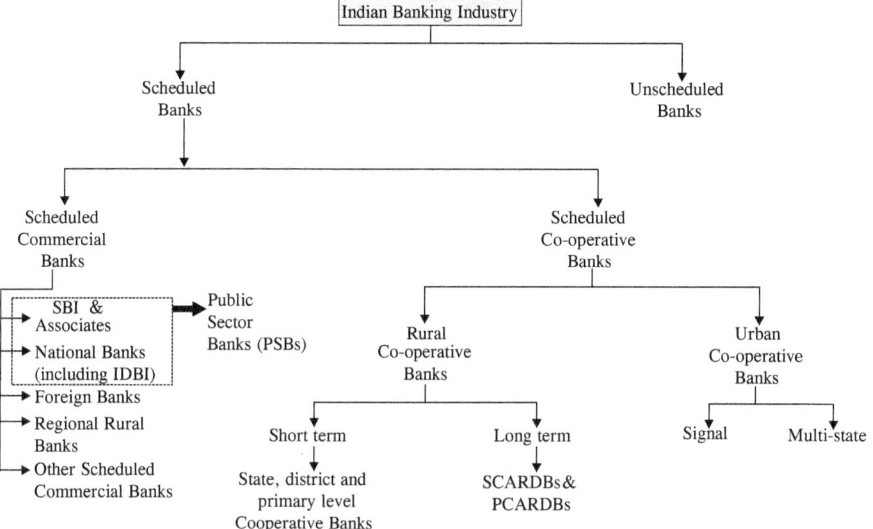

Regional Rural Banks (RRBs)

- Even after the nationalization of banks in 1969, there were cultural issues, which posed as a hindrance to the government – led commercial banks to lend money and support the farmers.

- To resolve the issue, the Narasimhan Working Committee was set up in 1975. Based on this group's recommendations, a Regional Rural Banks Ordinance was formulated in 1975, which was later replaced by the Regional Rural Banks Act in 1976.

- The RRB's shares were: Central Govt. – 50%, State Govt. – 15% and Sponsor Bank – 35%.

- The Public Sector Banks sponsor RRBs, subscribing to the share capital.

- The RRBs cater to the credit needs of the weaker sections of the society including farmers, artisans and small – scale entrepreneurs.

- RRBs were unable to sustain because of the mounting losses due to imprudent commercial policy. The Khusrau Committee recommended the RRB merger with the sponsor banks.

- The RRBs are being monitored by the NABARD currently and the government allowed the RRBs to grant loans to the non – priority sectors to improve their financial position.

Private Sector Banks

- The Private Sector Banks are those banks where the equity is held by the private shareholders and not by the government.

- The private sector banks have been categorized as old and new.

- The old banks existed prior to the nationalization in 1969 and were trivial to be nationalized. The Board of Directors for such banks consisted of eminent businessmen or prominent personalities, mostly.

- Some of the old private sector banks are City Union Bank, Dhanlaxmi Bank, J&K Bank and the Karur Vyasa Bank

- The banks which initiated operations after the liberalization in 1991, with the introduction of economic and financial reforms, are the new private sector banks.

- Some of the criteria for being enlisted were: banks should have minimum net worth of 200 crore; within 3 years of inception, the banks should be issuing shares to public and the net worth should rise to 300 crore and the promoters should be holding 25% of the paid – up capital.

- These banks are further classified into – Indian and Foreign banks. Some of the Indian banks are Kotak Mahindra Bank, Yes Bank, Bandhan Bank and ICICI Bank and some of the foreign players are HDFC Bank and Deutsche Bank.

Cooperative Banks

- These banks have been organized under the cooperative society's law of the states.

- The history of this concept dates back to the days of poverty and deprivation in Europe, when Hermann Schulze and Friedrich Wilhelm had proposed this idea.

- Te concept centered round the easy availability of credit to small businesses and for the poor sections of the society. Today, microfinance institutions follow a similar approach for economic development.

- In India, the cooperative banks have been classified into: Urban Cooperative Banks and Rural Cooperative Banks.

- Banking protocols of the Urban Cooperative Banks are monitored by the RBI and the Urban Cooperatives are further bifurcated into scheduled and non – scheduled institutions.

- Alternatively, the Rural Cooperatives are divided into short – term and long – term structures.

- The short – term structures include the State Cooperative Banks (operate at the state apex level), District Central Cooperative Banks (operate at the district levels) and the Primary Agricultural Credit Societies (operate at the village level).

- On the contrary, the long – term structures are bifurcated into State Cooperative Agriculture and Rural Development Banks (SCARDS) and Primary Cooperative Agriculture and Rural Development Banks (PCARDS)

- Since these banks follow a complex operational model, a forum called the State Level Task Force on Cooperative Union Banks (TAFCUB) has been established to supervise and address grievances related to duality of control (between the RBI and the NABARD).

Scheduled and Non – Scheduled Banks

- The RBI has classified the banks as scheduled and non – scheduled.

- The scheduled banks are those which have a paid – up capital and reserve an aggregate value of not less than 5 lakh.

- The scheduled banks form the majority of the banking spectrum and comprises of commercial banks (domestic and international), RRBs and the state – cooperative banks.

- For the banks which have not been included in the Second Schedule of the RBI Act, 1934, they were termed as the non – scheduled ones.

- Non – scheduled banks are also called Local Area Banks (LABs) are further classified into Coastal Local Area Banks (Andhra Pradesh), Capital Local Area Banks (Punjab), Krishna Bhima Samruddhi Local Area Bank Ltd (Karnataka and AP) and Subhadra Local Area Bank (Kolhapur).

INSURANCE SECTOR

IRDA

Insurance Regulatory and Development Authority (IRDA)

IRDA is a multimember nodal agency and is vested with regulatory powers in respect of the insurance sector similar to those vested in SEBI in respect of the capital markets and of RBI for the banking sector. The IRDA Act, 1999 cleared the way for private sector entry into the insurance business.

The IRDA has powers to lay down prudential norms and investment guidelines. It has ended the monopoly of LIC/GIC in the insurance sector, by permitting private players to enter, as recommended by Malhotra Committee.

Some of the functions of the authority include:

- To protect the interest of and secure fair treatment to policy holders.

- To bring about speedy and orderly growth of the insurance industry.

- To ensure speedy settlement of genuine claims and to prevent frauds and malpractices.

- Promote fairness, transparency and orderly conduct in financial markets dealing with insurance.

Life Insurance Corporation of India (LIC)

- A true saga of trust – the hallmark of LIC.

- The LIC was established on September 1, 1956, after nationalizing the existing private insurance companies.

- There are 250 million LIC customers.

- The Insurance Act 1938, was the first legislation governing not only life insurance but also non-life insurance to provide strict state control over insurance business.

- The demand for nationalization of life insurance industry was made repeatedly in the past but it gathered momentum in 1944 when a bill to amend the Life Insurance Act 1938 was introduced in the Legislative Assembly.

- However, it was much later on the 19th of January, 1956, that life insurance in India was nationalized. About 154 Indian insurance companies, 16 non-Indian companies and 75 provident were operating in India, at the time of nationalization.

- Today LIC functions with 2048 fully computerized branch offices, 113 divisional offices, 8 zonal offices and 1381 satellite offices. LIC's Wide Area Network covers 113 divisional offices and connects all the branches through a Metro Area Network.

- LIC continues to be the dominant life insurer even in the liberalized scenario of Indian insurance and is moving fast on a new growth trajectory surpassing its own past records.

- Some of the objectives of the LIC include increasing insurance cover; reaching out to the masses at reasonable

- prices; maximizing savings; catering to the insurance needs of the society and promoting satisfaction, ownership and dedication for the agents and employees for achieving corporate targets and market penetration.

- Besides conventional portfolios such as insurance plans, pension plans, unit plans, micro insurance plans, health plans and Aam Aadmi Bima Yojana, the LIC runs three schemes supported by SSF – Janashree Bima Yojana, Krishi Shramik Samajik Suraksha Yojana and Shiksha Sahayog Yojana, for the benefit of families below the poverty line.

- S. K. Roy is the Chairman of the LIC of India.

General Insurance Corporation of India (GIC)

- The entire general insurance business in India was nationalized by General Insurance Business (Nationalization) Act, 1972 (GIBNA).

- The Government of India, in order to streamline and benchmark the processes related to general insurance, took over the shares of 107 companies into the general insurance business, leading to the formation of the GIC.

- The GIC was incorporated on 22nd November, 1972.

- Gradually, after the mergers and alliances amongst the insurance players, four companies were left as fully owned subsidiary companies of GIC, namely National Insurance Company, United India Insurance Company, Oriental Insurance Company and New India Assurance Company.

- GIC Re is a wholly owned subsidiary of the Indian Government.

- The objectives include building long – term relationship with the business partners, setting ethical standards, using technological intervention to reach out to customers with innovative products and services and maximizing revenues.

- G. C. Gaylong is the GM & Director and GIC is headquartered in Mumbai.

- GIC re has recently gone global and enforced reinsurance programmes of several insurance companies in the SAARC countries.

- GIC provides Treaty and Facultative business on risk emanating from the international markets, based on merits of the business.

- A.M. Best has affirmed the financial strength rating of A (Excellent) and the issuer credit rating of "a" of General Insurance Corporation of India.

NON – BANKING FINANCIAL INSTITUTIONS (NBFIS)

Introduction

- Non – banking financial institutions lack a full banking license and cannot be regulated by a national or international banking regulatory authority.

- NBFIs supplement banks by providing the infrastructure to allocate surplus resources to individuals and companies with deficits. Additionally, NBFIs also introduces competition in the provision of financial services.

- While banks have standard products and services, NBFIs offer customized deals as per client requirements.

- A market – oriented financial system, juxtaposed with well – developed NBFIs is conducive for economic growth.

- On the brighter side of things, NBFIs provide additional options to transform an economy's savings into capital investment, which serves as back – up in case of an economic crisis.

- Flipside, since there is no regulatory intervention in the case of NBFIs, they could lead to destabilizing the financial system. An illustration of the same is the Asian Financial Crisis in 1997.

- According to the Economic Survey, there are four NBFI institutions in India, viz. Export Import Bank of India (EXIM), NABARD, National Housing Bank (NHB) and Small Industries Development Bank of India (SIDBI).

- These institutions are supervised by the RBI – as all – India FIs.

- There is an 'umbrella limit' for the total resources mobilized at any point of time by an FI, which should not exceed 10 times its net owned funds as per the latest audited balance sheet.

Export – Import Bank of India (EXIM)

- EXIM Bank is the premier export finance institution in India, established in 1982, under the Export – Import Bank of India Act, 1981.

- Since its incorporation, EXIM Bank has facilitated cross border trade and investments.

- EXIM Bank aides the small and medium scale industries, through a varied portfolio of products and services, in the complete business cycle, starting from import of technology, product development, marketing and export.

- EXIM Bank comprises of a Board of Directors including representatives from the Government, RBI, Export Credit Guarantee Corporation of India, public sector banks and the business community.

- The main objectives of EXIM Bank is financing, facilitating and promoting foreign trade in India. Also, it is responsible for discharging duties of coordinating the activities of various financial institutions, providing finances for export and import of goods and services.

- EXIM is known to manage finances to third world countries for export and is a wholly owned subsidiary of the Government of India.

NABARD

- NABARD was established based on the recommendation of the Shivaram Committee on July 12, 1982.

- NABARD is one of the premier agencies providing economic impetus and development in the rural areas.

- NABARD is India's specialised bank for Agriculture and Rural Development in India and started with an initial corpus of 100 crore.

- After RBI sold its stake in NABARD to the Indian Government, the former holds 99% stake and NABARD has a corpus of more than 5000 crore.

- NABARD has been entrusted with matters concerning policy, planning and operations in the verticals related to credit for agriculture and other economic activities in the rural areas of India.

- Through assistance of Swiss Agency for Development and Cooperation, NABARD set up the Rural Innovation Fund. The Rural Infrastructure Development Fund (RIDF) is another noted scheme of 51,283 crore and have been sanctioned for 2,44,651 projects covering irrigation, rural roads and bridges, health and education, soil and water conservation schemes.

- To provide mileage to the economic development of the villages, NABARD has process partnered with about 4000 organisations in promoting SHG-Bank Linkage programme, tree-based tribal communities' livelihoods initiative, watershed approach in soil and water conservation, increasing crop productivity initiatives through Lead Crop Initiative or disseminating flow of information to agrarian communities through Farmer Clubs.

National Housing Bank (NHB)

- National Housing Bank (NHB), a wholly owned subsidiary of Reserve Bank of India (RBI), was set up on 9 July 1988 under the National Housing Bank Act, 1987.

- NHB is a premier institution for housing.

- There was a dire need for the incorporation of the NHB because of the non – availability of long – term finance to individual households which was a major impediment to the development of the housing sector. Thus, the NHB essentially became an Act of the Parliament.

- Some of the objectives of the NHB include integrating housing finance system with the overall finance system, ensuring widespread access of housing facilities, promoting affordable housing credit, upgrading the housing stock in the country, encouraging public agencies to emanate as providers of serviced lands, for housing and gauging optimal utilization of resources.

- A major activity of the NHB includes extending financial assistance to eligible institutions in the housing sector by way of refinance and direct finance. The NHB is the regulator and supervisor of the Housing Finance Companies (HFCs) in the country.

Small Industries Development Bank of India (SIDBI)

- Small Industries Development Bank of India (SIDBI) was established as a wholly owned subsidiary of IDBI under the Small Industries Development Bank of India Act, 1989.

- SIDBI is the apex financial institution for promoting, financing and developing industries in the small scale sector.

- The operations were incorporated from April 2, 1990.

- Headquartered in Lucknow, SIDBI regulates the activities of agencies which provide funds to small enterprises.

- The entire portfolio of operations which were previously handled by the IDBI has been shifted to SIDBI.

- SIDBI provides assistance to the small scale industrial sector through additional institutions like State Financial Corporation (SFC), Commercial Banks and State Industrial Development Corporation.

- Besides share capital, SIDBI can increase resources by taking loans from the Government of India and RBI.

- The Indian Capital market does often provide loans to the SIDBI.

- SIDBI is also permitted to obtain loans from foreign sources through the 'Single Window Service.'

- SIDBI has contributed to the corpus of 88 venture capital funds which has catalyzed investment of more than 5600 crore across 472 MSMEs.

MICRO FINANCE

- Microfinance is a corpus of financial services for entrepreneurs and small businesses lacking access to banking and allied services.

- Mohammed Yunus, a Nobel Prize winner, introduced the concept of microfinance in Bangladesh in the form of the 'Grameen Bank.' The concept was bought by NABARD, under the flagship microfinance initiative.

- Microfinance accounts for a common link between SHGs, NGOs and banks.

- The main attributes of microfinance includes loans devoid of security, loans to people below the poverty line, regulating loan limits, assisting NGOs in deciding terms and conditions for granting loans to the poor and exploiting untapped business potential of the rural areas.

- Launched in 1992 as a pilot project, it has since provided its efficacy as a mainstream programme for banking by the poor, who mainly comprise the marginal farmers, landless labourers, artisans and craftsmen and people involved in hawking and vending business.

- Microfinance is advantageous as it ensures timely repayment of loans to banks, reduction in transactional costs, both to the poor and the banks and maintaining transparency and coherence in financial proceedings.

- There are currently a few social interventions that have been combined with micro financing to increase awareness of HIV/AIDS. Such initiatives like the "Intervention with Microfinance for AIDS and Gender Equity" (IMAGE) which incorporates microfinance with "The Sisters-for-Life" program; a participatory program that educates on different gender roles, gender-based violence, and HIV/AIDS infections to strengthen the communication skills and leadership of women.

- Few of the most reputed players are SKS Microfinance Ltd., BSS Microfinance Pvt. Ltd., Grameen Financial Services Pvt. Ltd., Janalakshmi Financial Services Pvt. Ltd., S.M.I.L.E Microfinance Ltd. and Utkarsh Microfinance Ltd.

FOREIGN BANKS

- The Mandate of the Department of Financial Services covers the functioning of Banks, Financial Institutions, Insurance Companies, Foreign Banks and the National Pension System.

- The Department is headed by the Secretary, who is assisted by an Additional Secretary, four Joint Secretaries and two Economic Advisers.

- The following tabular column represents some of the most reputed foreign banks, operating in India:

Sl. No.	Name of Bank	Country of Incorporation	Number of Banking Branches
1.	Autralia and New Zeeland Banking Group Ltd.	Australia	3
2.	National Australia Bank	Australia	1
3.	Westpac Banking Corporation	Australia	1

4.	Bank of Bahrain & Kuwait BSC	Bahrain	4
5.	AB Bank Ltd.	Bangladesh	1
6.	Sonali Bank Ltd.	Bangladesh	2
7.	Bank of Nova Scotia	Canada	3
8.	Industrial & Commercial Bank of China Ltd.	China	1
9.	BNP Paribas	France	8
10.	Credit Agricole Corporate & Investment Bank	France	5
11.	Societe Generate	France	4
12.	Deutsche Bank	Germany	17
13.	HSBC Ltd.	Hong Kong	26
14.	PT Bank Maybank Indonesia TBK	Indonesia	1
15.	Mizuho Bank Ltd.	Japan	5
16.	Sumitomo Mitsui Banking Corporation	Japan	2
17.	The Bank of Tokyo-Mitsubishi UFJ, Ltd.	Japan	5
18.	SBM Bank (Mauritius) Ltd.	Mauritius	4
19.	Cooperatieve Rabobank U.A	Netherlands	1
20.	Doha Bank	Qatar	3
21.	Qatar National Bank	Qatar	1
22.	JSC VTB Bank	Russia	1
23.	Sberbank	Russia	1
24.	DBS Bank Ltd.	Singapore	12
25.	United Overseas Bank Ltd.	Singapore	1
26.	FirstRand Bank Ltd.	South Africa	1
27.	Shinhan Bank	South Korea	6
28.	Woori Bank	South Korea	3
29.	KEB Hana Bank	South Korea	1
30.	Industrial Bank of Korea	South Korea	1
31.	Bank of Ceylon	Sri Lanka	1
32.	Credit Suisse A.G	Switzerland	1
33.	CTBC Bank Co., Ltd.	Taiwan	2
34.	Krung Thai Bank Public Co. Ltd.	Thailand	1
35.	Abu Dhabi Commercial Bank Ltd.	UAE	2
36.	Mashreq Bank PSC	UAE	1
37.	First Abu Dhabi Bank PJSC	UAE	1
38.	Emirates Bank NBD	UAE	1
39.	Barclays Bank Plc.	United Kingdom	6

40.	Standard Chartered Bank	United Kingdom	100
41.	The Royal Bank of Scotland plc	United Kingdom	1
42.	American Express Banking Corporation	USA	1
43.	Bank of America	USA	4
44.	Citibank N.A.	USA	35
45.	J.P. Morgan Chase Bank N.A.	USA	4
Total			**286**

- Not only do these foreign banks provide innovative financial services to customers, but also create an all new banking experience, using the power of technology.

- Foreign banks also play a significant role in shaping up a country's economy and is a relationship – building tool among nations, considering the concepts of macroeconomics.

- Though foreign banks bring with them all the technologies and expertise, yet none of them have been able to make a mark in this segment of the banking industry. In an era when retail sector accounts for 20% of all the credits, the disappearance of foreign sector banks could greatly undermine the competitiveness and efficiency of the Indian Retail Banking Industry.

- The RBI is primarily responsible for monitoring the regulatory framework with respect to the foreign banks.

EXERCISE

1. What are the three important components of the Indian Money Market?
   - (a) Liquid Money, White Money and Black Money
   - (b) Short – term money and Long – term money
   - (c) Call Money, Notice Money and Term Money
   - (d) Liquid Money, Notice Money and Term Money

2. Consider the following statements with respect to the Indian Money Markets
   - (i) In India, the privatization accounts for catering to the majority of the financial demands
   - (ii) Inter – Bank Market involves transactions between banks for creating financial equilibrium
   - (iii) Most of these exchanges take place considering floating interest rates.

   Which of the above statements are TRUE?
   - (a) (i) & (ii)   (b) (ii) & (iii)
   - (c) (i) & (iii)   (d) (i), (ii) & (iii)

3. What is T – Bills?
   - (a) Telephone Bills
   - (b) Telemarketing Bills
   - (c) Tenure Bills
   - (d) Treasury Bills

4. Which country's government used T – Bills for the first time?
   - (a) USA
   - (b) USSR
   - (c) UK
   - (d) India

5. Which of the following aspects are unique to the USP of the T – Bills?
   - (i) An auction process
   - (ii) Competitive returns as per customers' specifications
   - (iii) Government bears the responsibility of the final payment.

   Which of the above statements are TRUE?
   - (a) (i) and (ii)
   - (b) (ii) and (iii)
   - (c) (i) and (iii)
   - (d) (i), (ii) and (iii)

6. For which of the following amounts, can T – Bills be issued?
   - (a) ₹ 75, 000
   - (b) ₹ 70, 000
   - (c) ₹ 60, 000
   - (d) ₹ 45, 000

7. Which is the most significant utility of the commercial bill market?
   - (a) Timely collection of interests
   - (b) Short – term funds for business empowerment
   - (c) Create a stable seller – buyer relationship
   - (d) Identify payment trespassers.

8. What is the biggest challenge for the commercial bill?
   - (a) Big business conglomerates
   - (b) Private banks
   - (c) Consumers
   - (d) Sellers.

9. Consider the statements related to the Collateral Loan Market
   - (i) There is a huge risk involved in the high value loans
   - (ii) Collateral Loan Market facilitates loan sanction real fast
   - (iii) Maturities on such loans are no longer than one year.

   Which of the above statements are TRUE?
   - (a) (i) and (ii)
   - (b) (ii) and (iii)
   - (c) (i) and (iii)
   - (d) (i), (ii) and (iii)

10. Who are the lenders in the case of collateral loans?
    (a) Asset Management Companies
    (b) Banks
    (c) Insurance Companies
    (d) Credit Rating Agencies
11. Which financial enterprise assists in covering short – term obligations like payroll?
    (a) Commercial Bill Market
    (b) Collateral Loan Market
    (c) Treasury Bill Market
    (d) Commercial Paper Market
12. Consider the following attributes of gilt – edged securities.
    (i) Safe investment
    (ii) Complete liquidity
    (iii) Bulk investment
    Which of the above is TRUE?
    (a) (i) and (ii)
    (b) (i) and (iii)
    (c) (ii) and (iii)
    (d) (i), (ii) and (iii)
13. The first public sector bank in India which obtained license for Internet Banking from RBI is-
    (a) Punjab National Bank
    (b) Oriental Bank of Commerce
    (c) Corporation Bank
    (d) State Bank of India
14. Which of the following is not a function of the Securities and Exchange Board of India (SEBI)?
    (a) Supervising the working of the Stock Exchanges
    (b) Underwriting new capital issues
    (c) Regulating merchant banks and mutual funds
    (d) promoting the development of a healthy capital market
15. Inflation, in theory, occurs:
    (a) when the price of essential commodities outstrips income
    (b) when money supply grows at a higher rate than GDP in real terms

(c) when the exchange rate of a currency falls
(d) when fiscal deficit exceeds balance of payment deficit

16. According to the Chakravarthy Committee, one of the principal causes affecting price stability in India is:
    (a) existence of black money
    (b) violent fluctuation in agricultural production
    (c) India's precarious balance of payment position
    (d) fiscal deficit
17. Which of the following statements correctly expresses the difference between preference shares and equity shares?
    (a) equity shareholders have no voting right but preference shareholders have voting rights
    (b) preference shareholders have no have voting rights but equity shareholders have voting rights
    (c) preference shareholders have no right to profit whereas equity shareholders have a right to profit
    (d) preference shareholders get exemption from taxes while equity shareholders do not get any exemption
18. Which one of the following governmental steps has proved relatively effective in controlling the double digit rate of inflation in the Indian economy during recent years?
    (a) enhanced rate of production of all consumer goods
    (b) streamlined public distribution system
    (c) pursuing an export oriented strategy
    (d) containing budgetary deficit and unproductive expenditure
19. Which one of the following is not a feature of "Value Added Tax" ?
    (a) It is multi-point destination-based system of taxation.

(b)   It is a tax levied on value addition at each stage of transaction in the production distribution chain.

(c)   It is a tax on the final consumption of goods or services and must ultimately be borne by the consumer.

(d)   It is basically a subject of the central government and the state governments are only a facilitator for its successful implementation.

20.   Which one of the following statements is an appropriate description of deflation?

(a)   It is a sudden fall in the value of a currency against other currencies

(b)   It is a persistent recession in both the financial and real sectors of economy

(c)   It is a persistent fall in the general price level of goods and services

(d)   It is a fall in the rate of inflation over a period of time

21.   How do we define the terms bull and bear with regard to stock markets?

(a)   A bull is an optimistic operator who first buys and then sells shares in expectation of the price going up; a bear is a pessimistic market operator who sells the shares in expectation of buying them back at a lower price.

(b)   There is nothing significantly different as both operate in the capital market.

(c)   Bull is one who first sells a share and then buys it at a lower price; bear means one who first buys and then sells it in expectation of prices going up.

(d)   A bull is ready to buy any share; a bear only deals in government securities.

22.   A rise in 'SENSEX' means:

(a)   a rise in prices of shares of all companies registered with Bombay Stock Exchange

(b)   a rise in prices of shares of all companies registered with National Stock Exchange

(c)   an overall rise in prices of shares of group up companies registered with Bombay Stock Exchange

(d)   a rise in prices of shares of all companies belonging to a group of companies registered with Bombay Stock Exchange

23.   Which of the following could be a cause of demand inflation?

(a)   An increase in the cost of labour

(b)   An increase in domestic interest rates

(c)   An increase in the level of consumer spending

(d)   An increase in import prices, resulting from a depreciating dollar

24.   'SHG Bank Linkage Programme' is a programme which encourages India's banks to lend to self-help groups (SHGs) composed mainly of poor women, this has evolved into an important Indian tool for microfinance. This programme was initiated by ?

(a)   Reserve Bank of India (RBI)

(b)   Agricultural Refinance and Development Corporation (ARDC)

(c)   National Bank for Agriculture and Rural Development (NABARD)

(d)   Non-Banking Finance Companies (NBFC)

25.   Which of the following statements is not correct regarding the 'Banking Sector' of India?

(a)   At present there are 26 Nationalized Banks in India.

(b)   Foreign Banks and Regional Rural Banks do not come under the category of Scheduled Commercial Banks.

(c)   Banks have the freedom to regulate their own Savings Bank Deposit interest rates.

(d)   Narsimham Committee is related to Banking Sector reforms.

26. The concept of 'Universal Banking'
    was implemented in India on the
    recommendations of:
    (a)   Abid Hussain Committee
    (b)   R H Khan Committee
    (c)   S Padmanabhan Committee
    (d)   Y H Malegam Committee
27. When there is an inflationary trend in
    the economy, what would be trend in
    the pricing of the Bank Products?
    (a)   Increasing Trend
    (b)   Decreasing Trend
    (c)   Constant Trend
    (d)   There is no relevance of the
          inflation in pricing of the Banking
          Products
28. As per Section 24 (2A) of Banking
    Regulation Act 1949, every banking
    company in India has to maintain
    equivalent to an amount which shall
    not at the close of the business on
    _____________ be less than 25% of
    the total of its net demand and time
    liabilities, which is known as SLR.
    Which among the following is the
        correct option?
    (a)   Any Day
    (b)   Any Week
    (c)   Any Fortnight
    (d)   Any Month
29. For which of the following, the
    Reserve Bank of India has stipulated
    a   maximum   Capital   Adequacy
    Requirements in India?
    (a)   Private Sector Banks
    (b)   Banks that Undertake Insurance
          Business.
    (c)   Local Area Banks
    (d)   Scheduled Commercial Banks
30. Which one of the following Public
    Sector Bank's emblem figures a dog
    and the words 'faithful friendly, in it?
    (a)   Punjab National Bank
    (b)   Syndicate Bank
    (c)   Oriental Bank of Commerce
    (d)   State Bank of India

31. Which among the following would
    most likely follow if the Reserve
    Bank of India effects selling of the
    securities?
    (a)   The cash resources at the disposal
          of the commercial banks increase.
    (b)   The cash resources at the disposal
          of the commercial banks get
          diminished.
    (c)   The   cash   resources   of   the
          commercial   banks   remain
          unchanged.
    (d)   None of the above.
32. An excise duty is a charge on which of
    the following?
    (a)   Export of goods
    (b)   Production of goods
    (c)   Production or sale of goods
    (d)   Consumption of good
33. The most active segment of the Money
    Market in India is which one of the
    following?
    (a)   Call Money / Notice Money
          Market
    (b)   Repo / Reverse Repo
    (c)   Commercial Paper (CP)
    (d)   Certificate of Deposit (CD)
34. What does venture capital mean?
    (a)   A short-term capital provided to
          industries
    (b)   A long-term start-up capital
          provided to new entrepreneurs
    (c)   Funds provided to industries at
          times of incurring losses
    (d)   Funds provided for replacement
          and renovation of industries
35. Consider the following statements :
    The function of the Reserve Bank of
    India does not include:
    1.   Open market operations
    2.   Monitoring revenue collection
    3.   Supervising non-banking finance
         companies
    4.   Review of public expenditure

Which of the statement/s given above is/are correct?

(a) 1 only (b) 2 and 4
(c) 1, 3 and 4 (d) 1, 2, 3 and 4

36. Consider the following statements.
1. The National Housing Bank, the apex institution of housing finance in India, was set up as a wholly-owned subsidiary of the Reserve Bank of India.
2. The Small Industries Development Bank of India was established as a wholly-owned subsidiary of the Industrial Development Bank of India.

Which of the statement given above is/are correct?

(a) 1 only (b) 2 only
(c) Both 1 and 2 (d) Neither 1 nor 2

37. Why is the offering of "teaser loans" by commercial banks a cause of economic concern ?
1. The teaser loans are considered to be an aspect of sub-prime lending and banks may be exposed to the risk of defaulters in future.
2. In India, the teaser loans are mostly given to inexperienced entrepreneurs to set up manufacturing or export units.

Which of the statements given above is/are correct?

(a) 1 only
(b) 2 only
(c) Both 1 and 2
(d) Neither 1 nor 2

38. Name the 3 commodities in the Wholesale Price Index.
1. Primary articles
2. Fuel, power, light and lubricants
3. Manufactured products
4. Food articles and industrial raw materials

(a) 1, 2 and 3 (b) 2, 3 and 4
(c) 1, 3 and 4 (d) 1 and 3

39. Which of the following measures would result in an increase in the money supply in the economy?
1. Purchase of government securities from the public by the Central Bank
2. Deposit of currency in commercial banks by the public
3. Borrowing by the government from the Central Bank
4. Sale of government securities to the public by the Central Bank

Select the correct answer using the codes given below :

(a) 1 only (b) 2 and 4
(c) 1 and 3 (d) 2, 3 and 4

40. Consider the following statements:
1. High growth will lead to inflation.
2. High growth will lead to deflation.

Which of the statements given above is/are correct?

(a) Only 1 (b) Only 2
(c) Both 1 and 2 (d) Neither 1 nor 2

41. Which one among the following is an appropriate description of deflation?
(a) it is a sudden fall in the value of a currency against other currencies
(b) It is a persistent recession in the economy
(c) It is a persistent fall in the general price level of goods and services
(d) It is fall in the rate of inflation over a period of time

42. Consider the following statements regarding Non-Banking Finance Companies (NBFCs):
1. NBFCs can also engage in Micro-Finance Activities.
2. Housing-finance companies form a distinct sub-group of the NBFCs.
3. The deposit insurance facility of the Deposit Insurance and Credit Guarantee Corporation is not available for NBFC depositors.

Which among the above statement(s) is/are not correct?

(a) Only 1   (b) 1 and 3

(c) All of there   (d) None of these

43. Which among the following are the 'Credit-Rating Agencies' of India?

1. CRISIL   2. CARE

3. ICRA   4. ONICRA

(a) 1 and 3   (b) 1, 2 and 3

(c) 1, 3 and 4   (d) All of them

44. Which among the following are the wholly/partly owned subsidiaries of the Reserve Bank of India (RBI)?

1. Deposit Insurance and Credit Guarantee Corporation (DICGC)

2. National Housing Bank (NHB)

3. National Bank for Agriculture and Rural Development (NABARD)

4. Bharatiya Reserve Bank Note Mudran Private Limited (BRBNMPL)

(a) 1 and 4   (b) 1, 2 and 4

(c) 2, 3 and 4   (d) All of them

45. Consider the following steps:

1. Banking Department gets currency from the Issue Department

2. Government puts the currency in circulation

3. Central Government incurs a deficit in its Budget

4. Government Sells Treasury Bills to Banking Department of RBI

Which among the following is the correct order of the above steps?

(a) 1 2 3 4   (b) 2 3 4 1

(c) 3 4 1 2   (d) 4 3 2 1

46. Consider the following:

1. Commercial Banks

2. Central Bank of India

3. Government

Which among the above can create money?

(a) Only 1   (b) Only 1 & 2

(c) Only 3   (d) All 1 2 & 3

47. With reference to inflation in India, which of the following statements is correct?

(a) Controlling the inflation in India is the responsibility of the Government of India only

(b) The Reserve Bank of India has no role in controlling the inflation

(c) Decreased money circulation helps in controlling the inflation

(d) Increased money circulation helps in controlling the inflation

48. The Reserve Bank of India regulates the commercial banks in matters of:

1. liquidity of assets

2. branch expansion

3. merger of banks

4. winding-up of banks

Select the correct answer using the codes given below.

(a) 1 and 4 only

(b) 2, 3 and 4 only

(c) 1, 2 and 3 only

(d) 1, 2, 3 and 4

49. Which of the following grants / grant direct credit assistance to rural households?

1. Regional Rural Banks

2. National Bank for Agriculture and Rural Development

3. Land Development Banks

Select the correct answer using the codes given below.

(a) 1 and 2 only   (b) 2 only

(c) 1 and 3 only   (d) 1, 2 and 3

50. Which among the followings is the type of inflation?

1. Demand Pull Inflation

2. Cost Push Inflation

3. Stagflation

4. Hyperinflation

Choose the correct type.

(a) 1, 2, 3, 4   (b) 1, 2

(c) 3, 4   (d) 1, 4

51. What is the difference between Inflation and Deflation?
    1. Inflation is an increase in price of goods while Deflation is that state in which the value of money rises and the price of goods and services falls.
    2. Deflation is an increase in price of goods while Inflation is that state in which the value of money rises and the price of goods and services falls.
    3. Inflation is that state in which the value of money rises and the price of goods and services falls while deflation is an increase in price of goods.

    Choose the correct difference between Inflation and Deflation.
    (a) 1 only   (b) 2 only
    (c) 3 only   (d) 1, 2, 3

52. Which among the following is the type of organised sector of Indian money market?
    1. Call money market
    2. Treasury Bill Market
    3. Commercial Bill Market
    4. Collateral loan market

    Choose the correct code.
    (a) 1 and 2
    (b) 3 and 4
    (c) 1, 2, 3, 4
    (d) None of the Above

53. Consider the following statement:
    1. Ad hoc treasury bills are sold to the banks and public and are freely marketable.
    2. Regular treasury bills are not sold to the banks and the general public, and are not marketable.

    Choose the correct code.
    (a) 1 only
    (b) 2 only
    (c) 1 and 2
    (d) None of the Above

54. Which among the following are the Nationalised Banks?
    1. Bank of India
    2. Punjab National Bank
    3. Canara Bank
    4. United Commercial Bank

    Choose the code.
    (a) 1 and 2   (b) 3 and 4
    (c) 1 and 4   (d) 1, 2, 3, 4

55. What are the reforms of Narsimham Committee on Banking sector?
    1. Nationalisation of banks should not take place any more.
    2. Private and foreign banks should be set up to promote competition.
    3. There should be a phased reduction of CRR and SLR.

    Choose the correct option.
    (a) 1 only
    (b) 2 only
    (c) 3 only
    (d) All of the Above

56. Consider the following statement:
    1. As per recommendations of the Narasimham Committee, it has been decided that credit facilities granted by banks will be classified into performing and non-performing assets (NPA)
    2. NPA is a loan which is in default for more than nine months.

    Choose the incorrect statement.
    (a) 1 only
    (b) 2 only
    (c) 1 and 2
    (d) None of the Above

57. Choose the type of capital market:
    1. Securities Market
    2. Financial institutions
    3. Gill-edged market
    4. Incorporated securities

    Which among the following code is correct?
    (a) 1 and 4   (b) 1 and 3
    (c) 1 and 2   (d) 3 and 4

58. Consider the following statement:
    1. GIC was formed in November 1972.
    2. The 107 private companies operating in the field were grouped together into four - National Insurance Company, United India Insurance Company, Oriental Insurance Company and New India Assurance Company.

    Choose the incorrect statement.
    (a) 1 only   (b) 2 only
    (c) 1 and 2
    (d) None of the Above

59. Name of four institutions that are regulated by the RBI as all-India FIs:
    1. Export Import Bank of India (EXIM Bank)
    2. National Bank for Agriculture and Rural Development (NABARD)
    3. National Housing Bank (NHB)
    4. Small Industries Development Bank of India (SIDBI)

    Choose the correct answer.
    (a) 1 and 2
    (b) 3 and 4
    (c) 1, 3, 4
    (d) 1, 2, 3, 4

60. Consider the following statement:
    1. IRDA is a multimember nodal agency
    2. It is vested with regulatory powers in respect of the insurance sector similar to those vested in SEBI in respect of the capital markets and of RBI for the banking sector.
    3. The IRDA Act, 1999 cleared the way for private sector entry into the insurance business.

    Choose the correct statement.
    (a) 1 only
    (b) 2 only
    (c) 3 only
    (d) All of the Above

61. Which of the following markets are independently regulated by Forward Market Commission?
    (a) Mutual Funds
    (b) Commodity Futures Market
    (c) Stock Market
    (d) Foreign Exchange Markets

62. According to the Chakravarthy Committee, one of the principal causes affecting price stability in India is:
    (a) existence of black money
    (b) violent fluctuation in agricultural production
    (c) India's precarious balance of payment position
    (d) fiscal deficit

63. Which one of the following statements is an appropriate description of deflation?
    (a) It is a sudden fall in the value of a currency against other currencies
    (b) It is a persistent recession in both the financial and real sectors of economy
    (c) It is a persistent fall in the general price level of goods and services
    (d) It is a fall in the rate of inflation over a period of time

64. The International Development Association, a lending agency, is administered by the:
    (a) International Bank for Reconstruction and Development
    (b) International Fund for Agricultural Development
    (c) United Nations Development Programme.
    (d) United Nations Industrial Development Organization

65. A fall in 'SENSEX' means:
    (a) a fall in prices of shares of all companies registered with Bombay Stock Exchange
    (b) a fall in prices of shares of all companies registered with National Stock Exchange

   (c)   an overall fall in prices of shares of group up companies registered with Bombay Stock Exchange

   (d)   a fall in prices of shares of all companies belonging to a group of companies registered with Bombay Stock Exchange

66. From time to time, which among the following body publishes the "Exchange Control Manual" in context with the Foreign Exchange in India?

   (a)   Foreign Trade Promotion Board

   (b)   Department of Commerce

   (c)   Reserve Bank of India

   (d)   SEBI

67. The Laffer curve is the graphical representation of:

   (a)   The relationship between tax rates and absolute revenue these rates generate for the government.

   (b)   The inverse relationship between the rate of unemployment and the rate of inflation in an economy.

   (c)   The inequality in income distribution.

   (d)   The relationship between environmental quality and economic development.

68. Which among the following is true about "deficit financing"?

   (a)   Public expenditure in excess of public revenue

   (b)   Public revenue in excess of public expenditure

   (c)   New currency replaced by old currency

   (d)   None of above

69. What do we call an arrangement whereby an issuing Bank at the request of the Importer (Buyer) undertakes to make payment to the exporter (Beneficiary) against stipulated documents?

   (a)   Bill of Exchange

   (b)   Letter of Exchange

   (c)   Letter of Credit

   (d)   Bill of Entry

70. Consider the following statements:

   1.   Sensex is based on 50 of the most important stocks available on the Bombay stock Exchange (BSE).

   2.   For calculating the Sensex, all the stock are assigned proportional weightage.

   3.   New York Stock Exchange is the oldest stock exchange in the world.

   Which of the statements given above is/are correct?

   (a)   2 only   (b)   1 and 3

   (c)   2 and 3   (d)   none

71. Brent index is associated with :

   (1)   crude oil prices

   (2)   copper future prices

   (3)   gold future prices

   (4)   shipping rate index

   Which of the following is true?

   (a)   Only 1   (b)   Only 2

   (c)   Only 3   (d)   Only 4

72. Which of the following are the provisions of SARFAESI Act which enables banks to reduce their non-performing assets (NPAs)?

   1.   Enforcement of Security Interest by secured creditor (Banks/ Financial Institutions).

   2.   Transfer of non- performing assets to asset reconstruction company which will then dispose of those assets and realise the proceeds.

   3.   To provide a legal framework for securitization of assets.

   4.   Assisting banks in making the credibility track record of customers under Credit Information Bureau of India (CIBIL).

   (a)   1 and 2   (b)   1, 2 and 3

   (c)   2, 3 and 4 (d)   1, 2, 3 and 4

73. Which among the following are the 'Credit-Rating Agencies' of India?

   1.   CRISIL   2.   CARE

   3.   ICRA   4.   ONICRA

(a) 1 and 3   (b) 1, 2 and 3
(c) 1, 3 and 4   (d) All of them

74. Choose the type of capital market:
1. Securities Market
2. Financial institutions
3. Gill-edged market
4. Incorporated securities
Which among the following code is correct?
(a) 1 and 4   (b) 1 and 3
(c) 1 and 2   (d) 3 and 4

75. Consider the following statement:
1. Bombay Stock Exchange (BSE) is India's oldest stock exchange
2. It formally came into being in 1888
3. It was a regional exchange till 2002 when it became a national exchange
Choose the incorrect statement regarding BSE.
(a) 1 only
(b) 2 only
(c) 3 only
(d) None of the Above

76. _______ deals with long-term finance (more than 365 days) funds. It includes all facilities and institutional arrangements available for borrowing and lending of term funds (including medium-term).
1. Capital market
2. Stock market
3. Debit
4. Credit
Choose the correct answer.
(a) 1 only   (b) 2 only
(c) 3 only   (d) 4 only

77. Name of four institutions that are regulated by the RBI as all-India FIs:
1. Export Import Bank of India (EXIM Bank)
2. National Bank for Agriculture and Rural Development (NABARD)
3. National Housing Bank (NHB)
4. Small Industries Development Bank of India (SIDBI)

Choose the correct answer.
(a) 1 and 2   (b) 3 and 4
(c) 1, 3, 4   (d) 1, 2, 3, 4

78. Which of the following organisation provides guarantee to exporters?
(a) EXIM Bank
(b) Export Loan Guarantee Corporation
(c) RBI
(d) Commerce Ministry

79. Which of the following is not one of the features of the Special Economic Zones (SEZ) being set up for promoting exports ?
(a) The SEZ area will be treated as foreign territory for trade operations, duties and tariff.
(b) No licence is required for import into the zone.
(c) Foreign workers will be allowed free entry without visa restrictions.
(d) There will be no routine examination by customs authorities of import/export cargo.

80. TRIPS (Trade Related aspects of Intellectual Property Rights) agreements is administered by
(a) United Nations Conference on Trade and Development (UNCTAD)
(b) United Nations Organization (UNO)
(c) World Trade Organization (WTO)
(d) World Bank (WB)

81. Foreign Direct Investment involves:
(a) A speculator trying to make a profit by buying company shares on a foreign stock exchange.
(b) A UK energy company buying territory abroad where it expects to find oil reserves.
(c) A tourist purchasing foreign currency to spend on a holiday abroad.

(d) A company signing an agreement with a wholesaler to distribute its products in foreign markets.

82. What is meant by term Balance of Payment?
I.   Those transactions arising out of exports and imports (the visible items)
II. It is astatistical statement of all transactions made between one particular country and all other countries during a specified period of time
III. This account is the summary of all international trade transactions of the domestic country in one year
(a) I & III   (b) Only I
(c) Only II   (d) None of the above

83. Which of the below statements are correct regarding exchange trade?
I.   The value of rupee was managed by the state bank
II. The strict foreign exchange controls also encouraged hawala trade
III. India followed a strongly inward looking policy, laying stress on import substitution
(a) Only I   (b) Both II & III
(c) Only III   (d) All the above

84. What was the main reason of introducing trade reforms in 1991?
I.   Make exports competitive
II. Unshackle foreign trade from the clutches of a control regime
III. Allow import of most goods using only tariff as a restraint
(a) I & II   (b) Only II
(c) Only III   (d) All the above

85. Which is the correct statement according to FTP 15 – 20?
I.   FTP 2015-20 introduces two new schemes, namely "Merchandise Exports from India Scheme (MEIS)" and "Services Exports from India Scheme (SEIS)"
II. These schemes (MEIS and SEIS) replace multiple schemes earlier in place, each with different conditions for eligibility and usage.
III. Incentives (MEIS & SEIS) to be available for SEZs also e-Commerce of handicrafts, handlooms, books, etc. eligible for benefits of MEIS.
IV. FTP benefits from both MEIS & SEIS will be extended to units located in SEZs.
(a) I & II   (b) II & IV
(c) Only III   (d) All the above

86. Which points are correct regarding SEZ act?
I.   Exemption to SEZ developer and units from Minimum Alternate Tax.
II. Constitution of an authority for each SEZ with a view to providing greater administrative, financial and functional autonomy to these zones.
III. Establishment of designated courts and a single enforcement agency to ensure speedy trial and investigation of offences committed in SEZs.
(a) I & II   (b) Only II
(c) Only III   (d) All the above

87. Which among the following is the apex organization of Industrial Finance in India?
(a) IDBI   (b) ICICI
(c) IFCI   (d) RIDF

88. Which among the following is the correct full form of SIDO?
(a) Small Industries Development Organization
(b) Sick Industries Development Organization
(c) Small Industries Development Office
(d) State Industrial Development Organization

89. With reference to the National Investment Fund to which the disinvestment proceeds are routed, consider the following statements ?
    1. The assets in the National Investment Fund are managed by the Union Ministry of Finance.
    2. The National Investment Fund is to be maintained within the Consolidated Fund of India.
    3. Certain Asset Management companies are appointed as the fund managers.
    4. A certain proportion of annual income is used for financing select social sectors.

Which of the statements given above is/are correct ?
(a) 1 and 2
(b) 2 only
(c) 3 and 4
(d) 3 only

90. SEZs were established with the objective of _____ .
    1. attracting foreign investment directly.
    2. protect domestic market from competition from multinationals.
    3. providing more capital to agricultural and allied activities.
(a) 1 only
(b) 2 only
(c) 3 only
(d) All of the above

HINTS & EXPLANATIONS

1. **(c)** The three important components of the Indian Money Market are call money (one – day transactions), notice money (transaction between 2 – 14 days) and term money (transactions exceeding a fortnight).

2. **(b)** Options ii and iii are correct as Inter – bank market implies transaction (borrowing and lending) between banks and all these policies deploy floating rates of interest, as they are subjected to market risks.

3. **(d)** T – bills stands as an acronym for treasury bills.

4. **(a)** USA had introduced Treasury Bills for the first time in the history of short – term financial markets.

5. **(d)** All three options are appropriate as T – Bills are issued by a bidding process; for competitive T – Bills, the bidder has to specify returns and in case of maturity, the government pays the par value to the bearer.

6. **(a)** T – Bills can be issued for a minimum amount of ₹ 25, 000 and in multiples of the same. Thus option A suffices.

7. **(b)** A commercial bill provides short – term boost for business expansion

8. **(a)** The MNCs and big corporate do not abide by the principle of timely payment and hence challenges the conventional protocol of the commercial bill.

9. **(a)** The third statement is wrong as maturities on collateral loans are no longer than nine months.

10. **(b)** Banks are the lenders. In case of payment default, the property is seized by the hypothecary bank.

11. **(d)** Commercial paper market provides a means for corporations to borrow money to cover short-term debt obligations, such as payroll.

12. **(d)** Gilt–edged securities provide zero risk, 100% liquidity and massive returns.

13. **(a)**   14. **(b)**   15. **(b)**

16. **(b)**   17. **(c)**   18. **(d)**

19. **(d)** VAT is the State Subject.

20. **(c)** Deflation is a decrease in the prices of goods and services. It occurs when the annual inflation rate falls below 0%, which is negative inflation rate. This is different from Disinflation which is a slow-down in the inflation rate. This is a situation when inflation declines to lower levels but prices continue to rise.

21. **(a)**   22. **(c)**   23. **(c)**

24. **(c)**

25. **(b)** Foreign Banks and Regional Rural Banks also come under the category of Scheduled Commercial Banks. Now, the banks are free to determine their savings bank deposit interest rate, subject to the following two conditions:

   1. Each bank will have to offer a uniform interest rate on savings bank deposits up to ₹ 1 lakh,irrespective of the amount in the account within this limit.

   2. For savings bank deposits over ` 1 lakh, a bank may provide differential rates of interest, if it so chooses. However, there should not be any discrimination from customer to customer on interest rates for similar amount of deposit.

26. (b)   27. (a)   28. (a)

29. (c)

30. (b) Syndicate Bank. The symbol of dog implies that Bank is trustworthy and a friend. Its slogan is : Your faithful and friendly financial partner.

31. (b)   32. (c)   33. (a)

34. (b) Venture capital (VC) is a long term financial capital provided to early-stage, high-potential, start up companies or new companies.

35. (b)   36. (c)

37. (a) The statement (1) is correct because it includes the definition of teaser loans but the statement (2) is not correct, because in India teaser loan is provided to the home buyers not for setting up manufacturing or export units.

38. (a)   39. (c)

40. (a) Typically, higher inflation is caused by strong economic growth. If Aggregate demand in an economy expanded faster than aggregate supply, we would expect to see a higher inflation rate. If demand is rising faster than supply, then this suggests that economic growth is higher than the long run sustainable rate of growth.

41. (c) Deflation is defined as a fall in the general price level of goods and services. It is a negative rate of inflation. It means the value of money increases rather than decreases.

42. (d)   43. (d)   44. (d)

45. (c)   46. (d)

47. (c) When inflation becomes very high, the RBI decreases supply of money (to check inflation) by adopting light monetary policy.

48. (d) The Reserve Bank of India is the main monetary authority of the country and beside that, in its capacity as the central bank, acts as the bank of the national and state governments. Sometimes it happens that some of the banks close down due to non recovery of loans or such other issues. In such conditions people have to suffer as their money is with the bank then. For this reason there is provision for winding up of the banking company under the Banking Regulation Act, 1949. The power of winding up of Bank lies in the hand of Reserve Bank of India.

49. (c) Land development bank started financing long term loan for more significant rural development activities like rural and cottage industries, rural artisans etc. The main purpose of RRBs is to mobilize financial resources from rural / semi-urban areas and grant loans and advances mostly to small and marginal farmers, agricultural labourers and rural artisans.

50. (a) Types of inflation are Demand Pull Inflation, Cost Push Inflation, Stagflation, Hyperinflation.

51. (a) Inflation is an increase in price of goods while Deflation is that

state in which the value of money rises and the price of goods and services falls.

52. (c) The type of organised sector of Indian money market are Call Money Market, Treasury Bill Market, Commercial Bill Market and Collateral loan market

53. (d) Ad hoc treasury bills are not sold to the banks and the general public, and are not marketable while regular treasury bills are sold by Reserve Bank of India on behalf of the Central Government.

54. (d) The nationalised banks are Central Bank of India, Bank of India, Punjab National Bank, Canara Bank, United Commercial Bank, Syndicate Bank, Bank of Baroda, United Bank of India, Union Bank of India, Dena Bank, Allahabad Bank, Indian Bank, Indian Overseas Bank Bank of Maharashtra.

55. (d)

56. (b) NPA is a loan (whether term loan, cash credit, overdraft, or bills discounted), which is in default for more than six months.

57. (c) The securities market is further divided into the gilt-edged market and the corporate securities market.

58. (d) The GIC was formed in November 1972 consequent upon the nationalisation of general insurance business. The 107 private companies operating in the field were grouped together into four - National Insurance Company, United India Insurance Company, Oriental Insurance Company and New India Assurance Company, with GIC as the holding company.

59. (d) According to the Economic Survey, there are four Institutions, namely the Export Import Bank of India (EXIM Bank), National Bank for Agriculture and Rural Development (NABARD), the National Housing Bank (NHB) and Small Industries Development Bank of India (SIDBI).

60. (d) IRDA is a multimember nodal agency. It is vested with regulatory powers in respect of the insurance sector similar to those vested in SEBI in respect of the capital markets and of RBI for the banking sector.

   The IRDA Act, 1999 cleared the way for private sector entry into the insurance business.

61. (b)   62. (b)

63. (c) Deflation is a decrease in the prices of goods and services. It occurs when the annual inflation rate falls below 0%, which is negative inflation rate. This is different from Disinflation which is a slow-down in the inflation rate. This is a situation when inflation declines to lower levels but prices continue to rise.

64. (a) International Development Association (IDA), is a part of the World Bank that helps the world's poorest countries. It complements the World Bank's other lending arm— the International Bank for Reconstruction and Development (IBRD) which serves middle-income countries with capital investment and advisory services. IDA was created in 1960.

65. (c)   66. (c)
67. (a) In economics, the Laffer curve is a hypothetical representation of the relationship between government revenue raised by taxation and all possible rates of taxation. It is used to illustrate the concept of taxable income elasticity – which taxable income will change in response to changes in the rate of taxation.
68. (a) Deficit financing, practice in which a government spends more money than it receives as revenue, the difference being made up by borrowing or minting new funds. Although budget deficits may occur for numerous reasons, the term usually refers to a conscious attempt to stimulate the economy by lowering tax rates or increasing government expenditures. The influence of government deficits upon a national economy may be very great. It is widely believed that a budget balanced over the span of a business cycle should replace the old ideal of an annually balanced budget. Some economists have abandoned the balanced budget concept entirely, considering it inadequate as a criterion of public policy.
69. (c)
70. (a) The 'BSE SENSEX' is a value-weighted index composed of 30 stocks and was started in 1 January, 1986. The origin of the NYSE can be traced to 17 May, 1792. When the Buttonwood Agreement was signed by 24 stock brokers outside 68 Wall Street in New York under a buttonwood tree. Amsterdam Stock Exchange (1602) is considered oldest in the world and was established by the Dutch East India company.
71. (a) Brent Crude is a major trading classification of sweet light crude oil that serves as a major benchmark price for purchases of oil worldwide. Brent Crude is extracted from the North Sea and comprises Brent Blend, Forties Blend, Oseberg and Ekofisk crudes .The Brent Crude oil marker is also known as Brent Blend, London Brent and Brent petroleum. The index represents the average price of trading in the 25 day Brent Blend, Forties, Oseberg, Ekofisk (BFOE) market in the relevant delivery month as reported and confirmed by the industry media.
72. (b)   73. (d)
74. (c) The securities market is further divided into the gilt-edged market and the corporate securities market.
75. (c) Bombay Stock Exchange (BSE) India's oldest stock exchange formally came into being in 1887 and was a regional exchange till 2002 when it became a national exchange.
76. (a) Capital market deals with long-term finance (more than 365 days) funds. It includes all facilities and institutional arrangements available for borrowing and lending of term funds (including medium-term).
77. (d) According to the Economic Survey, there are four Institutions, namely the Export Import Bank of India (EXIM Bank), National Bank for Agriculture and Rural Development (NABARD),

the National Housing Bank (NHB) and Small Industries Development Bank of India (SIDBI).

78. (b)   79. (c)   80. (c)

81. (b)   The energy company will own and control the territory and the oil reserves it contains.

82. (c)   Balance of payments (BoP) is astatistical statement of all transactions made between one particular country and all other countries during a specified period of time. It also include export-import of visible and invisible items.

83. (b)

84. (d)   The major thrust was to make exports competitive, unshackle foreign trade from the clutches of a control regime and allow import of most goods using only tariff as a restraint.

85. (d)   These schemes (MEIS and SEIS) replace multiple schemes earlier in place, each with different conditions for eligibility and usage. Incentives (MEIS & SEIS) to be available for SEZs also e-Commerce of handicrafts, handlooms, books etc., eligible for benefits of MEIS. FTP benefits from both MEIS & SEIS will be extended to units located in SEZs.

86. (d)   87. (a)   88. (d)

89. (c)   On 27 January 2005, the Government had decided to constitute a 'National Investment Fund' (NIF) into which realization from sale of minority shareholding of the Government in CPSEs would be channelised. This fund is managed by professionals and a part of it is used for use in social sector – like education, health care and employment.

90. (d)

FOREIGN TRADE INVESTMENT IN INDIA

INTRODUCTION

- Foreign trade is exchange of capital, goods, and services across international borders or territories, which involves the activities of the government and individuals.
- In most countries, it represents a significant share of gross domestic product (GDP). Foreign trade in India, includes all imports and exports to and from India. At the level of Central Government it is administered by the Ministry of Commerce and Industry.

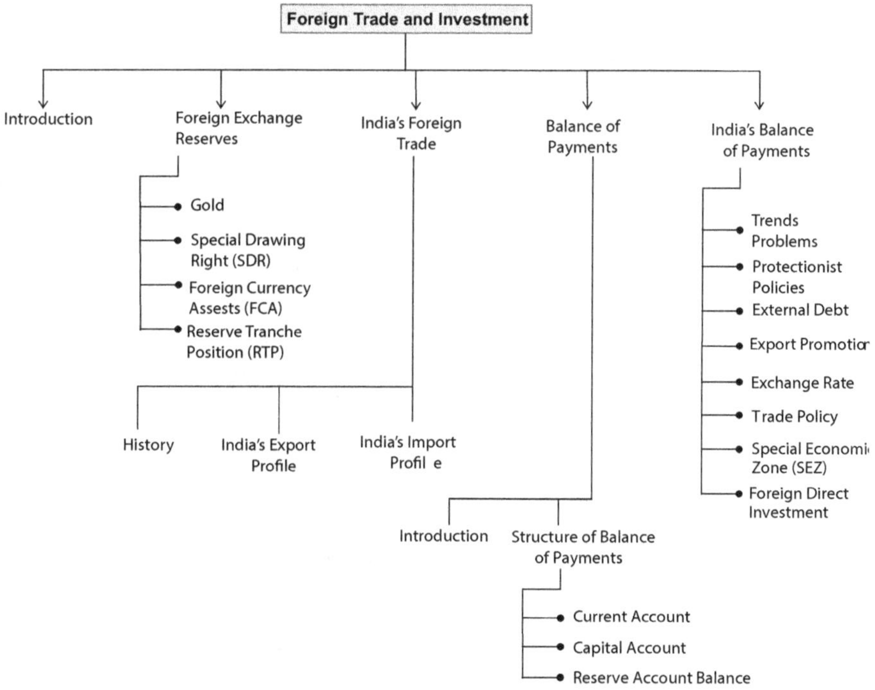

FOREIGN EXCHANGE RESERVES

- **Foreign exchange reserves** also called **forex reserves** or **FX reserves** are assets held by a central bank or other monetary authority, usually in various reserve currencies and used to back its liabilities, e.g. the local currency issued, and the various bank reserves deposited with the central bank by the government or by financial institutions.

- The foreign exchange reserves of India comprise of three elements:
  (i)   Gold,
  (ii)   Special Drawing Rights (SDR),
  (iii) Foreign Currency Assets (FCA).

Gold

- It accounts for only 5% of our foreign exchange assets.

Special Drawing Rights (SDR)

- An international type of monetary reserve currency, created by International Monetary Fund (IMF) in 1969 which operates as a supplement to the existing reserves of member countries.
- It is also known as **"paper gold"**, created in response to concerns about the limitations of gold and dollars as the sole means of settling international accounts, SDRs are designed to augment international liquidity by supplementing the standard reserve currencies.
- Its value is based on a *basket of five* key international currencies and SDRs can be exchanged for freely usable currencies. The basket of five international currencies includes *US dollar*, euro, *Chinese yuan*, *Japanese yen* and *British pound*.

Foreign Currency Assets (FCAs)

- Foreign currency assets include foreign exchange reserves less gold holdings, special drawing rights and India's reserve position in the IMF.

Foreign Exchange Management

- Foreign exchange management (FEM) can be managed in three possible ways: Fixed currency rates, floating currency rates and managed exchange rates.

Fixed Exchange rates

- Fixed rates are currency values which are tied to a precious metal such as gold, or anchored to another currency, like the US Dollar. This method was brought by the International Monetary Fund (IMF).
- The IMF system involved the US$ as the anchor for the system with the US$ given a specific value in terms of gold, and other currencies were then given a value in terms of the US$, such as £1 = $2.40. India was part of this regime too and in 1948, 1$ was equal to ₹ 3.30.
- However, the system collapsed in 1971 for a variety of reasons, including the build up of US debts abroad as a result of the need to fund the war in Vietnam, inflation in the USA and growing doubts about the stability of the US$.

Floating Exchange Rates

- Under a floating system, a currency can rise or fall due to changes in demand or supply of currencies on the foreign exchange market.
- The advantages of floating exchange rates are flexibility and automatic adjustment in case of balance of trade disequilibrium.

Managed Exchange Rates

- This is a combination of fixed and floating rates. In today's economic situation, almost all countries follow this system of exchange rate determination. The governments usually let the market determine the exchange rates but intervene whenever needed.

Reserve Tranche Position

- Each member of the IMF is assigned a quota, part of which is payable in SDRs or Specified usable currencies and part in the member's own currency.
- The difference between a member's quota and the IMF's holdings of its currency is a country's Reserve Tranche position (RTP).

INDIA'S FOREIGN TRADE

History of Foreign Trade in India

- Historically, India ran a trade surplus for centuries together through export of spices, handicrafts, textiles, etc. No restrictions on imports or exports were officially maintained.
- Before India got independence, import of goods from great Britain received official encouragement through Imperial preferences.
- Statutorily, it was the Sea Customs Act, 1878 that provided the basis for implementing the official bias in favour of imports from Britain.

- The Government of India Act, 1935 granted Central government the exclusive legislative powers to regulate import of goods into India and export of goods from India. However, this power was used when the Imports and Exports (Control) Act, 1947 was enacted.

- The initial life of the Imports and Exports (Control) Act, 1947 was three years but it was extended from time to time till 1971.

- To protect industries from influx of imported goods the government issued the Imports (Control) Order 1955 allowing most of the imports only against an import licence.

- In 1976 many changes were made to the Imports and Exports (Control) Act, 1947.

- Beginning mid-1991, the Government of India introduced a series of reforms to liberalise and globalise the Indian economy.

- The Import policies prior to 1992 contained an Open General Licence under which specific goods could be imported and exported by specific categories of importers and exporters subject to fulfilment of certain conditions.

- In 1992, the policy was amended to open general licence and allow imports and exports of all goods without a licence, except those specifically mentioned in a small negative list.

- In 1950s, India's share in the world trade was 1.78% which was decline to 0.59% in 1990 and remained low for many years. India's share in world trade is currently around 2% (2015) and our country has set for itself the ambitious target of gaining 3.5% of world trade by 2020.

- India has been pursuing a policy of market diversification directing her export promotion efforts at Asia and ASEAN, Latin America and Africa through Focus Market Initiatives and bilateral trade agreements.

BALANCE OF PAYMENTS (BOP)

Introduction

- Balance of payments (BOP) is statistical statement of all transactions made between one particular country and all other countries during a specified period of time. BOP compares the dollar difference of the amount of exports and imports, including all financial exports and imports.

- *A negative balance of payments* means that more money is flowing out of the country than coming in. The balance of *payment* is maintained by Central Bank of India, i.e. **Reserve Bank of India (RBI)**.

- Balance of payments may be used as an indicator of economic and political stability. For example, if a country has a consistently positive BOP, this could mean that there is significant foreign investment within that country. It may also mean that the country does not export much of its currency.

- BOP indicates trade balance, foreign investments and investment by foreigners. Even a negative BOP does not signify unfavourable climate for the economy. It is unfavourable only if the economy lacks the means to fill the gap created by negative BOP.

Balance of trade and balance of payment

- Balance of trade takes into account only those transactions arising out of exports and imports (the visible items). It does not consider the exchange of services rendered such as shipping. Balance of payment takes into account the exchange of both visible and invisible items.

- Hence, the balance of payments represents a better picture of a country's economic transactions with the rest of the world than the Balance of trade.

Structure of Balance of Payments

Accounts

A balance of payments statement is a summary of a nation's total economic transaction undertaken on international account. It is usually composed of three sectors:

1. Current account,
2. Capital account,
3. Reserve account balance.

Current Account

This account is the summary of all international trade transactions of the domestic country in one year. It records the following 3 items:

(i) **Visible items of trade**

- The balance of exports and imports of goods is called the balance of visible trade, e.g. Tea, Coffee, etc.

(ii) **Invisible Trade**

- The balance of exports and imports of services is called the balance of invisible trade. The invisible are divided into three categories: (a) **Services-** insurance, travel, transportation, miscellaneous (like communication, construction, financial, software, etc.), (b) **Income**, and (c) **Transfers** (grants, gifts, remittances, etc.).

(iii) **Unilateral transfers**

- Unilateral transfers are receipts which residents of a country make without getting anything in return, e.g. gifts, etc.

Capital Account

- This account is the summary of foreign capital transactions. **On the credit side** of this account receipt of foreign exchange due to Foreign Direct Investment (FDI), Foreign Capital Investment (FCI) and Foreign Borrowing (FB) is recorded.
- **On the debit side** of capital account payment of foreign exchange due to Direct Investment Abroad (DIA), Portfolio Investment Abroad (PIA) and Foreign Lending (FL) is recorded.
- While India made the rupee fully convertible under current account, it was felt that the economy was not yet ready for capital account convertibility (CAC).

Reserve Account Balance

- This is the adjusting account in balance of payment. It makes an adjustment between current account balance and capital account balance.
- If the deficit in the current account is followed by surplus in capital account than the excess foreign exchange is diverted into capital account to current account so that deficit in the current account is eliminated.
- The remaining surplus in the capital account is transferred to the Reserve account and recorded on the credit of reserve account. Therefore both Current Account and Capital Account is always balanced.
- The Reserve Account is also the indicator of *Forex Reserves of the country*. If surplus in the Capital Account is more than deficit in the Current Account, there is net increase in the Forex Reserves of the country at the end of the year.
- On the other hand if deficit in the current account is more than surplus in the Capital Account then there is net decrease in Foreign Reserves of the country at the end of the year.

Balance of Payment (BOP) Crisis

- If international reserves of a country are not enough to balance a combined deficit in current and capital account on a sustained basis, then the phenomenon is called a *BOP crisis*.

- It can be tackled by exporting more or by limiting imports through tariffs, quotas, etc.
- Contractionary fiscal and monetary policies can also tackle the crisis through lower import demand with fall in average income levels.
- Another short term solution is currency devaluation which encourages exports and discourages costlier imports.

India's Balance of Payment

- The international **Balance of Payments (BOP)** of a country reflects its economic strengths and weaknesses. A typical problem of the developing countries is that of a chronic BOP deficit, India being no exception.
- Our country has been facing BOP disequilibrium right since independence, culminating into a disaster in 1990-91, the year of the acute BOP crisis. India then had foreign exchange reserve of mere **1 billion dollar**, barely sufficient to finance a month's import bill. The country was on the verge of **defaulting**.
- This crisis led to the massive changes in the country's economic policy, popularly known as the **Structural Adjustment Program or New Economic Policy (NEP)** regime, focusing on liberalization and globalization of the economy.

Trends & Problems Of India's Bop – 1949-50 To 1999-2000.

- The disequilibrium in India's BOP has been caused by both internal as well as external factors. The need for development of such a big nation with a huge population is one of the main causes for the recurring BOP problem.
- The BOP is always under pressure and had huge deficits due to high imports of food grains and capital goods, the heavy external borrowings and its payment and poor exports.

- India faced a major BOP crisis in the early 1990s. We had to borrow from IMF to be able to sustain the economy. This loan came with a number of conditions. The following are some of the conditions that came with the medium term loan given by IMF to India for restructuring of the economy:
  - Government expenditure to be cut by 10% per annum,
  - Devaluation of rupee by 22%,
  - Excise duty to be increased by 20%,
  - Custom duty to be cut drastically from the peak of 130% to 30%.

Protectionist Policies

- The main objective of the Second Five Year Plan (1956-57 to 1960-61) was to attain self reliance through industrialization. Self reliance was to be achieved through import substitution.
- For this basic industries had to be set up which required import of capital goods. Exports were expected to automatically take-off with industrialization.
- All focus was on import substitution, with gross neglect of exports. Such inward looking protectionist policies did result in some self-reliance in the consumer goods industries, but the capital goods industries remained mostly import intensive.
- The high degree of protection to Indian industries led to inefficiency and poor quality products due to lack of competition. The high cost of production further eroded our competitive strength.
- Rising petroleum products demand, the two oil shocks, harvest failure, all put severe strain on the economy. The BOP situation remained weak throughout the 1980s, till it reached the crisis situation in 1990-91, when India was on the verge of defaulting due to heavy debt burden and constantly widening trade deficit.

External Debt

- India had to resort to large scale foreign borrowings for its developmental efforts in the field of basic social and industrial infrastructure. The country's resources were very much limited due to low per capita income and savings

- The situation worsened because Government of India resorted to heavy foreign borrowings to correct the BOP situation in the short run out of panicky. By the Seventh Five Year Plan, the debt service obligations rose sharply because of harder average terms of external debt, involving commercial borrowing, repayments to the IMF and a fall in concessional aid flow.

Export Promotion

Although by the Sixth Five Year Plan we had done away with the need of food grain imports and some crude oil was being produced domestically, BOP position was still not comfortable due to low exports. The need for export promotion was felt during the 1960s. The Third Five Year Plan introduced certain export promotion policies like cash compensatory schemes, tax exemptions, duty drawbacks, Rupee devaluation, etc. However our exports remained discouraging. Indian exports depended largely on world trade situation. We were mainly primary product exporters, the price of which fluctuated heavily with fluctuations in world market demand.

- Primary products exporting countries have an unfavorable term of trade. The earnings from primary product exports were low and unstable.
- Secondly, the quality of Indian products was not up to the world standards due to which we could not sustain markets.
- Third, only residue products were mainly exported. The fact that export earnings also contribute to economic development was overlooked. Cumbersome procedures for license, etc. served as disincentives for exporters. Domestic inflation further reduced the competitiveness of India's export.

Exchange Rate

- The instability of the exchange value of the rupee was another problem. The constant devaluations (to promote exports) raised the amount of external debt. The value of rupee was managed by the central bank (fixed exchange rate).
- The gap between official and market exchange rate created problems for the exporters and importers. The strict foreign exchange controls also encouraged hawala trade.
- India followed a strongly inward looking policy, laying stress on import substitution. Ideally, imports should be financed by export earnings. But because there was export pessimism, the deficit was financed either by the invisible earnings or by foreign aid or depletion of valuable foreign exchange reserve. Much import constraint to check trade deficit was also not possible because India's imports were mainly '*maintenance imports*'.
- On one hand import reduction was not possible and on the other exports suffered due to the recession in the 1980s.

  India's BOP was thus beset with several problems. The process of liberalization began from the mid 1980s. Restriction on certain imports were removed, particularly those which were used as inputs for export production. But by then the situation was already bad and all the mismanagement ultimately led to the 1990-91 BOP crisis.

Foreign Trade Policy 2015-20

Aiming to nearly double India's exports of goods and services to $900 billion by 2020, the government has announced several incentives in the five-year Foreign Trade Policy for exporters and units in the Special Economic Zones (SEZ). Unveiling the first trade policy of the NDA government,

Commerce Minister Nirmala Sitharaman said the FTP (2015-20) will introduce *Merchandise Exports from India Scheme* (MEIS) and *Services Exports from India Scheme (SEIS)* to boost outward shipments. The new policy aims at boosting India's exports and it is believed that PM Narendra Modi's pet projects, '*Make in India*' and '*Digital India*' will be integrated with the new Foreign Trade Policy.

Trade Policy (2015-20) Key Features

- India to be made a significant participant in world trade by 2020.
- Merchandize exports from India (MEIS) to promote specific services for specific Markets Foreign Trade Policy.
- FTP would reduce export obligations by 25% and give boost to domestic manufacturing.
- FTP 2015-20 introduces two new schemes, namely **"Merchandise Exports from India Scheme (MEIS)" and "Services Exports from India Scheme (SEIS)".** The 'Services Exports from India Scheme' (SEIS) is for increasing exports of notified services. These schemes (MEIS and SEIS) replace multiple schemes earlier in place, each with different conditions for eligibility and usage. Incentives (MEIS and SEIS) to be available for SEZs also e-Commerce of handicrafts, handlooms, books, etc. eligible for benefits of MEIS. FTP benefits from both MEIS and SEIS will be extended to units located in SEZs.
- Agricultural and village industry products to be supported across the globe at rates of 3% and 5% under MEIS.
- Higher level of support to be provided to processed and packaged agricultural and food items under MEIS.
- Industrial products to be supported in major markets at rates ranging from 2% to 3%.
- Served from India Scheme (SFIS) will be replaced with Service Export from India Scheme (SEIS).

- Branding campaigns planned to promote exports in sectors where India has traditional strength.
- SEIS shall apply to 'Service Providers located in India' instead of 'Indian Service Providers'.
- The criteria for export performance for recognition of status holder have been changed from Rupees to US dollar earnings.
- Manufacturers who are also status holders will be enabled to self-certify their manufactured goods as originating from India.
- Reduced Export Obligation (EO) to (75%) for domestic procurement under EPCG scheme.
- Online procedure to upload digitally signed document by Chartered Accountant/ Company Secretary/Cost Accountant to be developed.
- Inter-ministerial consultations to be held online for issue of various licences.
- No need to repeatedly submit physical copies of documents available on Exporter Importer Profile.
- Export obligation period for export items related to defence, military store, aerospace and nuclear energy to be 24 months instead of 18 months.
- Calicut Airport, Kerala and Arakonam ICDS, Tamil Nadu notified as registered ports for import and export; Vishakhapatnam and Bhimavarm added as Towns of Export Excellence.
- Certificate from independent chartered engineer for redemption of EPCG authorisation no longer required.

Special Economic Zone (Sez)

- Special Economic Zone (SEZ) is a specifically delineated duty-free enclave that has economic laws different from a country's typical economic laws, usually the goal is to increase foreign investments.
- India was one of the first in Asia to recognise the effectiveness of the

Export processing Zone (*EPZ*) model in promoting exports, with Asia's **first EPZ set up in *Kandla* in *1965*.** With a view to attract larger foreign investments in India, the *Special Economic Zones* (*SEZs*) Policy was announced in April 2000.

- Today, there are approximately 3,000 SEZs operating in 120 countries which account for over US $ 600 billion in exports and about 50 million jobs.
- As a major step forward meant to invoke confidence in investors and signal the government's commitment to a stable SEZ policy regime, a comprehensive Special Economic Zones Act, 2005 was passed by the Parliament in May 2005. It received Presidential assent on the 23rd of June 2005. This Act came into force w.e.f. February 10, 2006.

The main objectives of the SEZ Act

- Generation of additional economic activity.
- Promotion of exports of goods and services.
- Promotion of investment from domestic and foreign sources.
- Creation of employment opportunities.
- Development of infrastructure facilities.

The salient features of SEZs Act

- Exemption from customs duty, excise duty, etc. on import/domestic procurement of goods for the development, operation and maintenance of SEZs and the units therein.
- 100% income tax exemption for 5 years, 50% for the next 5 years and 50% of ploughed back export profits for 5 years thereafter for SEZs units.
- Exemption from capital gains on transfer of an undertaking from an urban area of SEZs.
- 100% income tax exemption to SEZ developers for a block of 10 years in 15 years.

- Exemption from dividend distribution tax to SEZ developers.
- 100% income tax exemption for 5 years and 50% for next five years for off shore Banking units located in SEZ.
- Exemption to SEZ developer and units from Minimum Alternate Tax.
- CST exemption to SEZ developer and units on inter-state purchase of goods.
- Constitution of an authority for each SEZ with a view to providing greater administrative, financial and functional autonomy to these zones.
- Establishment of designated courts and a single enforcement agency to ensure speedy trial and investigation of offences committed in SEZs.
- Encouragement to State Governments to liberalise State laws and delegate their powers to the Development Commissioners to the SEZs to facilitate *single window clearance*.

Export Oriented Units, Export processing Zone and Special Economic Zone Schemes

- The Government has liberalised the scheme for export-oriented units and export processing zones. Agriculture, horticulture, poultry, fisheries and dairying have been included in export-oriented units.
- Export processing zone units have also been allowed to export through trading and star trading houses and can have equipments on lease. These units have been allowed *cent per cent* participation in foreign equities.

1. Export Processing Zones

- Before getting converted into Special Economic Zones (SEZs), these Export Processing Zones (EPZs) were playing important role in promoting exports of the country. These zones were created to develop such an environment in the economy which may provide capability of facing international competition.

- The Export Processing Zone (EPZs) set up as enclaves, separated from the Domestic Tariff Area by fiscal barriers, were intended to provide a competitive duty free environment for export production.

- All the *8 EPZs, located at Kandla and Surat* (Gujarat), Santa Cruz (Maharshtra), Cochin (Kerala), Chennai (Tamil Nadu), Vishakhapatnam (Andhra Pradesh), Faeta (West Bengal) and Noida (U.P) have been converted into Special Economic Zones.

2. Export-Oriented Units

- Since 1981, the Government introduced a complementary plan of EPZ (Now converted into SEZ) scheme for promoting export units (making export of their cent per cent production. Under this scheme the Government provides various incentives to increase the production capacity of these units so as to increase exports of the country.

3. Export Houses, Trading Houses and Star Trading Houses

- To increase the marketable efficiency of exporters, the Government introduced the concept of export houses, trading houses and star trading houses.

- Since April 1, 1994 a new category named **Golden Super Star Trading Houses** was added by the Government which has the highest average annual foreign exchange earnings. On March 31, 2003 there were 4 Golden Super Star Trading House working in the country.

4. Export Promotion Industrial Parks (EPIP)

- A Centrally-sponsored 'Export Promotion Industrial Park (EPIP)' scheme was introduced in August 1994 with a view to involving the state governments in the creation of infrastructure facilities for export oriented production. It provides for 75% (limited to 10 crore) grant to state government towards creation of such facilities.

- The Central Government has so far approved 25 proposals for establishments of EPIPs in the states of Punjab, Haryana, Himachal Pradesh, Rajasthan, Karnataka, Kerala, Maharashtra, Tamil Nadu, Andhra Pradesh, U.P., Gujarat, Bihar, J&K, Assam, M.P., West Bengal, Odisha, Meghalaya, Manipur, Nagaland, Mizoram and Tripura.

- At present, the number of formally approved SEZs is 523, notified is 352 and operational is 196. The total number of units approved in SEZs is 4,102. A total investment of ₹ 3,48,983.22 crores has been done till 2015. Moreover, till now 15,04,597 persons have received employment through SEZs.

FDI

- Foreign direct investment (FDI) is an investment in a business by an investor from another country for which the foreign investor has control over the company purchased. The *Organisation of Economic Co-operation and Development (OECD)* defines control as owning 10% or more of the business. Businesses that make foreign direct investment are after called *Multinational Corporations* (*MNCs*) or *Multinational Enterprises (MNEs)*.

- A MNE may create a new foreign enterprise by making a direct investment, which is called a *greenfield investment*.

- A MNE may make a direct investment by the acquisition of a foreign firm, which is called an *acquisition* or *prownfield investment* .

Advantages FDI

1. Economic Development Stimulation.
2. Easy International Trade.
3. Employment and Economic Boost.
4. Development of human capital Resources.
5. Tax incentives.
6. Resource Transfer.
7. Reduced disparity between revenues and costs.
8. Increased productivity.
9. Increment in income.

Disadvantages of FDI

1. Hindrances to domestic Investment.
2. Risk from political changes.
3. Negative influence on exchange rates.
4. Higher costs.
5. Economic non-viability.
6. Expropriation.
7. Modern-day Economic colonialism.

- FDI, being a non-debt capital flow, is a leading source of external financing, especially for the developing economies. It not only brings in capital and technical know-how but also increases the competitiveness of the economy.

- The current phase of FDI policy is characterized by negative listing, permitting FDI freely except in a few sectors indicated through a negative list. Under the current policy regime, there are three broad entry options for foreign direct investors.

1. In some sectors, FDI is not permitted (*negative list*);
2. In another small category of sectors, foreign investment is permitted only till a specified level of foreign equity *participation, and*

3. The third category, comprising all the other sectors, is where foreign investment up to 100 % *of equity participation is allowed.* The third category has two subsets –
   a. one consisting of sectors where automatic approval is granted for FDI (often foreign equity participation less than 100 %), and
   b. the other consisting of sectors where prior approval from the Foreign Investment Approval Board (FIPB) is required.

- FDI policy changes increasingly reflect the requirements of industry and are based on stakeholder's consultation. Upfront listing of negative sectors has helped focus on reform areas, which are reflected in buoyant FDI inflows.

FDI Routes and Sector wise FDI Limits

- Many changes have been made to the Foreign Direct Investment (FDI) policy in the last few years. Further, FDI is also allowed through two different routes namely, Automatic and the Government route.

- The erstwhile Foreign Investment Promotion Board (FIPB) has been phased out recently. In the automatic route, foreign entities do not need the prior approval of the government to invest. However, they have to inform the RBI about the amount of investment within a stipulated time period.

- In the government route, any investment can be made only after the prior approval of the government. Various other conditions as defined in the consolidated FDI policy are applicable to various sectors. In specific sectors, the FDI is prohibited.

Sector wise FDI Limits

Sector	FDI Limit	Entry Route & Remarks
Agriculture & Animal Husbandry • Floriculture, Horticulture, Apiculture and Cultivation of Vegetables & Mushrooms under controlled conditions • Development and Production of seeds and planting material • Animal Husbandry(including breeding of dogs), Pisciculture, Aquaculture • Services related to agro and allied sectors	100%	Automatic
Plantation Sector • Tea sector including tea plantations • Coffee plantations • Rubber plantations • Cardamom plantations • Palm oil tree plantations • Olive oil tree plantations	100%	Automatic
Mining Mining and Exploration of metal and non-metal ores including diamond, gold, silver and precious ores but excluding titanium bearing minerals and its ores	100%	Automatic
Mining (Coal & Lignite)	100%	Automatic
Mining Mining and mineral separation of titanium bearing minerals and ores, its value addition and integrated activities	100%	Government
Petroleum & Natural Gas Exploration activities of oil and natural gas fields, infrastructure related to marketing of petroleum products and natural gas, marketing of natural gas and petroleum products etc	100%	Automatic
Petroleum & Natural Gas Petroleum refining by the Public Sector Undertakings (PSU), without any disinvestment or dilution of domestic equity in the existing PSUs.	49%	Automatic

Sector	FDI Limit	Entry Route & Remarks
Defence Manufacturing	100%	**Automatic up to 49% Above 49% under Government routein cases resulting in access to modern technology in the country**
Broadcasting • Teleports(setting up of up-linking HUBs/ Teleports) • Direct to Home (DTH) • Cable Networks (Multi System operators (MSOs) operating at National or State or District level and undertaking upgradation of networks towards digitalization and addressability • Mobile TV • Head end-in-the Sky Broadcasting Service(HITS)	100%	**Automatic**
Broadcasting Cable Networks (Other MSOs not undertaking up gradation of networks towards digitalization and addressability and Local Cable Operators (LCOs))	100%	**Automatic**
Broadcasting Content Services • Terrestrial Broadcasting FM(FM Radio) • Up-linking of 'News & Current Affairs' TV Channels	49%	**Government**
Up-linking of Non-'News & Current Affairs' TV Channels/ Down-linking of TV Channels	100%	**Automatic**
Print Media • Publishing of newspaper and periodicals dealing with news and current affairs • Publication of Indian editions of foreign magazines dealing with news and current affairs	26%	**Government**
Publishing/printing of scientific and technical magazines/specialty journals/ periodicals, subject to compliance with the legal framework as applicable and guidelines issued in this regard from time to time by Ministry of Information and Broadcasting.	100%	**Government**

Sector	FDI Limit	Entry Route & Remarks
Publication of facsimile edition of foreign newspapers	100%	Government
Civil Aviation – Airports Green Field Projects & Existing Projects	100%	**Automatic**
Civil Aviation – Air Transport Services • Scheduled Air Transport Service/ Domestic Scheduled Passenger Airline • Regional Air Transport Service (Foreign Airlines are barred from Investing in Air India)	100%	**Automatic up to 49% Above 49% under Government route 100% Automatic for NRIs**
Civil Aviation • Non-Scheduled Air Transport Service • Helicopter services/seaplane services requiring DGCA approval • Ground Handling Services subject to sectoral regulations and security clearance • Maintenance and Repair organizations; flying training institutes; and technical training institutions	100%	**Automatic**
Construction Development: Townships, Housing, Built-up Infrastructure	100%	**Automatic**
Industrial Parks (new & existing)	100%	**Automatic**
Satellites- establishment and operation, subject to the sectoral guidelines of Department of Space/ISRO	100%	**Government**
Private Security Agencies	74%	**Automatic up to 49% Above 49% & up to 74% under Government route**
Telecom Services	100%	**Automatic up to 49% Above 49% under Government route**
Cash & Carry Wholesale Trading	100%	**Automatic**

Sector	FDI Limit	Entry Route & Remarks
E-commerce activities (e-commerce entities would engage only in Business to Business (B2B) e-commerce and not in Business to Consumer (B2C) e-commerce.)	100%	Automatic
Single Brand retail trading Local sourcing norms will be relaxed up to three years and a relaxed sourcing regime for another five years for entities undertaking Single Brand Retail Trading of products having 'state-of-art' and 'cutting edge' technology.	100%	**Automatic up to 49%** **Above 49% under Government route**
Multi Brand Retail Trading	51%	Government
Duty Free Shops	100%	Automatic
Railway Infrastructure Construction, operation and maintenance of the following • Suburban corridor projects through PPP • High speed train projects • Dedicated freight lines • Rolling stock including train sets, and locomotives/coaches manufacturing and maintenance facilities • Railway Electrification • Signaling systems • Freight terminals • Passenger terminals • Infrastructure in industrial park pertaining to railway line/sidings including electrified railway lines and connectivities to main railway line • Mass Rapid Transport Systems.	100%	Automatic
Asset Reconstruction Companies	100%	Automatic
Banking- Private Sector	74%	**Automatic up to 49%** **Above 49% & up to 74% under Government route**
Banking- Public Sector	20%	Government
Credit Information Companies (CIC)	100%	Automatic

Sector	FDI Limit	Entry Route & Remarks
Infrastructure Company in the Securities Market	49%	Automatic
Insurance • Insurance Company • Insurance Brokers • Third Party Administrators • Surveyors and Loss Assessors • Other Insurance Intermediaries	49%	Automatic
Pension Sector	49%	Automatic
Power Exchanges	49%	Automatic
White Label ATM Operations	100%	Automatic
Financial services activities regulated by RBI, SEBI, IRDA or any other regulator	100%	Automatic
Pharmaceuticals(Green Field)	100%	Automatic
Pharmaceuticals(Brown Field)	100%	Automatic up to 74% Above 74% under Government route
Food products manufactured or produced in India Trading, including through e-commerce, in respect of food products manufactured or produced in India.	100%	Government

EXERCISE

1. Which of the following organisation provides guarantee to exporters?
   (a) EXIM Bank
   (b) Export Loan Guarantee Corporation
   (c) RBI
   (d) Commerce Ministry
2. Which of the following does not form part of current account of Balance of Payments?
   (a) Export and import of goods
   (b) Export and import of services
   (c) Income receipts and payments
   (d) Capital receipts and payments
3. Which institution is known as 'soft loan window' of World Bank?
   (a) IFC
   (b) IDA
   (c) IMF
   (d) Indian Development Forum
4. Global capital-flows to developing countries increased significantly during the nineties. In view of the East Asian financial crisis and Latin American experience, which type of inflow is good for the host country?
   (a) Commerical loans
   (b) Foreign Direct Investment
   (c) Foreign Portfolio Investment
   (d) External Commercial Borrowings
5. The earnings of India from diamond export is quite high. Which one of the following factors has contributed to it?
   (a) pre-independene stock-piling of diamonds in the country which are now exported
   (b) large production of industrial diamonds in the country
   (c) expertise available for cutting and polishing of imported diamonds which are then exported
   (d) as in the past, India produces huge quantity of gem diamonds which are exported

6. Which one of the following modes of privatization is the most comprehensive and complete?
   (a) introduction of private capital in public sector
   (b) contracting out management of public enterprises to the private sector
   (c) transferring ownership and management to the workers
   (d) transferring ownership and management to the private sector
7. Which one of the following types of borrowings from the IMF has the softest servicing conditions?
   (a) Second tranche loan
   (b) SAF
   (c) ESAF
   (d) Oil facility
8. Which unit of valuation is known as 'paper gold'?
   (a) Eurodollar   (b) Petrodollar
   (c) SDR   (d) GDR
9. Which of the following is not one of the features of the Special Economic Zones (SEZ) being set up for promoting exports ?
   (a) The SEZ area will be treated as foreign territory for trade operations, duties and tariff.
   (b) No licence is required for import into the zone.
   (c) Foreign workers will be allowed free entry without visa restrictions.
   (d) There will be no routine examination by customs authorities of import/export cargo.
10. Which of the following is considered lending for promotion of exports?
    (a) Packing Credit
    (b) Overdraft
    (c) Cash Credit Account
    (d) Bill Discounting

11. For National Manufacturing and Investment Zones (NMIZ), Special Economic Zone (SEZ) and EOUs (Exports-Oriented Units), which of the following statement is true?
    (a) NMIZs and EOUs will be located within SEZs
    (b) SEZs and EOUs will be located within NMIZs.
    (c) NMIZs are independent of SEZs and EOUs.
    (d) NMIZs and SEZs will be competitors in nature

12. Both Foreign Direct Investment (FDI) and Foreign Institutional Investor (FII) are related to investment in a country. Which one of the following statements best represents an important difference between the two ?
    (a) FII helps bring better management skills and technology, while FDI only brings in capital.
    (b) FII helps in increasing capital availability in general, while FDI only targets specific sectors.
    (c) FDI flows only into the secondary market while FII targets primary market
    (d) FII is considered to be more stable than FDI.

13. A great deal of Foreign Direct Investment (FDI) to India comes from Mauritius than from many major and mature economies like UK and France. Why?
    (a) India has preference for certain countries as regards receiving FDI
    (b) India has double taxation avoidance agreement with Mauritius
    (c) Most citizens of Mauritius have ethnic identity with India and so they feel secure to invest in India
    (d) Impending dangers of global climatic change prompt Mauritius to make huge investments in India

14. TRIPS (Trade Related aspects of Intellectual Property Rights) agreements is administered by

(a) United Nations Conference on Trade and Development (UNCTAD)
(b) United Nations Organization (UNO)
(c) World Trade Organization (WTO)
(d) World Bank (WB)

15. Which is the role of the International Monetary Fund (IMF)?
    (a) To implement and advance global trade agreements
    (b) To settle industrial and trade disputes between members
    (c) To help poorer countries with their economic development
    (d) To maintain international financial stability in global financial markets

16. Which of the following is not an argument for protectionism?
    (a) To protect infant industries
    (b) To increase the level of imports
    (c) To protect strategic industries
    (d) To improve the balance of payments

17. Dumping in the context of international trade refers to :
    (a) Exporting goods at prices below the cost of production
    (b) Exporting goods of inferior quality
    (c) Exporting goods only to re-import them at cheaper rates
    (d) Exporting goods without paying appropriate taxes in the receiving country

18. Foreign Direct Investment involves:
    (a) A speculator trying to make a profit by buying company shares on a foreign stock exchange.
    (b) A UK energy company buying territory abroad where it expects to find oil reserves.
    (c) A tourist purchasing foreign currency to spend on a holiday abroad.
    (d) A company signing an agreement with a wholesaler to distribute its products in foreign markets.

19. Many a times we read about Hot Money in newspapers. Which among the following options rightly describes hot money?

   (a) Hot money is useful and generally durable and is good for the country in all weathers

   (b) Hot money is dangerous and volatile and leaves the country in bad weather conditions

   (c) Hot money is good and adds to the development of the country & it comes from exports of services

   (d) Hot money is bad & useless as its arises from unusual activities like casinos, gambling, horse races, speculations etc.

20. A systematic record of all economic transactions completed between residents of a country and the rest of the world in a year is known as..?

   (a) Net Capital Flow

   (b) Balance of Payment

   (c) Balance of Trade

   (d) Absolute Flow

21. Asian Financial Crisis of 1997 started from which of the following countries?

   (a) Myanmar   (b) Thailand

   (c) Cambodia   (d) Malaysia

22. Many a times we read in the newspapers that when Foreign Capital is allowed to enter the country freely, it can affect the economy adversely. Which among the following is a correct reason for the above assumption?

   (a) It affects the balance of payments of the country by adversely affecting the Current Account

   (b) It poses risks to the value of the country's currency as well as management of local liquidity

   (c) The foreign capital earns profit in the country which is repatriated

   (d) The Balance of Trade of the country is badly affected by Foreign Capital Inflows

23. TANKAN is revision of the Industry Classification of the Short-term Economic Survey of Enterprises (usually quarterly) is used in following country ?

   (a) Japan   (b) South Korea

   (c) China   (d) All of them

24. Which among the following is the most important source region of NRI remittances to India ?

   (a) North America (b) Europe

   (c) Middle East   (d) Asia Pacific

   (e) South America

25. In context with the two way trade of India with different regions, which among the following region is India's largest trade partner?

   (a) EU Region   (b) Gulf Region

   (c) North America (d) Latin America

26. Which among the following will be a debit entry in India's balance of payments?

   (a) Imports of goods by India.

   (b) Income of Indian investments abroad.

   (c) Receipts of transfer payments.

   (d) Exports of services by India.

27. Which among the following countries is currently the biggest supplier of crude oil to India?

   (a) Iran   (b) Saudi Arabia

   (c) UAE   (d) Nigeria

28. IMF can grant loan to ___________?

   (a) Any sovereign country of the World

   (b) Any sovereign country of the World and Public Sector companies backed by Sovereign guarantee

   (c) Any Member country of IMF

   (d) Any Member country of IMF and Public Sector Companies backed by Sovereign guarantee of Member Country '

29. In which among the following forms, the Special Drawing Rights (SDR) are kept as currency of International Monetary Fund?

   (a) Paper Currency

   (b) Gold

   (c) Book Keeping Entry

   (d) A combination of all of three

30. A new term Lourdes Treatment and Resuscitation Option (LTRO) was making news in context with which among the following?

   (a) World Bank
   (b) International Monetary Fund
   (c) European Central Bank
   (d) Federal Reserve Bank of America

31. Christine Lagarde is the head of which among the following international agencies / bodies?
   (a) Asian Development Bank
   (b) Non-alignment Movement
   (c) International Atomic Energy Agency
   (d) International Monetary Fund

32. AoA in context with World Trade Organization is ___?
   (a) Article of Association
   (b) Agreement on Agriculture
   (c) Agreement on Association
   (d) Administration of Agriculture

33. Which of the following were the aims behind the setting up of the World Trade Organization (WTO)?
   1. promotion of free trade and resource flows across countries
   2. protection of intellectual property rights
   3. managing balanced trade between different countries
   4. promotion of trade between the former East Bloc countries and the Western World
   (a) 1, 2, 3 and 4   (b) 1 and 2
   (c) 2 and 3   (d) 1 and 4

34. Which of the following statement is not correct in relation to International Monetary Fund?
   1. India is a founder member of the IMF.
   2. IMF conducts regular review of India's economic status under Article IV.
   3. India's quota in the IMF is more than 2 per cent
   4. Finance Minister is ex-officio Governor of the IMF.
   (a) 1 and 4   (b) 3 only
   (c) 1 only   (d) 2 and 4

35. Consider the following:
   1. Balance of trade
   2. Net factor income
   3. Net transfer payments
   Which among the above make the part of the "Capital Account"?
   (a) Only 1   (b) 1 & 2
   (c) 2 & 3   (d) 1, 2 & 3

36. Which of the following constitute the Capital Account ?
   1. Foreign Loan.
   2. Foreign Direct Investment.
   3. Private Remittances.
   4. Portfolio Investment.
   Select the correct answer using the codes given below
   (a) 2 & 4   (b) 1 & 3
   (c) 1 & 2   (d) 1, 2 & 4

37. Which sentence is correct regarding foreign exchange?
   I. Foreign exchange reserves in India comprises of 6 elements.
   II. Foreign exchange management can be done in three possible ways: Fixed currency regime, floating currency regime and managed exchange rates.
   III. Silver is an element of foreign exchange reserve
   (a) I & II   (b) Only II
   (c) Only III   (d) None of the above

38. Which statement is correct regarding Current account?
   I. Those transactions arising out of exports and imports (the visible items)
   II. It is a statistical statement of all transactions made between one particular country and all other countries during a specified period of time
   III. This account is the summary of all international trade transactions of the domestic country in one year
   (a) I & II   (b) Only I
   (c) II & III   (d) Only III

39. What was the main reason of introducing trade reforms in 1991?
    I. Make exports competitive
    II. Unshackle foreign trade from the clutches of a control regime
    III. Allow import of most goods using only tariff as a restraint
    (a) I & II
    (b) Only II
    (c) Only III
    (d) All the above

40. Which points are correct regarding SEZ act?
    I. Exemption to SEZ developer and units from Minimum Alternate Tax.
    II. Constitution of an authority for each SEZ with a view to providing greater administrative, financial and functional autonomy to these zones.
    III. Establishment of designated courts and a single enforcement agency to ensure speedy trial and investigation of offences committed in SEZs.
    (a) I & II
    (b) Only II
    (c) Only III
    (d) All the above

41. Which statement is correct regarding Export houses?
    I. To increases the marketable efficiency of exporters, the Government introduced the concept of export houses, trading houses and star trading houses.
    II. Those registered exporters who have shown good export performances over past few years have been given the status of export houses, and trading houses.
    III. Units having such classification are required to achieve the prescribed average export performance level and earning of foreign exchange.
    (a) Only III
    (b) I & II
    (c) II & III
    (d) All the above

42. Foreign exchange reserves of India comprise of which elements?
    I. Gold
    II. Special Drawing Rights (SDR)
    III. Foreign currency assets
    IV. Reserve Tranche Position (RTP) in the IMF
    (a) I & II
    (b) II & III
    (c) Only III
    (d) All the above

43. Which one of the following groups of items is included in India's foreign-exchange reserves?
    (a) Foreign-currency assets, Special Drawing Rights (SDRs) and loans from foreign countries
    (b) Foreign-currency assets, gold holdings of the RBI and SDRs
    (c) Foreign-currency assets, loans from the World Bank and SDRs
    (d) Foreign-currency assets, gold holdings of the RBI and loans from the World Bank

44. Balance of payments of a country includes:
    (a) Current account
    (b) Moentary account
    (c) Capital account
    (d) All of above

45. India's foreign trade policy be best described as
    (a) Free trade
    (b) Controlled free trade
    (c) Laizzez faire
    (d) None of these

46. Which of the following is not seen as an advantage of the gold standard?
    (a) For a given stock of gold, a rise in real money supply can only occur if the price level declines.
    (b) Inflation is unlikely to emerge as a significant problem.
    (c) No country needs to serve at the centre of this fixed exchange rate system.
    (d) The monetary mechanism has credibility.

47. Special drawing rights are not...
    (a) a credit line allocated by the IMF to member countries according to each country's quota.
    (b) backed by US dollars.
    (c) the IMF's unit of account.
    (d) a basket of four currencies.

48. Special Drawing Rights (SDR) facility is available at:

(a) International Monetary Fund (IMF)

(b) International Bank for Reconstruction and Development (IBRD)/World Bank

(c) International Development Association (IDA)

(d) Organisation of Economic Co-operation and Development (OEC

49. Free Trade Policy refers to a policy where there is :

(a) absent of tariff

(b) restriction on the movement of goods

(c) existence of anti-dumping policy

(d) encouragement for balances growth

50. Specially developed economic zones in India where some of the economic laws and restrictions of the land are relaxed with the purpose of giving incentives to investors, are commonly known as :

(a) Special Economic Zone

(b) Preferential Zones

(c) Industrial Parks

(d) Economic corridors

51. 'Trade Gap' means :

(a) Gap between total imports and total exports

(b) Gap between total GDP and total consumption

(c) Gap between available liquidity and expected demand

(d) Gap between budgeted revenue collection and actual collection of the same

52. In which one of the following places was Asia's first Export Processing Zone (EPZ) set up ?

(a) Kandla   (b) Cochin

(c) Surat   (d) Santa Cruz

HINTS & EXPLANATIONS

1. (b)

2. (d) Capital receipts and payments do not form part of current account of Balance of Payment.

3. (b) 4. (b) 5. (c) 6. (d) 7 (c)

8. (c) 9. (c) 10. (a) 11. (b) 12. (b)

13. (b) India has comprehensive Double Taxation Avoidance Agreements (DTAA) with 23 countries. This means that there are agreed rates of tax and jurisdiction on specified types of income arising in a country to a tax resident of another country. Under the Income Tax Act 1961 of India, there are two specific provisions, Section 90 and Section 91, which provide specific relief to taxpayers to save them from DTAA. Section 90 is for taxpayers who have paid the tax in a country with which India has signed DTAA, while Section 91 provides relief to taxpayers who have paid tax to a country with which India has not signed a DTAA. Thus, India gives relief to both kind of taxpayers Mauritius by itself is a low tax counting.

14. (c) 15. (d)

16. (b) Protectionism would reduce the level of imports into an economy.

17. (a)

18. (b) The energy company will own and control the territory and the oil reserves it contains.

19. (b) 20. (b) 21. (b) 22. (b) 23. (a)

24. (a) 25. (b) 26. (b) 27. (b) 28. (c)

29. (c)

30. (c) European Central Bank European Central Bank's (ECB's) LTRO — Long Term Refinancing Operation is more appropriately termed the Lourdes Treatment and Resuscitation Option.

31. (d)

32. (b) Different agreements of WTO are:
    1. Multi-Fiber agreement (MFA).
    2. Agreement on agriculture (AOA).
    3. Trade related investment measures (TRIMS).
    4. Trade related intellectual property right (TRIPS).
    5. General agreement on trade and services (GATS)

33. (b) 34. (b) 35. (d) 36. (d)

37. (b) Foreign exchange management can be done in three possible ways: Fixed currency regime, floating currency regima and managed exchange rates. The foreign exchange reserves of India comprise of four elements.

38. (d) This account is the summary of all international trade transactions of the domestic country in one year

39. (d) The major thrust was to make exports competitive, unshackle foreign trade from the clutches of a control regime and allow import of most goods using only tariff as a restraint.

40. (d)

41. (d) To increases the marketable efficiency of exporters, the Government introduced the concept of export houses, trading houses and star trading houses. Those registered exporters who have shown good export performances over past few years have been given the status of export houses, and trading houses. Units having such classification are required to achieve the prescribed average export performance level and earning of foreign exchange. These units are provided some special facilities and benefits by the Government.

42. (d)

43. (b) Foreign-exchange reserves (also called forex reserves or FX reserves) is money or other assets held by a central bank or other monetary authority so that it can pay if need be its liabilities, such as the currency issued by the central bank, as well as the various bank reserves deposited with the central bank by the government and other financial institutions.

44. (d) The balance of payments, also known as balance of international payments and abbreviated BoP, of a country is the record of all economic transactions between the residents of the country and the rest of the world in a particular period (over a quarter of a year or more commonly over a year).

45. (b)

46. (a) A gold standard is a monetary system in which the standard economic unit of account is based on a fixed quantity of gold.

47. (b) Special Drawing Rights (currency code XDR also abbreviated SDR) are supplementary foreign exchange reserve assets defined and maintained by the International Monetary Fund (IMF).

48. (a)

49. (a) Free trade is a policy followed by some international markets in which countries' governments do not restrict imports from, or exports to, other countries.

50. (a) A special economic zone (SEZ) is an area in which business and trade laws differ from the rest of the country.

51. (a) Exp. Trade gap is a situation in which a country buys more from other countries than it sells to other countries

52. (a) India set up its first EPZ in Kandla in 1965. EPZs were envisaged to boost our slackening exports and route in foreign exchange.

INSURANCE

INTRODUCTION OF INSURANCE

Everyone is vulnerable to risk at one point of Life. In the ancient time, it was the contribution made by others which made-up for the loss. In the present day, the life has become increasingly complex, and to meet for the losses Insurance business offers a remedy. Insurance helps an individual or family to cover the losses faced due to adversity at certain moments of life.

For commerce and industry, Insurances plays a vital role. All business lives in uncertainty and risks. This may include plant, machinery, raw materials, premises etc. Such goods are susceptible to damage and be destroyed by flood or fire. At such eventualities, some of the incidents can be avoided, whilst, others are unavoidable. Insurances protect these unavoidable risks.

Types of Insurance

The major types of Insurances are listed below:

a. Life Insurance
b. Health Insurance
c. Motor Insurance
d. Property Insurance
e. Travel Insurance
f. Group insurance

Life Insurance

It is a financial cover for a contingency which is linked with human life, namely death, disability, accident, retirement etc. Human life is subject to unprecedented risks of death and disability, which may arise due to natural and accidental causes. When human life is lost or a person is disabled permanently or temporarily, there is loss of income to the household.

Health Insurance:

It relates to the type of insurance, which covers medical expenses. Health Insurance policy is a contract between the insurer and the individual/group, wherein the insurer agrees to provide specified health insurance cover to a particular "premium', which is subject to terms and conditions specified in the insurance policy.

Motor Insurance

This insurance renders protection to the owner of the vehicle, when:

Damages to the vehicle

On pays to Third Party Liability, which are determined by law against the owner of the vehicle

The Third Party Insurance is a statutory requirement. The Vehicle owner is legally liable for any injury or damage on third party life or property, which is caused with the use of the vehicle in a public place. As per the Motor Vehicles Act, 1988, driving a motor vehicle without insurance in a public place is a punishable offence.

Property Insurance:

It means the insurance of buildings, stocks, machinery etc, against potential Fire and Allied Perils, Burglary Risks and so forth. Marine Cargo Insurance insures for those goods in transit through sea, air railways, roads or courier. While Marine Hull Insurance, insures hulls of ships and boats. Aviation Insurance Policy has specialized policy to secure insurance for planes and helicopters. This has broad coverage of General Insurance, and the cover is as per the type of property the sought to be covered.

Travel Insurance

This Insurance offers protection while travelling. One should consider, whether the policies cover domestic travel or overseas travel or both in travel insurance. It protects you and the family against travel related accidents, unexpected medical expenditure during travel, baggage loss, passport loss etc. It also includes interruption or delays in the flights for baggage delay.

Group Insurance

Group Insurance is provided by insurance companies to certain classes of individuals, with benefits of insurance coverage at moderate cost.

Types of Insurance Policies:

There are usually five types of insurance policies. They are as follows:

(a). Whole life

(b). Term Insurance

(c). Life annuity

(d). Endowment

(e). Investment – linked

(a) Whole life Insurance:

Life insurance policy that normally covers an individual until his or her death, unless it lapses due to non-payment of premium or is cancelled, builds up a cash value (called cash surrender value),pays a fixed death benefit. The insured or policyholder may obtain a loan (called policy loan) against the accumulated cash value. Also, called as continuous premium whole life insurance, ordinary life insurance, permanent life insurance, or straight life insurance.

(b) Term Insurance:

Term insurance is the most traditional life insurance policy wherein the insured gets death benefit if any contingency happens within the policy term. The insured is, however, not entitled to receive any survival benefit if he outlives the policy term.

Term insurance policies are available in the range of 10-30 years term. These plans are relatively cheaper than endowment policies, money back policies and ULIPs. The benefits in a term insurance policy can be availed only in the event of the death of the insured.

Simplest and usually the cheapest type of life insurance that stays in effect for a specified period or until a certain age of the insured. It pays the face amount of the policy in case the insured dies within the coverage period (term) but pays nothing if he or she outlives it. Also, (unlike in whole life insurance) whereas it premium cost is low in younger years, it generally increases rapidly with the age of the insured. Term life insurance is used commonly as an insurance cover for a loan repayment or post-death liabilities such as estate taxes.

(c) Life Annuity:

Life annuity is an insurance product in which the annuitant receives a series of future payments for his/her lifetime after retirement. The annuitant has to pay a predetermined payment or a series of regular payments till he/she is working.

Life annuity provides financial support to the retires and helps them maintain a similar standard of living as before retirement. In a life annuity the uncertainty of the annuitant's life span is shifted to the insurer.

Series of payments at fixed intervals, guaranteed for a fixed number of years or the lifetime of one or more individuals. Similar to a pension, the money is paid out of an investment contract under which the annuitant(s) deposit certain sums (in a lump sum or in instalments) with an annuity guarantor (usually a government agency or an insurance firm). The amount paid back includes principal and interest, either or both of which (depending on the local regulations) may be tax exempt. An annuity is not an insurance policy but a tax-shelter.

(d) Endowment Insurance:

Life insurance policy that pays the assured sum (face amount) on a fixed date or upon the death of the insured, whichever comes earlier. Endowment policies carry premiums higher than those on conventional whole life policies and term insurance, but are useful in meeting special lump sum needs such as college expenses or for buying a retirement home. Also called endowment life policy or endowment policy.

(e) Health Insurance and Medical insurance

Health insurance is a type of insurance coverage that pays for medical and surgical expenses that are incurred by the insured. Health insurance can either reimburse the insured for expenses incurred from illness or injury or pay the care provider directly. Health insurance is often included in employer benefit packages as a means of enticing quality employees.

HISTORY OF LIFE INSURANCE

Let's know the history of Life Insurance chronologically.

Ancient System of Insurance:

Insurance, in India, has well-entrenched history since centuries. The concept for "*Yogakshema*" in the Rig-Veda literally means *'prosperity, well being and security of people'*. Other reference of insurances can be found in the Manusmrithi, Dharmashastra and Arthashastra. The understating of the term, however, is referred to as the 'pooling of resources', which could be supplied when succumbed to natural calamities, namely fire, floods, famine and epidemics. The modern day meaning of Insurance has derived its essence from these references.

Insurance of Modern Day:

In the year 1818, the modern day form of Life Insurance came of India. It was realized with the establishment of Oriental Life Insurance Company in Calcutta. The company however had its fall in 1834. The Madras Equitable had commenced in 1829, to transact life Insurance business in the Madras Presidency. Subsequently, in the year 1870 the enactment of the British Insurance Act and added in the later decades of 19th Century were the Bombay Mutual (1871), and the Empire of India (1874) saw its light in the Bombay Residency.

- The significant aspects of this period consisted in the following:

- The established Insurance companies aided solely to the needs of the Europeans community and neglected the interest of the Indian Natives.

- Initiatives by renowned Babu Mauttyal Seal sought to bring changes, but the Indian lives were treated as sub-standard, and the burdened with high premium charges.

- A new shade of light came in with first Indian Life Insurance Company, namely Bombay Mutual Life Assurance Society in the year 1870. It reduced the premium charges to normal rates. Nationalism inspired one Bharat Insurance Company (1896) to be for the people. There was flowering of many insurance companies during the Swadeshi Movement [1905-1907], namely, The United India in Madras, National Indian and National Insurance in Calcutta and Co-operative Assurance at Lahore.

- Major transformation came about in 1914, with Government of India initiative to publish returns for Insurance Companies in the Indian Soil. The first statutory measure initiated with the view to regulate life business come in 1912 through Indian Life Assurance Companies Act.

- Thereafter in the year 1928, Indian Insurance Companies Act granted the Government to collect statistical information, of both Indian and foreign insurers on both life and non-life business transacted in the Indian soil. A greater emphasis in the protection of the interest of insurance public came into force in the 1938, with the consolidation of the earlier legislation, and was amended to form the Insurance Act of 1938. It has ample of provision for effective control over the activities of the insurers in India.

Life Insurance of India: It's Birth

Life insurance in India was nationalized on 19th January, 1956. By this time, there were about 154 Indian Insurance companies, about 16 non-Indian companies, and over 75 provident were in operation.

The insurance was accomplished in twofold ways:

First, by means of ordinance, the management of the companies was take over

Secondly, the ownership was taken over by means of comprehensive bill

In the 90s LIC had an all-pervading monopoly, but with its avenues open for the private sector, the dominance has reduced to a considerable extent.

HISTORY OF GENERAL INSURANCE

The beginning of General Insurance dates back to the time of Industrial Revolution, 17th century in the west. It has its legacy during the British Occupation. The roots are traced back to the establishment of Triton Insurance Company Ltd. by the British at Kolkata in the year 1850. The establishment of Indian Mercantile Insurance Ltd. in the year 1907 gave birth to General insurance, as it was the first company to transact it.

The other developments of General Insurance are as follows:

The transformation came in the year 1957, with a wing of the Insurance Association of India. The code of conduct for ensuring fair conduct and sound business practices across Non-Life/ General Insurance sector was framed by the General Insurance Council.

The Insurance Act was amended in the year 1968, to regulate investments and set minimum solvency margins. In the same year, the Tariff Advisory Committee was established.

The General Insurance Business (Nationalization) Act passed in 1972 nationalized the general insurance business, with its effect from 1st January. About 107 insurers were grouped into 4 companies, namely, the National Insurance Company Ltd., the New, India Assurance Company Ltd., the Oriental, Insurance Company Ltd and the United India & Insurance Company Ltd. After its incorporation, the General Insurance Corporation of India commended its business on 1st January 1973.

Malhotra Committee:

The Recommendations of Malhotra Committee changed the nature of General Insurance in India. The government in the year 1993 set up a committee under the chairmanship of RN Malhotra, former Governor of RBI, with the view to propose recommendations for reforms in the insurance sector.

The Malhotra Committee had the following recommendations to make:

The submitted report in 1994, paved a way for private sector to be permitted to enter the insurance industry.

The committee stated that the foreign companies be allowed through MOU (Memorandum of Understanding) to enter by floating Indian Companies, preferably a joint venture with Indian Partners.

Effect of Malhotra Committee: Birth of IRDA

In accordance of the recommendation of Malhotra committee, the Indian Parliament passed the Insurance Regulatory and Development Authority (IRDA) Act in 1999.

The key feature of this act consists in:

- It opened the Indian Insurance market by the invitation of application for registration proposal in August 2000.

- 26% participation was allowed for Foreign Companies to enter into the Indian Insurance sector. The power to frame the regulations was granted under section 114A of the Insurance Act, 1938.

- IRDA has framed numerous regulations since 2000, pertaining to the insurance business for the protection of Indian Policyholders' interest, which includes the registration of Life & Non-Life (General) Insurance Companies.

KNOW ABOUT IRDAI

Insurance Regulatory and Development Authority (IRDAI) directs the Indian insurance industry to secure the interests of the policyholders, and works for the systematic expansion of the industry.

Background of IRDAI:

- Year 1991: Government of India commenced the economic reforms programme and financial sector reforms

- Year 1993: Committee on Reforms in the Insurance Sector, headed by Mr. R. N. Malhotra, (Retired Governor, RBI) set up to suggest reforms

- Year 1994: The Malhotra Committee proposed certain reforms after having studied the Insurance sector and hearing out the stakeholders

The Birth of IRDAI

IRDA (Insurance Regulatory and Development Authority) set up as autonomous body under the **IRDA Act, 1999.** It had the following features:

Mission of IRDAI: To protect the interests of policy holders, to regulate, promote and ensure orderly growth of the insurance industry and for matters connected therewith or incidental thereto.

Activities of IRDAI: Frames regulations for insurance industry in terms as of Section 114A of the Insurance Act 1938

Since the year 2000 has enrolled new insurance companies in accordance with regulations.

IRDAI Monitors insurance sector activities for healthy development of the industry and protection of policyholders' interests

IRDAI: Functions and Duties

The powers, duties and functions of IRDA are recorded under Section 14 of the IRDA Act, 1999. Here are the functions and duties:

- Registering and regulating insurance companies

- Protecting policyholders' interests

- Licensing and establishing norms for insurance intermediaries

- Promoting professional organisations in insurance

- Regulating and overseeing premium rates and terms of non-life insurance covers

- Specifying financial reporting norms of insurance companies

- Regulating investment of policyholders' funds by insurance companies
- Ensuring the maintenance of solvency margin by insurance companies
- Ensuring insurance coverage in rural areas and of vulnerable sections of society

INDIAN INSURANCE MARKET

Of the 53 Insurance companies in Indian Insurance industry, 24 are life insurance business and 29 are non-life insurers. Life Insurance Corporation (LIC) is the only public sector company, among the life insurers.

And out of 29 non-life insurance companies, 6 companies are known to be public sector insurers, but two are specialized insurers, namely Agriculture Insurance Company Ltd for Crop Insurance and, Export Credit Guarantee Corporation of India, which is meant for Credit Insurance.

There are 5 registered private sector insurers which deal on policies exclusively related to Health, Personal Accident and Travel insurance segments. These 5 private sector insurers include Star Health and Allied Insurance Company Ltd, Max Bupa Health Insurance Company Ltd, Religare Health Insurance Company Ltd, Apollo Munich Health Insurance Company Ltd, and Cigna TTK Health Insurance Company Ltd.

General Insurance Corporation of India is the only national re-insurer, apart from the 53 Insurance companies. In the Indian Insurance market, there are other stakeholders which include, approved insurance agents, Web- Aggregators, Brokers, licensed Corporate Agents, Common Service Centres, Surveyors, and Third Party Administrators Servicing Health Insurance claims.

The Insurance Laws (Amendment) Act, 2015 provides for the improvement of the Foreign Investment Cap for an Indian Insurance Company, from 26% to an Explicitly Composite Limit of 49% with the intention to protect Indian Ownership and Control.

ULIP (UNIT LINKED INSURANCE PLAN): INTRODUCTION

Unit Linked Insurance Plan (ULIP) is a life insurance product, which grants cover on risk for the policyholder, with investment options to invest in numerous qualified investments, namely, stocks, bonds, and other mutual funds.

The investments made in ULIP are subjected to ample risks associated with capital markets. The investment risk in the investment portfolio is shouldered by the policyholder. The policyholder should make the investment, only after considering the risk involved and the needs.

UPLIP: Fees, Charges & Deductions/ Types

The charge structure by different insurers differs considerably. The fees, charges, and deductions are subject to rise over time to time.

There are different types of fees and charges. Listed below are the different types of charges and fees.

Premium Allocation Charge:

Under this charge, a percentage of the premium appropriated before allocating the united under the policy. It includes the initial and renewal expenses exclusive of the commission expenses.

Mortality Charges:

Mortality charges are the charges to provide the cost for insurance coverage under the plan. It depends upon a list of factors, like the age, the state of health, amount of coverage, etc.

Fund Management Fees:

These are fees charged for the management for the fund(s) and are deducted prior to arriving at the NAV (Net Asset Value).

Policy/ Administration charges:

These charges are made for the administration of the plan and are levied by the cancellation of units. The charges could either be flat till the end of the policy term or change at a pre-determined rate.

Fund Switching Charge:

This is applicable with subsequent switches, which exceeds the number of funds switches allowed each year without any charge.

Service Tax Deductions:

A risk portion of the premium is deducted prior to the allotment of the units as the applicable service tax. It is utilized for purchasing units.

PUBLIC SECTOR INSURANCE COMPANIES

Listed below are the Public Sector Insurance Companies:

- Life Insurance Corporation of India (LIC)
- General Insurance Corporation of India (GIC)
- The new India assurance company limited (NIACL)
- United India insurance company limited (UIIC)
- The oriental insurance company limited (OICL)
- National insurance company limited (NICL)
- Agriculture insurance company of India limited (AICIL)

Life Insurance Corporation of India

Head office - Mumbai

Chairman - Shri S. K. Roy

The Parliament of India enacted the Life Insurance Corporation Act on the 19th of June 1956, and the Life Insurance Corporation of Indian was established on 1st September, 1956, with the objective of spreading life insurance much more widely and in particular to the rural areas with a view to reach all insurable persons in the country, providing them adequate financial cover at a reasonable cost.

General Insurance Corporation

Head office - Mumbai

Chairman - Mrs. Alice G. Vaidyan

General Insurance Corporation of India (GIC Re) was approved as 'Indian Reinsurer' on 3rd November, 2000. As an Indian reinsurer GIC has been giving reinsurance support to four public sector & other private general insurance companies.

The New India Assurance Company Limited

Head office- Mumbai

Chairman - G. Srinivasan

It is the "largest general insurance company of India on the basis of gross premium collection inclusive of foreign operations". It was founded by Sir Dorabji Tata in 1919, and was nationalised in 1973.

National Insurance Company Limited (NICL)

Head office- Kolkata

Chairman - Shri A.V. Girija Kumar

It is a state owned general insurance company in India. The company was established in 1906 and nationalised in 1972. It's portfolio consists of a multitude of general insurance policies, offered to a wide arena of clients encompassing different sectors of the economy.[3] Apart from being leading insurance provider in India, NICL also serves Nepal.

United India Insurance Company Limited

Head office - Chennai

Chairman - Milind Kharat

Under Department of Financial Services, Ministry of Finance (India), is a public sector General Insurance Company of India and one of the top General Insurers in Asia. With the net worth of Rs 5407 crores and profit of Rs 528 crores, the company has collected gross premium of Rs 9709 crores as of in the financial year 2013-14. The company has more than seven decades of experience in Non-life Insurance business and was formed to its present form by the merger of 22 companies, consequent to the nationalisation of General Insurance companies in India.

Oriental Insurance Company Limited

Head office - New Delhi

Chairman - Dr. A.K.Saxena

It was established on September 12, 1947 in the then Bombay. It was a completely owned subsidiary of Oriental Government Security Life Assurance Company Ltd. It was created with the mandate of executing its parent body's general insurance operations.

GLOSSARY OF INSURANCE TERMS:

A.

Actuary- A professional who is trained in the mathematics of insurance and risk management, including the calculations of premiums, policy reserves and other values

Agent- The insurance company representative who sells policies on behalf of the insurer, or an independent agent represents more than one company; a captive agent represents only one company.

Applicant- Prospective policyholder; completes and signs the insurance application.

Assets- The items on a balance sheet showing the value of property owned.

Assuming Company- An insurance company that accepts the risk transferred from another insurance company in a reinsurance transaction.

B.

Billing Clerk- Person who is responsible for revenue billing

Broker- Represents the interests of the insured in searching for insurance coverage at the lowest cost and highest benefit to the insured. The broker may also be an agent of the insurer for purposes of policy collection and delivery of the policy.

C.

Catastrophic- Event An event that causes loss to many people at once. Also called catastrophe, several examples are tornados, hurricanes and plane crashes.

Cede- To transfer to a reinsurer all or part of the insurance or reinsurance written by a ceding company.

Ceding Company- The company that transfers its risk to a reinsurer. Also called the Cedant.

Claim Adjuster- The person who investigates insurance claims for losses and recommends an effective settlement.

Claim Service Representative- Also called CSR; they are responsible for clerical completion of all claim files.

Clause- A section of an insurance policy dealing with various coverage, exclusions, duties of the insured, locations covered and conditions that terminate coverage.

Combined Ratio- The sum of the loss ratio and the expense ratio.

Commercial Lines- Insurance for

businesses, professionals and commercial establishments.

Compulsory- Mandatory or enforced.

Contract- Legally binding agreement between two parties who wish to exchange some sort of consideration (anything of value, e.g. money or goods).

Coverage- The insurance afforded under a contract of insurance.

D.

Declaration- Part of the insurance policy that identifies the named insured, policy period and

limit of insurance.

Deductible- The amount of money the policy holder must pay on a loss.

Direct Loss- A loss which is a direct consequence of a peril.

Disability Insurance- Covers wage loss for the disabled person.

E.

Earned Premiums- The portion of the premium for which protection has been provided. If an insured has an annual premium and makes monthly payments, each month the insurer earns 1/12th of the premium.

Endorsement- A written agreement attached to the insurance policy which alters the

provisions of the contract.

Exclusion- A provision in the insurance policy that indicates what is denied coverage.

Expense Ratio- The ratio of all operating expenses divided by the premiums written.

Exposure to Loss- The policyholder's possibility of loss

F.

Fire Insurance- The foundation of today's property insurance. Covers loss to property caused by a fire or lightning

Flood Insurance- Insurance to reimburse property owners from loss due to the peril of flood

Fortuitous Losses- Unintentional loss occurring by accident or chance

Frequency of Loss- Refers to the actual numbers or times the same or similar loss occurs.

Frequency-Severity Matrix- Matrix used to determine which type of risk treatment is appropriate for a risk.

G.

General Liability- Insurance to protect an owner or operator of a business from a wide range of liability exposures.

H.

Hazard- A condition that creates or increases the chance or severity of a loss due to a peril

Homeowners- Policy Insurance against property and liability perils to which a homeowner or renter is exposed.

I.

IBNR- Incurred but not reported losses. This is for losses which have occurred during a stated period, usually a calendar year, but have not yet been reported to the insurer.

Indemnification- Insurance principle which states that the insured, after a loss, should be restored in whole or in part by payment, repair or replacement by the insurer

Independent Adjuster- An adjuster hired by the insurer to investigate and settle claims on behalf of the insurance company.

Indirect Loss- A loss resulting from a peril but not caused directly by that peril.

Insurance- Economic device whereby the individual or business pays a cost (premium) in exchange for protection against financial loss. The agreement is a contract also known as an insurance policy.

Insured- The policy holder protected in case of a loss or claim.

Insurer- The party who pays for losses in an insurance arrangement.

L.

Law of Large Numbers- States that the larger the number of risks or exposures, the more closely the actual loss experience will approach the expected loss experience.

Legal Hazard- Characteristics of the legal system that increase the frequency or severity of losses.

Legislated- Determined by law.

Liability- The obligation of financial responsibility that may arise by negligence, contract or tort committed.

Liability Insurance- Protects the policyholder against a suit or claim for another's bodily injury and property damage.

Loss- An undesired and unplanned reduction of financial value.

Loss Control- The process of identifying and acting upon situations which may lead to losses.

Loss Ratio- A formula used by insurers to relate loss expenses to earned premiums.

Loss Reserve- Money set aside to pay losses.

M.

Marine Insurance- Covers loss or damage to ships, cargo or injuries to ship crew members

Moral Hazard- Dishonesty or character defects that increase the chance of loss

Morale Hazard- Carelessness or indifference to a loss because of the existence of insurance

N.

Negligence- Failure to use that degree of care which an ordinary person of reasonable prudence would use to protect others from harm.

P.

P&C- Property and Casualty Insurance.

Peril- A cause of loss.

Physical Hazard- A physical condition that increases the chance of loss

Policy- The written insurance contract that may include all clauses, riders and endorsements.

Policy Service Representative- Also called PSR; they are responsible for premium rating and issuing policy files.

Policyholder- The insured protected in case of a loss or claim.

Pooling- The method by which each member of an insurance pool shares in every risk written by other pool members.

Premium- The price of insurance protection, paid by the policyholder to the insurer.

Premium Auditor- Person that reviews charges to ensure that the premium paid is fair for the coverage furnished.

Private Insurance- Voluntary programs that are available from the government or private firms.

Proximate Cause- The immediate or actual cause of loss or damage.

Public Adjuster- Hired by the insured, an adjuster who operates independently from insurance companies to investigate and settle claims.

R.

Re-Inspector- Person who double-checks the work of the original adjuster.

Reserves- The funds an insurance company sets aside to pay for reported but outstanding claims.

Rider- An endorsement to an insurance policy that modifies its clauses and provisions, including or excluding certain conditions from coverage.

Risk- The uncertainty concerning the occurrence of a financial loss.

Risk Avoidance- Avoiding the risk altogether

Risk Control- Techniques used to control the frequency and magnitude of losses.

Risk Control Consultant- A person with expertise in risk management techniques that reduce the frequency and severity of losses.

Risk Management- The identification of loss exposures and treatments for those exposures.

Risk Retention- Retaining or bearing the risk.

Risk Transfer- Transferring the financial consequences of a loss to another party, such as an insurance company.

S.

Severity of Loss- Refers to the size or cost of the loss to the organization.

T.

Tort- An injury or wrong committed against an individual.

U.

Umbrella Policy- Insurance policy over and above a basic liability policy.

Underwriter- The professional responsible to assess the merits of each risk and decide a suitable premium for accepting all or part of the risk.

Underwriting- The process of scrutinizing a risk to determine whether or not to insure that risk.

Underwriting Assistant- Assists the underwriter. Also called underwriting technician or underwriting associate.

W.

Waiver- Relinquishment of a legal right to act.

Workers' Compensation- Benefits paid to an employee as a result of occupational injury.

Written Premiums- The total premiums on all policies written by an insurer during a specified period of time, regardless of what portions have been earned.

IMPORTANT ABBREVIATIONS RELATED TO INSURANCE INDUSTRY

A.

ARM – Associate in Risk Management

B.

BAP – Business Auto Policy

BOP – Business Owners Policy

BIFR- Board for Industrial and Financial Reconstruction

C.

CIC – Certified Insurance Counsellor

CISR – Certified Insurance Service Representative

CRISIL- Credit Rating Information Services of India Limited

D.

DSU – Delay in Start-Up Insurance

DOD – Date of Death

E.

EAP – Estimated Annual Premium

ETB – Engaged In Trade or Business

EEI- Electronic Equipment Insurance

F.

FMV – Air Market Value

FDA- Food and Drug Administration

FII- Foreign Institutional Investor

FDI- Foreign Direct Investment

G.

GAP – Guaranteed Auto Protection

GL – General Liability

GWP – Gross Written Premium

GIPSA- General Insurance Public Sector Association of India

GNP- Gross National Product

GBIC- Governing Body of Insurance Council

H.

HII – Health Insurance Institute

HLV – Human Life Value

I.

IPO- Initial Public Offer

IRDA- Insurance Regulatory and Development

IGMS- Integrated Grievance Management System

IBAI- Insurance Brokers Association of India

IIRM- Institute of Insurance and Risk Management

IIB- Insurance Information Bureau of India

L.

LOC – Letter Of Credit

LIC- Life Insurance Corporation

M.

M&D – Minimum and Deposit

MDO – Monthly Debit Ordinary Life Insurance

MPL – Maximum Possible Loss

MPP – Managed premium plan

N.

NSDL- National Security Depository Limited

NAV- Net Asset Value

NASSCOM- National Association of Software and Services

NDS- Negotiated Dealing System

NCLT- National Company Law Tribunal

O.

ORFS – Operational Risk Financing Securities

P.

PAP – Personal Auto Policy

PLI- Public Liability Insurance

R.

RAM – Reverse-Annuity Mortgage

S.

SPAP – Special Personal Auto Policy

SEZ- Special Economic Zone

SEBI- Securities and Exchange Board of India

T.

TDI – Trade Disruption Insurance

TERI – Targeted Enterprise Risk Insurance

TPA – Third-party administrator

TRIM- Trade Related Investment Measures

TPA - Third Party Administration

TRAI- Telecom Regulatory Authority of India

U.

UL – Umbrella Liability

ULIP- Unit Linked Insurance Plan

UHIS- Universal Health Insurance Scheme

Y.

YRT – Yearly Renewable Term

Employment State Insurance Scheme (ESIS)

ESIS (Employment State Insurance Scheme) is a multi-dimensional social security system which is designed to provide socio-economic protection to the worker population and their dependants covered under the scheme.

It offers full medical care to self and the dependants, which is admissible from the first day of insurable employment. More so, the insured persons are also entitled to a variety of other cash benefits in times of physical distress due to sickness, temporary or permanent disablement etc. This may result to the loss of earning capacity, the confinement in respect of insured women or dependants of insured persons who die in industrial accidents or because of employment injury or occupational hazard are entitled to a monthly pension called the dependants benefit.

SCHEMES RELATED TO INSURANCE (PMFBY, PMJJBY, PMSBY ETC.)

Pradhan Mantri Fasal Bima Yojana [PMFBY]

The majority of the rural population in India depends on Agriculture. On 13th January 2016, Prime Minister Shri Narendra Modi initiated this new scheme.

The features are as follows:

Uniform premium of only 2% to be paid by farmers for all Kharif crops and 1.5% for all Rabi crops. About 5% of the premium to be paid, for all annual commercial and horticultural crops.

- In PMFBY Premium rates to be paid by farmers are very low. The balance premium will be paid by the Government to provide full insured amount to the farmers against crop loss in any natural calamities.

- No upper limit on Government subsidy. The government bears the balance premium even if it is 90%.

- In PMFBY farmers will get a claim against full sum insured without any reduction, bringing changes to the previous provision of capping the premium rate which has low claims paid to the farmers.

- This scheme encouraged the use of technology to a great extent. The use of smart-phones, remote sensing drone & GPS technologies' ought to be used to capture and upload data for crop cutting, to reduce the delay in the process of claim payment.

Pradhan Mantri Suraksha Bima Yojana [PMSBY]

Following are the features of this Scheme:

- It is Indian Government's accidental Insurance cover, announced in 2015 budget.

- Provides personal accident insurance to the high-risk category, which includes mechanics, labourers, and truck drivers involving a lot of travel. PMSBY is the cheapest insurance cover. It covers also both partial and permanent disability cover.

- Available between the ages of 18-70 years, who should have a bank account. Excluding the service tax, Rs. 12 is the annual premium.

- Automatic debit from the bank account for the scheme holder is made for the premium amount. Amount of Rs. 2 Lakh is paid to the nominee, in case of subscribers' death, by accident or is fully disabled.

- Amount of Rs. 1 lakhs is paid if the holder meets with an accident and suffers partial permanent disability.

Pradhan Mantri Jeevan Jyoti Bima Yojana (PMJJBY)

The PMJJBY is offered to people in the age group of 18 to 50 years having a bank account who have given their approval to join/enable auto-debit.

Aaadhar would be the primary KYC for the

bank account. The life cover of Rs. 2 lakhs shall be for the one year period starting from 1st June to 31st May and will be renewable. Risk coverage under this scheme is for Rs. 2 Lakh in case of death of the insured, regardless of the reason.

The premium is Rs. 330 per annum is to be auto-debited in one instalment from the subscriber's bank account as per the option is given by him on or before 31st May of each annual coverage period under the subscribed scheme. The PMJJBY is provided by Life Insurance Corporation and all other approved life insurers who are willing to offer the product on similar terms with necessary approvals and tie up with banks for this purpose.

Insurance Current Affairs, Insurance Ombudsman, Banccassurance, Current insurance schemes.

INSURANCE CURRENT AFFAIRS

Pradhan Mantri Fasal Bima Yojana [PMFBY] revised its operational guidelines to make it more effective. Here are the operational guidelines:

- 12% interest to be paid to farmers by the insurance companies for the delay in settlement claims beyond two months as prescribed to be the cut-off date.

- 12% interest to be paid by the state government for delay in the release of state share of subsidy beyond 3 months of the prescribed cut-off date submission by insurance companies.

- Standard Operating Procedure for evaluation of insurance companies initiated, which removes them if found ineffective in the services.

- The new operational guidelines include Perennial Horticultural crops on pilot basis under the ambit of PMFBY.

- Localised calamites like cloud burst and natural fire, included to the unseasonal and cyclonic rainfalls, landslide, hailstorms and inundation in the post harvest losses.

- Crop loss due to attack of wild animals on pilot basis are provided coverage under this scheme, to be borne by the concerned state government.

- Incorporates definition of major crops, unseasonal rainfall and the inundation for clarity and proper coverage.

- To avoid the duplication of beneficiaries, aadhaar number is mandatorily

- Insurance companies are given the target for enrolling 10% more non-loaned farmers than the previous corresponding seasons.

- A mandatorily expense of 0.5% of gross premium per company per season for publicity and awareness of the scheme is required.

- 50% of 80% total share of subsidy of corresponding season of previous year as subsidy is required to be released of upfront premium subsidy at the beginning of the season.

- Under these new operational guidelines, Balance Premium will be paid as a second instalment based on the specific approved business statistics on the portal for settlement of claims.

- The Final instalment will be paid after reconciliation of the entire coverage date on portal based on the final business statistics. These guidelines will reduce the delay in settling the claims of farmers to great extent.

Insurance Ombudsman

In view of providing a forum for resolving disputes and complaints of the aggrieved insured public or their legal heirs against the Insurance Companies, the Govt. of India, framed "Redressal Public Grievances Rules,1998", as per the power vested on it 114(1) of the Insurance Act, 1938. It aims at resolving complaints relating to the settlement of disputes with the Insurance Companies on the personal lines of Insurance, through cost effective, efficient and impartial manner.

Located in 12 cities, the rules apply to all Insurance companies operating in General Insurance business and Life Insurance business, in Public and Private Sectors.

Features of Insurance Ombudsman:

- Individuals aggrieved and has taken insurance policy on personal lines (deceased, the legal heir(s) under such policy) can approach Insurance Ombudsman.

- Representation should be made of the Insurance company & either an unsatisfactory reply should have been received or the representation should stand as un-replied for at least one month.

- Complaint must be lodged within 1 year of the events.

- Total relief sought must be within an amount of Rs.20 lakhs

- The grievance/ complaint should not currently be or have earlier been before any court or consumer Forum.

- There are no charges to be paid/no fees.

- Ex-gratia payment will be awarded, if the circumstance is considered fit.

- Various complaints can be addressed pertaining to repudiation of claims totally or partially, any disputes on the legal construction of the policies, delay in the settlement of claims, despites regarding premiums paid/ or payable and non-issue of insurance documents.

- Personal life of insurance, policy taken or given in an individual capacity, for instance life insurance, personal accident insurance, medical insurance, insurance of personal property of the individual like motor vehicle, household articles etc, can be raised.

Who can approach Ombudsman for complaint?

- If you have first approached the insurance company with complaint

- If not resolved,

- If not resolved to the satisfaction

- Not responded to it for 30 days

- The complaint pertains to any of the polices taken in the capacity as an individual,

- Value of the claim including the expense claimed should not be above Rs, 20 Lakhs

What the complaint is about?

- Any partial or total repudiation of claims by an insurer

- Any dispute about premium to be paid or payable as per the policy terms

- Disputes on the legal construction of the policies as far as it relates to the claims

- Delay in the settlement of claims

- Non-issue of insurance document to you, after you have paid your premium

- On the settlement process

Banccassurance:

It means selling of insurance products through the banks. The insurance companies along with the banks come up in a partnership, and the bank sells the insurance products of the tied insurance company's to its clients. This Bank Insurance Model is termed as Banccassurance.

1. 'Simply click' credit card scheme is launched by which of the following Banks? **[UPPCS PRE 2016]**

    (a) IDBI   (b) ICICI

    (c) B.O.B.   (d) S.B.I.

2. Which one of the following countries is the largest exporter of tea in the world? **[UPPCS PRE 2016]**

    (a) India   (b) China

    (c) Kenya   (d) Sri Lanka

3. Tatipaka Oil Refinery is located in the State of **[UPPCS PRE 2016]**

    (a) Assam   (b) Uttar Pradesh

    (c) Karnataka   (d) Andhra Pradesh

4. Which one of the following segments of population is not included in the scheme of Inclusive development? **[UPPCS PRE 2016]**

    (a) Marginal farmers

    (b) Landless agricultural labours.

    (c) Scheduled Castes/Scheduled Tribes

    (d) People living in semi-urban areas

5. What is the effect of deficit financing on economy? **[UPPCS PRE 2016]**

    (a) Reduction in taxes

    (b) Increase in wages

    (c) Increase in money supply

    (d) Decrease in money supply

6. 'e-Biz' refers to **[UPPCS PRE 2016]**

    (a) Electronic commerce

    (b) single window financial transactions

    (c) single window for business inquiries

    (d) single window for approach to government services

7. The committee which has recommended abolition of Tax Rebates under Section - 88 of the Income Tax Act of India, is **[UPPCS PRE 2016]**

    (a) Chelliah Committee

    (b) Kelkar Committee

    (c) Shome Committee

    (d) Rangrajan Committee

8. Which among the following is not a parameter for estimating Global Gender Gap Index of World Economic Forum? **[UPPCS PRE 2017]**

    (a) Health   (b) Education

    (c) Economy   (d) Leisure

9. What is meant by a Bullock – Capitalist **[UPPCS PRE 2017]**

    (a) Farmers who are poor

    (b) Farmers who arc rich.

    (c) Farmers who have some resources but are not rich.

    (d) Farmers who are big Zamindars.

10. Which bank has been established in China by BRICS countries? **[UPPCS PRE 2017]**

    (a) New Industrial Development Bank

    (b) New Agricultural Development Bank

    (c) New Development Bank

    (d) New Commercial Bank

11. SEZ India mobile app has been launched in January 2017 by **[UPPCS PRE 2017]**

    (a) Ministry of Labour and Employment.

    (b) Ministry of Finance

    (c) Ministry of Commerce and Industry

    (d) Ministry of Corporate Affairs.

12. With affect from 1 April, 2017 the minimum wage for unskilled labour in Uttar Pradesh has been fixed at
    [UPPCS PRE 2017]
    (a) ₹ 7000 per month
    (b) ₹ 7400 per month
    (c) ₹ 7800 per month
    (d) ₹ 8200 per month

13. Which among the following statements are true about 'Urja Ganga' project?
    [UPPCS PRE 2017]
    1. It is a gas pipe line project
    2. It was launched in October 2016
    3. It runs from Iran to India

    Choose the correct answer from the code given below :

    Codes :
    (a) Only 2 and 3 are correct
    (b) Only 1 and 2 are correct
    (c) Only 1 and 3 are correct
    (d) All 1, 2 and 3 are correct

14. Which among the following services is not provided under Integrated Child Development Services [ICDS] scheme?
    [UPPCS PRE 2017]
    (a) Supplementary feeding
    (b) Immunization
    (c) Distribution of free books and school dress to the children
    (d) Health and Nutrition Education to 3-6 year old children

15. As per the Economic Survey 2015 – 16, which one of the following has been constructed as the Chakravyuha Challenge of the Indian economy?
    [UPPCS PRE 2017]
    (a) Movement of Indian Economy from socialism to capitalism
    (b) Movement of Indian Economy from socialism with limited entry to marketism with exit
    (c) Movement of Indian Economy from socialism with limited entry to marketism without exit
    (d) Movement of Indian Economy from mixed economy to capitalism

16. What is India's rank in the 2017 Sustainable Development Goal Index?
    [UPPCS PRE 2017]
    (a) 116th   (b) 125th
    (c) 108th   (d) 95th

17. Which among the following is not included in the ten main themes of the Union budget for the financial years 2017-18?   **[UPPCS PRE 2017]**
    (a) Export performance
    (b) The poor and the underprivileged
    (c) Youth
    (d) Rural population

18. Which of the following is/are not the supply-side factor/s responsible for inflation?   **[MPPCS PRE 2018]**
    1. Increase in export
    2. Store
    3. Increase in credit creation
    4. Famine
    (a) Only a and b   (b) Only c and d
    (c) Only d   (d) Only c

19. Which of the following factors are not responsible for poverty?
    [MPPCS PRE 2018]
    1. Inflation
    2. Increase in Government expenditure
    3. Deficit Financing
    4. Short savings and Capital formation
    (a) Only a and c   (b) Only a, c and d
    (c) Only b and d   (d) Only b and c

20. "Absence of minimum income to get the minimum needs of life" is concerned with which of the following types of poverty?
    [MPPCS PRE 2018]
    (a) Absolute poverty
    (b) Relative poverty
    (c) Both the above
    (d) None of the above

21. Which of the following factors is/are concerned in the calculation of Green National Income [GNI]?
[MPPCS PRE 2018]
    1. National Income
    2. Depletion of Natural Resources
    3. Environmental Degradation
    (a) Only a and c   (b) Only a
    (c) Only a and b   (d) All of the above

22. The concept of Human Poverty Index [HPI] was introduced in the
[MPPCS PRE 2018]
    (a) Human Development Report, 1990
    (b) Human Development Report, 1997
    (c) Human Development Report, 2001
    (d) Human Development Report, 2014

23. The policy regarding Special Economic Zones (SEZ) was announced in
[UPPCS PRE 2018]
    (a) April, 2000   (b) April, 2001
    (c) April, 2002   (d) April, 2003

24. Which of the following is known as market clearing price?
(SSC Steno. 2017)
    (a) Equilibrium price
    (b) Disequilibrium price
    (c) Ceteris paribus
    (d) No option is correct

25. Which of the following is the not a small-scale industry in India?
(SSC Steno. 2017)
    (a) Sugar Industry
    (b) Cotton Industry
    (c) Petroleum Industry
    (d) Handloom Industry

26. What is GST?   **(SSC Steno. 2017)**
    (a) A direct tax   (b) An indirect tax
    (c) A corporate tax (d) A municipal tax

27. Which one of the following statement is True regarding rate of interest:
(SSC MTS 2017)
    (a) Rate of interest may be zero

    (b) Rate of interest increases with economic growth
    (c) Rate of interest can not be zero
    (d) Rate of interest cannot be determined

28. In an inflationary situation, which of the following statements is false for a country?   **(SSC MTS 2017)**
    (a) Cost of living rises
    (b) Profits rise faster than wages
    (c) Value of money falls
    (d) Country's export's become more competitive

29. Area which supports the economy and export trade of a sea port is called its:
(SSC MTS 2017)
    (a) economic zone (b) export basin
    (c) umland   (d) hinter land

30. The law of demand states that when :
(SSC MTS 2017)
    (a) income and price rises demand rises
    (b) price rises demand rises
    (c) price falls demand rises
    (d) income rises demand rises

31. The state with largest gap in male and female literacy is :   **(SSC MTS 2017)**
    (a) Rajasthan   (b) Kerala
    (c) Uttar Pradesh   (d) Madhya Pradesh

32. What was the main objective of the 5th Five Year Plan?(SSC Sub. Ins. 2017)
    (a) Removal of poverty and achievement of self-reliance
    (b) Faster, more inclusive and sustainable growth
    (c) Inclusive growth
    (d) None of these

33. Which of the following is a basic characteristic of 'Oligopoly'?
(SSC Sub. Ins. 2017)
    (a) Many sellers, many buyers
    (b) Few sellers, few buyers
    (c) Few sellers, many buyers
    (d) Many sellers, few buyers

34. Banking comes under which of the following sector?
    (SSC Sub. Ins. 2017)
    (a) Primary sector
    (b) Secondary sector
    (c) Tertiary sector
    (d) Both Secondary and Tertiary sectors

35. In which situation, wages and prices chase each other at a very quick speed? **(SSC Sub. Ins. 2017)**
    (a) Disinflation   (b) Reflation
    (c) Stagflation   (d) Hyper-inflation

36. What is the full form of FDI?
    (SSC Sub. Ins. 2017)
    (a) Foreign Direct Input
    (b) Foreign Direct Investment
    (c) Fiscal Direct Investment
    (d) Fiscal Direct Input

37. An increase of 1% per annum in the rate of growth of the money supply will increase inflation in the long run by __________. **(SSC CHSL 2017)**
    (a) Zero percent   (b) One percent
    (c) 0.5 percent   (d) More than one percent

38. 7 workers work in a printing press. Each gets paid 450 per day. The 8th worker demands 500 per day. If this worker is hired then all other workers must be paid 500. The marginal resource (labour) cost of the 8th worker is ______. **(SSC CHSL 2017)**
    (a) 50 (b)   850
    (c) 400   (d) 100

39. Which among the following is an example of micro – economic variable? **(SSC CGL 2017)**
    (a) National Income
    (b) Aggregate Supply
    (c) Employment
    (d) Consumer's Equilibrium

40. Which one of the following is not an instrument of credit control in India?
    (SSC CGL 2017)
    (a) Rationing of credit
    (b) DirectAction
    (c) Open Market operations
    (d) Variable cost reserve ratios

41. Which of the following is not true about a Demand Draft? **(SSC CGL 2017)**
    (a) It is a negotiable instrument.
    (b) It is a banker's cheque.
    (c) It may be dishonoured for lack of funds.
    (d) It is issued by a bank.

42. Who gave the 'General Equilibrium Theory'? **(SSC CGL 2017)**
    (a) J.M. Keynes   (b) Leon Walras
    (c) David Ricardo (d) Adam Smith

43. What is the accepted average Calorie requirement for rural area in India?
    (SSC CGL 2017)
    (a) 2100   (b) 2200
    (c) 2300   (d) 2400

44. Which one of the following is a component of Food Security System?
    (SSC CGL 2017)
    (a) Buffer stock
    (b) Minimum support price
    (c) Fair price shops
    (d) Mid day meals

45. Movement along the supply curve is known as______. **(SSC CGL 2017)**
    (a) Contraction of supply
    (b) Expansion of supply
    (c) Increase in supply
    (d) Expansion and contraction of supply

46. At which rate, Reserve Bank of India borrows money from commercial banks? **(SSC CGL 2017)**
    (a) Bank Rate
    (b) Repo Rate
    (c) Reverse Repo Rate
    (d) Statutory Liquidity Rate

47. A philosophy that the worker should share in industrial decisions is termed as **(SSC Sub. Ins. 2014)**

   (a) industrial democracy

   (b) worker sovereignty

   (c) industrial socialism

   (d) worker dictatorship

48. 'Investing opportunities model' was proposed by **(SSC Steno. 2016)**

   (a) Revenstein   (b) Davis

   (c) E.S. Lee   (d) S.A. Stouffer

49. The market system in which there are only two buyers facing a large number of sellers is called **(SSC Steno. 2016)**

   (a) monopsony   (b) duopsony

   (c) duopoly   (d) oligopoly

50. One of the following is NOT a component of foreign exchange reserves in India **(SSC Steno. 2016)**

   (a) Gold stock of RBI

   (b) SDR holdings of government

   (c) Foreign exchange assets of RBI

   (d) Foreign exchange assets of government

51. An indirect instrument of monetary policy is **(SSC Steno. 2016)**

   (a) Open market operations

   (b) Statutory liquidity ratio

   (c) Bank rate

   (d) Cash reserve ratio

52. Who fixes the REPO rate in India ? **(SSC Steno. 2016)**

   (a) WTO - World Trade Organization

   (b) SEBI - Securities and Exchange Board of India

   (c) RBI - Reserve Bank of India

   (d) IMF - International Monetary Fund

53. According to the law of diminishing marginal utility, as the amount of a good consumed increases, the marginal utility of that good tends to **[CDS 2018-1]**

   (a) improve

   (b) diminish

   (c) remain constant

   (d) first diminish and then improve

54. Consider the following statements about impact of tax: **[CDS 2018-1]**

  1. A tax is shifted forward to consumers if the demand is inelastic relative to supply.

  2. A tax is shifted backward to producers if the supply is relatively more inelastic than demand.

   Which of the statements given above is/are correct?

   (a) 1 only   (b) 2 only

   (c) Both 1 and 2   (d) Neither 1 nor 2

55. Which one of the following events is not correctly matched with the year in which it happened? **[CDS 2018-1]**

   (a) Inauguration of the SWIFT system of electronic interbank fund transfers worldwide—1985

   (b) Conclusion of the Uruguay Round of GATT—1994

   (c) Inauguration of the World Trade Organization—1995

   (d) Establishment of the first wholly electronic stock exchange (Nasdaq)—1971

56. Growth in production (in percent) of which one of the following core industries in India during the period 2015-2016 was negative? **[CDS 2018-1]**

   (a) Natural gas

   (b) Refinery products

   (c) Fertilizer

   (d) Coal

57. Which of the following statements about the India Post Payments Bank (IPPB) is/are correct? **[CDS 2018-1]**

  1. It has been incorporated as a Public Limited Company.

  2. It started its operation by establishing two pilot branches at Hyderabad and Varanasi.

   Select the correct answer using the code given below.

   (a) 1 only   (b) 2 only

   (c) Both 1 and 2   (d) Neither 1 nor 2

58. The Reserve Bank of India has recently constituted a high-level task force on Public Credit Registry (PCR) to suggest a road map for developing a transparent, comprehensive and near-real-time PCR for India. The task force is headed by **[CDS 2018-1]**

    (a) Sekar Karnam

    (b) Vishakha Mulye

    (c) Sriram Kalyanaraman

    (d) Y. M. Deosthalee

59. Which one of the following statements about Exchange-Traded Fund (ETF) is not correct? **[CDS 2018-1]**

    (a) It is a marketable security.

    (b) It experiences price changes throughout the day.

    (c) It typically has lower daily liquidity and higher fees than mutual fund shares.

    (d) An ETF does not have its net asset value calculated once at the end of every day.

60. Which one of the following is not an exclusive right of the concerned coastal nations over Exclusive Economic Zone (EEZ)? **[CDS 2018-1]**

    (a) Survey and exploitation of mineral resources of ocean deposits

    (b) Exploitation of marined water energy and marine organisms including fishing

    (c) Conservation and management of marine resources

    (d) Navigation of ships and laying down submarine cables

61. Who among the following scholars argued that "capital created underdevelopment not because it exploited the underdeveloped world, but because it did not exploit it enough"? **[CDS 2017-II]**

    (a) Bill Warren   (b) Paul Baran

    (c) Geoffrey Kay   (d) Lenin

62. Match List-I with List-II and select the correct answer using the code given below the Lists : **[CDS 2017-II]**

	List-I	List-II
	(Type of Deficit)	(Explanation)
A.	Fiscal Deficit	1. Total Expenditure– Revenue Receipts & Non-debt
B.	Revenue Deficit	2. Revenue Expenditure – Revenue Receipts
C.	Effective Revenue	3. Revenue Deficit –Grants for Deficit Creation of Capital Assets
D.	Primary Deficit	4. Fiscal Deficit – Interest Payments

Code :

	A	B	C	D
(a)	1	2	3	4
(b)	1	3	2	4
(c)	4	2	3	1
(d)	4	3	2	1

63. In India, the base year of the new GDP series has been shifted from 2004-05 to **[CDS 2017-II]**

    (a) 2007 - 08   (b) 2008 - 09

    (c) 2010 - 11   (d) 2011 - 12

64. Which of the following indicators have been used by the World Economic Forum to calculate Global Competitiveness Index for 2016–2017? **[CDS 2017-II]**

    1. Efficiency enhancer subindex

    2. Innovation and sophistication factors subindex

    3. Life expectancy enhancer subindex

    Select the correct answer using the code given below.

    (a) 1 and 2 only   (b) 2 and 3 only

    (c) 1 and 3 only   (d) 1, 2 and 3

65. Devaluation of currency will be more beneficial if prices of   **[CDS 2017-II]**
    (a) domestic goods remain constant
    (b) exports become cheaper to importers
    (c) imports remain constant
    (d) exports rise proportionately

66. The monetary policy in India uses which of the following tools?
    [CDS 2017-II]
    1. Bank rate
    2. Open market operations
    3. Public debt
    4. Public revenue
    Select the correct answer using the code given below.
    (a) 1 and 2 only   (b) 2 and 3 only
    (c) 1 and 4 only   (d) 1, 2, 3 and 4

67. Arrange the following events in sequential order as they happened in India :   **[CDS 2017-II]**
    1. Mahalanobis Model
    2. Plan Holiday
    3. Rolling Plan
    Select the correct answer using the code given below.
    (a) 1, 2, 3   (b) 3, 2, 1
    (c) 2, 3, 1   (d) 1, 3, 2

68. BREXIT refers to the Great Britain leaving which one of the following?
    [CDS 2017-I]
    (a) International Monetary Fund
    (b) Commonwealth
    (c) World Trade Organization
    (d) European Union

69. Which one of the following sectors is not affected by the changes made in the Foreign Direct Investment Policy in June 2016?   **[CDS 2017-I]**
    (a) Multi-brand retailing
    (b) Defence
    (c) Private security agencies
    (d) Manufacturing of small arms and ammunitions covered under the Arms Act, 1959

70. Goods and Services Tax likely to be levied in India is not a   **[CDS 2017-I]**
    (a) gross value tax (b) value-added tax
    (c) consumption tax (d) destination-based tax

71. The Most Favoured Nation (MFN) Clause under WTO regime is based on the principle of   **[CDS 2017-I]**
    (a) non-discrimination between nations
    (b) discrimination between nations
    (c) differential treatment between locals and foreigners
    (d) uniform tariff across commodities

72. The Twelfth Five-Year Plan focussed on inclusive growth. Which of the following were considered as challenges for inclusiveness ?
    [CDS 2017-I]
    1. Poverty
    2. Group inequality
    3. Regional imbalance
    4. Unemployment
    Select the correct answer using the code given below.
    (a) 1, 3 and 4 only
    (b) 1, 2, 3 and 4
    (c) 1, 2 and 4 only
    (d) 2 and 3 only

73. In the year 2016, the Government of India announced a ₹ 6,000 crore special package for the textile and apparel sector to   **[CDS 2017-I]**
    1. create one crore jobs within three years
    2. create jobs equally for men and women
    3. provide tax and production incentives for the entrepreneurs
    Select the correct answer using the code given below.
    (a) 1 only   (b) 2 and 3 only
    (c) 1 and 3 only   (d) 1, 2 and 3

74. Which of the following statements about Bitcoin is/are correct?
    [CDS 2017-I]

1. It is a decentralized virtual currency.
2. It is generated through complex computer software systems.
3. The Reserve Bank of India recognized it as a legal tender in January 2016.

Select the correct answer using the code given below.

(a) 1 only   (b) 1 and 2 only
(c) 2 and 3 only   (d) 1, 2 and 3

75. Which of the following statements about the Trans-Pacific/ Partnership (TPP) is / are correct? **[CDS 2017-I]**
1. The TPP was signed by 12 Pacific Rim nations in the year 2015.
2. The TPP is likely to be a game-changer in global trade as member countries account for about 40 percent of global GDP.
3. India is a founder member of TPP.

Select the correct answer using the code given below.

(a) 1, 2 and 3   (b) 1 and 2 only
(c) 2 and 3 only   (d) 1 only

76. The 76% growth rate registered by Indian economy during the year 2015-16 is based on **[CDS 2017-I]**
(a) Gross National Product at market prices
(b) Gross Value Added at constant prices
(c) Gross Domestic Product at market prices
(d) Gross Domestic Product at constant prices

77. TRIPS Agreement pertains to
[CDS 2017-I]
(a) international tariff regime
(b) intellectual property protection
(c) international practices on trade facilitation
(d) international taxation of property

78. Which one of the following is not a component of Revenue Receipts of the Union Government? **[CDS 2017-I]**

(a) Corporate tax receipts
(b) Dividends and profits
(c) Disinvestment receipts
(d) Interest receipts

79. Consider the following statements about the Second Five-Year Plan :
[CDS 2017-I]
1. It was drafted under the leadership of K. N. Raj.
2. It proposed that industries like electricity, railways, steel, machineries and communication could be developed in the public sector.
3. The drafters found balancing industry and agriculture very difficult.
4. The drafters found balancing industry and agriculture really easy.

Which of the statements given above is/are correct?

(a) 1 only   (b) 1 and 2
(c) 2 and 3   (d) 3 and 4

80. Which one of the following statements is correct? **[CDS 2017-I]**

For the purpose of Census 2011
(a) a person aged seven and above who can both read and write with understanding in any language is treated as a literate
(b) a person aged eight and above who can both read and write with understanding in any language is treated as a literate
(c) a person aged nine and above who can both read and write with understanding in any language is treated as a literate
(d) a person aged ten and above who can both read and write with understanding in any language is treated as a literate

81. Who among the following is the Chairman of the Fourteenth Finance Commission? **[CDS 2016-II]**

(a) C. Rangarajan (b) Vijay Kelkar

(c) Y. V. Reddy (d) Rakesh Mohan

82. Which one of the following is/are credit rating agency/ agencies in India?

[CDS 2016-II]

(a) CRISIL (b) CARE

(c) ICRA (d) All of the above

83. In India, the term 'hot money' is used to refer to [CDS 2016-II]

(a) Currency + Reserves with the RBI

(b) Net GDR

(c) Net Foreign Direct Investment

(d) Foreign Portfolio Investment

84. Which one of the following statements is correct with respect to the composition of national income in India

[CDS 2016-II]

(a) The share of manufacturing sector has declined.

(b) The share of services sector has increased sharply.

(c) The share of agriculture has remained static.

(d) The share of services sector has declined.

85. Which one of the following statements is not correct? **[CDS 2016-II]**

(a) Creation of National Investment and Infrastructure Fund (NIIF) was announced in the Union Budget, 2015-16.

(b) NIIF is a fund for enhancing infrastructure facility in the country.

(c) NIIF and NIF (National Investment Fund) are the names of the same organization,

(d) NIIF can have more than one alternative investment fund.

86. Capital deepening refers to

[CDS 2016-II]

(a) going for more fixed capital per worker

(b) emphasis on social overhead capital

(c) constant capital-output ratio

(d) increasing capital-output ratio

87. According to the Classical Theory of Employment, deviations from the state of full employment are **[CDS 2016-II]**

(a) purely temporary in nature

(b) permanent in nature

(c) imaginary situations

(d) normal situations

88. Which of the following will be the outcome if an economy is under the inflationary pressure? **[CDS 2016-II]**

1. Domestic currency heads for depreciation.

2. Exports become less competitive with imports getting costlier.

3. Cost of borrowing decreases.

4. Bondholders get benefitted.

Select the correct answer using the code given below.

(a) 1 and 2 (b) 2 and 3

(c) I and 3 only (d) 1, 3 and 4

89. Which of the following with regard to the term 'bank run' is correct?

[CDS 2016-II]

(a) The net balance of money a bank has in its chest at the end of the day's business

(b) The ratio of bank's total deposits and total liabilities

(c) A panic situation when the deposit holders start withdrawing cash from the banks

(d) The period in which a bank creates highest credit in the market

90. The headquarters of 'Economic and Social Commission for Asia and the Pacific' is located at **[CDS 2016-II]**

(a) Singapore (b) Manila

(c) Bangkok (d) Hong Kong

91. Which of the following statements (s) are true with respect to the concept of "efficiency" as used in mainstream economics? **[CDS 2016-II]**

1. Efficiency occurs when no possible recorganisation of production can make anyone better off with out making someone else worse off

2. An economy is elearly inefficient if it is inside the Production Possibility Frontier (PPF)

3. At a minimum, an efficient economy is on its Production Possibility Frontier (PPF)

4. The terms such as ' Pareto Efficiency', 'Pareto Optimality' and 'Allocative Efficiency' are all essentially one and same which denote 'efficiency in resource allocation'

Select the correct answer using the code given below :

(a) 1 and 4 only   (b) 1 and 3 only

(c) 2 and 3 only   (d) 1, 2, 3 and 4

92. Which of the following is / are the example (s) of Transfer Payment(s)? **[CDS 2016-II]**

1. Unemployment Allowance
2. Payment of salary
3. Social Security Payment
4. Old age Pension

Select the correct answer using the code given below :

(a) 1 and 3 only

(b) 1, 2 and 3 only

(c) 1, 3 and 4 only

(d) None of the above

93. Which of the following is not a 'Public Good'? **[CDS 2016-I]**

(a) Electricity

(b) National Defence

(c) Light House

(d) Public Parks

94. Which of the following statement (s) is /are false? **[CDS 2016-I]**

1. Wage Boards are tripartite in nature, with representatives from workers, employers and independent members.

2. Except for the wage Board for Journalists and Non - Jouralists, all the other wage boards are statutory in nature

3. Second National Commission on labour has recommended against the utility of wages boards.

Select the correct answer using the code given below:

(a) 1 only   (b) 2 only

(c) 1 and 2 only   (d) 1, 2 and 3

95. Which of the following statements are correct? **[CDS 2016-I]**

1. Ability to pay principle of taxation holds that the amount of taxes people pay should relate to their income or wealth

2. The Benefit Principle of taxation states that individuals should be taxed in proportion to the benefit they receive from Government programmes

3. A progressive tax takes a larger share of tax from poor families than it does from rich families

4. Indirect taxes have the advantage of being cheaper and easier to collect

Select the correct answer using the code given below:

(a) 1 and 3 only   (b) 2 and 4 only

(c) 1, 2 and 4 only (d) 1, 2, 3 and 4

96. Which one of the following is not a thrust area in the railway budget 2015-16? **[CDS 2016-II]**

(a) Online booking of disposable bed rolls

(b) Defence Travel System to eliminate Warrants

(c) 180 days in advance ticket booking facility for passengers

(d) Bio - Toilets

97. Which one of the following terms is used in Economics to denote a technique for avoiding a risk by making a counteracting transaction? **[CDS 2016-I]**

(a) dumping   (b) Hedging

(c) Discounting   (d) Deflating

98. Which of the following is /are example (s) of 'Near Money'? **[CDS 2016-I]**
  1. Treasury Bill
  2. Credit Card
  3. Saving accounts and small time deposits
  4. Retail money market mutual funds

  Select the correct answer using the code given below:
  (a) 1 only   (b) 2 only
  (c) 1, 2 and 3   (d) 1, 3 and 4

99. Which of the following statements is / are true with respect to Phillips curve?
  [CDS 2016-I]
  1. It shows the trade - off between unemployment and inflation
  2. The downward sloping curve of Phillips curve is generally held to be valid only in the short run.
  3. In the long run , Phillips Curve is usually thought to be horizontal at the non accelerating inflation rate of unemployment (Nairu)

  Select the correct answer using the code given below:
  (a) 1 only   (b) 2 and 3 only
  (c) 1 and 2 only   (d) 1, 2 and 3

100. Which one of the Five Year Plans had a high priority to bring inflation under control and to achieve stability in the economic situation? **[CDS 2016-I]**
  (a) Fourth Plan (1969 - 74)
  (b) Fifth Plan (1974 - 79)
  (c) sixth Plan (1980 - 85)
  (d) Seventh Plan (1985 - 90)

102. In the context of Indian economy, 'Open Market Operations' refers to
  [CDS 2013 - I]
  (a) borrowing by scheduled banks from the RBI
  (b) lending by commercial banks to industry and trade
  (c) purchase and sale of government securities by the RBI
  (d) None of the above

103. The terms 'Marginal Standing Facility Rate' and 'Net Demand and Time Liabilities', sometimes appearing in news, are used in relation to
  [CDS 2014 - I]
  (a) banking operations
  (b) communication networking
  (c) military strategies
  (d) supply and demand of agricul tural products

104. The national income of a country for a given period is equal to the
  [CDS 2013 - I]
  (a) total value of goods and services produced by the nationals
  (b) sum of total consumption and investment expenditure
  (c) sum of personal income of all individuals
  (d) money value of final goods and services produced

105. Which of the following is a most likely consequence of implementing the 'Unified Payments Interface (UPI)'?
  [CDS 2017-I]
  (a) Mobile wallets will not be necessary for online payments.
  (b) Digital currency will totally replace the physical currency in about two decades.
  (c) FDI inflows will drastically increase.
  (d) Direct transfer of subsidies to poor people will become very effective.

106. Disguised unemployment generally means   **[CDS 2013 - I]**
  (a) large number of people remain unemployed
  (b) alternative employment is not available
  (c) marginal productivity of labour is zero
  (d) productivity of workers is low

107. In the 'Index of Eight Core Industries', which one of the following is given the highest weight? **[CDS2015-I]**
(a) Coal production
(b) Electricity generation
(c) Fertilizer production
(d) Steel production

108. Which of the following brings out the 'Consumer Price Index Number for Industrial Workers'? **[CDS 2015-I]**
(a) The Reserve Bank of India
(b) The Department of Economic Affairs
(c) The Labour Bureau
(d) The Department of Personnel and Training

109. Recently, India's first 'National Investment and Manufacturing Zone' was proposed to be set up in
[CDS 2016-I]
(a) Andhra Pradesh (b) Gujarat
(c) Maharashtra (d) Uttar Pradesh

110. The value of goods and services in terms of money is **[IBPS - 2017 MAIN]**
(a) M1 (b) NNP
(c) GDP (d) PPP
(e) M3

111. Which of the following is correct regarding dematerialization?
[IBPS - 2017 MAIN]
(a) It is the process by which an Investor can get physical certificates converted into electronic form
(b) The investors can dematerialize only those share certificates that are already registered in their name
(c) The electronic certificates are maintained in an account with the Depository Participant
(d) Both 1 and 3
(e) All of the above

112. A Mutual Fund's NAV calculated on a day is known as **[IBPS - 2017 MAIN]**
(a) Asset value per Fund
(b) Price value per share
(c) Asset value per stock
(d) Price value per Fund
(e) Net asset price

113. NABARD stands for
[IBPS - 2017 MAIN]
(a) National Association for Building Asset Reconstruction Department
(b) National Bank for Agriculture and Rural Development
(c) National Agency of Banking Regulatory Directives
(d) National Asset Building and Reconstruction Department
(e) None of these

114. In a mutual fund, investors subscriptions are accounted for as **[IBPS-2017 MAIN]**
(a) Liabilities (b) Deposits
(c) Unit Capital (d) Assets
(e) None of these

115. Which of the following is an unsecured money market instrument ?
[IBPS - 2017 MAIN]
(a) Treasury Bills
(b) Certificates of Deposit
(c) Commercial Paper
(d) Bankers' Acceptances
(e) All of these

116. What does MSF stand for?
[IBPS - 2017 MAIN]
(a) Mutual Secure Finance
(b) Marginal Standing Facility
(c) Minimum Structured Finance
(d) Material Securitized Fund
(e) Minimum Social Fund

117. What is the term when a seller tries to sell the same good at different prices ?
[IBPS - 2017 MAIN]
(a) Price Differential
(b) Dumping
(c) Price Discrimination
(d) Bullying
(e) None of these

118. What is the term for fixing high price for new product? **[IBPS - 2017 MAIN]**
    - (a) Decoy Pricing
    - (b) Skimming
    - (c) Freemium
    - (d) Absorption Pricing
    - (e) Odd Pricing

119. What does SEBI stand for ?

    [IBPS - 2017 MAIN]
    - (a) Securities and Exchange Board of India
    - (b) Service and Employment Building of India
    - (c) Securities Exchange Board of India
    - (d) Service Estimated by Banks in India
    - (e) None of these

120. BSDA stands for **[IBPS - 2017 MAIN]**
    - (a) Basic Securities Demat Account
    - (b) Bombay Soft Drinks Association
    - (c) Basic Services Demat Account
    - (d) Basic Service. Development Authority
    - (e) None of these

121. When the signature of the drawer of a cheque is not genuine, such a cheque is called   **[SBI PO-2017 MAIN]**
    - (a) Cross Cheque
    - (b) Stale cheque
    - (c) Forged cheque
    - (d) Postdatedcheque
    - (e) None of these

122. The Regulatory Consistency Assessment Programme (RCAP), which evaluates a country's readiness for Basel III norms, is conducted by

    [SBI PO - 2017 MAIN]
    - (a) ADB   (b) BIS
    - (c) IMF   (d) World Bank

123. The deposit of cash under cash reserve ratio(CRR) requirement with the RBI is a

    [SBI PO - 2017 MAIN]
    - (a) Contributory requirement
    - (b) Discretionary requirement
    - (c) Mandatory requirement
    - (d) Voluntary requirement
    - (e) None of these

124. Credit cards are also knows as which of the following? **[SBI PO - 2017 MAIN]**
    - (a) Plastic money   (b) Hard money
    - (c) Silver money   (d) Easy money
    - (e) None of these

125. Who can file a criminal case against the drawer of a dishonoredcheque?

    [SBI PO - 2017 MAIN]
    - (a) The payee
    - (b) The holder in due course
    - (c) Both of the above
    - (d) The paying banker
    - (e) None of these

126. A cheque is considered as stale when it has been in circulation for

    [SBI PO - 2017 MAIN]
    - (a) More than forty eight hours
    - (b) More than one year
    - (c) More than six months unless otherwise specified
    - (d) More than three months
    - (e) None of these

127. Which of the following bank is generally not considered as Commercial bank?

    [SBI PO - 2017 MAIN]
    - (a) Public Sector Bank
    - (b) Private Sector Bank
    - (c) Development Bank
    - (d) Foreign Bank
    - (e) None of these

128. Which one of the following rates is not decided by RBI?

    [SBI PO - 2017 MAIN]
    - (a) Repo rate
    - (b) Prime Lending Rate
    - (c) Bank rate
    - (d) Marginal Standing Facility (MSF) rate
    - (e) None of these

129. The financial assistance of loans of ` 10000 by bank to a small borrower will be called...?   **[SBI PO - 2017 MAIN]**
  (a) Business finance
  (b) Government finance
  (c) Micro finance
  (d) Small finance
  (e) KYC finance

130. Insurance works on the principle of:
  (LIC ADO -2015)
  (a) Sharing of losses
  (b) Probabilities
  (c) Large numbers
  (d) Randomness
  (e) All of the above

131. Insurance helps to: **(LIC ADO -2015)**
  (a) Prevent adverse situations from occurring
  (b) Reduce the financial consequences of adverse situations
  (c) Negate all consequences of adverse situations
  (d) Make assets continuously productive
  (e) All of the above

132. The term 'Risk' includes:
  (LIC ADO -2015)
  (a) Damage to machinery and property
  (b) Impact on the health or life of a person
  (c) Leakage of toxic products into the atmosphere
  (d) Effect on the healthy life of the neighbourhood
  (e) All of the above

133. Which of the following intermediaries do not require IRDA's licence/ approval to operate in India? **(LIC ADO -2015)**
  (a) Insurance Brokers
  (b) Insurance Agents
  (c) Third Party Administrators
  (d) Surveyors
  (e) All the above intermediaries require IRDA's licence/ approval

134. An actuary is expected to:
  (LIC ADO -2015)
  (a) Make an exact forecast of the future liabilities of policies
  (b) Make a reasonable forecast of the future liabilities of policies
  (c) Calculate the premium required to cover a risk on a long-term basis
  (d) Find the probability of an insured event to happen in non-life policies
  (e) All the above statements are incorrect

135. The principle of ____________ ensures that an insured does not profit by insuring with multiple insurers
  (LIC ADO -2015)
  (a) Subrogation
  (b) Contribution
  (c) Co-insurance
  (d) Indemnity
  (e) Particular Average

136. The principle of average applies when the value is ____________ in the proposal   **(LIC ADO -2015)**
  (a) Understated
  (b) Overstated
  (c) Not ascertainable
  (d) Negligible
  (e) Only sentimental

137. CTL as used in insurance
  (LIC ADO -2015)
  (a) Contributory Total Loss
  (b) Constructive Total Loss
  (c) Construction Totally Lost
  (d) Contractors' Total Loss
  (e) Co-insurer's Tally of Loss

138. Which of the following terms matches closest with 'Family Floater'?
  (LIC ADO -2015)
  (a) Health insurance
  (b) Property insurance
  (c) Accidental injury
  (d) Consequential loss
  (e) Marine Partial Loss

139. Which of the following terms is dissimilar to the other four options?

    (LIC ADO -2015)

    (a) Post-hospitalisation expenses

    (b) Expenses on treatment of pre-existing diseases

    (c) Reinstatement value

    (d) Funeral expenses

    (e) Ambulance charges

140. In cases where a Life Insurance Agent collects the premium from the policyholder and remits it to the insurer's office, he is acting as an agent of __________ :   **(LIC ADO -2015)**

    (a) IRDA

    (b) the Insurance Company

    (c) the Policyholder

    (d) the broker

    (e) the general public

141. A policy where the policyholder makes a one-time payment of premium, is known as a _____ : **(LIC ADO -2015)**

    (a) Money-back policy

    (b) Single premium policy

    (c) Salary Savings Scheme policy

    (d) Half-yearly policy

    (e) Annual policy

142. Which of the following is an important reason for insurers to sell life insurance policies through agents?

    (LIC ADO -2015)

    (a) The benefits of life insurance policies are simple and clear to all

    (b) People can decide which policy is best for them

    (c) Agents have to earn their commissions

    (d) Agents have to meet their marketing targets

    (e) Many people require personalised guidance for selecting the right policy

143. Compared to the premium for a Whole Life plan, the premium for an Endowment plan will be __________ for the same age   **(LIC ADO -2015)**

    (a) more   (b) less

    (c) the same   (d) double

    (e) half

144. As per structured formula under the Motor Vehicle Act, victims of fatal injuries are paid compensation on the basis of: **(LIC ADO -2015)**

    (a) Age and sex

    (b) Age and number of dependents

    (c) Income and size of family

    (d) Age and income

    (e) Income and number of dependents

145. Time Policies relate to: **(LIC ADO -2015)**

    (a) Fire insurance

    (b) Hull insurance

    (c) Personal Accident insurance

    (d) Workmen's Compensation insurance

    (e) Motor vehicles insurance

146. Which clause specifies the perils insured in a scheduled form of policy?

    (LIC ADO -2015)

    (a) Preamble Clause

    (b) Recital Clause

    (c) Operative Clause

    (d) Consideration Clause

    (e) Attestation Clause

147. The minimum paid up capital required for a General Insurance Company is Rs. —   **(LIC ADO -2015)**

    (a) 25 crores   (b) 50 crores

    (c) 75 crores   (d) 100 crores

    (e) 200 crores

148. Select the expanded form of ALOP used in insurance.   **(LIC ADO -2015)**

    (a) Advance Loss of Profits insurance

    (b) Agreed Loss of Profits insurance

    (c) Additional Loss of Profits insurance

    (d) Associated Loss of Profits insurance

    (e) Authorised Loss of Profits insurance

149. Which of the following terms matches closest with 'Professional indemnity cover'?   **(LIC ADO -2015)**
   (a) Hospitals Nursing homes
   (b) Insurance Companies
   (c) Commercial Banks
   (d) Fast Moving Consumer Goods
   (e) Practicing Surgeons

150. Insurance business is transacted in India primarily as per the provisions of:
                (LIC ADO -2015)
   (a) Insurance Regulatory and Development Authority Act, 1999
   (b) Insurance Act, 1938
   (c) Life Insurance Corporation Act, 1956
   (d) Employees State Insurance Act, 1948
   (e) Motor Vehicles Act 1938

151. Section 64 C of the Insurance Act, 1938 contains provisions relating to:
                (LIC ADO -2015)
   (a) Insurance Regulatory and Development Authority
   (b) Life Insurance Corporation of India
   (c) The Life Insurance Council
   (d) General Insurance Corporation of India
   (e) Tariff Advisory Committee

152. As per IRDA Regulations, insurers should ensure that their advertisements present a correct picture. This provision is most important in the case of:
                (LIC ADO -2015)
   (a) The Government
   (b) Insurance Regulatory and Development Authority
   (c) Auditors
   (d) Policyholders
   (e) Shareholders

153. Which provision of the Insurance Act 1938 specifies about nomination by policyholder?   **(LIC ADO -2015)**

   (a) Section 38
   (b) Section 39
   (c) Section 40
   (d) Section 41
   (e) Section 45

154. Which Regulation of IRDA provides for a Grievance Redressal Procedure?
                (LIC ADO -2015)
   (a) IRDA (Policyholders' Interests) Regulations, 2002
   (b) IRDA (Meetings) Regulations, 2000
   (c) IRDA (Regulation of Indian Insurance Companies) Regulations, 2000
   (d) IRDA (Reinsurance Advisory Committee) Regulations, 2001
   (e) IRDA (Micro-insurance) Regulations, 2005

155. Redressal of Public Grievances Rules, 1998 created the system of _____
                (LIC ADO -2015)
   (a) Insurance Agency
   (b) Insurance Surveyors
   (c) Insurance Ombudsman
   (d) State Commission
   (e) Consumer Forum

156. The technique of making small deposits in various financial institutions so that they do not attract the attention of legal/ enforcement authorities is called ________   **(LIC ADO -2015)**
   (a) Phishing
   (b) Smurfing
   (c) Internet surfing
   (d) Know Your Customer
   (e) Subrogation

157. Select the expanded form of AML as used in insurance   **(LIC ADO -2015)**
   (a) Anti-Money Laundering
   (b) Anti-Money Lending
   (c) Adjuster of Monetary Losses
   (d) Averages of Marine Losses
   (e) Adjustment of Motor Losses

158. Select the expanded form of ULIP used in insurance **(LIC ADO -2015)**
  (a) Unit Linked Investment Policy
  (b) Universal Life Insurance Policy
  (c) Umbrella Life Insurance Policy
  (d) Unit Linked Insurance Policy
  (e) Underwriting Linked Insurance Policy

159. Which of the following terms matches closest with 'Nomination'? **(LIC ADO -2015)**
  (a) Loss of Property Documents
  (b) Loss of Merchandise
  (c) Loss of Life
  (d) Loss of Baggage
  (e) Loss of Passport

160. The 8th BRICS summit 2016 was held in ____. **(LIC AAO - 2016)**
  (a) Brazil
  (b) China
  (c) India
  (d) South Africa
  (e) Russia

161. The Food and Agriculture Organization (FAO) of UN has declared the year 2016 as the __? **(LIC AAO - 2016)**
  (a) International Year of Soils
  (b) International Year of Family Farming
  (c) International Year of Quinoa
  (d) International Year of Pulses
  (e) None of these

162. The World Malaria Day (WMD) is observed on which date? **(LIC AAO - 2016)**
  (a) April 20
  (b) April 15
  (c) April 24
  (d) April 25
  (e) None of these

163. In which of the following states is the Gorumara National Park located? **(LIC AAO - 2016)**
  (a) Kerala
  (b) West Bengal
  (c) Haryana
  (d) Madhya Pradesh
  (e) None of these

164. Copenhagen is the capital of which country? **(LIC AAO - 2016)**
  (a) Ireland
  (b) Australia
  (c) Denmark
  (d) South Africa
  (e) Germany

165. What is the currency of Austria? **(LIC AAO - 2016)**
  (a) Kwanza
  (b) Euro
  (c) Ngultrum
  (d) Real
  (e) Pula

166. Which one of the following is a purpose of 'UDAY', a scheme of the Government? **(LIC AAO - 2016)**
  (a) Providing technical and financial assistance to start-up entrepreneurs in the field of renewable sources of energy.
  (b) Providing electricity to every household in the country by 2018.
  (c) Replacing the coal-based power plants with natural gas, nuclear, solar, wind and tidal power plants over a period of time.
  (d) Financial turnaround and revival of power distribution companies.
  (e) None of the above

167. Who among the following won the Polly Umrigar Award 2015 – 16? **(LIC AAO - 2016)**
  (a) Gautam Gambhir
  (b) Rohit Sharma
  (c) MS Dhoni
  (d) R. Ashwin
  (e) Virat Kohli

168. Women's Cricket World Cup 2017 was held in ____. **(LIC AAO - 2016)**
  (a) Australia
  (b) South Africa
  (c) England
  (d) New Zealand
  (e) India

169. By which of the following year, India has set the target of eliminating malaria in the country? **(LIC AAO - 2016)**
  (a) 2020
  (b) 2022
  (c) 2025
  (d) 2030
  (e) None of these

170. Who is the author of the book "The White Tiger"?   **(LIC AAO - 2016)**
  (a) Maneesh Tripathi
  (b) Aravind Adiga
  (c) Arvind Joshi
  (d) Vijay Lohkare
  (e) Kiran Desai

171. LAMITYE 2016 is a joint military training exercise held between India and______.   **(LIC AAO - 2016)**
  (a) Maldives   (b) France
  (c) Sri Lanka   (d) Seychelles
  (e) Japan

172. The Union Government has launched the Stand Up India Scheme to promote entrepreneurship among SC/ST and women entrepreneurs through banks. Under the scheme, the loans are for green field enterprises in the non-farm sector and will range between ________.
          (LIC AAO - 2016)
  (a) Rs 1 lakh and Rs 10 lakh
  (b) Rs 1 lakh and Rs 20 lakh
  (c) Rs 1 lakh and Rs 50 lakh
  (d) Rs 10 lakh and Rs 50 lakh
  (e) Rs 10 lakh and Rs 1 crore

173. Which among the following cities has emerged as the cleanest city for the second year in a row?   **(LIC AAO - 2016)**
  (a) Chandigarh   (b) Visakhapatnam
  (c) Mysore   (d) Lucknow
  (e) Mumbai

174. Which bank has launched 'Japan Desk' to facilitate Japanese corporate investing in India? **(LIC AAO - 2016)**
  (a) State Bank of India
  (b) Punjab National Bank
  (c) Bank of Baroda
  (d) Dena Bank
  (e) None of these

175. Which of the following committees is formed to suggest changes in the Cinematograph act? **(LIC AAO - 2016)**
  (a) Shyam Benegal Committee
  (b) Nilesh Jha Committee
  (c) Chand Kiran Salooja Committee
  (d) Rastogi Committee
  (e) None of these

176. Indian Railways partnered with French company Alstom to manufacture 800 "super high-power" locomotives and decided to set up the factory in which state?   **(LIC AAO - 2016)**
  (a) Madhepura, Bihar
  (b) Chennai, Tamil Nadu
  (c) Visakhapatnam, Andhra Pradesh
  (d) Ahmedabad, Gujarat
  (e) None of these

177. The 103rd Indian Science Congress held in ____.   **(LIC AAO - 2016)**
  (a) Kochi, Kerala
  (b) Chennai, Tamil Nadu
  (c) Kolkata, West Bengal
  (d) Mysuru, Karnataka
  (e) Jaipur, Rajasthan

178. The Woody Island is located in which of the following sea?   **(LIC AAO - 2016)**
  (a) Arabian Sea
  (b) Bay of Bengal
  (c) South China Sea
  (d) Red Sea
  (e) None of these

179. Who among the following is the new chairman of the Empowered Committee of State Finance Ministers on Goods and Services Tax (GST)?
          (LIC AAO - 2016)
  (a) Saurabh Patel
  (b) Amit Mitra
  (c) Pradip Kumar Amat
  (d) G. Parameshwara
  (e) None of these

180."Apka Bhala and Sabki Bhalayi" is the tagline for which of the following banks? **(LIC AAO - 2016)**
   (a) IDFC
   (b) Bandhan Bank
   (c) Canara Bank
   (d) Allahabad Bank
   (e) UCO Bank

181.Which of the following country has decided to sell nuclear-capable F-16 fighter jets to Pakistan?
   (LIC AAO - 2016)
   (a) United States
   (b) United Kingdom
   (c) China
   (d) France
   (e) None of these

182.Paani Foundation has announced to work with which state government to resolve water crisis in the state?
   (LIC AAO - 2016)
   (a) Bihar　　　　(b) Gujarat
   (c) Maharashtra　(d) Odisha
   (e) None of these

183.Banaras Hindu University was founded by ___. **(LIC AAO - 2016)**
   (a) Annie Besant
   (b) Lord Hardig
   (c) Madan Mohan Malaviya
   (d) Vibhuti Narayan Singh
   (e) Motilal Nehru

184.The South Eastern Coalfields Limited (SECL), a subsidiary of the Coal India Limited (CIL), will set up India's largest coal washery in which state?
   (LIC AAO - 2016)
   (a) Madhya Pradesh
   (b) Jharkhand
   (c) Chhattisgarh
   (d) Uttar Pradesh
   (e) None of these

185.Which pair has won the 2016 St Petersburg Ladies Trophy (WTA)?
   (LIC AAO - 2016)
   (a) Laura Siegemund and Monica Niculescu
   (b) Arantxa Parra Santonja and Anabel Medina Garrigues
   (c) Martina Hingis and Sania Mirza
   (d) Lucie Hradecka and Andrea Hlavackova
   (e) None of these

186.Which country has successfully launched the ASTRO-H space observation satellite? **(LIC AAO - 2016)**
   (a) United States　(b) China
   (c) France　　　　(d) Japan
   (e) Russia

187.The first ever 2016 G – 20 Summit which was recently hosted by China in which city? **(LIC AAO - 2016)**
   (a) Shanghai　　　(b) Hangzhou
   (c) Tianjin　　　　(d) Beijing
   (e) Taipei

188.Who became the first ever lyricist to enter the Guinness Book of World Records for penning the most number of songs in Bollywood?
   (LIC AAO - 2016)
   (a) Gulzar
   (b) Javed Akhtar
   (c) Sameer Anjaan
   (d) Anand Bakshi
   (e) None of these

189.Rajaji National Park is an Indian National Park & Tiger Reserve that encompasses the Shivaliks, near the foothills of the Himalayas, located in which state? **(LIC AAO - 2016)**
   (a) Uttarakhand
   (b) Madhya Pradesh
   (c) Rajasthan
   (d) Odisha
   (e) Chhattisgarh

190. What is the Full form of UNCTAD –
     (LIC HFL – 2018)
     (a) United Nations Conference on Trade and Development
     (b) United Nations Committee on Trade and Development
     (c) United Nations Conference on Transport and Development
     (d) United Nations Committee for Transport Authority Development
     (e) United Nations Conference on Trade Audit Development

191. Bhimbetka is located in which state? –
     (LIC HFL – 2018)
     (a) Madhya Pradesh
     (b) Rajasthan
     (c) Maharashtra
     (d) Chhattisgarh
     (e) Odisha

192. Every year, Kalidas Samman given by which Indian state? – **(LIC HFL – 2018)**
     (a) Rajasthan
     (b) Madhya Pradesh
     (c) Bihar
     (d) Uttar Pradesh
     (e) Himachal Pradesh

193. In January 2018, Padma Shri award given to which cricketer –
     (LIC HFL – 2018)
     (a) MS Dhoni
     (b) Virat Kohli
     (c) Sikhar Dhawan
     (d) Rohit Sharma
     (e) Yuvraj Singh

194. 13 February is celebrated as which day? – **(LIC HFL – 2018)**
     (a) World Radio Day
     (b) World AIDS Day
     (c) World Health Day
     (d) World Earth Day
     (e) World Red Cross Day

195. Ganeshi Lal is the governor of which Indian State? **(LIC HFL – 2018)**
     (a) Assam   (b) Kerala
     (c) Sikkim   (d) Odisha
     (e) West Begal

196. Kathak is the classical dance from which state? **(LIC HFL – 2018)**
     (a) Tamil Nadu
     (b) Andhra Pradesh
     (c) Uttar Pradesh
     (d) Gujarat
     (e) Kerala

197. Which country hosting the Women T20 world cup 2018? – **(LIC HFL – 2018)**
     (a) West Indies   (b) England
     (c) Australia   (d) South Africa
     (e) India

198. Gangtok is the capital of which Indian State? **(LIC HFL – 2018)**
     (a) Arunachal Pradesh
     (b) Sikkim
     (c) Assam
     (d) Tripura
     (e) Meghalaya

199. Where is the Headquarters of the organization for the prohibition of chemical weapons located?
     (LIC HFL – 2018)
     (a) The Hague, Netherlands
     (b) Vienna, Austria
     (c) Ottawa, Canada
     (d) London, England
     (e) None of these

200. In Live and Let Die, who played the role of James bond?- **(LIC HFL – 2018)**
     (a) Thomas Cruise
     (b) Matt Damon
     (c) Roger Moore
     (d) Leonardo DiCaprio
     (e) None of these

201. What is the Ratio of female per thousand male in Kerala? **(LIC HFL – 2018)**
  (a) 1012   (b) 994
  (c) 1028   (d) 1084
  (e) 1092

202. Which organization is Sole re-insurer of India? **(LIC HFL – 2018)**
  (a) Bajaj Allianz Life Insurance
  (b) Bharti AXA Life Insurance
  (c) Birla Sun Life Insurance
  (d) General Insurance Corporation of India
  (e) None of these

203. Commonwealth games 2018 were held in which country – **(LIC HFL – 2018)**
  (a) Ottawa, Canada
  (b) Gold Coast, Australia
  (c) Glasgow, Scotland
  (d) Kuala Lumpur, Malaysia
  (e) None of these

204. Where has Samsung opened its biggest mobile factory? **(LIC HFL – 2018)**
  (a) Gurgaon   (b) Pune
  (c) Indore   (d) Cennai
  (e) Noida

205. Which person has been appointed as First CFO of RBI? **(LIC HFL – 2018)**
  (a) Sudha Balakrishnan
  (b) J Packirisamy
  (c) Karnam Sekar
  (d) Padmaja Chunduru
  (e) Suresh Sethi

206. Who has become first woman firefighter in Airport Authority of India –
(LIC HFL – 2018)
  (a) Taniya Sanyal
  (b) Anjali Bhargaw
  (c) Mohini Dhakad
  (d) Avani Mathur
  (e) None of these

207. Which Jain Muni has passed away recently – **(LIC HFL – 2018)**
  (a) Pulaksagar
  (b) Acharya Vidyasagar
  (c) Pramansagar
  (d) Tarun Sagar
  (e) None of these

208. What is the venue of Summer Olympics 2020? **(NICL AO- 2017)**
  (a) Tokyo   (b) Beijing
  (c) Moscow   (d) New York
  (e) Los Angeles

209. Which organisation regulates Pension products in India? **(NICL AO- 2017)**
  (a) IRDA   (b) RBI
  (c) PFRDA   (d) SIDBI
  (e) SEBI

210. What does "I" stands in TIES –
(NICL AO- 2017)
  (a) Institute   (b) International
  (c) Information   (d) Infrastructure
  (e) Import

211. Which city becomes first in India to get Underground water metro Tunnel?
(NICL AO- 2017)
  (a) New Delhi   (b) Mumbai
  (c) Kolkata   (d) Ahmedabad
  (e) Bengaluru

212. Dudhwa National park is located in which of the following State?
(NICL AO- 2017)
  (a) Uttar Pradesh
  (b) Madhya Pradesh
  (c) Rajasthan
  (d) Gujarat
  (e) Chhattisgarh

213. Kamuthi solar Power Plant is located in which Indian state? **(NICL AO- 2017)**
  (a) Kerala
  (b) Tamil Nadu
  (c) Odisha
  (d) Telangana
  (e) Andhra Pradesh

214. South Asian Speakers Summit 2017 held in which of the following city?
(NICL AO- 2017)
(a) Ranchi
(b) New Delhi
(c) Hyderabad
(d) Indore
(e) Nagpur

215. How much fund allotted for MGNREGA in Budget 2017?
(NICL AO- 2017)
(a) Rs. 30,000 crore
(b) Rs. 48,000 crore
(c) Rs. 28,000 crore
(d) Rs. 52,000 crore
(e) Rs. 40,000 crore

216. According to Economic Survey, what is the Industrial growth rate in FY17?
(NICL AO- 2017)
(a) 5.2%
(b) 6.0%
(c) 4.8%
(d) 6.4%
(e) 5.5%

217. Which day is observed on 20th June every year? **(NICL AO- 2017)**
(a) World Forestry Day
(b) International Customs Day
(c) International Women's Day
(d) World Consumer's Day
(e) World Refugee day

218. Life insurance contract designed to pay a lump sum after a specific term or on death – **(NICL AO- 2017)**
(a) Child Policy
(b) Retirement Policy
(c) Endowment Policy
(d) Money Back Policy
(e) None of these

219. A person or company registered as an adviser related to insurance cover on behalf of a client –
(NICL AO- 2017)
(a) Buyer
(b) Broker
(c) Dealer
(d) Consumer
(e) None of these

220. "Yves Meyer" receives Abel prize given in which field? **(NICL AO- 2017)**
(a) Mathematics
(b) Chemistry
(c) Physics
(d) Medical
(e) None of these

221. Sunder lal Patwa recently died, was the former Chief Minister of which State?
(NICL AO- 2017)
(a) Punjab
(b) Rajasthan
(c) Jharkhand
(d) Madhya Pradesh
(e) Bihar

222. What does "S" Stands for what in FSDC? **(NICL AO- 2017)**
(a) Saving
(b) Stability
(c) Stock
(d) Sustainability
(e) Standing

223. India by Nile 2017 festival held in which country? **(NICL AO- 2017)**
(a) Egypt
(b) Libya
(c) Morocco
(d) South Sudan
(e) Sudan

224. The final of the FIFA U-17 World cup will be held in which of the following Stadium? **(NICL AO- 2017)**
(a) Fatorda Stadium, Goa
(b) Jawaharlal Nehru Stadium, Kochi
(c) Salt Lake Stadium, Kolkata
(d) Shree Shiv Chhatrapati Sports Complex, Pune
(e) Bangalore Football Stadium, Bangalore

225. Indiafirst life insurance is a joint venture between which two Banks?
(NICL AO- 2017)
(a) Andhra Bank & Bank of Baroda
(b) Canara Bank & Central Bank of India
(c) Federal Bank & ICICI Bank
(d) IDBI Bank & Indian Bank
(e) Kotak Bank & Laxmi Vilas Bank

226. Which banks are authorized to give loans under PMMY? **(NICL AO- 2017)**
    (a) Commercial Banks
    (b) Scheduled Commercial Banks
    (c) Non-scheduled Commercial Banks
    (d) Co-operative banks
    (e) Regional Rural Banks

227. Brahmaputra Literary Festival 2017 held in which state? **(NICL AO- 2017)**
    (a) Sikkim
    (b) Arunachal Pradesh
    (c) Assam
    (d) Manipur
    (e) West Bengal

228. What is the Male Literacy rate in India according to census 2011 ?
    (NICL AO- 2017)
    (a) 70%
    (b) 74.30%
    (c) 78.75%
    (d) 85.05%
    (e) 82.14%

229.1 Which Indian State has recently signs MoU with Bill & Melinda Gates Foundation? **(NICL AO- 2017)**
    (a) Odisha
    (b) Maharashtra
    (c) Karnataka
    (d) Telangana
    (e) Uttar Pradesh

230.1 MSME day is celebrated on which date – **(RBI Grade B – 2018)**
    (a) 27 June
    (b) 20 July
    (c) 12 March
    (d) 9 April
    (e) 18 August

231. Which of the following bank listed as Best bank in private sector?
    (RBI Grade B – 2018)
    (a) HDFC
    (b) IDBI
    (c) ICICI
    (d) Yes Bank
    (e) Axis Bank

232. India & Russia Conclude Negotiations for which of the following Missile?
    (RBI Grade B – 2018)
    (a) R-1.01
    (b) A-100
    (c) M-2.0
    (d) S-400
    (e) P-6

233. Rohingya tribe people belongs to which country? **(RBI Grade B – 2018)**
    (a) Bangladesh
    (b) India
    (c) China
    (d) Tajikistan
    (e) Myanmar

234. Reserve Bank of India is conducting Financial Literacy Week from –
    (RBI Grade B – 2018)
    (a) June 4
    (b) May 10
    (c) April 1
    (d) March 31
    (e) February 12

235. First nuclear bomb dropped in which of the following city –
    (RBI Grade B – 2018)
    (a) Hiroshima
    (b) Yokohama
    (c) Osaka
    (d) Nagasaki
    (e) Kagoshima

236. Committee set up by RBI to make a Public Credit Registry (PCR) is headed by whom – **(RBI Grade B – 2018)**
    (a) Nandan Nilekani
    (b) H.R. Khan
    (c) Kishore Sansi
    (d) Aruna Sharma
    (e) Y.M. Deosthalee

237. World environment day 2018 was hosted by which country?
    (RBI Grade B – 2018)
    (a) India
    (b) China
    (c) Japan
    (d) Canada
    (e) France

238. Which of the following country is the last to join BRICS association in 2010?
    (RBI Grade B – 2018)
    (a) Brazil
    (b) India
    (c) South Africa
    (d) China
    (e) Russia

239. Jallikattu is typically practised in the which Indian State as a part of Pongal celebrations?   **(RBI Grade B – 2018)**
    (a) Kerala
    (b) Tamil Nadu
    (c) Andhra Pradesh
    (d) Telangana
    (e) Odisha

240. "Banglore Tiger" Book is based on which Indian IT company –
    (RBI Grade B – 2018)
    (a) Wipro   (b) TCS
    (c) Infosys   (d) Rolta India
    (e) None of these

241. Buddha Mountain, a Seven mountain temple is located in which country?
    (RBI Grade B – 2018)
    (a) China   (b) Japan
    (c) South Korea   (d) Thailand
    (e) None of these

242. "Our Tree is still grown in" is written by which author –
    (RBI Grade B – 2018)
    (a) Aravind Adiga
    (b) Chetan Bhagat
    (c) Robin Sharma
    (d) Ruskin Bond
    (e) None of these

243. Where is Salar Jung Museum located –
    (RBI Grade B – 2018)
    (a) Hyderabad
    (b) Nagpur
    (c) Lucknow
    (d) New Delhi
    (e) None of these

244. What does W stands in WLTF?
    (RBI Grade B – 2018)
    (a) World   (b) Wholesale
    (c) Widerange   (d) Widespread
    (e) None of these

245. The 2018 BRICS summit is the tenth annual BRICS summit, was held in which country –**(RBI Grade B – 2018)**
    (a) South Africa   (b) China
    (c) India   (d) Russia
    (e) Brazil

246. What is the Minimum age for loksabha candidate?**(GIC Officer Scale-1 – 2018)**
    (a) 18 Years   (b) 21 Years
    (c) 25 Years   (d) 30 Years
    (e) 35 Years

247. Who won the 2018 National award for best actress   **(GIC Officer Scale-1 – 2018)**
    (a) Hema Malini
    (b) Madhuri Dixit
    (c) Aishwarya Rai
    (d) Sridevi
    (e) Kajol

248. Rat temple (Karni Mata Temple) is situated in which state?
    (GIC Officer Scale-1 – 2018)
    (a) Rajasthan   (b) Punjab
    (c) Bihar   (d) Uttar Pradesh
    (e) Madhya Pradesh

249. Who is the Chairman of Payments council of Indian?
    (GIC Officer Scale-1 – 2018)
    (a) R. A. Sankara Narayanan
    (b) Atul Kumar Goel
    (c) Rajnish Kumar
    (d) Mukesh Kumar Jain
    (e) Vishwas Patel

250. Who is the Chief Minister of Himachal pradesh – **(GIC Officer Scale-1 – 2018)**
    (a) Jai Ram Thakur
    (b) Kamal Nath
    (c) Ashok Gahlot
    (d) Sarbananda Sonowal
    (e) Bhupesh Baghel

251. Who is the first Indian women's cricket team captain - **(GIC Officer Scale-1 – 2018)**
   - (a) Shantha Rangaswamy
   - (b) Diana Edulji.
   - (c) Shubhangi Kulkarni.
   - (d) Purnima Rau.
   - (e) Anju Jain.

252. Indian cricketer name recently inducted into ICC Hall of fame-
   (GIC Officer Scale-1 – 2018)
   - (a) Gautam Gambhir
   - (b) Virender Sehwag
   - (c) Rahul Dravid
   - (d) MS Dhoni
   - (e) None of these

253. Indian Science Congress 2019 will be held in which city/State?
   (GIC Officer Scale-1 – 2018)
   - (a) Andhra Pradesh
   - (b) Goa
   - (c) Himachal Pradesh
   - (d) Punjab
   - (e) Delhi

254. Name the Continent with maximum countries -
   (GIC Officer Scale-1 – 2018)
   - (a) Africa
   - (b) Asia
   - (c) North America
   - (d) Europe
   - (e) South America

255. Who is the Chief election commissioner of India - **(GIC Officer Scale-1 – 2018)**
   - (a) Om Prakash Rawat
   - (b) Sushil Chandra
   - (c) Sunil Arora
   - (d) Ashok Lavasa
   - (e) None of these

256. Palme d'or award is presented in the field of – **(GIC Officer Scale-1 – 2018)**
   - (a) Science
   - (b) Music
   - (c) Movie
   - (d) Art
   - (e) Journalism

257. Country's largest flag hoisted in Belagavi, is located in
   (GIC Officer Scale-1 – 2018)
   - (a) Kerala
   - (b) Maharashtra
   - (c) Karnataka
   - (d) Tamil Nadu
   - (e) Odisha

258. Oscar Award for Best Motion Picture 2018 – **(GIC Officer Scale-1 – 2018)**
   - (a) Shape of Water
   - (b) Aquaman
   - (c) Black Panther
   - (d) A Star is Born
   - (e) Ready Player One

259. Golden Globe award 2018 winner in Musical/comedy –
   (GIC Officer Scale-1 – 2018)
   - (a) Lady Bird
   - (b) Scarlett Ingrid Johansson
   - (c) Mila Kunis
   - (d) Emma Stone
   - (e) Eva Green

260. Who is the current Minister of State in Skill Development and Entrepreneurship?
   (GIC Officer Scale-1 – 2018)
   - (a) D.V. Sadananda Gowda
   - (b) Ramvilas Paswan
   - (c) Radha Mohan Singh
   - (d) Anant Kumar Hegde
   - (e) None of these

261. Indian Army conducted 'Vijay Prahar' military exercise in which State?
   (GIC Officer Scale-1 – 2018)
   - (a) Uttar Pradesh
   - (b) Gujarat
   - (c) Haryana
   - (d) Rajasthan
   - (e) Uttarakhand

262. Tata Steel have signed a definitive agreement to create a 50:50 joint venture with German company –
     (GIC Officer Scale-1 – 2018)
     (a) Estel   (b) Hoesch AG
     (c) Otto Wolff   (d) Ferrostaal
     (e) Thyssen Krupp

263. One question related to MoU signed between Indian state and Singapore –
     (GIC Officer Scale-1 – 2018)
     (a) Haryana   (b) West Bengal
     (c) Telangana   (d) Karnataka
     (e) Uttarakhand

264. In the given options, who is one of the deputy governors of RBI? M.K. Jain
     (GIC Officer Scale-1 – 2018)
     (a) Sunil Arora
     (b) Rajiv Mehrishi
     (c) Arvind Saxena
     (d) Pradeep Kumar Sinha
     (e) M. K. Jain

265. What is the plate colour for electric vehicles with the font in white colour?
     (GIC Officer Scale-1 – 2018)
     (a) Red   (b) Yellow
     (c) Green   (d) Black
     (e) None of these

266. What is the meaning of "S" in PMGSY –
     (OICL AO – 2017)
     (a) Samman   (b) Sadak
     (c) Samajik   (d) Seva
     (e) None of these

267. Which state government has received three gold awards at the 20th National Conference on E-Governance -
     (OICL AO – 2017)
     (a) Assam
     (b) Odisha
     (c) Andhra Pradesh
     (d) Karnataka
     (e) None of these

268. Cassini is one of the most ambitious efforts in planetary space exploration by-   **(OICL AO – 2017)**
     (a) NASA   (b) ISRO
     (c) JAXA   (d) Roscosmos

269. The book "I am HIV positive, so what?" has been authored by-
     (OICL AO – 2017)
     (a) Saurabh Kumar
     (b) R. Bhatnagar
     (c) Jayanta Kalita
     (d) Abhinadan Bose
     (e) None of these

270. H.S Prannoy is associated with which sport –   **(OICL AO – 2017)**
     (a) Hockey   (b) Badminton
     (c) Tennis   (d) Football
     (e) None of these

271. Where is the headquarter of National Insurance Company Limited (NICL)-
     (OICL AO – 2017)
     (a) Mumbai   (b) New Delhi
     (c) Bengaluru   (d) Kolkata
     (e) None of these

272. 2017 AIBA world boxing championships held in which country –   **(OICL AO – 2017)**
     (a) Germany   (b) Canada
     (c) Austria   (d) UAE
     (e) None of these

273. Who is the Chancellor of Germany-
     (OICL AO – 2017)
     (a) Liz Mohn
     (b) Steffi Graf
     (c) Angela Merkel
     (d) Andrea Nahles
     (e) None of these

274. What is the Constituency of Union Minister Radha Mohan singh –
     (OICL AO – 2017)
     (a) Lucknow (Uttar Pradesh)
     (b) Bhopal (Madhya Pradesh)
     (c) Nagpur (Maharashtra)
     (d) Bathinda (Punjab)
     (e) Purvi Champaran (Bihar)

275. The 2017 BRICS summit was the ninth annual BRICS summit held in
(OICL AO – 2017)
(a) Xiamen   (b) New Delhi
(c) Beijing   (d) Salvador
(e) None of these

276. Tata Teleservices to merge consumer business with- **(OICL AO – 2017)**
(a) Idea   (b) Bharti Airtel
(c) Reliance   (d) Vodafone
(e) None of these

277. Sardar Patel Stadium is located in which city – **(OICL AO – 2017)**
(a) Ahmedabad   (b) Nagpur
(c) Dharamshala   (d) Cuttack
(e) None of these

278. North East Calling event is being organised by the Ministry of Development of North Eastern Region in- **(OICL AO – 2017)**
(a) New Delhi
(b) Bhopal
(c) Chandigarh
(d) Shimla
(e) None of these

279. Which language is not present in 8th schedule of constitution –
(OICL AO – 2017)
(a) Pali   (b) Urdu
(c) Sanskrit   (d) Maithili
(e) None of these

280. What does P stands for in VVPAT –
(OICL AO – 2017)
(a) Press   (b) Print
(c) Paper   (d) Post
(e) None of these

281. Who will represent the International Boxing Association (AIBA) at International Olympic Committee Athletes' Forum – **(OICL AO – 2017)**
(a) L. Sarita Devi
(b) Mary Kom
(c) Katie Taylor
(d) Delfine Persoon
(e) None of these

282. Saubhagya Scheme completed by –
(OICL AO – 2017)
(a) July, 2018
(b) March, 2018
(c) December, 2018
(d) October, 2018
(e) August, 2018

283. Where is the head office of NICL –
(OICL AO – 2017)
(a) Indore   (b) Chandigarh
(c) Jaipur   (d) New Delhi
(e) Kolkata

284. What is the full form of TPA in insurance- **(OICL AO – 2017)**
(a) Two Party Administrator
(b) Third Party Administrator
(c) Total payment Asset
(d) Time Per Assests
(e) None of these

285. Bathukamma festival is celebrated in which state- **(UIIC Assist – 2017)**
(a) Telangana
(b) Arunachal Pradesh
(c) Sikkim
(d) Karnataka
(e) Odisha

286. Agricultural leadership award 2017 given to whom – **(UIIC Assist – 2017)**
(a) Chief Minister Shivraj Singh
(b) Chief Minister Raman Singh
(c) Chief Minister K. Chandrasekhar Rao
(d) Chief Minister Vasundhara Raje Scindia
(e) None of the Above

287. RBI issue currencies in which system –
(UIIC Assist – 2017)
(a) Forex Reserve System
(b) Maximum Fiduciary system
(c) Minimum Reserve system
(d) Proportional Reserve system
(e) None of these

288. Under the aegis of Pradhan Mantri Mudra Yojana (PMMY), MUDRA has created as CGFMU. In the term CGFMU, G stands for –
(UIIC Assist – 2017)
(a) Guarantee   (b) Grade
(c) Gross   (d) General
(e) None of these

289. G20 summit 2017 is recently held in which country –**(UIIC Assist – 2017)**
(a) Germany   (b) Austria
(c) Belgium   (d) UK
(e) None of these

290. Salim Ali Bird Sanctuary is located in which of the following state –
(UIIC Assist – 2017)
(a) Madhya Pradesh
(b) Gujarat
(c) Kerala
(d) Goa
(e) None of these

291. Valley of flowers National Park is located in which of the state –
(UIIC Assist – 2017)
(a) Himachal Pradesh
(b) Uttarakhand
(c) Sikkim
(d) Kerala
(e) Tamil Nadu

292. What is the Capital of Kazakhstan-
(UIIC Assist – 2017)
(a) Manama   (b) Amman
(c) Astana   (d) Doha
(e) None of these

293. A type of insurance policy that covers property that is easily movable and provides additional coverage over what normal insurance policies do not-
(UIIC Assist – 2017)
(a) Floater Insurance
(b) Flood insurance
(c) Liability insurance
(d) General insurance
(e) Travel insurance

294. The Task Force on Supportive Policy and Regulatory Framework for Micro-finance set up – **(UIIC Assist – 2017)**
(a) RBI   (b) NABARD
(c) SIDBI   (d) IRDA
(e) None of these

295. Indravati dam is located in which of the following state? **(UIIC Assist – 2017)**
(a) Punjab   (b) Rajasthan
(c) Uttar Pradesh   (d) Odisha
(e) None of the above

296. What is the Constituency of Nirmala Sitharaman? **(UIIC Assist – 2017)**
(a) Andhra Pradesh, Rajya Sabha
(b) Bangalore, Rajya Sabha
(c) Bihar, Rajya Sabha
(d) Haryana, Rajya Sabha
(e) None of these

297. Headquarters of BMEL is located in –
(UIIC Assist – 2017)
(a) Bangalore
(b) Indore
(c) Raipur
(d) Chennai
(e) None of the above

298. Simbex Exercise is conducted between which two countries?
(UIIC Assist – 2017)
(a) India & Singapore
(b) India & China
(c) India & Japan
(d) India & Malaysia
(e) None of these

299. Which of the following day is celebrated on October 24th?
(UIIC Assist – 2017)
(a) United Nations Day
(b) International Day of Yoga
(c) International Labour Day
(d) World Literacy Day
(e) None of these

300. Which is fully state-owned Insurance company?   **(UIIC Assist – 2017)**
    (a) Life Insurance Corporation of India
    (b) SBI Life Insurance
    (c) Shriram Life Insurance
    (d) Bharti AXA Life Insurance
    (e) None of these

301. Green bond are issued for collecting fund for –   **(UIIC Assist – 2017)**
    (a) Renewable Energy
    (b) Chemical Energy
    (c) Physical Energy
    (d) Both A and B
    (e) None of these

302. In the term ASBA, B stands for what?
          (UIIC Assist – 2017)
    (a) Bank   (b) Buyer
    (c) Blocked   (d) Balance
    (e) None of these

303. Salar Jung Museum is an art museum located in which of the following state?
          (UIIC Assist – 2017)
    (a) Andhra Pradesh
    (b) Punjab
    (c) Karnataka
    (d) Telangana
    (e) None of these

304. What does "I" stands for in NID –
          (UIIC Assist – 2017)
    (a) Instruments   (b) Investment
    (c) Insurance   (d) Institute
    (e) None of these

305. Anupam Mishra who recently passed away belonged to which field?
          (NIACL AO- 2017)
    (a) Environmentalist
    (b) Physicist
    (c) Chemist
    (d) Author

    (e) None of these

306. Consumer grievance OCMC recently launched. What doers M stand for –
          (NIACL AO- 2017)
    (a) Member   (b) Medical
    (c) Meditation   (d) Money
    (e) None of these

307. Where is Balpakram National Park –
          (NIACL AO- 2017)
    (a) Meghalaya   (b) Sikkim
    (c) Assam   (d) Mizoram
    (e) Tripura

308. Health insurance under which insurance?   **(NIACL AO- 2017)**
    (a) Life insurance
    (b) Home insurance
    (c) General insurance
    (d) Liability insurance
    (e) None of these

309. 10000 POS Machine given by NABARD at which cost ?
          (NIACL AO- 2017)
    (a) Rs. 120 crore
    (b) Rs. 110 crore
    (c) Rs. 100 crore
    (d) Rs. 90 core
    (e) None of these

310. In LAF, what does A stand for –
          (NIACL AO- 2017)
    (a) Advance   (b) Availity
    (c) Adjustment   (d) Advance
    (e) None of these

311. Where is Gurdongmong lake?
          (NIACL AO- 2017)
    (a) Sikkim
    (b) Odisha
    (c) Rajasthan
    (d) Himachal Pradesh
    (e) Uttarakhand

312. Utkarsh gets license from RBI for – **(NIACL AO- 2017)**
    (a) Small Finance Bank
    (b) Insurance Company
    (c) Cooprative Bank
    (d) Private Bank
    (e) None of these

313. 49% FDI in insurance must be approved by- **(NIACL AO- 2017)**
    (a) FIPB   (b) CCEA
    (c) IRDAI   (d) SEBI
    (e) All of the above

314. March 8 observed as which day? **(NIACL AO- 2017)**
    (a) World Leprosy Day
    (b) World Population Day
    (c) International Labour Day
    (d) International Women's day
    (e) None of these

315. Tanset Satellite launched by which country – **(NIACL AO- 2017)**
    (a) China
    (b) South Korea
    (c) Japan
    (d) Thailand
    (e) None of these

316. Zhuhaui Airshow conducted by which country? **(NIACL AO- 2017)**
    (a) China
    (b) Thailand
    (c) North Korea
    (d) Maldives
    (e) None of these

317. Sashmita Malik related to which sports – **(NIACL AO- 2017)**
    (a) Football   (b) Hockey
    (c) Badminton   (d) Cricket
    (e) None of these

318. Institute of skills in which city – **(NIACL AO- 2017)**
    (a) Kanpur
    (b) Lucknow
    (c) Noida
    (d) Allahabad
    (e) None of these

319. International telecommunication Union Headquater – **(NIACL AO- 2017)**
    (a) Mexico
    (b) Ottawa
    (c) New York
    (d) Geneva
    (e) None of these

320. Judima Festival celebrated in – **(NIACL AO- 2017)**
    (a) Meghalaya   (b) West Bengal
    (c) Sikkim   (d) Assam
    (e) None of these

321. Koyna Hydro project in which state – **(NIACL AO- 2017)**
    (a) Andhra Pradesh
    (b) Maharashtra
    (c) Gujarat
    (d) Odisha
    (e) Telangana

322. INSAT 3DR launched by ISRO is which type of satellite? **(NIACL AO- 2017)**
    (a) Radio Satellite
    (b) Communications Satellite
    (c) Geostationary Satellites
    (d) Weather Satellite
    (e) None of these

323. Chairman of Insolvency and Bankruptcy Board- **(NIACL AO- 2017)**
    (a) Pradeep Kumar Sinha
    (b) V. K. Yadav
    (c) Sanjay Mitra
    (d) M.S. Sahoo
    (e) None of these

324. Which company launched a single Quick Response (QR) code between Visa, MasterCard, Rupay –

(NIACL AO- 2017)

(a) Adyen   (b) Oxigen

(c) Alipay   (d) Barclaycard

(e) BTCC

325. Which bank is first to support U17 FIFA World Cup – **(NIACL AO- 2017)**

(a) Bank of Baroda

(b) State Bank of India

(c) American Bank

(d) HDFC

(e) None of these

326. Agni V Missile Range –

(NIACL AO- 2017)

(a) 3000 Km   (b) 4000 Km

(c) 5000 Km   (d) 6000 Km

(e) None of the above

327. Which Bank to transform 100 villages in Digital village – **(NIACL AO- 2017)**

(a) ICICI Bank   (b) HDFC Bank

(c) IDBI Bank   (d) SBI

(e) None of these

328. Who tops the list of Forbes India highest earning celebrities list – **(NIACL AO- 2017)**

(a) Salman Khan

(b) Amitabh Bachchan

(c) Shahrukh Khan

(d) Amir Khan

(e) None of these

329. Good Governance day –

(NIACL AO- 2017)

(a) Birth anniversary of Indira Gandhi

(b) Birth anniversary of Lal Bahadur Shastri

(c) Birth anniversary of Jawaharlal Nehru

(d) Birth anniversary of Atal Bihari Vajpayee

(e) None of these

330. Which Bank has launched Easy-pay app for merchants–   **(NIACL AO- 2017)**

(a) Canara Bank

(b) ICICI bank

(c) Kotak Mahindra Bank

(d) Axis Bank

(e) None of these

331. Receivables Exchange of India (RXIL) is a joint venture company set up by –

(NIACL AO- 2017)

(a) NSE and SIDBI

(b) NSE and ICICI

(c) SIDBI and SBI

(d) SBI and ICICI

(e) None of these

332. As per Oxford Economic, which city is to be the world's fastest-growing city during 2019-35?   **(NIACL AO- 2018)**

(a) Noida   (b) Kolkata

(c) Surat   (d) Mumbai

(e) None of these

333. Where was the ASEAN-India Youth Summit held?   **(NIACL AO- 2018)**

(a) Guwahati   (b) Shillong

(c) Imphal   (d) Kolkata

(e) None of these

334. Who is the Chairman of NGT?

(NIACL AO- 2018)

(a) Sanjiv Puri

(b) K.Goel

(c) Atul Sahai

(d) Pradosh Kumar

(e) None of these

335. What is the Full form of CPA?

(NIACL AO- 2018)

(a) Compulsory Personal Accident

(b) Credit Permanent Asset

(c) Commercial Payable Authority

(d) Commodity Payment Assets

(e) None of these

336. What is the name of the cyber insurance policy launched by HDFC ERGO? **(NIACL AO- 2018)**
   (a) Pay@Insure
   (b) E@Secure
   (c) U@Money
   (d) Mo@Invest
   (e) None of these

337. HDFC Standard Life Insurance changed its name to? **(NIACL AO- 2018)**
   (a) HDFC Life Insurance
   (b) Secure Life HDFC
   (c) HDFC Standard Insurance
   (d) HDFC Insurance
   (e) None of these

338. Which Indian institute is 1st & 3rd Globally to offer BTech Program in Artificial Intelligence? **(NIACL AO- 2018)**
   (a) IIT-Hyderabad
   (b) IIT-Mumbai
   (c) IIT-Delhi
   (d) IIT-Roorkee
   (e) None of these

339. India and which country signed protocol for tobacco export? **(NIACL AO- 2018)**
   (a) Nepal
   (b) Japan
   (c) China
   (d) Qatar
   (e) None of these

340. Where is India's 1st Aqua Mega Food Park commissioned? **(NIACL AO- 2018)**
   (a) Tamil Nadu
   (b) Andhra Pradesh
   (c) Maharashtra
   (d) Odisha
   (e) None of these

341. Where was India's latest communication satellite, GSAT-31 was successfully launched from? **(NIACL AO- 2018)**
   (a) Spaceport in French Guyana
   (b) Wenchang Satellite Launch Center
   (c) Vikram Sarabhai Space Centre, Kerala
   (d) Rocket Launch Site Berlin
   (e) None of these

342. What was India's rank in Global Corruption Index 2019? **(NIACL AO- 2018)**
   (a) 67
   (b) 103
   (c) 78
   (d) 92
   (e) None of these

343. Where will ISRO be setting India's first Human Spaceflight Centre? **(NIACL AO- 2018)**
   (a) Bangalore
   (b) Kolkata
   (c) Chennai
   (d) Visakhapatnam
   (e) None of these

344. In which state is Kiru Hydroelectric Power Project situated? **(NIACL AO- 2018)**
   (a) Uttarakhand
   (b) Jammu and Kashmir
   (c) Himachal Pradesh
   (d) Haryana
   (e) None of the above

345. LIC completes acquisition of 51% stake in? **(NIACL AO- 2018)**
   (a) Axis Bank
   (b) ICICI
   (c) HDFC
   (d) IDBI
   (e) None of these

346. Who becomes first female cricketer to play 200 ODIs? **(NIACL AO- 2018)**
   (a) Mithali Raj
   (b) Poonam Raut
   (c) Smriti Mandhana
   (d) Jhulan Goswami
   (e) None of these

347. Which country assumes chairmanship of G77, UN's largest bloc? **(NIACL AO- 2018)**
   (a) Palestine
   (b) Armenia
   (c) Azerbaijan
   (d) Bahrain
   (e) None of these

348. What is the Minimum Entry Age for Pradhan Mantri Vaya Vandana Yojana?
(NIACL AO- 2018)
   (a) 50 Years
   (b) 18 years
   (c) 60 years
   (d) 35 Years
   (e) None of these

349. Which city is named as World Capital of Architecture for 2020?
(NIACL AO- 2018)
   (a) Rio de Janeiro (Brazil)
   (b) Paris (France)
   (c) Tokyo (Japan)
   (d) Seoul (South Korea)
   (e) None of these

350. Which state topped in Ease of Doing Business? **(NIACL AO- 2018)**
   (a) Tamil Nadu
   (b) Andhra Pradesh
   (c) Sikkim
   (d) Gujarat
   (e) None of these

351. Which Indian state is set to become the first state in India to roll out Universal Basic Income? **(NIACL AO- 2018)**
   (a) Sikkim
   (b) Assam
   (c) West Bengal
   (d) Jharkhand
   (e) None of these

352. Which country's central bank banned Indian Notes above Rs 100?
(NIACL AO- 2018)
   (a) Nepal
   (b) Singapore
   (c) Bangladesh
   (d) Bhutan
   (e) None of these

353. Which organisation has formed a committee to investigate the systemically important insurers? **(NIACL AO- 2018)**
   (a) IRDAI
   (b) SEBI
   (c) SIDBI
   (d) RBI
   (e) None of these

354. Which state launched 'One Family, One Job' scheme? **(NIACL AO- 2018)**
   (a) Kerala
   (b) Himachal Pradesh
   (c) Nagaland
   (d) Sikkim
   (e) None of these

HINTS & EXPLANATIONS

1. (d)
2. (c) 3. (d) 4. (d) 5. (c) 6. (d)
7. (b) 8. (d) 9. (c) 10. (c) 11. (c)
12. (b) 13. (b) 14. (c) 15. (c) 16. (a)
17. (a) 18. (d) 19. (d) 20. (a) 21. (c)
22. (b) 23. (a)

24. (a) Equilibrium Price is the market price where the quanti by of goods supplied is equal to the quantity of goods demanded. It is also known as market clearing Price.

25. (c) The Petroleum Industry is not a small scale Industry. Small scale Enterprise is one in which the investment in plant and macniroy is between ₹ 25 Lakhs to ` 10 crores.

26. (b) Goods and Services Tax is an indirect tax which was introduced in India on 1 July 2017 and was applicaple throughout India, which replaced multiple cascading taxes levied by the central and state governments.

27. (a) Rate of Interest may be zero is true regarding rate of interest.

28. (d) In an inflationary Situation, country's export's declines as the goods which were cheaply available earlier now becomes expensive.

29. (b) Export Basin is the area which supports the economy and export trade of a sea port.

30. (c) In microeconomics, the law of demand states that, "Other things being equal, as the price of a good increases its demand decreases and vice versa."

31. (a) Rajasthan is the state with largest gap in male and female literacy.

32. (a) The Fifth Five–year Plan (1974–1978) laid emphasis on employment, poverty and achievement of self reliance.

33. (c) Oligopoly is a market structure in which a small number of firms has the large majority of market share.

34. (c) Banking sector is a services sector. Therefore, it comes under Tertiary sector.

35. (d) Hyper – Inflation is a situation in which the price increases at a very high rate.

36. (b) FDI full form is Foreign Direct Investment.

37. (b)   38.   (b)

39. (d) Microeconomics is the study of the behaviour of the individual units (like an individual firm or an individual consumer) of the economy. Consumer's Equilibrium is the example of microeconomic variable.

40. (b) Credit Control Instruments used by RBI are rationing of credit, Open Market operations, Variable cost reserve ratios, Bank rate policy, Statutory Liquidity Ratio (SLR), and Selective Credit Control (SCC). Direct action is not the credit control instrument used by RBI.

41. (c) The Demand Draft is a pre-paid Negotiable Instrument, wherein the drawee bank undertakes to make payment in full when the instrument is presented by the payee for payment. So it may not be dishonored for lack of funds.

42. **(b)** Leon Walras developed general equilibrium theory to solve a much-debated problem in economics.

43. **(d)** The accepted average calorie requirement in India is 2400 calories per person per day in rural areas and 2100 calories per person per day in rural area.

44. **(a)** There are three major components of food security; Availability (Buffer stock), Access and utilization/consumption.

45. **(d)** The movement in supply curve can be of two types - extension and contraction. Extension in a supply curve is caused when there is increase in the price or quantity supplied of the commodity while contraction is caused due to decrease in the price or quantity supplied of the commodity.

46. **(c)** The RBI borrows from the commercial banks as per the monetary demand & supply and to control the liquidity in the market. It borrows at an interest rate called the Reverse Repo Rate.

47. **(a)** Industrial democracy is an arrangement which involves workers making decisions, sharing responsibility and authority in the workplace.

48. **(d)**   49. **(c)**   50. **(c)**

51. **(a)** The indirect instruments of monetary policy generally operate through repurchase (repos) and outright transactions in government securities (open market operations).

52. **(c)**

53. **(b)** The law of diminishing marginal utility states that as a person increases consumption of a product while keeping consumption of other products constant, there is a decline in the marginal utility that person derives from consuming each additional unit of that product.

54. **(c)** The tax incidence depends on the relative price elasticity of supply and demand. When supply is more elastic than demand, buyers bear most of the tax burden. When demand is more elastic than supply, producers bear most of the cost of the tax. Tax revenue is larger the more inelastic the demand and supply are.

55. **(a)** The Society for Worldwide Interbank Financial Telecommunication (SWIFT) was founded in Brussels in 1973 under the leadership of its inaugural CEO, Carl Reuterskiöld , and was supported by 239 banks in fifteen countries. It started to establish common standards for financial transactions and a shared data processing system and worldwide communications network designed by Logica and developed by The Burroughs Corporation. Fundamental operating procedures, rules for liability, etc., were established in 1975 and the first message was sent in 1977. SWIFT's first United States operating center was inaugurated by Governor John N. Dalton of Virginia in 1979.

56. **(a)** Growth in production (in percent) of natural gas industries in India during the period 2015 - 2016 was negative. Production of refinery products, crude oil, natural gas, steel and cement dwindled in the period whereas fertilisers,

coal and cement reported healthy output numbers. Electricity had no fluctuation from last year.

57. (a) India Post Payments Bank is incorporated as a Public Sector Bank under the Department of Posts with 100% GOI equity. IPPB was launched on January 30th, 2017 in Ranchi and Raipur with the objective of being present in all corners of India by the end of the year.

58. (d) The Reserve Bank of India has constituted a 10-member 'High Level Task Force on Public Credit Registry (PCR) for India', which is headed by YM Deosthalee, ex-CMD, L&T Finance Holdings.

59. (c) An ETF, or exchange-traded fund, is a marketable security that tracks an index, a commodity, bonds, or a basket of assets like an index fund.

60. (a) An exclusive economic zone (EEZ) is a sea zone prescribed by the United Nations Convention on the Law of the Sea over which a state has special rights regarding the exploration and use of marine resources, including energy production from water and wind. It stretches from the baseline out to 200 nautical miles (nmi) from its coast. The term does not include either the territorial sea or the continental shelf beyond the 200 nmi limit.

61. (c) Geoffrey Kay has given the famous dictum- 'capital created underdevelopment not because it exploited the underdeveloped world, but because it did not exploit it enough.'

62. (a) A-1,B-2,C-3 and D-4 is the correct answer.

63. (d) In January 2015, the Ministry of Statistics & Programme Implementation has released the new series of national accounts, revising the base year from 2004-05 to 2011-12. The base year of national accounts was last revised in January 2010.

64. (b) GCI scores are calculated on basis of 12 categories called 'pillars of competitiveness which covers both business and social indicators. It includes pillars such as institutions, infrastructure, health and primary education, labour market efficiency, financial market development, technological readiness and market size.

65. (a) Devaluation of currency will be more beneficial if prices of domestic goods remains constant.

66. (a) Monitory policy in India uses 7 tools viz. cash reserve ratio, statutory liquidity ratio, repo and reserve repo rates, bank rate, marginal standing funding and open market operations.

67. (a) Mahalanobis model in India occurred as an analytical framework for India's Second Five Year Plan in 1955. The duration of plan holiday was from 1966 to 1969. The main reason behind the plan holiday was the Indo-Pakistan war & failure of third plan. During this plan annual plans were made and equal priority was given to agriculture its allied sectors and the industry sector. Rolling Plan was started with an annual plan for 1978-79 and as a continuation of the terminated fifth year plan.

68. (d) Brexit refers to Great Britain's expected withdrawal from the European Union (EU). A referendum was held on 23 June 2016, in which 52% of votes were in favor of leaving the EU. UK's economy was expected to be affected by the Brexit vote.

69. (a) Changes in Foreign Direct Investment (FDI) policy affected single brand trading, defense, and private security sectors, manufacturing of small arms, pharmaceuticals. Eight year relaxation for single brand retail is proposed, FDI limit for defense sector has been made applicable for small arms, and FDI limit is raised to 74% for private security agency.

70. (a) GST would be applied at each stage of sale/purchace of goods services, according to value added.

71. (a) Most-favoured-nation (MFN) Clause under the WTO regime ensured that countries should not discriminate between their trading nations and also that national and international business entities get equal treatment. The clause forms the first article of the General Agreement on Tariffs and Trade (GATT). Reducing tariffs and non-tariff barriers is also highlighted by the clause.

72. (a) 12th Five Year Plan (2012 - 2017) aimed at achieving growth rate of 8% by focusing on inclusive growth. The government aimed reducing poverty by 10 per cent during the plan. Skill Development Strategies needed for increasing employment. Promoting regional balances will promote equal economic growth of all states.

73. (c) In 2016, the Union Government of India announced a Rs. 6,000 crore special package for the textile and apparel industry to create one crore jobs, mostly for women, in the next three years. The package included several tax and production incentives. The government also planned to bring in more flexibility in labor laws to increase productivity.

74. (b) Bitcoin is a digital currency and was invented on October 31, 2008 by an unidentified programmer, or group of programmers called Satoshi Nakamoto. It uses complex computer software for its generation called Bitcoin mining. Reserve Bank of India (RBI) does not allow the use of Bitcoins, and warned those investing in it.

75. (b) The Trans-Pacific Partnership (TPP) is a trade agreement between 12 Pacific Rim nations including Australia, Brunei, Canada, Chile, Japan, Malaysia, Mexico, New Zealand, Peru, Singapore, the United States (until January 23, 2017) and Vietnam. These members account for 40 percent of global GDP. India is not a member of the TPP.

76. (d) Real GDP or Gross Domestic Product (GDP) growth of India at constant prices in the year 2015-16 is estimated at 7.56 percent in comparison to the growth rate of 7.24 percent in 2014-15. Real Gross Value Added growth at basic constant prices in 2015-16 is 7.3 per cent. Gross National Product is

the total value of goods produced and services provided by a country during a year.

77. **(b)** The Agreement on Trade-Related Aspects of Intellectual Property Rights (TRIPS) is an international legal agreement between the members of the World Trade Organization regarding setting standards for the regulation of intellectual property by national governments. It has 162 member nations and became effective on January 1, 1995.

78. **(c)** Government receipts which create liability or reduce assets is called capital receipts and the receipts which neither create liability nor reduce assets of Government are called revenue receipts. Corporate tax receipt, dividends and profits and interest receipt are revenue receipts (increase income), but disinvestment receipt is capital receipt (reduces asset).

79. **(c)** Indian economist K. N. Raj drafted sections of India's first Five-Year Plan. Second Five-Year Plan (1956-61) was drafted by scientist and statistician P.C. Mahalanobis, and mainly focused on heavy industries and transportation, particularly in the public sector.

80. **(a)** In 2011 Census, a person aged seven years and above who can both read and write in any language, is treated as 'literate'. In the Censuses prior to 1991, children below five years of age were treated as illiterates, but later, keeping in mind that the ability to read and write with understanding is not generally achieved until one has time to develop these skills, the defining age for the literate category was raised to seven in the Censuses of 2001 and 2011.

81. **(c)** Y. V. Reddy is the Chairman of Fourteenth Finance Commission of India.

82. **(d)** All three CRISIL,CARE and ICRA are credit rating agencies

83. **(d)** Hot money is cash that investors from foreign countries will invest during the short term in search of the highest interest rate possible. With the opening up of debt and equity markets to foreign portfolio investors, the FPI (Foreign Portfolio Investment) has emerged as the leading form of quick money flows globally.

84. **(b)** The contribution of Services Sector of India to overall GDP has increased sharply, from 41% in 1990-91 to 66% in 2014-15.

85. **(c)** The purpose of the National Investment Fund (NIF) is related to disinvestment proceedings of central public sector enterprises and to invest the same to generate earnings without depleting the corpus.
National Investment and Infrastructure Fund (NIIF) is a fund created by the Government of India for enhancing infrastructure financing in the country.

86. **(d)** Capital Deepening is the process of increasing the amount of capital per worker.

87. **(a)** Full employment is the employment level at which every individual who desires to work at the existing wage rate gets employed. If the condition of unemployment

occurs, it is a temporary/abnormal condition in the economy.

88. (c) If an economy is under inflationary pressure the most likely effects include the depreciation of domestic currencies and the cost of borrowing also decreases.

89. (c) A bank run occurs when a large number of customers of a bank or another financial institution withdraw their deposits simultaneously due to concerns about the bank's solvency. The panic situation arises when depositors withdraw their part fearing that the bank will be unable to repay their deposits in full and on time,

90. (c) The Economic and Social Commission for Asia and the Pacific (ESCAP) is the regional development arm of the United Nations for the Asia-Pacific region. It is a conglomerate of 53 Member States and 9 Associate Members. The headquarters of ESCAP is in Bangkok.

91. (d) When the re-organisation of production is not possible which can make any one better off with out making someone else worse off then efficiency occurs. Pareto Efficiency, pareto Optimality and Allocative Efficiency are all the same and indicates "efficiency in resource allocation".

92. (c) Transfer payment is a payment of money to individuals by government without taking any goods or services.

Examples :-
- Un employment allowance
- Social security payments
- Old age pension
- Student grant
- Subsidies to farmers, exporters & manufacturer.

93. (a) Electricity is not public good but it is club good including roads, bridges, gas, sewage, wires, telecom.

94. (b) Besides for the Wage Boards for journalists and non-journalists newspaper and new-agency employees being Statutory Wage Board, all other wage boards are non-statutory in application. That is why recommendations made by these boards are out of enforceable by the law.

95. (c) A progressive tax receives a larger percentage from the income of higher earners than it acts from low income person.

96. (c) The Advance Reservation Period (ARP) for booking tickets in trains is 120 days.

97. (b) Hedging is used in limiting or offsetting probability of loss from fluctuations in the prices of commodities, currencies or securities.

98. (d) Near Money is a term used in economics to describe highly liquid assets that can easily be converted into cash.

100. (c) The long-run Phillips curve is now seen as a vertical line at the natural rate of unemployment, where the rate of inflation has no effect on unemployment.

101. (b) The Fifth Five year plan (1974-79) had a high priority to bring inflation under control and to achieve stability in the economic situation.

102. (c) It is an activity by a central bank(RBI) to buy or sell government securities. The aim of open market operations is to manipulate the short term interest rate and the supply of base money in an economy, and indirectly control the total money supply.

103. (a) Marginal Standing Facility rate is the rate at which banks borrow funds overnight from the Reserve Bank of India (RBI) against approved government securities. Net Demand and time liability is the sum of demand and time liability of Banks with public and other banks wherein assets with other banks is subtracted to get net liability of other bank.

104. (d) National Income is the money value of all the final goods and services produced by a country during a period of one year. National Income consists of a collection of different types of goods and services of different types.

105. (a) "A" is the most appropriate choice. Mobile wallets will not be necessary, because your mobile number is directly linked with the bank account using bank's 'customized app' which is built on the UPI platform.

106. (c) Disguised unemployment is a situation when people do not have productive full-time employment, but are not counted in the official unemployment statistics.

107. (b) Electricity generation (weight: 10.32%) increased by 3.5% in July, 2015. Its cumulative index during April to July, 2015-16 increased by 2.0 % over the corresponding period of previous year.

108. (c) The labour Bureau brings out "consumer price index numbers" for industrial workers.

109. (a) In order to boost 'Make in India' campaign, first national investment and manufacturing zone to come up in Andhra Pradesh. The state assured the Centre of availability of 10 sq km of land in one place in Prakasham district.
Ref: Economic Times/ET Bureau Sep 21, 2015. http://articles.economictimes.indiatimes.com/2015-09-21/news/66760948_1_andhra-pradesh-nimz-manufacturing-zone

110. (c) The value of all commodities and services could be measured in terms of money, but money cannot be measured through itself. Since money is used to measure and exchange the goods and services produced in any economy, it is better to evaluate money value in proportion of Gross Domestic Products (GDP). The value of GDP at Market Prices in proportion of Broad Money may reveal lowest value of Money whereas Value of GDP at Market Prices in proportion to currency with the public reveals the highest money value.

111. (e) Dematerialization in short called as Demat' is the process by which an investor can get physical certificates converted into electronic form maintained in an account with the Depository Participant. The investors can dematerialize only those share certificates that are already registered in their name and belong to the list of securities admitted for dematerialization at the depositories.

112. (b) The mutual fund's NAV is its net asset value, or price per share. A

mutual fund calculates its NAV by adding up the current value of all the stocks, bonds and other securities (Including cash) In Its portfolio, subtracting the managers salary and other operating expenses, and dividing that figure by the fund's total number of shares. Each end of the business day. net asset value are calculated and referred as net asset value per share. The mutual fund's net asset value is changing daily because of market fluctuations affecting the investments of funds.

113. (b) National Bank for Agriculture and Rural Development (NABARD) is an apex development bank. In India having headquarters based in Mumbai (Maharashtra) and other branches are all over the country. It was established on 12 July 1982 by a special act by the parliament and its main focus was to uplift rural India by increasing the credit flow for elevation of agriculture & rural non farm sector.

114. (b) When goods are sold at higher prices so that fewer sales are needed to break even, it is known as creaming or skimming. Selling a product at a high price, sacrificing high sales to gain a high profit is therefore 'skimming' the market. Skimming is usually employed to reimburse the cost of investment of the original research into the product: commonly used in electronic markets when a new range, such as DVD players, are firstly dispatched into the market at a high price. This strategy is often used to target early adopters" of a product or service.

115. (a) The Securities and Exchange Board of India (frequently abbreviated SEBI) is the regulator for the securities market In India. It was established in the year 1988 and given statutory powers on 12 April 1992 through the SEBI Act, 1992. It Is mandated protect the interests of investors in securities and to promote the development of, and to regulate the securities market and for matters connected therewith.

116. (c) Indian market regulator SEBI recently introduced new type of Demat Account to woo small Investors In Opting securities in Demat form. This type of Demat account is called 'Basic Services Demat Account (BSDAY). This initiative is to reach the IPOs to ret all Investors and promoting small Investors to have their securities In Demat form. It became effective from 1 October 2012.

117. (c)	118. (b)	119. (c)	120. (a)
121. (c)	122. (d)	123. (c)	124. (b)
125. (c)	130. (e)	131. (b)	132. (e)
133. (e)	134. (b)	135. (b)	136. (a)
137. (b)	138. (a)	139. (c)	140. (b)
141. (b)	142. (e)	143. (a)	144. (d)
145. (b)	146. (c)	147. (d)	148. (a)
149. (e)	150. (b)	151. (c)	152. (b)
153. (b)	154. (a)	155. (c)	156. (b)
157. (a)	158. (d)	159. (c)	160. (c)
161. (d)	162. (d)	163. (b)	164. (c)
165. (b)	166. (d)	167. (e)	168. (c)
169. (d)	170. (b)	171. (d)	172. (e)
173. (c)	174. (a)	175. (a)	176. (a)
177. (d)	178. (c)	179. (b)	180. (b)
181. (a)	182. (c)	183. (c)	184. (c)
185. (c)	186. (d)	187. (b)	188. (c)
189. (a)	190. (a)	191. (a)	192. (b)
193. (a)	194. (a)	195. (d)	196. (c)
197. (a)	198. (b)	199. (a)	200. (c)
201. (d)	202. (d)	203. (b)	204. (e)
205. (a)	206. (a)	207. (d)	208. (a)
209. (c)	210. (d)	211. (c)	212. (a)
213. (b)	214. (d)	215. (b)	216. (a)
217. (e)	218. (c)	219. (b)	220. (a)
221. (d)	222. (b)	223. (a)	224. (c)
225. (a)	226. (b)	227. (c)	228. (e)

229. (a)	230. (a)	231. (a)	232. (d)
233. (e)	234. (a)	235. (a)	236. (e)
237. (a)	238. (c)	239. (b)	240. (a)
241. (c)	242. (d)	243. (a)	244. (b)
245. (a)	246. (c)	247. (d)	248. (a)
249. (e)	250. (a)	251. (b)	252. (c)
253. (d)	254. (a)	255. (a)	256. (c)
257. (c)	258. (a)	259. (a)	260. (d)
261. (d)	262. (e)	263. (c)	264. (e)
265. (c)	266. (b)	267. (c)	268. (a)
269. (c)	270. (b)	271. (d)	272. (a)
273. (c)	274. (e)	275. (a)	276. (b)
277. (a)	278. (a)	279. (a)	280. (c)
281. (b)	282. (c)	283. (e)	284. (b)
285. (a)	286. (c)	287. (c)	288. (a)
289. (a)	290. (d)	291. (b)	292. (c)

293. (a)	294. (b)	295. (d)	296. (b)
297. (a)	298. (a)	299. (a)	300. (a)
301. (a)	302. (c)	303. (d)	304. (a)
305. (a)	306. (c)	307. (a)	308. (c)
309. (a)	310. (c)	311. (a)	312. (a)
313. (a)	314. (a)	315. (a)	316. (a)
317. (a)	318. (a)	319. (d)	320. (d)
321. (b)	322. (d)	323. (d)	324. (b)
325. (a)	326. (c)	327. (a)	328. (a)
329. (d)	330. (b)	331. (a)	332. (c)
333. (a)	334. (b)	335. (a)	336. (b)
337. (a)	338. (a)	339. (c)	340. (b)
341. (a)	342. (c)	343. (a)	344. (b)
345. (d)	346. (a)	347. (a)	348. (c)
349. (a)	350. (b)	351. (a)	352. (a)
353. (a)	354. (d)		

LOK SABHA ELECTION 2019: AT A GLANCE

The 2019 Lok Sabha Election Results are declared, the Bhartiya Janata Party (BJP) has won 303 seats on its own, surpassing its previous record of 282 seats in 20The 16th Lok Sabha has been dissolved with the acceptance of the resignation of Prime Minister Narendra Modi and his Council of Ministers by President Ram Nath Kovind on May 24, 20

However, President Kovind requested the Government to continue to serve till the new Government assumes office. The term of the 16th Lok Sabha will officially end on June 3, 20Hence, the 17th Lok Sabha will be constituted prior to that.

Lok Sabha Election Results 2019	
BJP	303
Congress	52
Dravida Munnetra Kazhagam (DMK)	23
Trinamool Congress (TMC)	22
Yuvajana Sramika Rythu (YSR) Congress	22
Shiv Sena	18
Janata Dal (United)	16
Biju Janata Dal	12
Bahujan Samaj Party	10
Telangana Rashtra Samithi	9
Others	55
Total	**542**

RBI releases 'Vision 2021' for e-payment system:

The Reserve Bank of India (RBI) on May 15, 2019 released 'Payment and Settlement Systems in India: Vision 2019 – 2021', a vision document for safe, secure, quick and affordable e-payment system.

Highlights of Payment Systems Vision 2021:

- The Payment Systems Vision 2021 states 36 specific action points and 12 specific outcomes.

- The document deliberates on boosting customer awareness, setting up a 24X7 helpline and self-regulatory organisation for e-payment service providers.

- The main agenda of the vision document is the 'no-compromise' approach towards safety and security of payment systems.

UNDRR confers P.K. Mishra with prestigious Sasakawa Award 2019:

The United Nations Office for Disaster Risk Reduction (UNDRR) on May 16, 2019 honoured Dr Pramod Kumar Mishra, Additional Principal Secretary to Prime

Minister Narendra Modi, with the 'Sasakawa Award 2019 for Disaster Risk Reduction'. The award was announced during the 6th Session of 'Global Platform for Disaster Risk Reduction' (GPDRR) 2019, which is being held at Geneva, Switzerland.

India's GS Lakshmi appointed first female match referee by ICC:

Former Indian cricketer, GS Lakshmi was on May 14, 2019 appointed by the International Cricket Council as the first-ever woman referee on the international panel of match referees.

Indian Postal Department released Postage Stamp to commemorate 750th Birth Anniversary of Sri Vedanta Desika:

In order to commemorate the 750th birth anniversary of Sri Vedanta Desikan, Vice President, M. Venkaiah Naidu unveiled a postage stamp in New Delhi on May 2, 20The stamp has been released by Indian postal department. Born in 1268 CE, he was Sri Vaishnava philosopher and one of the most brilliant stalwarts of Sri Vaishnavism in the post-Ramanuja period.

PayPal India launched One Touch with the help of Google Smart Lock for seamless transactions:

PayPal India used Google Smart Lock and launched its OneTouch experience in India. The launch of the One Touch feature permits Indian consumers to register their android device with PayPal and stay logged into PayPal for further PayPal purchases on that device, thus removing the issue of repeated log-ins and enabling a seamless payments experience.

LIC HFL initiated UDYAM -a skill development centre for marginalized youth in Bangalore:

As a part of Corporate Social Responsibility (CSR), LIC Housing Finance Ltd (LIC HFL) in association with Lok Bharti Education Society has unveiled a skilling centre named "UDYAM" in Bangalore, which will provide skill development training to marginalized youth in the sectors of BFSI, Retail and IT/ITES.

First Bi-monthly Monetary Policy Statement 2019-20 :

- Monetary Policy Committee (MPC) decided to reduce the policy repo rate under the liquidity adjustment facility (LAF) by 25 basis points to 6.0 per cent from 6.25 per cent with immediate effect

- Reverse repo rate under the LAF stands adjusted to 5.75 per cent, and the marginal standing facility (MSF) rate and the Bank Rate to 6.25 per cent.

- GDP growth for 2019-20 is projected at 7.2 per cent – in the range of 6.8-7.1 per cent in H1:2019-20 and 7.3-7.4 percent in H2. The next meeting of the MPC is scheduled during June 3, 4 and 6, 2019.

Monetary Policy Rate	
Repo Rate	6.00%
MSF Rate	6.25%
CRR	4%
Repo Rate	6.00%
MSF Rate	6.25%
CRR	4%

RBI sells entire stake in NHB, Nabard to govt for Rs. 1,470 crore:

- The Reserve Bank of India (RBI) has divested its entire stake in Nabard and National Housing Bank (NHB) for Rs. 20 crore and Rs. 1,450 crore, on 26 February and 19 March, respectively. With this, the Government of India now holds 100% stake in both the financial institutions.

- RBI held 100% shareholding in NHB, which was divested on 19 March 20The current change in the capital structure of both the financial institutions was brought in by the Government of India through amendments to the NABARD Act, 1981 and the NHB Act, 19

RBI became the first APAC central bank to begin interest rate easing cycle

- The Reserve Bank of India is the first central bank in the Asia-Pacific region to begin an explicit interest rate easing cycle. The monetary policy committee led by Shaktikanta Das cut the repo rate by 0.25 percentage point in February 2019 and again by 0.25 percentage point in March 2019, taking the total repo rate down to 6 per cent, the lowest in about nine years since 2010

- Inflation at 2.9 per cent has remained within the RBI's comfort zone of 4 per cent (+/- 2 per cent).

Fitch has predicted GDP growth rate of 6.8% in FY20 for India.

- RBI extends ombudsman scheme to non-deposit taking NBFCs:

- Reserve Bank of India has announced to extend the ambit of Ombudsman scheme for NBFCs to all eligible non deposit taking NBFCs as well. The scheme which lays down rules for redressal mechanism in cases of customer complaints was earlier applicable only to deposit-taking NBFCs.

- All Non-Deposit Taking Non-Banking Financial Companies having customer interface, with assets size of Rupees 100 crore or above will come within the ambit, and shall comply with the provisions of the Ombudsman Scheme for Non Banking Financial Companies.

- The scheme still excludes various NBFC groups such as Infrastructure Finance Companies (NBFC-IFC), Core Investment Company (CIC), Infrastructure Debt Fund-Non-Banking Financial Company (IDF-NBFC) and also NBFCs under liquidation.

Karnataka Bank signs MOU with Bharti Axa Life Insurance :

- Karnataka Bank has entered into a memorandum of understanding with Bharti AXA Life Insurance Company to distribute the latter's life insurance products

- This is the third such tie-up by the bank after PNB MetLife Life Insurance Company and LIC of India, both of which continue to provide insurance solutions to the customers of Karnataka Bank.

Bank of India to sell 25% stake in life insurance JV SUD Life Insurance for Rs. 1,106 crore

- Public sector lender Bank of India offered to sell a 25 per cent stake in its joint venture company Star Union Dai-ichi Life Insurance Co Ltd for approximately Rs. 1,106 crore ($159.87 million).

- Star Union Dai-ichi Life Insurance Co. Ltd. (SUD Life) is a joint venture (JV) of Bank of India, Union Bank of India and Dai-ichi Life, a leading life insurance company of Japan

- Bank of India to sell 6.49 crore shares, or 25.02 per cent stake, in Star Union Dai-ichi Life Insurance Co at a floor price of 170.50 per share.

Canara Bank, Canara HSBC OBC Life launch „Webassurance:

- Public sector lender Canara Bank and its life insurance partner Canara HSBC Oriental Bank of Commerce Life Insurance announced the launch of 'Webassurance'.

- Four life insurance products of Canara HSBC OBC Life would be made available to customers of Canara Bank, covering the key needs of child future, savings and investments, retirement planning and protection.

- Canara HSBC OBC Life is jointly owned by two public sector banks Canara Bank (51 per cent) and Oriental Bank of Commerce (23 per cent) and HSBC Insurance (Asia Pacific) Holdings (26 per cent), the Asian insurance arm of banking and financial services groups HSBC.

IRDAI asks insurers to share status of claims with policyholders:

- The Insurance Regulatory and Development Authority of India (IRDAI) has advised all the insurance company to devise a framework to share the status of claims by developing a tracking mechanism for policyholders so as to enable them to know the status of their claim.

- Insurance companies will have to inform about claim settlement status to policyholders at various stages of processing

NATIONAL

World's largest solar park launched in Karnataka :

Karnataka's Chief Minister, Siddaramaiah has launched the world's largest solar park in the state. The solar park has been set up with an investment of ` 16,500 crore at Pavagada in Karnataka's Tumakuru district. The 2000 MW park is named as 'Shakti Sthala' and spans across 13000 acres. It is spread over five villages and is a benchmark in the unique for people's participation in power model put on ground.

National Conference on Doubling Farmers' Income by 2022 :

The conference ''Agriculture 2022 - Doubling Farmers' Income'' was inaugurated by Union Minister for Agriculture and Farmers Welfare Shri Radha Mohan Singh. Prime Minister Narendra Modi attended the last session of this two day conference organized at National Agriculture Science Complex (NASC), Pusa, New Delhi.

The conference was organized in the backdrop of Ashok Dalwai Panel, which was set up for doubling of farmers' income.

The panel pointed out that real income of farmers' need to register a compound annual growth rate of 10.4% for farmers' income to double by 20

The summit was attended by Farmers, senior officials from the Central and State Governments, scientists, economists, representatives from professional associations, academicians, Industry and NGOs.

Pradhan Mantri Jan Arogya Abhiyaan :

Prime Minister Narendra Modi recently rolled out the Centre's flagship scheme — Pradhan Mantri Jan Arogya Abhiyaan, also known as Ayushman Bharat.

Ayushman Bharat is the National Health Protection Scheme, which will cover over 10 crore poor vulnerable families (around 50 crore beneficiaries) providing coverage of up to ₹ 5 lakh (per family per year) for secondary and tertiary care hospitalisation. It will subsume the on-going centrally sponsored schemes – Rashtriya Swasthya Bima Yojana (RSBY) and the Senior Citizen Health Insurance Scheme (SCHIS). It will be an entitlement based scheme with entitlement decided on the basis of deprivation criteria in the SECC database.

Yuva Sahakar Scheme :

National Cooperative Development Corporation (NCDC) has come up with a youth-friendly scheme 'Yuva Sahakar-Cooperative Enterprise Support and Innovation Scheme.''

About the scheme:

- NCDC has created a dedicated fund with liberal features enabling youth to avail the scheme

- The scheme will be linked to ` 1000 crore 'Cooperative Start-up and Innovation Fund (CSIF)' created by the NCDC.

- The funding for the project will be up to 80% of the project cost for these special categories as against 70% for others.

Witness Protection Scheme 2018 :

The Supreme Court has approved the Centre's draft witness protection scheme and has asked all the states to implement it till Parliament comes out with a legislation. The court has also made some changes in the scheme.

The draft witness protection scheme has been finalised in consultation with the National Legal Services Authority (NALSA) and Bureau of Police Research and Development (BPRD). The types of protection measures envisaged under the scheme are to be applied in proportion to the threat and they are not expected to go on for infinite time.

Chennai Became The World's Largest Rail Coach Manufacturer:

Indian Railways Integral Coach Factory (ICF) has surpassed the top Chinese manufacturers after creating a 40% record increase in its production.

Kiru Hydro Electric (HE) Project:

The Cabinet Committee on Economic Affairs has approved the investment sanction for construction of Kiru Hydro Electric (HE) Project (624 MW) in Jammu & Kashmir.

Atal Solar Krushi Pump Yojana:

Maharashtra government has launched Atal Solar Krushi Pump Yojana. Under the scheme, the government of Maharashtra has decided to give two LED bulbs, a DC fan and a mobile charging socket as freebies to farmers. The scheme provides a subsidy of up to 95% on solar pump sets. The State plans to install one lakh solar pumps.

ISRO Launches PSLV C-45 Carrying EMISAT And 28 Nano Satellites:

The Indian Space Research Organisation (ISRO) has launched a Defence Intelligence Satellite, EMISAT in its 47th Polar Satellite Launch Vehicle (PSLV) mission, along with 28 other customer satellites onboard the advanced PSLV-C45 Rocket.

Indian Army Builds Longest Suspension Bridge Over River Indus In Leh-Ladakh:

The Indian Army has successfully built the longest suspension bridge 'Matiri Bridge' over the Indus River in the Leh-Ladakh region. Built in a record time of 40 days 'Maitri Bridge' is longest Suspension Bridge over Indus River.

NuGen Mobility Summit To Be Held in November 2019:

The International Centre for Automotive Technology (ICAT) is organizing a NuGen Mobility Summit, 2019, at Manesar, NCR, from 27th to 29th November 20

BSNL Gets Licence For WiFi On Flights:

State-owned telecom service provider Bharatiya Sanchar Nigam Limited (BSNL) has received a licence from the Department of Telecommunications to provide Internet and mobile services on flights.

India's 1st Indigenously Built Dhanush Howitzer Inducted In Army:

India's first indigenously designed and developed Dhanush artillery gun was inducted in the Indian Army during a ceremony held at Ordnance Factory in Jabalpur, MP. The Army had placed an order for more than 110 of these guns with the Ordnance Factory.

Guwahati Railway Station 1st To Get ISO Certification In India:

The Guwahati Railway Station has become the first ever railway station in the Indian Railways to get an ISO certification from the National Green Tribunal (NGT) for "providing passenger amenities in a clean and green environment."

President Launches 'CRPF Veer Parivar' App For Families of Martyred CRPF Troops:

President Ram Nath Kovind launched 'CRPF Veer Parivar' app, a mobile application for families of CRPF personnel killed in the line of duty. The app was launched after the President paid his tributes to the fallen troops at the National Police Memorial in Delhi on the occasion of the CRPF's 'Valour Day'.

Namami Gange Gets Global Recognition At World Summit:

The National Mission for Clean Ganga (NMCG) was awarded the distinction of "Public Water Agency of the Year" by Global Water Intelligence at the Global Water Summit in London.

India Successfully Test Fires Sub-Sonic Cruise Missile 'Nirbhay':

India has successfully test-fired first indigenously designed and developed long-range sub-sonic cruise missile 'Nirbhay' from a test range in Odisha. The all-weather missile has a 1,000-kilometre strike range.

First-Of-Its-Kind 'Voter Park' Inaugurated In Gurugram:

India's first-of-its-kind 'Voter Park' was inaugurated in Gurugram, Haryana, aimed at increasing voter awareness and educating people about the electoral process.

India's First Foreign Interactive Bird Park Launched In Mumbai:

India's first exotic Bird Park 'Essel World Bird Park' was launched by Essel World Leisure Pvt. Ltd, the entertainment arm of the $6-billion Essel Group in Mumbai.

New Railway Zone Announced For Andhra Pradesh:

Union Railway Minister Piyush Goyal announced a new railway zone for Andhra Pradesh, that is the Southern Coast Railway and it will be headquartered in Visakhapatnam. It will be the 18th zone in the country.

PM Launches 'One Nation One Card':

PM Narendra Modi launched the indigenously-developed National Common Mobility Card (NCMC) to enable people to pay multiple kinds of transport charges, including metro services and toll tax across the country.

INTERNATIONAL

Tesla Builds Its 'Largest Energy Storage System In Asia':

Tesla has developed its 'largest power storage system in Asia' at Osaka train station in Japan to reduce energy demand and provide emergency backup power to trains in Japan. It was launched in partnership with Kintetsu, a railway operator in Japan's Osaka. 7 megawatt-hours (MWh) system is its largest energy storage project in Asia and the fourth largest in the greater Asia-Pacific (APAC) region.

China Launches Its 2nd Generational Data Relay Satellite, Tianlian II-01:

China has successfully launched the first of its new-generation data relay satellite, Tianlian II-01 into orbit that will provide data relay, measurement, and control services for its manned spacecraft.

Google Launches Its 1st Drone Delivery Service In Australia:

Google parent Alphabet has beaten Amazon to launch one of the first commercial drone delivery businesses.

Emirates Islamic Becomes World's 1st Islamic Bank To Launch Banking Via WhatsApp:

Emirates Islamic has announced the launch of Chat Banking services for customers via WhatsApp, marking a global first in the Islamic banking sector.

India To Be Guest of Honour Country At ADIBF 2019 :

The UAE has announced that India will be the Guest of Honour country at the Abu Dhabi International Book Fair, ADIBF 2019, to be held at the end of April 2019.

UAE To Host World's Foremost Artificial Intelligence Summit:

UAE is set to host the world's foremost Artificial Intelligence (AI) Summit to empower global dialogue on the future of government, business and society. The inaugural 'AI Everything', AIE will take place at the Dubai World Trade Centre.

China Develops World's First Armed Amphibious Drone Boat:

The world's first armed amphibious drone boat named 'Marine Lizard' and guided by China's BeiDou Navigation Satellite System, has been successfully tested by China.

IMF & World Bank Launched 'Learning Coin' For In-House Purposes:

The International Monetary Fund (IMF) and the World Bank have together launched a private blockchain with a pseudo-token. The new token, called "Learning Coin" and only accessible within the IMF and World Bank, has a purpose to teach relevant individuals within the organizations about blockchain.

Sri Lanka's 1st Satellite 'Raavana-1' Launched Into Space:

Sri Lanka's first satellite 'Raavana-1' was launched into space from NASA's Flight Facility on Virginia's east shore. 'Raavana 1' weighs around 1.05 kg and the lifespan of the satellite is around one and a half years.

Russia Successfully Tests World's First Floating Nuclear Power Plant:

Russia has successfully tested the world's first floating nuclear power plant (NPP), Akademik Lomonosov, a subsidiary of Rosatom nuclear corporation stated. Reactors of the floating atomic block were launched in November 2018.

Sary-Arka-Antiterror 2019 - SCO joint anti-terrorism exercise:

The Shanghai Cooperation Organization's (SCO) member states will hold a joint anti-terrorism exercise "Sary-Arka-Antiterror 2019." The decision to hold a joint exercise was announced during the 34th meeting of the RATS council held in Tashkent, Uzbekistan.

ENVIRONMENT UPDATES

National Clean Air Program:

The government has announced the National Clean Air Programme (NCAP). This is the first ever effort in the country to frame a national framework for air quality management with a time-bound reduction target.

Fire Alert System (FAST) Version 3.0:

The Forest Survey of India (FSI), a body under the Environment Ministry, which is responsible for assessment and monitoring India's forest resources, launched the beta-version of the Large Forest Fire Monitoring Program.

Climate Change Performance Index (CCPI) 2019:

To encourage political and social pressure on those countries which have up to now failed to take ambitious actions on climate protection as well as to highlight countries with best-practice climate policies. The 2019 edition of the Climate Change Performance Index (CCPI) has been released.

- Globally, Sweden is in top position, followed by Morocco and Lithuania in the CCPI 2019.

- The bottom five in the list are Saudi Arabia, U.S., Iran, South Korea and Taiwan.

UN Environment Assembly:

The Fourth Environment Assembly was held in Nairobi, focusing on the theme "Innovative solutions for environmental challenges and sustainable consumption and production".

India's first forest-certification scheme gets global recognition:

The council of Programme for Endorsement of Forest Certification (PEFC), a Geneva-based non-profit organisation, has decided to endorse the Certification Standard for Sustainable Forest Management (SFM) developed by Network for Certification and Conservation of Forests (NCCF), an Indian non-profit organisation.

SPORTS

Asian Games 2018: India ends Asian Games campaign with best medal haul :

The 18th edition of Asian Games concluded in Jakarta, Indonesia on September 2. India concluded its run at the Asian Games with a record show that boasted of a total of 69 medals, including 15gold, 24 silver and 30 bronze. The previous highest medal tally for India was at the 2010 edition in Guangzhou, China where they had finished 6th with14 gold, 17silver and 34 bronze.

India has also created new national records in several sports and registered many firsts, some of which are listed below:

- PV Sindhu became the first badminton player to win silver in Asian Games.
- Rahi Sarnobat became the first Indian woman to win a gold medal in shooting at the Asian Games.
- Vinesh Phogat became the first Indian woman wrestler to win a gold medal at the Asian Games.
- Swapna Barman gave India its first-ever Asiad gold in women's heptathlon event.
- Neeraj Chopra became the first Indian javelin thrower to win an Asiad gold.
- Fouaad Mirza became the first Indian to win an Asian Games individual equestrian medal since 19
- India also won its first medal in sepaktakraw at the 18th Asian Games.

National Sports Awards 2018:

Union Ministry of Youth Affairs and Sports has announced The Na tional Sports Awards 2018 were on 20th September, 20Cricket captain Virat Kohli and world champion weightlifter Mirabai Chanu has been jointly conferred with Rajiv Gandhi Khel Ratna award 2018, India's highest sporting honour.

8 coaches of different discipline have been conferred with Dronacharya Awards. Arjuna Award, dhayanchand Award, Rashtriyakhel Protsahan Puruskar and Maulana Abulkalam Azad Trophy were also given to the players of different discipline.

Asian Para Games 2018: India records best-ever show with 72 medals

India has concluded its campaign at the 2018 Asian Para Games in Jakarta, Indonesia with a record medal haul, winning a total of 72 medals that included 15gold, 24 silver and 33 bronze medals. India was placed 9th in the overall tally.

Government to set up National Sports Stadium for differently-abled in Meghalaya:

The Union Minister of Social Justice and Empowerment, Thaawarchand Gehlot has announced that a stadium of international standard for differently-abled persons will be set up in Meghalaya. The stadium will be constructed at an estimated cost of over ` 200 crore.

India's Vedangi Kulkarni becomes fastest Asian to cycle the globe:

Indian woman Vedangi Kulkarni has become the fastest Asian to cycle the globe. The 20-year-old completed the 29,000 kilometers' distance required to qualify as bicycling across the globe on December 23, 20Overall, Kulkarni spent 159 days peddling up to 300 km a day in 14 countries.

Starting off from Perth in July, she will now be flying back to the Australian city to complete the record by cycling a 15 km distance to reach the same place from where she started.

Smriti Mandhana named ICC Women's Cricketer of the Year:

Smriti Mandhana has been named as Best player of the year, ODI Player of the Year and included in ICC Women's Team of the Year 20The cricketer had played a crucial role in India's semi-final appearance at the ICC Women's World T20 in the West Indies.

Mary Kom becomes 'World No 1' Boxer in latest AIBA World Rankings :

'Magnificent Mary' became the most successful boxer in world championships history when she claimed the 48kg category top honours in November 2018, her unprecedented sixth world title triumph.

Vinesh Phogat becomes first Indian athlete to be nominated in Laureus World Comeback of Year Award

Indian star wrestler Vinesh Phogat has become the first Indian athlete to be nominated for the prestigious Laureus World Comeback of the Year Award. Phogat has been nominated for the award alongside US Tour Championship winner Tiger Woods, who won his first tournament in five years.

XXI Commonwealth Games:

The XXI Commonwealth Games inaugurated in Gold Coast, Australia. The Venue of the Opening Ceremony was Carrara Stadium. 'Borobi' is officially named as the mascot of the 2018 Commonwealth Games which will formally conclude on 15th April. The Commonwealth Games have been conducted by the Commonwealth Games Federation and held at an interval of every four years. Since the first British Empire Games were held in Hamilton (Canada, 1930) the Games have grown from an event featuring 11 countries and 400 athletes to a sporting extravaganza with 71 nations and territories and over 6,600 athletes and team officials.

2018 FIFA World Cup Football:

France has won 2018 FIFA World Cup Football by defeating Croatia by 4-2 goals in the final match held at the Luzhniki Stadium in Moscow, Russia. It was France's second World Cup crown after it had own it in 1998 (by defeating Brazil) on home soil. With this, victory France joins Uruguay and Argentina in winning World Cup for a second time. It was Croatia's first World Cup final appearance and smallest country ever to reach final in the modern era.

2018 FIFA World Cup Awards:

Top 4 team rankings: France (1st, Winner), Croatia (2nd, Croatia), Belgium (3rd) and England (4th). Golden Ball award: Luka Modric (Croatia).

Golden Ball award: Luka Modric (Croatia)

Golden Boot award: Harry Kane (England captain) for scoring six goals across six games

Golden Glove award: Thibaut Courtois (Belgium). FIFA Young Player award: 19-year-old Kylian Mbappe (France)

FIFA Fair Play Award: Spain for superb disciplinary record

2018 Wimbledon Championships :

The 2018 Wimbledon Championships, the 132nd edition of the Championships took place at the All England Lawn Tennis and Croquet Club in Wimbledon, London, United Kingdom. The main tournament began on 2 July 2018 and finished on 15 July 20The results are as follows:

Men's Singles title: Serbia's Novak Djokovic (World Number 21) won the 2018 Wimbledon title in men's singles category by defeating Kevin Anderson (South Africa) in straight sets 6-2, 6-2, 7-6.

Women's Singles title: Angelique Kerber

(Germany) won the 2018 Wimbledon title in women's singles category by defeating Serena Williams (United States) in straight sets 6–3, 6–3.

Men's Doubles: It was won by Mike Bryan and Jack Sock pair from United States. They defeated Raven Klaasen (South Africa) and Michael Venus (New Zealand) pair by 6-3, 6-7(7-9), 6-3, 5-7, 7-5.

Women's Doubles: It was won by Barbora Krejčíková and Kateřina Siniaková pair from Czech Republic.

Mixed Doubles: It was won by Alexander Peya (Austria) and Nicole Melichar (United States) pair. They had defeated Jamie Murray (United Kingdom) and Victoria Azarenka (Belarus) by 7-6(7-1), 6-3.

India To Host U-17 Women's Football World Cup In 2020:

India will host the Under-17 Women's Football World Cup in 2020.This was announced by the President of International Football Federation (FIFA) Gianni Infantino after the council meeting in Miami, USA.

Virat Kohli Named Wisden's Leading Cricketer:

Team India captain Virat Kohli has been named as the Wisden Almanack's 'Leading Cricketer of the Year' for the third straight time. The 30-year-old smashed 2,735 runs in 47 international innings at an average of 68.37 in 2018, including 11 hundred and nine fifties.

Smriti Mandhana Named Wisden's Leading Women's Cricketer Of The Year:

Team India opener Smriti Mandhana has been named as the Wisden Almanack's 'Leading Women's Cricketer of the Year'.

Meena Kumari Maisnam Clinches Gold In Boxing World Cup 2019:

India bagged a Gold and two Silver medals at the Boxing World Cup at Cologne in Germany. Meena Kumari Maisnam (from Manipur) claimed the Gold medal in the 54 kg category.

Bajrang Regains Top Spot In World Wrestling Rankings:

India's Bajrang Punia has regained the world number one spot in the men's 65-kilogram freestyle category rankings. The rankings were released by United World Wrestling.

Bajrang Punia Wins Gold In Asian Wrestling Championship:

World number one Bajrang Punia won gold at Asian Wrestling Championship in China's Xian. He defeated Kazakhstan's Sayatbek Okassov in a nail-biting 65kg men's freestyle final.

Deepak Singh Wins Gold At Makran Cup In Boxing:

National Boxing champion Deepak Singh (49 kg) was the only Indian boxer to notch up the gold medal, while five others claimed silver medals in the Makran Cup in Chabahar, Iran.

AWARDS & HONOURS

Gandhi Peace Prize for 2018:

WHO Goodwill ambassador Yohei Sasakawa will get Gandhi Peace Prize for 20The award was given to Mr Sasakawa in recognition of his work towards the eradication of the disease in India and across the world.

Nari Shakti Puraskar 2018:

To acknowledge Women's achievements, the Government of India confers Nari Shakti Puraskars on eminent women and institutions in recognition of their service towards the cause of women empowerment. The award is given by the Ministry of Women and Child Development. The award carries a cash award of Rs.1 Lakh and a certificate for individuals and institutions.

PM Modi Awarded Russia's Highest State Honour:

Prime Minister Narendra Modi was decorated with Order of St Andrew the Apostle – the highest state decoration of Russia, for exceptional services in promoting special and privileged strategic partnership between the two countries.

Shanti Swarup Bhatnagar Prizes Conferred For Science & Tech:

Prime Minister Narendra Modi conferred the Shanti Swarup Bhatnagar Prizes for Science and Technology for the years 2016, 2017 and 2018 in New Delhi.

2 West Bengal Government Schemes Win UN Awards:

Two schemes of the West Bengal government for skill development-"Utkarsh Bangla" and distribution of bicycles to students "Sabooj Sathi" have won the prestigious World Summit on the Information Society (WSIS) awards of the United Nations. The "Utkarsh Bangla" project aims at creating a pool of skilled candidates who are industry ready, while under the "Sabooj Sathi" scheme, bicycles are distributed to students between class IX and XII studying in government-run and government-aided schools and madrasas of the state.

Telugu Poet K Siva Reddy Selected For Prestigious Saraswati Samman 2018:

Telugu poet K Siva Reddy has been selected for the prestigious Saraswati Samman, 2018 for his collection of poetry titled Pakkaki Ottigilite. The award carries a cash prize of 15 lakh rupees, a citation and a plaque.

Dr A K Singh Conferred With Lifetime Achievement Award:

Dr. A K Singh, director at Life Sciences, DRDO has been honoured with Lifetime Achievement Award 2019 during 4th APJ Abdul Kalam Innovation Conclave at Chandigarh University, Mohali.

NY Times, Wall Street Journal Win Pulitzers For Trump Probes:

The New York Times and The Wall Street Journal were awarded Pulitzer Prizes for their separate investigations of President Donald Trump and his family.

Indian Bank Receives Best Bank Award From The State Government Of Tamil Nadu:

Indian Bank, a Public Sector Bank (PSB), headquartered at Chennai, Tamil Nadu has been awarded the Best Bank Award by the Tamil Nadu government for successfully meeting the needs of women's self-help groups (SHGs).

'Notun Disha' Initiated By Tripura Government:

The government of Tripura announced 'Notun Disha' (New Direction) for assessing the academic level of students in classes III-VIII and then improving their current level. It was launched by state Education Minister Ratan Lal Nath.

President presents Swachh Survekhshan - 2019 Awards:

President Ram Nath Kovind has presented Swachh Survekhshan-2019 Awards in New Delhi. Indore bagged award for the cleanest city for the third straight year in Swachh Survekshan.

Dr Rajendra Joshi Conferred With 'Pravasi Bhartiya Samman':

Swiss-based NRI scientist Dr Rajendra Joshi has been conferred with the Pravasi Bhartiya Samman Award by the President of India Ram Nath Kovind.

President's Certificate of Honour & Maharshi Badrayan Vyas Samman Awards:

Vice President Venkaiah Naidu conferred President's Certificate of Honour and Maharshi Badrayan Vyas Samman Awards at New Delhi.

APPOINTMENTS

Ajay Narayan Jha joined as 15th Finance Commission:

Ajay Narayan Jha joined the Fifteenth Finance Commission, headed by former Planning Commission member N K Singh, is mandated to recommend distribution of net proceeds of taxes between the Union and the states, for a period of five years - April, 2020 to March, 2025, among others.

Ramesh Chand : Director-General of FAO:

Mr Chand's candidature is challenged by China, Cameroon, France and Georgia. To get elected to the post of Director-General of FAO, the candidate needs to secure a simple majority of the 194 members.

Justice P.C. Ghose Named India's First Lokpal:

Former Supreme Court judge Justice Pinaki Chandra Ghose was recommended to be the first Lokpal or anti-corruption ombudsman of India. Justice Ghose, 67, is a member of the National Human Rights Commission (NHRC) since June 2017.

Manu Sawhney Takes Over As Chief Executive of ICC:

Manu Sawhney took over as the International Cricket Council (ICC) Chief Executive Officer (CEO). Sawhney has been working alongside the outgoing CEO David Richardson for the last six weeks to ensure a smooth transition within the organization.

David Malpass Named World Bank President:

David Malpass has been appointed as the President of the World Bank. He was US President Donald Trump's nominee and won unanimous approval from the institution's executive board.

SUN Group Chairman Vikramjit Sahney Elected As President of ICC India:

SUN Group Chairman Vikramjit Singh Sahney elected as the new president of International Chamber of Commerce (ICC) - India. The chamber would work with the government to promote India's external trade.

Gargi Kaul Appointed Secretary of Defence Finance:

In a bureaucratic reshuffle, the Centre has appointed Gargi Kaul as Secretary, Defence Finance. She is a 1984-batch officer of the Indian Audit and Accounts Service (IA&AS). Kaul was earlier Financial Advisor, Defence Services in the Defence Ministry.

BK Nayak Appointed FIH Health And Safety Committee Chair:

Bibhu Kalyan Nayak became the first Indian to be appointed Chair of International Hockey Federation (FIH) Health and Safety Committee by the world governing body.

Pranay Kumar Verma Appointed As India's Ambassador To Vietnam:

Ministry of External Affairs has appointed Pranay Kumar Verma as India's Ambassador to the Socialist Republic of Vietnam.

Ausaf Sayeed appointed new Ambassador of India to Saudi Arabia:

Dr. Ausaf Sayeed, presently High Commissioner of India to the Republic of Seychelles, has been appointed as the next ambassador of India to Saudi Arabia.

Subhash Chandra Garg Appointed As Finance Secretary:

The Appointments Committee of the Cabinet has approved designating Shri Subhash Chandra Garg, lAS, Secretary, Department of Economic Affairs, Ministry of Finance as Finance Secretary.

MR Kumar Appointed LIC Chairman:

The government has appointed MR Kumar as the Chairman of Life Insurance Corporation (LIC) and Vipin Anand and TC Suseel Kumar as the managing directors (MDs).

Praful Patel became first Indian in FIFA Council:

Praful Patel, the President of All India Football Federation has become the first

Indian to be elected as a member of the FIFA Executive Council. The election was held during the 29th Asian Football Confederations Congress in Kuala Lumpur on April 5, 2019.Patel's term in the council will be for a period of four years, from 2019 to 2023

IMPORTANT DAYS:

International Day of Happiness: 20 March

International Day of Happiness is celebrated every year on March The theme for IDH 2019 is 'Happier Together', focusing on what we have in common, rather than what divides us.

World Water Day: 22 March

International World Water Day is held annually on 22 March as a means of focusing attention on the importance of freshwater and advocating for the sustainable management of freshwater resources. The theme for World Water Day 2019 is 'Leaving no one behind,' which is the central promise of the 2030 Agenda for Sustainable Development.

World Health Day: 7th April:

April 7 of each year marks the celebration of World Health Day. The theme of World Health Day 2019 is 'Universal health coverage (UHC): Everyone, Everywhere', according to WHO.

World Homoeopathy Day: 10th April

The World Homoeopathy Day 2019 will be observed across the world on April 10 to commemorate the birth anniversary of the founder of Homoeopathy, Dr Christian Fredrich Samuel Hahnemann. On the occasion of the World Homoeopathy Day 2019, the Central Council for Research in Homoeopathy (CCRH), an autonomous research organisation under the Union Ministry of AYUSH organised a two-day convention (on 9th and 10th April) at Dr. Ambedkar International Centre in New Delhi.

International Day of Human Space Flight: 12 April

The General Assembly declared 12 April as the International Day of Human Space Flight to celebrate each year at the international level the beginning of the space era for mankind.

World Book Day: 23 April

World Book Day is celebrated every year on 23 April. It is also known as World Book and Copyright Day, or International Day of the Book. It is organized by UNESCO to promote reading, publishing, and copyright. It was first celebrated on 23 April 19For the year 2019, Sharjah, UAE has been declared as the World Book Capital. It will be preceded by Kuala Lumpur, Malaysia in the year 2020.

World Wildlife Day: March 3

On this day, the Convention on International Trade in Endangered Species of Wild Fauna and Flora (CITES) was signed. The theme for World Wildlife Day 2019 is 'Life below water: for people and planet' which corresponds to goal 14 of the Sustainable Development Goals (SDGs) which is 'Life below water'.

World Consumer Rights Day: 15th March

World Consumer Rights Day is celebrated every year on 15 March as part of an initiative by Consumer International, a membership organization for consumer groups around the world. The theme for World Consumers day 2019 is "Trusted Smart Products".

SCIENCE & TECHNOLOGY:

Google Launches New Cloud Platform Anthos:

Google launched Anthos, a new open platform from Google Cloud that lets users run applications from anywhere.

Airtel, FICCI Ladies Organisation Launch Women's Safety App:

Bharti Airtel and the FICCI Ladies Organisation (FLO, the women business wing of apex trade body FICCI) launched a carrier agnostic safety app named 'My Circle' which has been designed to empower women in the event of any distress or panic situation.

IRCTC Launches Its Own Digital Payment Gateway 'IRCTC iPay':

IRCTC launched its own digital payment aggregator called 'IRCTC iPay'. With iPay, passengers will not need any third-party platforms as it will provide payment options like credit card, debit card, unified payment interface and international card.

ISRO Launches 'Yuva Vigyani Karyakram' For School Children:

Indian Space Research Organisation has launched 'Yuva VIgyani Karyakram', a 'Young Scientist Programme' for the School Children to be studying in the 9th standard.

Google Launches Reading Tutor App 'Bolo' For Kids in India:

Google launched a free app called "Bolo" that parents can download to help primary grade children improve their Hindi and English reading skills. Launched in India first, the app is designed to work offline and comes with a built-in reading buddy, "Diya", who encourages, aids, explains, and corrects the child, as they read aloud.

Microsoft Launched Project 'Sangam' To Boost India's Swachh Bharat Mission:

Microsoft has announced that it has partnered with The Ministry of Housing and Urban Affairs (MoHUA) to promote its Project 'Sangam' which is developed to accelerate Swachh Bharat Mission (SBM) in India.

World's most powerful rocket launches its maiden commercial flight :

The first commercial flight of famous private American aerospace manufacturer and space transportation services company SpaceX's Falcon Heavy rocket successfully lifted off from the Kennedy Space Center in Cape Canaveral, Florida. It carried Arabsat 6A satellite, a 13,200-pound Saudi telecommunications satellite into Earth orbit.

Aurora Supercomputer:

The United States has decided to build the fastest supercomputer titled 'Aurora supercomputer'.

EXERCISE

1. Who among the following has been appointed as the Chairman of Life Insurance Corporation (LIC)?
   (a) MR Kumar
   (b) Umesh Anand
   (c) TC Suseel Kumar
   (d) Vipin Anand
   (e) Gunjan Kapoor

2. As per RBI notification, _________ has been categorized as a private sector lender following the acquisition of majority stake by Life Insurance Corporation.
   (a) Dena Bank
   (b) HDFC Bank
   (c) ICICI Bank
   (d) IDBI Bank
   (e) BoB

3. Aviva Life Insurance announced the launch of __________, a specially designed mentorship program to empower the female workforce.
   (a) Woman (b) Wings
   (c) Together(d) Empower
   (e) High-heels

4. ICICI Lombard and _______announced a strategic partnership to provide cyber-insurance cover.
   (a) GooglePay
   (b) PhonePay
   (c) Paytm
   (d) Mobikwik
   (e) AmazonPay

5. Indian Space Research Organisation (ISRO) has successfully launched a Satellite from the Sriharikota, recently. What is the name of that satellite?
   (a) KALAMSAT-2B
   (b) BISAT-2A
   (c) RISAT-2B
   (d) ISSAT-2C
   (e) TRISAT-1B

6. As per the report by the United Nations, India's economy is projected to grow at _____ in the fiscal year 20
   (a) 7.5%   (b) 7.4%
   (c) 7.2%   (d) 7.1%
   (e) 7.3%

7. With which of the following bank, the World Bank has teamed up to enable recording of secondary market bond trading using blockchain tech?
   (a) Commonwealth Bank of Australia
   (b) Commonwealth Bank of Italy
   (c) Commonwealth Bank of India
   (d) Commonwealth Bank of Austria
   (e) Commonwealth Bank of Portugal

8. Name the Ride-hailing company that has launched a Credit Card in partnership with SBI Card.
   (a) Uber
   (b) Ola
   (c) Meru
   (d) Taxi4sure
   (e) Mycabs

9. As per Election Commission of India, the 2019 Lok Sabha elections witnessed a voter turnout of __________, which is the highest ever voter turnout in the history of general elections.
   (a) 69.10%
   (b) 68.10%
   (c) 66.10%
   (d) 67.10%
   (e) 65.10%

10. Name the company/lender that has toppled state-owned Indian Oil Corporation (IOC) to become the country's biggest company by revenue.
    (a) HDFC Ltd
    (b) SBI
    (c) Reliance Industries
    (d) ONGC
    (e) TCS

11. Which of the following firm has launched a new initiative HeART, that aims to mentor, partner and invest in real estate technology companies.
    (a) National Bank for Agriculture and Rural Development
    (b) ICICI Prudential Life Insurance Company
    (c) HDFC Capital Advisors
    (d) ICICI Prudential Asset Management Company
    (e) National Housing Bank

12. Which State became the first state to tap into masala bond market by listing KIIFB's masala bond worth of USD 312 million (Rs 2,150 crore) in London Stock Exchange (LSE)'s International Securities Market (ISM).
    (a) Kerala
    (b) Maharashtra
    (c) Sikkim
    (d) Punjab
    (e) Telangana

13. In which city, the 11th Joint Consular Committee meeting between India and Iran took place?
    (a) Kolkata
    (b) Tehran
    (c) New Delhi
    (d) Isfahan
    (e) Chennai

14. Leading stock exchange BSE has launched________app to enable more participation and help mutual fund distributors process transactions faster.
    (a) BSE M Fund
    (b) BSE MF Rock
    (c) BSE StAR MF
    (d) M Fund
    (e) Star Fund BSE

15. Ujjivan Small Finance Bank Limited has appointed________as its next Managing Director and Chief Executive Officer (CEO) from December 1, 2019.
    (a) Ravi Kumar Batra
    (b) Somitra Ghose
    (c) Nitin Chugh
    (d) Vipin Kumar Kant
    (e) Ashish Deval

16. IBM India has tied-up with________Company to co-create new Artificial Intelligence (AI)-based solutions.
    (a) HDFC ERGO General Insurance
    (b) Aditya Birla General Insurance
    (c) Bharti AXA General Insurance
    (d) Digit General Insurance
    (e) Apollo Munich General Insurance

17. Who among the following is the current MD and CEO of Ujjivan Small Finance Bank Limited?
    (a) Anubhav Chandra
    (b) Adarsh Kumar Goel
    (c) Kamal Narayan Murthi
    (d) Samit Ghosh
    (e) Sunil Chandra

18. Digital payments company Paytm, in association with ________________, has launched its first credit card called Paytm First Card.
    (a) ICICI Bank
    (b) SBI
    (c) Yes Bank
    (d) Citi Bank
    (e) HDFC Bank

19. Which Telecom company and HDFC Life Insurance have tied up to offer life cover for customers who get a prepaid recharge done?
    - (a) Bharti Airtel
    - (b) Vodafone
    - (c) BSNL
    - (d) Jio
    - (e) Idea

20. The Reserve Bank of India has appointed its former Deputy Governor, R Gandhi, on the board of private sector lender _________________ as an additional director.
    - (a) HDFC Bank
    - (b) Yes Bank
    - (c) Axis Bank
    - (d) ICICI Bank
    - (e) Kotak Mahindra Bank

21. CEAT Cricket Rating (CCR) Awards 2019 were announced in Mumbai. Name the player who bagged International Cricketer of the Year award.
    - (a) David Warner
    - (b) Virat Kohli
    - (c) MS Dhoni
    - (d) Rohit Sharma
    - (e) Shikhar Dhawan

22. Doordarshan has launched an online souvenir store for its viewers on ______ so that one can easily access it.
    - (a) Netflix
    - (b) Hotstar
    - (c) Viu
    - (d) Amazon India
    - (e) Flipkart

23. Name the Lender that has announced the launch of a co-branded multi-currency card with online travel booking portal Goibibo.
    - (a) IDBI Bank
    - (b) HDFC Bank
    - (c) Axis Bank
    - (d) ICICI Bank
    - (e) Karnataka Bank

24. LIC Mutual Fund appointed ___ as the company's Chief Executive Officer (CEO).
    - (a) Hemant Bhargava
    - (b) M R Kumar
    - (c) Dinesh Pangtey
    - (d) B Venugopal
    - (e) T.C. Suseel Kumar

25. BharatPe– India's first Fintech start-up enabling payments for merchants through interoperable UPI QR codes, has announced its foray into merchant services with a new app. What is the full form of UPI?
    - (a) Universal Payments Interface
    - (b) Unified Payments Interface
    - (c) Unified Programme Interface
    - (d) Unified Payments Industrial
    - (e) Unified Payments Institute

26. Who has been appointed as the new President of the United Nations General Assembly?
    - (a) Mohammed Ishtayeh
    - (b) Soumeylou Boubeye Maiga
    - (c) Joseph Nanven Garba
    - (d) Maria Fernanda Espinosa Garces
    - (e) Tijjani Mohammad Bande

27. The IBSA (India, Brazil & South Africa) Sherpas' Meeting, following the 9th IBSA Trilateral Ministerial Meeting, was held in ______.
    - (a) Imphal
    - (b) Nagpur
    - (c) Cochin
    - (d) Visakhapatnam
    - (e) Mumbai

28. _________ has decided to enhance the housing loan limits for Regional Rural Banks (RRBs) and Small Finance Banks (SFBs) for eligibility under priority sector lending, in a bid to give them a level playing field with other Scheduled Commercial Banks.
    (a) NITI Aayog (b) NIIF
    (c) NABARD   (d) SEBI
    (e) RBI

29. Which of the following organisation has launched 'Udyam', a skilling center in Bengaluru?
    (a) SBI
    (b) TCS
    (c) LIC HFL
    (d) Infosys
    (e) ONGC

30. Which of the following bank had announced that it will link its interest rate on savings account with a balance above Rs1 lakh and short-term loans like overdraft and cash credit facility to Reserve Bank of India's repo rate, effective 1 May 2019?
    (a) BoB   (b) IOB
    (c) PNB   (d) SBI
    (e) ICICI Bank

31. Bharti AXA General Insurance, a private non-life insurer, has tied up with financial marketplace Wishfin's insurance arm _________to offer two-wheeler insurance to customers via WhatsApp.
    (a) Wishpool   (b) Likepolicy
    (c) Wishrules   (d) Makeawish
    (e) Wishpolicy

32. Markets regulator SEBI directed ______to pay more than Rs 625 crore in the case of misuse of its co-location facility.
    (a) Tata Steel   (b) NSE
    (c) BSE   (d) Facebook
    (e) Paytm

33. Canara Bank and its life insurance partner Canara HSBC Oriental Bank of Commerce Life Insurance launched _________to enable its customers to purchase life insurance in a convenient and hassle-free way.
    (a) Bankruptcy Code
    (b) Webassurance
    (c) Webffidavit
    (d) Insuraisal
    (e) Bank Custodian

34. The RBI has divested its entire stake held in NHB and NABARD to the government, which now holds ____________ in these entities.
    (a) 99%   (b) 95%
    (c) 100%   (d) 75%
    (e) 50%

35. Which of the following bank has launched the first debit card-based authentication solution on NPCI's e-Mandate (electronic mandate) API (Application Program Interface) platform recently?
    (a) Kotak Mahindra Bank
    (b) HDFC Bank
    (c) IndusInd Bank
    (d) Axis Bank
    (e) State Bank of India

36. Which General Insurance company has launched a product– cyber defence insurance to protect businesses from financial and reputational losses due to cyber-attacks recently?
    (a) SBI General Insurance
    (b) Royal Sundaram General Insurance
    (c) Universal Sompo General Insurance Company
    (d) IFFCO Tokio General Insurance Company Limited
    (e) HDFC ERGO General Insurance Company

37. Bajaj Allianz General Insurance in collaboration with Bajaj Allianz Life Insurance have launched their first product. The name of the product is?
    (a) Cyber Defence Insurance Protection
    (b) Insurance Plan to Take Care
    (c) Take Care of Customers Health
    (d) Total Health Secure Goal
    (e) Customer Health Activity Secure

38. Which of the following diversified global analytics company, will transfer its rating business to its proposed new wholly-owned subsidiary?
    (a) CRISIL
    (b) ICRA
    (c) CARE
    (d) SMERA
    (e) CIBIL

39. India's largest app for financial services has integrated with Unified Payment Interface (UPI) as a payment method recently. Name the app.
    (a) Moneycontrol
    (b) Etmoney
    (c) Stock Watch
    (d) Investar
    (e) NSE Mobile

40. Which of the following bank has received approval from the Competition Commission of India (CCI) for the proposed scheme of amalgamation of Gruh Finance with the bank?
    (a) UCO Bank
    (b) Corporation Bank
    (c) Canara Bank
    (d) Bandhan Bank
    (e) Laxmi Vilas Bank

41. Which of the following bank has partnered with M1Xchange Trade Receivables Discounting System (TReDS) platform for MSME bill discounting?
    (a) Deutsche Bank
    (b) ICICI Bank
    (c) Axis Bank
    (d) ING Vysya Bank
    (e) Bank of Maharashtra

42. India ranked______out of 180 countries in the World Press Freedom Index 2019, released by Reporters Without Borders.
    (a) 97th   (b) 131st
    (c) 140th   (d) 177th
    (e) 159th

43. Which of the following country has announced that it will be hosting the G20 summit in November 2020?
    (a) Israel   (b) UAE
    (c) Japan   (d) India
    (e) Saudi Arabia

44. Which organisation has reduced the minimum subscription requirement as well as defined trading lots for Real Estate Investment Trusts (REITs) and Infrastructure Investment Trusts (InvITs)?
    (a) NABARD   (b) TRAI
    (c) IRDAI   (d) RBI
    (e) SEBI

45. Who is to head Supreme Court Committee on Prison Reforms?
    (a) Justice Ranjana Prakash Desai
    (b) Justice Ranjan Gogoi
    (c) Justice Amitava Roy
    (d) Justice Arun Kumar Mishra
    (d) Justice Alok Kumar

46. When is International Day for the Total Elimination of Nuclear Weapons observed?
    (a) 25th September
    (b) 26th September
    (c) 27th September
    (d) 28th September
    (e) 25th October

47. Consider the following statements about Beti Bachao Beti Padhao (BBBP) scheme?

    I. PM Modi has expanded BBBP scheme to all 640 districts of the country.

    II. Earlier it was existed in the districts of Gujarat & Maharashtra only.

    Which of the statements given above is/are correct?

    (a) I Only
    (b) II Only
    (c) Both I and II
    (d) Neither I nor II
    (e) Cannot be determined

48. Which of the following states are involved in the dispute of water share of river Cauvery?

    (a) Karnataka & Tamilnadu
    (b) Karnataka & Maharashtra
    (c) Tamilnadu & Maharashtra
    (d) Tamilnadu & Andhra Pradesh
    (e) None of these

49. The Central Institute of Indian Languages (CIIL) which protects and preserves endangered languages of the country is located at

    (a) New Delhi(b)   Mumbai
    (c) Chennai(d)   Mysore
    (e) Punjab

50. Which committee has been constituted by Union Government to expedite capital acquisition for Armed Forces modernization?

    (a) Vinay Sheel Oberoi committee
    (b) Rabindra Thapa committee
    (c) Vijayan Kumar committee
    (d) Narendra Singh committee
    (e) None of these

51. Which country has become the world's first country to repeal same-sex marriage?

    (a) Greece
    (b) Portugal
    (c) South Africa
    (d) Bermuda
    (e) None of these

52. Which Bank has been awarded the prestigious Celent Model Bank 2019 Award in the category of Financial Inclusion, for 'Redesigning Lending to Reach Small Businesses'?

    (a) Utkarsh Small Finance Bank
    (b) Equitas Small Finance Bank
    (c) Au Small Finance Bank
    (d) Fincare Small Finance Bank
    (e) Ujjivan Small Finance Bank

53. In January 2019, LIC has completed the process of picking up a controlling ______ stake in the nearly crippled IDBI Bank.

    (a) 49%   (b) 75%
    (c) 51%   (d) 25%
    (e) 100%

54. The 2nd edition of Belt and Road Forum (BRF) was held in Beijing, China from April 25 to 27, 20Which one of the following countries did not participate in this edition?

    (a) Pakistan,   (b) Laos,
    (c) Thailand   (d) India
    (e) None of these

55. Which space agency has recorded the first "marsquake," quake on the mars due to volcanic eruptions or land tides?

    (a) JAXA   (Japan   Aerospace Exploration Agency)
    (b) NASA (National Aeronautics and Space Administration)
    (c) ISRO (Indian Space Research Organisation)
    (d) Italian Space Agency
    (e) None of these

56. Who has been awarded by the Rabindranath Tagore Literary Prize 2019?
    (a) Santosh Rana
    (b) Nalini Bera
    (c) Leeladhar Jagudi
    (d) Rana Dasgupta
    (e) None of these

57. How many medals in total India won in Asian Wrestling championship tournament, 2019 held in Xian, China?
    (a) 12 (b) 14
    (c) 16 (d) 20
    (e) 24

58. Which of the following Institutes researcher developed a method for reading documents in Bharati Script by using a multi-lingual optical character recognition (OCR) scheme?
    (a) IIT Madras
    (b) Indian Council of Agricultural Research
    (c) Centre for Studies in Social Sciences, Calcutta
    (d) IIT Roorkee
    (e) IIT Mumbai

59. Which of the following countries has collaborated with India Post for digitizing 1.5 lakh post offices in India, for creating World's Biggest EPostal Network?
    (a) Tata Consultancy Services (TCS)
    (b) International Business Machines (IBM)
    (c) Intel Corporation
    (d) Microsoft Corporation
    (e) None of these

60. Which Crypto currency Exchange in India has launched the first Indian Platform for Wholesale Crypto currency Trading.?
    (a) Zebpay (b) Belfrics
    (c) BuyUcoin(d) Coinsecure
    (e) None of these

61. With reference to Money Loji' app, consider the following statements:
    I. It is launched to bring fastest solutions of financial needs for rural people.
    II. Consumers having a minimum income of 20,000 annually and a minimum age of 23 years will eligible for the benefit.
    Which of the statements given above is/are correct?
    (a) I only
    (b) II only
    (c) Both I and II
    (d) Neither I nor II
    (e) Either I or II

62. Name the lady person who has become the first woman umpire to stand in a men's ODI in the final match of ICC World Cricket League 2?
    (a) Ashleigh Gardner
    (b) Claire Polosak
    (c) Meg Lanning
    (d) Nicola Carey
    (e) None of these

63. Khushi Scheme to provide free sanitary napkins to school girls across the state belongs to which state?
    (a) Kerala
    (b) Haryana
    (c) Tamil Nadu
    (d) Odisha
    (e) Punjab

64. Which organisation has launched a 5G Use Cases Lab for banking and financial sector recently?
    (a) NHB
    (b) BRBNMPL
    (c) RBI
    (d) SEBI
    (e) IDRBT

65. Which Bank has launched 'NRI-Insta-Online' account opening process for NRIs residing in the Financial Action Task Force (FATF) member countries?
    (a) HDFC Bank
    (b) Bank of Baroda
    (c) State Bank of India
    (d) IDBI Bank
    (e) Axis Bank

66. IDRBT is an institution exclusively focused on banking technology. What is the full form of IDRBT?
    (a) Institute for Development & Research in Branches Technology
    (b) Institute for Development & Research in Banking Technology
    (c) Institute for Department & Research in Banking Technology
    (d) Indian for Development & Research in Banking Technology
    (e) Institute for Development & Revenue in Banking Treaty

67. Who has been appointed as the President of the World Bank recently?
    (a) Chrystia Freeland
    (b) Robert Lighthizer
    (c) David Malpass
    (d) Wilbur Ross
    (e) Larry Kudlow

68. Reserve Bank of India (RBI) has appointed 5-member committee under the chairmanship of ______ to strengthen digital payments as well as to boost financial inclusion through Financial Technology.
    (a) Nandan Nilekani
    (b) Vishal Sikka
    (c) NR Narayana Murthy
    (d) Salil Parekh
    (e) Sunil Bharti Mittal

69. The International Monetary Fund (IMF) and the World Bank have together launched a private blockchain with a pseudo-token. The new token called-?
    (a) Learning Sikka
    (b) Learning Coin
    (c) Learning Cash
    (d) Learning Money
    (e) Learning Dollar

70. The Centre has announced a new Rs ___ - coin which will come in 12-edged polygon (dodecagon) shape.
    (a) Rs 10 coin
    (b) Rs 20 coin
    (c) Rs 05 coin
    (d) Rs 02 coin
    (e) Rs 50 coin

71. Bank of Baroda has become the ______ largest bank in the country.
    (a) sixth   (b) fourth
    (c) first   (d) second
    (e) third

72. Which country recently has withdrawn itself from UN refugee programme?
    (a) Tanzania   (b) USA
    (c) Myanmar   (d) India
    (e) Nepal

73. Who has been re-elected as the Bangladesh president for another five-year term?
    (a) Abdul Hamid
    (b) Aminul Haqu
    (c) Sheikh Hasina
    (d) Zilur Rahman
    (e) Iajuddin Ahmed

74. The mission of the OECD is to promote policies that will improve the economic and social well-being of people around the world. What is the full form of OECD?

    (a) Organisation for Economic Co-operation and Dividend

    (b) Organisation for Economic Chamber and Development

    (c) Organisation for Economic Council and Development

    (d) Organisation for Economic Co-operation and Department

    (e) Organisation for Economic Co-operation and Development

75. Which Bank is the first to offer a fully digital and paperless banking system in India?

    (a) Airtel Payments Bank

    (b) State Bank of India

    (c) Yes Bank

    (d) Canara Bank

    (e) ICICI Bank

76. The Indian Museum is the largest and oldest museum in India and has rare collections of antiques, armour and ornaments, fossils, skeletons, mummies, and Mughal paintings. It was located in-

    (a) Hyderabad   (b) Lucknow

    (c) New Delhi   (d) Patna

    (e) Kolkata

77. Reliance Stadium or Indian Petrochemicals Corporation Ltd Sports Complex Ground also known as the IPCL Ground is located in-

    (a) Ranchi, Jharkhand

    (b) Vadodara, Gujarat

    (c) Mumbai, Maharashtra

    (d) Kochin, Kerala

    (e) Bengaluru, Karnataka

78. Which country will host the 17th G20 Summit in 2022?

    (a) Japan   (b) Saudi Arabia

    (c) Qatar   (d) India

    (e) None of these

79. Where was the First State Level Awareness Program on Agriculture Export Policy to create awareness among farmers and stakeholders held on 2nd February 2019?

    (a) Shimla   (b) Pune

    (c) Raipur   (d) Chennai

    (e) None of these

80. No income tax for earnings up to _____ rupees, as per the Interim Budget for 2019 presented by Union Finance Minister Piyush Goyal in Parliament on February 1, 2019?

    (a) Rs. 4 Lakh

    (b) Rs. 5 Lakh

    (c) Rs. 6 Lakh

    (d) Rs. 7 Lakh

    (d) None of these

81. Recently, Band Darwaja Campaign Part 2 was launched by Swachh Bharat Mission Gramin in association with _________.

    (a) IMF

    (b) World Bank

    (c) WHO

    (d) UNICEF

    (e) None of these

82. What is the name of Indian women Cricketer, who has won the International Women Cricketer of Year Award in CEAT International Cricket Awards 2019?

    (a) Smriti Mandhana

    (b) Mithali Raj

    (c) Harmanpreet Kaur

    (d) Jhulan Goswami

    (e) Shikha Pandey

83. IAAF World Relays 2019 was held in Nissan Stadium, Yokohama, Japan from May 11 to 12, 20IAAF refers to –

(a) Indian Association of Athletics Foundation

(b) International Association of Athletics Federations

(c) Inter Atlantic Federations of Athletics

(d) International Federations of Athletics Association

(e) None of these

84. What is the name of programme, which launched by ISRO to a 2-week long summer vacation residential programme?

(a) Yuvika-2019

(b) Summer – 2019

(c) Akash – 2019

(d) Udaan – 2019

(e) Vigyani – 2019

85. Who is the youngest BJP candidate to win in the Lok Sabha Elections 2019?

(a) Nusrat Jahan

(b) Tejaswi Surya

(c) Praveen Nishad

(d) Mukut Bihari

(e) None of these

86. Which seat of Uttar Pradesh was not won by the Bhartiya Janata Party in Lok Sabha Elections 2019?

(a) Pilibhit   (b) Rampur

(c) Gorakhpur   (d) Baghpat

(e) None of these

87. In Lok Sabha Election 2019 results which candidate has won from Begusarai Lok Sabha constituency?

(a) Gopal Jee Yadav

(b) Ravi Shankar Prasad

(c) Giriraj Singh

(d) Dinesh Chandra Yadav

(e) None of these

88. What is the present strength of Judges in the Supreme Court, as on May 24, 2019?

(a) 23   (b) 26

(c) 29   (d) 31

(e) None of these

89. Which of the following country has successfully launched its first satellite from Virginia in the United States?

(a) Indonesia

(b) Malaysia

(c) Nepal

(d) Egypt

(e) Philippines

90. Which of the following country will host the Under-17 Women's Football World Cup in 2020?

(a) UAE

(b) Indonesia

(c) Singapore

(d) Sri Lanka

(e) India

91. Which of the following organisation has released the 6th edition of the Global Environment Outlook (2019) titled 'Healthy Planet, Healthy People'?

(a) IMF   (b) UNEP

(c) World Bank   (d) NIIF

(e) ADB

92. Who among the following has been named the winner of the Commonwealth Youth Award for the Asian region?

(a) Rashmi V Mahesh

(b) Satyendra Dubey

(c) Ashok Khemka

(d) Sanjukta Parashar

(e) Padmanaban Gopalan

93. World Consumer Rights Day is celebrated every year on ______.

(a) 18 March   (b) 9 March

(c) 11 March   (d) 15 March

(e) 20 March

94. What is the theme for World Consumers day 2019?
    - (a) We Stand Against Market Abuses
    - (b) Trusted Smart Products
    - (c) Social Injustices And Consumer's Right
    - (d) Internet And Trusted Products
    - (e) None of the above option is the right answer

95. 4th Agri Leadership Summit 2019 was held at _____________.
    - (a) Sonipat, Haryana
    - (b) Jaipur, Rajasthan
    - (c) Dehradun, Uttarakhand
    - (d) Gangtok, Sikkim
    - (e) Ludhiana, Punjab

96. Which of the following state's Legislative Assembly passed the bills to end the minimum education criterion for panchayat and civic polls candidates?
    - (a) Sikkim
    - (b) Rajasthan
    - (c) Gujarat
    - (d) Haryana
    - (e) Punjab

97. In which of the following city union culture minister Mahesh Sharma inaugurated India's very first 'Fulldome 3D Digital Theatre'?
    - (a) New Delhi
    - (b) Chennai
    - (c) Kolkata
    - (d) Pune
    - (e) Ahmadabad

98. Which of the following state has set up a committee to review various schemes being implemented for the welfare of tribals in the state?
    - (a) Uttarakhand
    - (b) Karnataka

- (c) Maharashtra
- (d) Madhya Pradesh
- (e) Goa

99. Under _____________, government has aimed at equipping 9 lakh classrooms in schools and colleges across the country with digital facilities for teaching by 2022.
    - (a) Operation Digital Board
    - (b) Sarv Shiksha Abhiyan
    - (c) Digital Shiksha Mission
    - (d) Operation Digital Shiksha
    - (e) Operation Black Board

100. 1Which of the following city hosted the 4th India-ASEAN Expo and Summit?
    - (a) Bangalore
    - (b) New Delhi
    - (c) Nagpur
    - (d) Navi Mumbai
    - (e) Imphal

101. In January 2019, LIC has completed the process of picking up a controlling _____________ stake in the nearly crippled IDBI Bank.
    - (a) 49%
    - (b) 75%
    - (c) 51%
    - (d) 25%
    - (e) 100%

102. The Finance Ministry has decided to infuse _____________ crores into state-owned Bank of Baroda (BoB) after of the merger of two other public sector lenders Dena Bank and Vijaya Bank with BoB.
    - (a) Rs 4,342 crore
    - (b) Rs 5,042 crore
    - (c) Rs 6,742 crore
    - (d) Rs 7,745 crore
    - (e) Rs 8,321 crore

103. Which Bank has been categorized as a private sector lender following the acquisition of majority stake by Life Insurance Corporation?
    (a) Corporation Bank
    (b) IDBI Bank
    (c) State Bank of India
    (d) UCO Bank
    (e) Vijaya Bank

104. D-SIBs has already been phased-in from 01st April 2016 and fully effective from 01st April 20What is the full form of D-SIBs?
    (a) Dividend Systemically Important Banks
    (b) Domestic Security Important Banks
    (c) Domestic Systemically Important Banks
    (d) Domestic Systemically International Banks
    (e) Domestic Systemically Interface Banks

105. RBI has released 6th Bi-Monthly Monetary Policy Statement in February 20In this statement, RBI has reduced the policy repo rate under the Liquidity Adjustment Facility (LAF) by _______________ basis points.
    (a) 50 basis points
    (b) 25 basis points
    (c) 125 basis points
    (d) 10 basis points
    (e) 75 basis points

106. The Goods and Services Tax (GST) Council met for its 33rd meeting and slashed GST rate on under-construction residential properties and the affordable housing projects. The revised rates will be applicable from-
    (a) 01st May 2019
    (b) 01st August 2019
    (c) 31st March 2019
    (d) 01st June 2019
    (e) 01st April 2019

107. The Organisation for Economic Co-Operation & Development forecast in its interim outlook report that the world economy would grow _______ percent in 2019 and _________ percent in 2020.
    (a) 3.6% and 3.9%
    (b) 3.9% and 3.10%
    (c) 3.3% and 3.4%
    (d) 3.7% and 3.9%
    (d) 3.2% and 3.6%

108. NBHC has released Kharif Crop estimation for the year 2018-20According to the report, the basmati rice production is expected to decline by 9.24% to _____________________ million metric tonnes.
    (a) 5.18 million metric tonnes
    (b) 7.23 million metric tonnes
    (c) 9.67 million metric tonnes
    (d) 11.34 million metric tonnes
    (e) 13.87 million metric tonnes

109. The RBI cut its repo rate by 25 basis points to __________ in its first bi-monthly policy review of 2019-20.
    (a) 18%   (b) 12%
    (c) 8.5%   (d) 6%
    (e) 4 %

110. The Reserve Bank has announced that it will transfer an interim surplus of _____________________ crore rupees to the central government for the half-year ended 31st December 2018.
    (a) 92,000 crore rupees
    (b) 28,000 crore rupees
    (c) 65,000 crore rupees
    (d) 40,000 crore rupees
    (e) 16,000 crore rupees

111. Korea Exim Bank has come forward to extend a ________________ crore loan for Visakhapatnam (VIZAG) Metro Rail project.
    (a) Rs 2,000 crore
    (b) Rs 2,300 crore
    (c) Rs 3,000 crore
    (d) Rs 3,100 crore
    (e) Rs 4,100 crore

112. According to Reserve Bank of India, bank credit rose to __________ percent for the fortnight to 29 March 2019?
    (a) 11.24%
    (b) 12.31%
    (c) 13.24%
    (d) 14.31%
    (e) 15.31%

113. The RBI cut its repo rate by 25 basis points to __________ in its first bi-monthly policy review of 2019-20.
    (a) 3%   (b) 6%
    (c) 7.5%   (d) 18%
    (e) 12%

114. Karnam Sekar has been appointed as the MD and CEO of this bank, recently.
    (a) Canara Bank
    (b) Vijaya Bank
    (c) Indian Overseas Bank
    (d) KVB Bank
    (e) SBI Bank

115. Which bank celebrated its 114th Foundation Day on 12th March 2019?
    (a) Indian Bank
    (b) Corporation Bank
    (c) ICICI Bank
    (d) Canara Bank
    (e) SBI Bank

116. Which bank partners with Credit-Vidya to leverage customer experience?
    (a) Punjab National Bank
    (b) IDBI Bank

    (c) Yes Bank
    (d) Citibank
    (e) RBL Bank

117. Which bank plans to to raise up to Rs.50,000 crore by issuing bonds?
    (a) Axis Bank(b) ICICI Bank
    (c) Kotak Mahindra Bank
    (d) HDFC Bank
    (e) IDBI Bank

118. What is the new Repo Rate revised by the six-member monetary policy committee chaired by RBI Governor Shaktikanta Das?
    (a) 5.75%
    (b) 6.00%
    (c) 6.25%
    (d) 6.50%
    (e) 6.75%

119. Kotak Mahindra Bank (Kotak) stated that it will charge customers for UPI transactions starting 1st of May 20Where is the headquarters of Kotak Mahindra Bank?
    (a) Bengaluru   (b) Mumbai
    (c) Hyderabad   (d) Chennai
    (e) Cochin

120. Name of the Bank which becomes first lender to charge for UPI use?
    (a) Yes Bank
    (b) Axis Bank
    (c) Kotak Mahindra Bank
    (d) ICICI Bank
    (e) IDBI Bank

121. Which bank received a capital infusion of Rs 5,042 Crore from the government, recently?
    (a) IDBI Bank
    (b) Dena Bank
    (c) Bank of Baroda
    (d) Union Bank of India
    (e) ICICI Bank

122. Which of the following Bank has raised Rs.1,251.30 crore by issuing Basel III-compliant bonds?
    (a) SBI
    (b) Axis
    (c) IDBI
    (d) HDFC
    (e) ICICI Bank

123. Which of the following banks have been designated as the RBI's list of D-SIBs?
    (a) PNB, BoB, Dena Bank
    (b) SBI, BoB and ICICI Bank
    (c) HDFC, ICICI, and Axis Bank
    (d) SBI, ICICI and HDFC Bank
    (e) SBI, Yes, and Axis Bank

124. Which of the following bank has been categorized as a private sector lender following the acquisition of majority stake by Life Insurance Corporation?
    (a) Axis Bank
    (b) IDBI Bank
    (c) HDFC Bank
    (d) Punjab National Bank
    (e) ICICI Bank

125. Which bank has sanctioned a loan Rs 689 crore to over 1,600 Micro, Small and Medium Enterprises (MSMEs)?
    (a) Union Bank of India
    (b) Axis Bank
    (c) Punjab National Bank
    (d) Bank of Baroda
    (e) ICICI Bank

126. Which Bank acquired 9.9% stake in Kisan Finance for cash consideration of Rs 17.82 crore?
    (a) Kotak Mahindra Bank
    (b) IDBI Bank
    (c) Axis Bank(d) HDFC Bank
    (e) ICICI Bank

127. Ravneet Gill is appointed as MD and CEO of which of the following Bank?
    (a) KVB Bank
    (b) IDBI Bank
    (c) Axis Bank
    (d) Yes Bank
    (e) ICICI Bank

128. Which bank will pay Rs 28,000 Crore as Interim Dividend to the Government?
    (a) SBI
    (b) RBI
    (c) HDFC
    (d) axis
    (e) OBC Bank

129. RBI has recently raised the limit for collateral-free agriculture loans from Rs 1 Lakh to __________ .
    (a) Rs 1.3 lakh
    (b) Rs 1.4 lakh
    (c) Rs 1.5 lakh
    (d) Rs 1.6 lakh
    (e) Rs. 1.7 lakh

130. Reserve Bank of India (RBI) approved the appointment of V Vaidyanathan as MD and CEO of which bank for a period of three years?
    (a) IDFC First Bank
    (b) IDBI Bank
    (c) RBL Bank(d) Axis Bank
    (e) ICICI Bank

131. CAC means the ability of the domestic residents to converts the local currency to any foreign currency at will. What does 'A' stands for in 'CAC'?
    (a) Account
    (b) Act
    (c) Agenda
    (d) Agency
    (e) Application

132. Which bank recommended Unconditional Cash Transfer to farmers to alleviate the agrarian distress instead of Universal Basic Income (UBI) scheme?

(a) NABARD(b) SBI

(c) Punjab National Bank

(d) Corporation Bank

(e) OBC Bank

133. The Local Area Banks (LABs) are conceived as low-cost structures which would provide efficient and competitive financial intermediation services in a limited area of operation primarily in rural and semi-urban areas. What is the minimum capital requirement of a Local Area Bank?

(a) Rs 20 crore

(b) Rs 2,3 crore

(c) Rs 3,0 crore

(d) Rs 10 crore

(d) Rs 5 crore

134. Which of the following bank will inject Rs 37,500 crore through OMO in February?

(a) HDFC

(b) SBI

(c) RBI

(d) Axis

(e) OBC Bank

135. The Reserve Bank of India (RBI) named State Bank of India (SBI), ICICI Bank and ________________________ as D-SIBs, which in other words mean banks that are too big to fail.

(a) Bank of Baroda

(b) Axis Bank

(c) Punjab National Bank

(d) HSBC Bank

(e) HDFC Bank

136. India's new e-commerce policy came into effect from 01st February 20Which of the is not the highlights of this policy?

(a) The e-commerce retailer and whole seller shall be deemed to own the inventory of a vendor if over 50% of the purchases of such a vendor are through it.

(b) Bars online retailers from selling products through vendors in which they have an equity interest

(c) All online retailers will be required to maintain a level playing field for all the vendors selling their products on the platform, and it shall not affect the sale prices of goods in any manner

(d) Restricts marketplaces from influencing prices in a bid to curb deep discounting. With this, special offers like cashback, extended warranties, faster deliveries to some brands will be prohibited, with the view to provide a level playing field

(e) Disallows e-commerce players to control the inventory of the vendors. Any such ownership over the inventory will convert it into inventory based model from marketplace based model, which is not entitled to FDI

137. Which Bank has launched a new service called 'YONO Cash' for its customers using which customers can withdraw money from ATMs without using debit cards?

(a) State Bank of India

(b) HDFC Bank

(c) Union Bank of India

(d) Bank of Baroda

(e) ICICI Bank

138. Reserve Bank of India has provided no objection to ________________ for the proposed acquisition of Gruh Finance.

(a) Lakshmi Vilas Bank

(b) IDFC Bank

(c) Kotak Mahindra Bank

(d) India Post Payments Bank

(e) Bandhan Bank

139. Which bank has launched doorstep banking service for senior citizens over 70 years of age and differently-abled customers?
    (a) Axis Bank
    (b) ICICI Bank
    (c) HDFC Bank
    (d) State Bank of India
    (e) Indian Overseas Bank

140. Which organisation has taken off Allahabad Bank, Corporation Bank and Dhanlaxmi Bank from the Prompt Corrective Action (PCA) framework allowing them to resume their normal lending activities recently?
    (a) NABARD
    (b) SBI
    (c) RBI
    (d) SEBI
    (e) IRDAI

141. he Ahmedabad bench of the NCLT has approved the Rs 42,000-crore resolution plan submitted by Arcelor Mittal for the debt-ridden Essar Steel Ltd. What is the full form of NCLT?
    (a) National Company Law Treaty
    (b) National Council Law Tribunal
    (c) National Corporation Lease Tribunal
    (d) National Company Law Transit
    (e) National Company Law Tribunal

142. This bank raises Rs 487 crore through private placement of Tier II bonds.
    (a) Kotak Mahindra Bank
    (b) Indian Overseas Bank
    (c) Karur Vysya Bank
    (d) Federal Bank
    (e) IDBI

143. The BFS met to review the performance of banks under PCA and noted that the government has infused fresh capital into various banks including some of the banks currently under the PCA framework. What is the full form of BFS?
    (a) Board for Financial Society
    (b) Board for Financial System
    (c) Board for Financial Service
    (d) Banking for Financial Supervision
    (e) Board for Financial Supervision

144. The Central government has Relaxed angel tax norms for Start-ups from 7 years to _____________ years.
    (a) 05 years   (b) 10 years
    (c) 12 years   (d) 15 years
    (e) 20 years

145. Which bank launched 'YONO cash', cardless withdrawal of cash?
    (a) Axis
    (b) ICICI
    (c) SBI
    (d) HDFC
    (e) IDBI

146. India with immediate effect has boosted the Customs Duty on all the goods imported from Pakistan to-
    (a) 200%   (b) 300%
    (c) 400%   (d) 500%
    (d) 1000%

147. Which of the following is the name of Bank, which has signed a bancassurance deal with private life insurer HDFC Life Insurance Company to take advantage of HDFC Life's expertise in life insurance products, distribution and customer service recently?
    (a) Corporation Bank
    (b) Vijaya Bank
    (c) Oriental Bank of Commerce
    (b) UCO Bank
    (e) United Bank of India

148. Ajay Tyagi is present Chairperson of-
    (a) RBI
    (b) NABARD
    (c) IRDAI
    (d) TRAI
    (e) SEBI

149. RBI allows HDFC Bank to hold how much percent in Bandhan Bank?
    (a) 8.4
    (b) 9.9
    (c) 12
    (d) 18.6
    (e) 20.8

150. NBHC has released Kharif Crop estimation for the year 2018-20According to the report, the basmati rice production is expected to decline by 9.24% to _______ million metric tonnes.
    (a) 5.18 million metric tonnes
    (b) 7.23 million metric tonnes
    (c) 9.67 million metric tonnes
    (d) 15.34 million metric tonnes
    (e) 20.87 million metric tonnes

151. Name the India's largest bank which has signed an MoU with the Bank of China to boost business opportunities.
    (a) Canara Bank
    (b) State Bank of India
    (c) ICICI Bank
    (d) Bank of India
    (e) Vijaya Bank

152. FPI consists of securities and other financial assets passively held by foreign investors. What is the full from of FPI?
    (a) Financial Portfolio Investors
    (b) Foreign Product Investors
    (c) Foreign Portfolio Indian
    (d) Foreign Prompt Investors
    (e) Foreign Portfolio Investors

153. RBI denies a proposal to change the name of this bank.
    (a) IDBI Bank
    (b) Yes Bank
    (c) Dena Bank
    (d) Vijaya Bank
    (e) ICICI Bank

154. Where is the headquarters of World Bank?
    (a) New York
    (b) Paris
    (c) Vienna
    (d) Washington, DC
    (e) Geneva

155. ICICI Prudential Mutual Fund launched ICICI Prudential Bharat Consumption Scheme to get advantage from the Indian consumption market. The minimum investment of this scheme is;
    (a) Rs 2,000
    (b) Rs 3,000
    (c) Rs 4,000
    (d) Rs 5,000
    (e) Rs 8000

156. Where is the headquarters of Organisation for Economic Co-Operation & Development (OECD)?
    (a) Geneva
    (b) New York
    (c) London
    (d) Paris
    (e) Vienna

157. For which bank Reserve Bank of India has slapped a penalty of Rs 2 crore for non-compliance of regulatory directions?
    (a) IDBI Bank
    (b) Bank of Baroda
    (c) Punjab National Bank
    (d) Syndicate Bank
    (e) Canara Bank

158. Which of the following bank/company has crossed the Rs. 6 trillion market capitalization mark for the first time, making it only the third Indian firm-after Tata Consultancy Services Ltd

(TCS) and Reliance Industries Ltd (RIL) to achieve the milestone?

(a) HDFC Bank Limited

(b) State Bank of India

(c) ICICI Bank

(d) Oil and Natural Gas Corporation

(e) Wipro Limited

159. How much billionis accepted by Reserve Bank of India(RBI) from banks at its currency swap auction to ease liquidity?

(a) $2 billion   (b) $4 billion

(c) $5 billion   (d) $7 billion

(e) $9 billion

160. Markets regulator Securities and Exchange Board of India (SEBI) withdrew the ___________ limit on investments by Foreign Portfolio Investors in corporate bonds of an entity.

(a) 45%

(b) 30%

(c) 35%

(d) 25%

(e) 20%

161. IFFCO Tokio General Insurance has launched 'bank locker protector policy', the first stand-alone bank locker cover offered by any insurance company with a plan to protect the contents of a bank locker such as jewelry, title documents, and other valuables. Where is the headquarters of IFFCO Tokio General Insurance?

(a) Gurugram

(b) Pune

(c) Lucknow

(d) Kochin

(e) Hyderabad

162. Name the bank which has signed an MoU with Bharti AXA Life Insurance Company for Insurance Products recently?

(a) Axis Bank

(b) Karnataka Bank

(c) Canara Bank

(d) Punjab National Bank

163. The Reserve Bank of India (RBI) has set up an expert committee to suggest how the central bank should handle its reserves and whether it can transfer its surplus to the government. This committee headed by-

(a) Duvvuri Subbarao

(b) C Rangarajan

(c) YV Reddy

(d) Bimal Jalan

(e) Arvind Subramanian

ANSWER KEYS

1. (a)	17 (d)	33 (b)	49 (d)	65 (d)	81 (b)	97 (c)	113. (b)	129. (d)	145. (c)	161. (a)
2. (d)	18 (d)	34 (c)	50 (a)	66 (b)	82 (a)	98 (c)	114. (c)	130. (a)	146. (a)	162. (b)
3. (b)	19 (a)	35 (a)	51 (d)	67 (c)	83 (b)	99 (a)	115. (b)	131. (a)	147. (e)	163. (d)
4. (d)	20 (b)	36 (a)	52 (d)	68 (a)	84 (a)	100 (b)	116. (e)	132. (b)	148. (e)	
5. (c)	21 (b)	37 (d)	53 (c)	69 (b)	85 (a)	101. (c)	117. (d)	133. (e)	149. (b)	
6. (d)	22 (d)	38 (a)	54 (d)	70 (b)	86 (b)	102. (b)	118. (b)	134. (c)	150. (a)	
7. (a)	23 (d)	39 (b)	55 (b)	71 (e)	87 (c)	103. (b)	119. (b)	135. (e)	151. (b)	
8. (b)	24 (c)	40 (d)	56 (d)	72 (a)	88 (d)	104. (c)	120. (c)	136. (a)	152. (e)	
9. (d)	25 (b)	41 (e)	57 (c)	73 (a)	89 (c)	105. (b)	121. (c)	137. (a)	153. (a)	
10. (c)	26 (e)	42 (c)	58 (a)	74 (e)	90 (e)	106. (e)	122. (a)	138. (e)	154. (d)	
11 (c)	27 (c)	43 (e)	59 (a)	75 (a)	91 (b)	107. (c)	123. (d)	139. (d)	155. (d)	
12 (a)	28 (e)	44 (e)	60 (c)	76 (e)	92 (e)	108. (a)	124. (b)	140. (c)	156. (d)	
13 (c)	29 (c)	45 (c)	61 (d)	77 (b)	93 (d)	109. (d)	125. (c)	141. (e)	157. (c)	
14 (c)	30 (d)	46 (b)	62 (b)	78 (d)	94 (b)	110. (b)	126. (e)	142. (c)	158. (a)	
15 (c)	31 (e)	47 (a)	63 (d)	79 (b)	95 (a)	111. (e)	127. (d)	143. (e)	159. (c)	
16. (a)	32 (b)	48 (a)	64 (e)	80 (b)	96 (b)	112. (c)	128. (b)	144. (b)	160. (e)